For Fred and Jan

Best wishes,

Livingston

MOVING TOGETHER

MOVING TOGETHER

DANCE AND PLURALISM IN CANADA

Allana C. Lindgren, Batia Boe Stolar, & Clara Sacchetti, editors

This book has been published with the help of a grant from the Canadian Federation for the Humanities and Social Sciences, through the Awards to Scholarly Publications Program, using funds provided by the Social Sciences and Humanities Research Council of Canada. Wilfrid Laurier University Press acknowledges the support of the Canada Council for the Arts for our publishing program. We acknowledge the financial support of the Government of Canada through the Canada Book Fund for our publishing activities. This work was supported by the Research Support Fund.

Library and Archives Canada Cataloguing in Publication

Title: Moving together : dance and pluralism in Canada / edited by Allana C. Lindgren, Batia Boe Stolar, Clara Sacchetti.

Other titles: Moving together (Waterloo, Ont.)

Names: Lindgren, Allana, [date], editor. | Stolar, Batia Boe, [date], editor. | Sacchetti, Clara, [date], editor.

Description: Includes bibliographical references and index.

Identifiers: Canadiana (print) 2020029671x | Canadiana (ebook) 20200296779 | ISBN 9781771124836 (hardcover) | ISBN 9781771124843 (EPUB) | ISBN 9781771124850 (PDF)

Subjects: LCSH: Dance—Social aspects—Canada. | LCSH: Cultural pluralism—Canada.

Classification: LCC GV1588.6 .M68 2021 | DDC 792.8/0971—dc23

Cover and interior design by John van der Woude, JVDW Designs.
Front-cover image by master1305 via *iStock.com*.

Waterloo, Ontario, Canada
www.wlupress.wlu.ca

Printed in Canada

We dedicate this book to the choreographers and performers who shared their love of dance with us.

CONTENTS

III. IDENTITY FORMATION AND ARTISTIC AGENCY

IV. EDUCATION AND THE PROCESSES OF NORMALIZATION

V. BUILDING COALITIONS / BELONGING TO COMMUNITIES

LIST OF ILLUSTRATIONS

ACKNOWLEDGEMENTS

Moving Together: Dance and Pluralism in Canada has been in process for a long time. Along the way, the project has benefited from the generosity of many people. First and foremost, we would like to thank our contributors for their insightful research, goodwill, and patience.

We would also like to thank our families, colleagues, and friends for their questions and feedback about this project, which helped us to think more deeply about dance and pluralism. A special word of appreciation goes to Selma Odom, who forwarded an article within hours of a request. Her professionalism and collegiality continue to inspire and instruct.

The aid of our academic institutions was a great help. We acknowledge the support of the Faculty of Social Sciences and Humanities at Lakehead University, the Faculty of Fine Arts at the University of Victoria, and the University of Victoria Book and Creative Work Subvention Fund.

We have been fortunate to work with excellent freelance copy editors. Emma Woodley provided skilled assistance for an early draft of the manuscript. We are especially indebted to Hayley Evans, a gifted and meticulous editor, who worked closely with us as the project evolved.

Many thanks to our colleagues at Wilfrid Laurier University Press. Lisa Quinn welcomed our proposal and helped us through the initial stages. We also extend our thanks to the two anonymous external readers who were invited by WLU Press to comment on the manuscript. Our collection has benefited immensely from their investment of time as well as their constructive suggestions. Murray Tong, the managing editor, and WLU Press were wonderful to work with as they transformed our manuscript into a book. Thanks to Judi Gibbs, our lovely indexer. Finally, we would like to express our sincere gratitude to Siobhan McMenemy, the senior editor at WLU Press. This collection would never have come to fruition without her wise counsel and staunch support.

INTRODUCTION

CONTEXTS AND CHOICES

Allana C. Lindgren and Batia Boe Stolar

Canada has a long history of racial and ethnic diversity with a transnational circulation of people and cultural influences. Although the federal government, under the leadership of then Prime Minister Pierre Elliott Trudeau, officially adopted multiculturalism as a policy in 1971, as Lloyd Wong and Shibao Guo have asserted, "Multiculturalism existed demographically in Canada at the time of confederation when the country was formed."[1] They note, however, that diversity is not necessarily synonymous with equality, as the politically dominant culture in 1867 was still oriented towards the British Empire, rendering the multiplicity of races and ethnicities present in the Dominion of Canada at the time little more than "inequalitarian pluralism."[2]

Barely 150 years later, diversity has become a key part of the Canada's self-defined identity; it is a key concept the country uses and celebrates to distinguish itself from other nations. Echoing his father's sentiments, in a speech delivered in London, UK, in 2015, Prime Minister Justin Trudeau stated, "Canadians understand that diversity is our strength. We know that Canada has succeeded—culturally, politically, economically—because of our diversity, not in spite of it."[3]

Notwithstanding the Prime Minister's words, racial and ethnic disparities have been another defining aspect of the nation's colonialist history. The majority of hate crimes in Canada are motivated by racial or ethnic animosity (followed closely by religious prejudice).[4] In 2017, for instance, Barbara Kentner, an Indigenous woman, was killed from injuries after being hit by a trailer hitch thrown at her by a person in a moving vehicle in Thunder Bay—a city where almost 30 percent of the hate crimes in Canada that are specifically aimed at Indigenous people have occurred.[5] An attack on a mosque in Québec City, also in 2017, left six Muslim men dead and numerous other worshippers wounded. In 2018 and 2019, neo-Nazi recruiting posters were reported in Toronto and Winnipeg. The latter case has led to an investigation of an alleged neo-Nazi with explosives training who had been serving in the army reserves.[6] These examples—just a few of the incidents that occur on a yearly basis—demonstrate the urgent need to address violence sparked by racial and ethnic hatred.

In this light, the policies and laws pertaining to inclusivity that are grappled with on the legislative floors of government and then policed in streets and tested in the courts have real consequences for people's lives. Similarly, the everyday practices of pluralism—and marginalization—found in places of worship and educational institutions, on city streets and rural roads, in print and online media, on television and other modes of popular culture, and on national, city, and indie stages, collectively function as contributing factors that both shape and test the limits of inclusivity and tolerance, sharply foregrounding the uneven contours of opportunity and equity in Canada.

This collection asserts that the arts, specifically dance, have a significant, yet largely unexamined, role to play in the questioning and crafting of our pluralist society. At first, the pairing of dance and the issues of pluralism might seem incongruent. For some, dance may be viewed as apolitical or an activity far removed from attempts to achieve parity when it comes to disproportionate political power. Indeed, the effects of dance endeavours can be fleeting and soon forgotten. Some might suggest that dance activities forestall real change by providing relief from the mounting pressures of intolerable inequity.

The chapters in this collection do not dispute these critiques, but instead ask readers to consider how teachers, choreographers, dancers, presenters, arts administrators, audiences, and reviewers practise pluralism in Canada. Their choreographic works, performance conventions, and attendant media responses reveal how identities and notions of difference are perceived within and beyond racially and ethnically defined communities. Their successes and challenges serve as exemplars and cautions not only for other artists, but also as models that can be transposed into broader contexts of pluralism. Most notably, like other forms of soft diplomacy, dance can help to "set the stage" for social change. Dance brings people together to engage in non-threatening, non-legislated ways.[7] It provides opportunities to learn about cultures that are different from one's own. It facilitates moments when groups of people who have been historically marginalized take centre stage—literally and figuratively—and exercise agency. In other words, over the course of this collection, we argue that dance is an effective mode of inquiry to highlight the shifting concerns of pluralism in Canada.

Mindful of this focus, the title of the collection—*Moving Together: Dance and Pluralism in Canada*—can be interpreted in a number of ways. It proposes that dance can and does bring different communities of people together. It invites readers to think about the powerful visual symbolism of having people transcend racial and ethnic divides to dance with and for each other. Paradoxically, this collection also queries if the phrase "moving together" can apply to a single person. In thinking about subjectivity within the context of plurality, how might personal identities be forged from a broad swath of racial and ethnic characteristics? These markers are often further augmented or complicated by gender, class, age, and ability identifications. In this way, how might one's ever-accruing identities be "moving together" in acknowledgement that intersectionality is a dynamic element in the processes of identity formation and the plurality that defines each one of us?

The aim of this collection is to prompt discussion about the desirability and complications of what exactly "moving together" can mean. Does the phrase indicate the kind of unity in which it is possible to maintain one's individual identity while forging new alliances, or does "moving together" suggest conformity? While many of the case studies examined in this collection implicitly advance the perspective that dance can be a positive contributor to social change, readers are encouraged to consider the tensions and blind spots that sometimes accompany artistic activism.

THE POLITICS OF TERMINOLOGY

Throughout this collection, readers will encounter different terms used to discuss racial and ethnic inclusivity. Recognizing the range of descriptors in circulation in the dance community in Canada, no attempt has been made to achieve terminological uniformity. Nevertheless, it is acknowledged that the debates and critiques that some of the most pertinent terms have raised help to contextualize the issues addressed in these pages.

Most notably, although "multiculturalism" continues to be the preferred term within the Canadian federal government, it has become highly contentious in other sectors, contexts, and countries; for instance, multiculturalism as practiced in Europe has been resolutely denounced as a failure by several political leaders, including German Chancellor Angela Merkel, British Prime Minister David Cameron, and French President Nicolas Sarkozy.[8]

Within Canada there are divergent views about multiculturalism. One understanding of multiculturalism that has been advanced by Charles Taylor and Will Kymlicka, two prominent Canadian philosophers, is liberal multiculturalism.[9] According to Rita Dhamoon, "though varied in their normative positions and in terms of the practices they advocate, liberal multicultural theorists broadly claim that the equal treatment of 'minorities' requires public institutions to acknowledge, rather than ignore or downplay, cultural particularities."[10] While this approach is arguably more nuanced than the universalism underpinning perspectives that assume no differences between racial and ethnic groups and their positions within society or their relationships with the government, some scholars, including Dhamoon, have argued that there are problematic gaps between the idealism of liberal multiculturalist theory and how it is actually operationalized.[11] In other words, some critics have argued that, despite the rhetoric of inclusion, the policies and practices of liberal multiculturalism in Canada emphasize difference, separating—and ultimately ghettoizing—communities.[12] Multiculturalism has been critiqued for emphasizing superficial presentations and performances of diversity while essentially glossing over serious problems like racism and imbalanced access to political power.[13] Indeed, some scholars have contended that multiculturalist policies and practices have placated desires to promote Canada as a socially progressive and pluralist society without acknowledging that "diversity" is not synonymous with "parity." In this way, it can be argued that multiculturalism obfuscates the need to remedy raced-based and ethnically motivated discrimination.

A further critique involves attempts to include Indigenous peoples within the context of multiculturalism. Some scholars have resisted doing so because, as David B. MacDonald and others have asserted, the concept and practices of multiculturalism in Canada "insufficiently recognize the *sui generis* or inherent rights of Aboriginal peoples which existed before colonization and continue still. Aboriginal people are, through the expedient of multicultural policies, often placed alongside perceived ethnic minorities"—a distinction that can potentially help to evade action on land claims and treaty rights.[14]

Addressing theatre practices, Ric Knowles has suggested: "multiculturalism as performed through arts funding practices kept othered cultures in their static, nostalgic, and dehistoricized ethnic place, allowing dominant cultural expression to flourish within an established European tradition."[15] Similarly, Rustom Bharucha has argued that encounters between cultures are problematic if the politically dominant culture sets the terms of engagement, particularly if the artistic outcome is one of appropriation, extraction, and/or the exoticization of the other—or, more accurately, the Othered—culture.[16] Peter Brook's theatrical production of *The Mahabharata* (1985) exemplifies the kind of misguided and injurious approach that Bharucha critiques.[17] More generally, the mantra of some scholars (including Richard Schechner, one of the founders of Performance Studies) that suggests everything, including sacred ceremonies and religious rituals, can be viewed as "performance," is also problematic because it demonstrates a white/Western proclivity to assume the authority to classify and determine meaning while potentially trivializing spiritual rites by recasting them as "entertainment."[18]

At the same time, however, the agency and ingenuity of artists to work within and outside federal policies perceived as restrictive needs to be recognized as catalysts for artistic, social, and policy change. Despite the shortcomings of multiculturalism, there is a long list of artists in Canada who have found ways to bypass restrictive narratives that would limit them to performing superficial and historically static versions of their heritages. Or, as Knowles has stated, these performers—including, for example, artists associated with Native Earth Performing Arts, Cahoots Theatre Projects, and fu-GEN Asian Canadian Theatre, among others—have subverted "the official script in ways that ignore the folkloric enclaves into which they have been slotted, forming horizontal networks, performing into being new diasporic subjectivities, and establishing relationships and solidarities across acknowledged difference."[19] In this way, these artists have rejected what Jacqueline Lo and Helen Gilbert call "small 'm' multiculturalism," which often involves "folkloric displays" that tend to fetishize cultural difference: "Folkloric theatre trades in notions of history, tradition, and authenticity in order to gain recognition for the cultural capital of disenfranchised groups."[20] Instead, there is a growing number of artists in Canada whose work exemplifies Lo and Gilbert's concept of "big 'm' multiculturalism," which supports "a counterdiscursive practice that aims to promote cultural diversity, access to cultural expression, and participation in the symbolic space of the national narrative."[21]

In the wake of criticism of multiculturalism, many scholars have sought less contested terms to characterize the goals of racial and ethnic equality. In reviewing a few of these words, it becomes clear that just as "multiculturalism" has resonated in problematic ways in different countries and throughout time in Canada, other options also have troublesome baggage. One such word is "interculturalism."[22] This term has many proponents within arts scholarship, yet many early users of the term often simply perpetuated a universalism from a politically dominant white/Western perspective.[23] It is only in more recent scholarship that writers have recuperated the term to pursue the two-directional cultural exchange embedded in "interculturalism" as a promissory word.[24] However, beyond theatre, and even as recently as 2017, the term "interculturalism" has been used to represent hierarchical relationships between cultures. For example, "multiculturalism" is usually called "interculturalism" in Québec. As Stéphane Dion, the former leader of the Liberal Party of Canada and Canada's Ambassador to Germany and Special Envoy of the Prime Minister to the European Union and Europe suggests, the term "interculturalism" is preferred in Québec because it is seen "to emphasize the need to encourage newcomers to learn French and adopt cultural traits that distinguish Quebec."[25] Dion's comments unwittingly suggest that "interculturalism" is open to the same criticism of assimilation in the guise of diversity that has been levelled at multiculturalism.

Proponents of "new interculturalism"—a rethinking of interculturalism within Theatre Studies and Performance Studies spheres—have tried to recalibrate the strategies to achieve what Charlotte McIvor identified as "possibilities for both revisionist and future-oriented modes of critical engagement."[26] In so doing, one of new interculturalism's strategies is to decentre the West as a constant participant and referent in the intercultural engagement.[27]

Terminology is also of consequence for funding agencies. In addition to having an Equity Office and a "Diversity Evaluation Tool," which is accessible on its website, the Canada Council for the Arts has created a glossary that offers definitions for a range of terms and phrases such as "equity-seeking groups," and "minoritized culture"—words that all suggest sensitivity towards inclusivity.[28] Yet, once again, how a term is defined can yield challenging results. For example, the Canada Council defines "cultural diversity" as "the presence, expressions and participation of many different individuals and communities co-existing in the general culture of a society, and the explicit recognition that the contribution and participation of all peoples, particularly marginalized people, have the potential of equal value and benefit to the society at large."[29] This definition is troubling. The lack of clarity in the phrase "general culture" is evident. What does it mean? Whose culture is accepted as the general culture? Who defines which culture(s) are constitutive of the general culture? Likewise, what is implied by the inclusion of the term "potential" in the statement that "all peoples, particularly marginalized people, have the potential of equal value and benefit to the society at large"? As it stands, the phrasing can be interpreted to mean that marginalized people have the potential of equal value and benefit, but are not currently of equal value and benefit to Canadian society. This reading of the Canada Council's definition might be viewed as unfairly discounting the presumed goodwill that motivated the funding agency to create its glossary, but the slipperiness of definitions complicates and potentially contradicts the avowal of empowerment that "cultural diversity" might otherwise make.[30]

Regardless of terminological complexities, it is undisputable that dance artists in Canada have pursued the creative and liminal potential diversity. In so doing, many have adopted the term "hybridity," a concept closely associated with Homi Bhabha that has been used in dance in Canada largely as a way to describe cross-cultural collaborations based on respect.[31] Hybridity is not, however, the only word currently used to convey a commitment to bringing together artists from different aesthetic and cultural backgrounds. The phrase "fusion choreography" appears to be preferred by Menaka Thakkar, one of Canada's longest-practicing and most distinguished Bharatanatyam and Odissi artists, to describe the cross-cultural choreographic works she has been co-creating with other artists, including Robert Desrosiers, Claudia Moore, Danny Grossman, and William Lau, among others, since the 1980s.[32]

Despite this profusion of terminology, and while respecting the range of options chosen by our contributors, we have looked elsewhere for a word to use in the title of this collection that could be constructively be placed in conversation with the various connotations of the phrase "moving together." We chose "pluralism" in acknowledgement of the term's increasing currency within Canada by organizations such as the Global Centre for Pluralism in Canada, which was founded in Ottawa in 2006 by the federal government and His Highness the Aga Khan "to advance positive responses to the challenge of living peacefully and productively together in diverse societies."[33] In foregrounding this word in the title, this volume is aligned with the Global Centre's goal to engage with the ongoing experiment of diversity in Canada. We also chose the word in recognition of its longstanding presence in conversations about inclusivity in Canada. It has appeared in Hansard records of House of Commons debates, as well as in scholarship about racial and ethnic diversity in Canada extending back to the 1970s.[34] Furthermore, it was selected in response to the fact that in the early twenty-first century, the word is beginning to emerge as a preferred term within some sectors of the Canadian arts community.[35] Notably, the Cultural Pluralism in the Arts Movement Ontario, which was established in 2009 with the mandate "to open opportunities for Indigenous and racialized professionals and organizations," has been a strong advocate for "pluralism" as a term favoured by artists involved directly in debates about accessibility and equality.[36]

PREVIOUS DANCE SCHOLARSHIP

In addition to situating *Moving Together* within the ever-shifting terminology related to pluralism, it is important to acknowledge that this collection owes a debt to the existing body of literature about dance and the politics of inclusivity. While it is not possible to account for the entire publication list in this ever-growing field, there are several publications worth noting that will help readers to contextualize this volume within an ongoing discussion about diversity and Dance Studies. First, previous scholars have addressed the question of why dance is a particularly apt art form to assist in the examination of how collective identities are formulated. *The Oxford Handbook of Dance and Ethnicity* editors Anthony Shay and Barbara Sellers-Young suggest dance has multiple roles to play in the formation and representation of ethnic identities:

> Dance is a vehicle in the construction and exploration of danced ethnicity as specific embodiment of heritage, a form to explore new constructions of ethnicity, a choreographic framework for creating national unity through a shared experience of moving bodies, a space of resistance within the act of

> dancing to the imposition of social cultural forces, and a space in which to engage in dialogue about the meaning of race, gender, and lifestyle and their relationship to ethnic identity.[37]

Susan A. Reed adds to this assessment by noting that through the specificities of movement, costumes, and music, dance performances can be a way to resist cultural homogenization and to assert cultural heritage.[38] Following the lead of these scholars, many chapters in this collection explore the potential of dance to facilitate cultural harmony in Canada while at the same time functioning as a positive means through which identity is constituted and asserted.

Dance has also been used to blur the distinctions between cultural identities and nationalist sentiments. As Reed suggests, dance has long been used as a tool of cultural nationalism: "Since the late nineteenth and early twentieth centuries, with the rise of cultural nationalism in Europe and its colonies, dance has figured prominently in the creation of many ethnic and national 'cultures.'"[39] Part of dance's attractiveness in this regard is its malleability—or, again turning to Reed: "As a highly portable, largely nonthreatening, and relatively accessible medium, dance is easily packaged and staged as cultural tradition."[40]

Dance can, however, also contribute to ongoing inequity. Like their counterparts in other fields, Dance Studies scholars have been wary of the problems of seemingly progressive or celebratory modes of diversity. Echoing critiques expressed in other disciplines, Yutian Wong has succinctly stated: "'Multicultural celebrations' are often comprised of a collection of uncontextualized, ahistoricized, and apoliticized practices."[41] Attentive to the implications of language, Susan Leigh Foster parses the unquestioned assumptions about the phrases "world arts" and "world stage" at her home department, the Department of World Arts and Cultures at the University of California, Los Angeles, noting that these classifications can "gloss over the colonial legacy of racialized and class-based hierarchizations of the arts."[42] Although some of the contributors to this collection focus on celebratory events, they heed the cautions of Wong and Foster by offering analyses that are not to meant to unthinkingly commend. Instead, they present case studies that will provoke a range of responses about how pluralism is defined and practised in Canada.

In addition to critiquing celebratory multiculturalism, dance scholars have also addressed the tensions between tradition and innovation. As Anthony Shay has observed—and Hari Krishnan confirms in this volume—folk festival presenters and audiences can perpetuate expectations that folk or ethnic dance practices are always oriented towards the past.[43] In so doing, they suspend dance styles—and the cultures in which they were created—in the past, robbing them of the ability to demonstrate innovation or to have contemporary relevance and agency. In examining the transnational circulations of Bharatanatyam, Janet O'Shea broaches the tensions between the dance form's classicist champions and the proponents who value Bharatanatyam's artistic elasticity, diplomatically counselling, "I think we should keep asking... questions; I just don't think we should necessarily lock down the answers to them."[44]

The tradition/innovation binary has garnered a lot of attention, in part because it inevitably leads to questions about authenticity, and ultimately distils into questions about power and ownership of cultural expressions. For instance, addressing the commercialization of traditional Kānaka Maoli culture in Hawai'i, Stephanie Nohelani Teves (Kānaka Maoli)—in alignment with scholars like Dhamoon—has argued that multiculturalism has yoked Indigenous peoples to prescribed expectations of Indigeneity:

> While it might appear that the cultures of 'the other' are now being accepted and celebrated, this often happens through a frame of liberal multiculturalism that depoliticizes and diminishes difference by emphasizing a surface-level celebration of cultural diversity that does not fully engage a transformative struggle against racism and white supremacy... This means that Indigenous peoples have to properly perform culture in order to be seen as Indigenous to begin with, thus binding indigeneity solely to cultural difference and denying Indigenous political self-determination.[45]

To counter the cultural calcification and political marginalization that can result from the label "traditional," it is helpful to consider Emily Wilcox's use of the phrase "dynamic inheritance" to describe some Chinese dance artists' inclination to pursue creativity within the context of their movement lineages:

> [Dynamic inheritance] is guided by the premise that cultural traditions inherently change and that they thus require continual innovation to maintain relevance to the contemporary world. In a basic sense, dynamic inheritance refers to the idea that cultural inheritance and individual innovation are mutually reinforcing processes."[46]

Other scholars, both in Dance Studies and beyond, have considered how national narratives reverberate in new ways when placed within global contexts.[47] The transnational circulation of aesthetic and political ideas embodied by dancers has been examined by a number of Dance Studies scholars, including Susan Manning, who insightfully reminds readers that transnationalist approaches can lead to alternate histories "as artists and educators move between the frames of myriad states."[48] The discussions about racial and ethnic diversity in this volume hopefully will facilitate reflection on the engagement between cultures and influences. Indeed, most of our contributors probe how dance styles from other countries have been reconceptualized within Canada while exploring how the international is localized.

At the same time, this volume clearly attends to—and reinforces—the continued validity of the nation-state as a topic of investigation. In *Staging the UK*, Jen Harvie opines that national identities can create real consequences for citizens "because they produce and distribute power, power that can be both oppressive and enabling."[49] Additionally, we also agree with Harvie that the arts do not simply *reflect* the nation, but that they are also actively involved in the fluctuant nature of nation-making: "if national identities are dynamic, they can be changed, and such change might contribute to social improvement—or decline."[50] As our authors demonstrate through the range of case studies they collectively explore, the ideas and images of "Canada" that are created and conveyed through dance-related practices and performances have an impact, not only on the individual participants, but also in the way they accrue to contribute to our larger understanding of what it means to be Canadian at different moments in the nation's history.

CONTINUING THE CONVERSATION: OUR CONTRIBUTORS

Despite efforts by dance artists, policymakers, and scholars dedicated to promoting pluralism in Canada, there is still work to do as cultural ignorance remains as a significant and troubling problem. Kevin A. Ormsby, dance artist, Artistic Director of KasheDance, and Program Manager for Cultural Pluralism in the Arts Movement Ontario, has succinctly articulated the issue: "Culturally diverse artists, regardless of generation, face marginality because of a lack of understanding of diverse art forms."[51] In other words, plurality requires more than "widening the circle" of social participation. Optimally, a heterogenetic Canada involves embracing cultural difference. Respect, in turn, is based on knowledge, and knowledge is attained through education and a desire to learn about cultures beyond one's own; yet, dance artist Natasha Bakht has pointedly noted that the effort to educate the politically dominant demographic has often fallen to the traditionally marginalized—a situation that demonstrates and reinforces the lack of equilibrium in the process of moving Canada towards equality:

> As I got older, I grew impatient with the questions and began to tire of explaining to wide-eyed white people what this charming form of dance was. This is the load that multiculturalism insists that some of us carry, while allowing other Canadians to take no responsibility for their own learning. What amazes me when I attend these events today is that the questions have not changed. The burden of educating people about bharata natyam still rests on the shoulders of young women, usually women of colour. Today, when someone asks me "what is bharata natyam?" I feel like saying, "google it."[52]

Heeding Bakht's objection, we have gathered a mix of scholars and artists who draw from a range of methodologies to explore on how pluralism has been practised in dance studios and stages across Canada. The variety of topics and themes they address and the spectrum of perspectives they offer hopefully will be instructive and provide a broad introduction to the possibilities that dance facilitates, as well as illuminating the limits of artistic interventions.

Section One, "Setting the Stage," contains one chapter, "Dancing Pluralism in Canada: A Brief Historical Overview," which examines how pluralism has been embodied by dancers in Canada. As the selection of case studies in this chapter demonstrate, dance has been used to resist assimilation while exposing exclusionary cultural policies and discriminatory assumptions about "high" and "low" art. Dance has also facilitated self-defined definitions of racial and ethnic subjectivity, and has provided creative opportunities for cross-cultural collaborations and advocacy. In other words, this brief overview invites readers to consider the power of dancing bodies throughout Canada's history.

The chapters in Section Two, "The Discourses of Pluralism," showcase how the various discourses of pluralism have been used to support nation-building exercises that, paradoxically, undermine and/or absorb cultural and regional differences. In so doing, they remind readers of the real ways that the discursive power of language has influenced the history of pluralism in Canada. Together, the chapters in this section advocate for a more nuanced approach to the examination of pluralism in Canada, even if—particularly if—doing so undermines pretensions of racial and ethnic harmony and cohesiveness.

In Chapter Two, "Embodying the Canadian Mosaic: The Great West Canadian Folk Dance, Folk Song, and Handicraft Festival, 1930," Anne Flynn examines the 1930 Canadian Pacific Railway (CPR) Folk Festival in Calgary. She outlines how the CPR festivals were promoted as a celebration of Canadian diversity unified into what organizer John Murray Gibbon coined as the "Canadian mosaic." Yet, as Flynn demonstrates, the festival actually functioned as a process of acculturation that normalized colonial hierarchies by capitalizing on the anti-modernist appeal of the "folk" and exploiting dance as a "renewable cultural resource." In this way, the commercialization of the folk in Canada underscores how the promotion of the Great West Canadian Folk Dance, Folk Song, and Handicraft Festival co-opted pluralism as an advertising tool to attract customers to CPR hotels.

In the next chapter, "Olé, eh?: Canadian Multicultural Discourses and Atlantic Canadian Flamenco," Batia Boe Stolar explores the media responses to El Viento Flamenco, a Flamenco group founded by three local St. John's, Newfoundland, residents in 1996. Most reviewers were initially perplexed by what they perceived as the incompatibility of Flamenco in Newfoundland: how could a "hot" Andalusian art be transposed to the "cold" Atlantic Canadian environment? By the time the group dispersed, however, reviewers had shifted their understanding of the Flamenco group by promoting "cultural hybridity as distinctly Canadian." Assessing this turn in perception, Stolar emphasizes the need to remain attentive to the ways that cultural difference is discussed.

In Chapter Four, "Illuminating a Disparate Diaspora: Fijian Dance in Canada," Evadne Kelly is interested in how the conflicts between Fijian-Canadian communities in Vancouver are conveyed and perpetuated through dance-related events. Specifically, she examines public dance performances by the diasporic Fijian community in Vancouver to disclose deep tensions between Fijians of Indian descent and Indigenous Fijians (iTaukei). As a result, Kelly suggests that "the two Fiji Day celebrations and the Christian Meke push against the Canadian discourse of multiculturalism, which erases tensions and differences and contradictions within so-called ethnic groups."

While Kelly illuminates the complexities and dissension between different factions of Fijian Canadians in Vancouver, in Chapter Five, "Ukrainian Theatrical Dance on the Island: Speaking Back to National and Provincial Images of Multicultural Cape Breton," Marcia Ostashewski shows how the diverse demographics in Cape Breton have been minimized in favour of easily packaged regional stereotypes. According to Ostashewski, the cultural branding of Cape Breton as Scottish, Acadian, and Mi'kmaq is limiting, as it does not recognize Nova Scotia's full range of cultural diversity. Using examples of dance activities to assert the energy and artistic presence of Ukrainian immigrants and their descendants, Ostashewski argues that it is possible to rewrite stereotypical narratives about the province in ways that provide a more accurate understanding of the rich range of cultural experiences in this part of Canada.

"Zab Maboungou: Trance and Locating the Other," Bridget E. Cauthery's contribution, draws attention to the inconsistencies between the ideals of pluralism and its practices by examining the work of Montréal-based dancer and choreographer Zab Maboungou, whose work subverts "both the homogenizing gaze and constructed narratives that seek to contain her and the art she creates." In particular, as Cauthery's analysis makes clear, dancers/choreographers, audiences, and funding agencies define culture and cultural identities in multiple and sometimes contradictory ways that reveal entrenched colonial assumptions and expectations.

The chapters in Section Three, "Identity Formation and Artistic Agency," explore how dance artists exercise agency. Issues related to intersectionality, working within and beyond cultural traditions, the politics of intercultural/intracultural identities, and the complex relationship between artistic inspiration and cultural infringement are all considered in this section.

In Chapter Seven, "A Contemporary Global Artist's Perspective," Hari Krishnan, a self-proclaimed "global artist," reflects on the connections between gender, race, and ethnicity in his life and how they have all enriched his work as an artist. Emphatically rejecting the limits of binary thinking, his open-minded curiosity has embraced Bharatanatyam and contemporary dance vocabularies to explore new ideas about race and, importantly, gender. Weaving personal experience with scholarly insight, Krishnan passionately discusses how dance has inspired him to embrace his own intersectionality as a source of power.

Following Krishnan's account of personal agency, in "Re-imagining the Multicultural Citizen: 'Folk' as Strategy in the Japanese Canadians' 1977

Centennial National Odori Concert," Lisa Doolittle examines the six-city National Odori Concert tour that was performed by thirty Japanese Canadian girls known as the Nikka Festival Dancers. According to Doolittle, the tour "consciously and strategically mobilized 'folk' to forge community cohesion, cross-cultural comprehension, and more fully enfranchised citizenship for Japanese Canadians." The resulting self-defined image of Japanese Canadians was one that was respectful of tradition, motivated by a strong sense of community, and eager for new artistic possibilities.

In her chapter, "Dance as a Curatorial Practice: Performing Moving Dragon's *Koong* at the Royal Ontario Museum," Allana C. Lindgren analyzes *Koong*, a choreographic work performed in the Gallery of Chinese Architecture in Toronto's Royal Ontario Museum (ROM) by Chengxin Wei and Jessica Jone, the husband-and-wife founders and artistic directors of Moving Dragon, a dance company based in Vancouver. Lindgren suggests that through *Koong*, these artists recontextualize the objects in the gallery and, in so doing, situate themselves as Chinese Canadians and artists.

In "Kinetic Crossroads: Chouinard, Sinha, and Castello," the title of Chapter Ten, Dena Davida examines the ways in which three choreographers—Marie Chouinard, Roger Sinha, and Maria Castello—adapt racially and ethnically diverse sources of inspiration in Québec. She invites readers to think about the potential for creativity—and problems—in the interface between artistic agency and cultural appropriation. Originally published in 1994, Davida has added an epilogue for this collection in which she reflects on the changes within the critical debates among dance scholars, as well as the ways in which the same arguments continue to inform practices of hybridity and generate questions about agency in the work of contemporary Montréal choreographers.

Several writers in the collection are interested in the importance of education in cultivating social change. This topic is explored in Section Four, "Education and the Processes of Normalization." Together, these chapters explore educational contexts and strategies for the normalization of positive racial and ethnic identities that can be implemented within studios, stages, post-secondary institutions, and on the street.

In Chapter Eleven, "From Inclusion to Integration: Intercultural Dialogue and Contemporary University Dance Education," Danielle Robinson and Eloisa Domenici advocate for recalibrating the curricula of university dance programs, arguing that the dominance of ballet and modern dance techniques should be supplanted with a pluralist focus. Intercultural integration, and not simply inclusion, is the goal.

Janelle Joseph writes about the sense of "kinaesthetic groupness" she experienced as part of a flash mob performing dances from different cultures in Chapter Twelve, "A Dance Flash Mob, Canadian Multiculturalism, and Kinaesthetic Groupness." She asserts that flash mobs disturb the social order, as well as provide opportunities for both performers and audience members to cast themselves as participants in diverse communities. She suggests that while flash mobs are unlikely to create permanent social change, they have the potential to inspire new social images and perceptions of pluralism and, in so doing, become a form of "public pedagogy" in which understanding and empathy can be fostered.

The goal of dance is to educate and empower: this message underpins Chapter Thirteen, "Contemporary Indigenous Dance in Canada," a conversation between dance scholars Carolyne Clare and Samantha Mehra, and Indigenous dance artist Santee Smith. In reading the resulting transcript of this discussion, it becomes clear that Smith's successes as a dancer, teacher, choreographer, and Artistic Director provide helpful strategies that can supplant racial stereotypes with more productive images of Indigenous agency.

In Chapter Fourteen, "'There Is the Me That Loves to Dance': Dancing Cultural Identities in Theatre for Young Audiences," Heather Fitzsimmons Frey addresses the educational value of dance in helping children appreciate diverse cultural identities through positive images. She writes that dance in Theatre for Young Audiences (TYA) productions "can inspire children to ask challenging questions about cultural and racially constructed differences—about who they are, who they would like to be, and what it means to be Canadian." In this way, dance is an effective conduit for conveying messages of empowerment to children.

How can dance be used to influence the development of racially and ethnically specific communities? Conversely, how can dance facilitate the construction of culturally pluralistic communities? Do you need to share the racial or ethnic heritage of a group to belong? These are some of the questions addressed in Section Five, "Building Coalitions / Belonging to Communities"—questions that encourage readers to think about the parameters of membership in cultural organizations and communities that are defined in racial and ethnic terms.

In Chapter Fifteen, "The Presence and Future of Danish Folk Dancing in Canada," Suzanne Jaeger laments the diminishing membership in the Danish folk dance group she has performed with for a number of years. Jaeger offers potential strategies for attracting new members, including joining forces with other Scandinavian dance groups, adapting the dances or introducing new dances that better reflect the contemporary diversity of Denmark, adopting gender-neutral terminology for the steps, or finding innovative ways to combine Danish dance with other dance styles.

Chapter Sixteen, "Glimpses of a Cultural Entrepreneur," a conversation between P. Megan Andrews and Yasmina Ramzy, a dance artist and teacher, draws the reader's attention to an important yet often overlooked aspect of dance: the business and economics of "world dance" in Canada. As a longstanding leader in belly dance in Canada, Ramzy has been key in building appreciation of and participation in the art form. At the same time, she acknowledges the tensions between wanting to explore the creative potential of belly dance and the limited financial support that keeps the belly dance community largely marginalized in this country.

In Chapter Seventeen, "Dance and the Fulfillment of Multicultural Desire: The Reflections of an Accidental Ukrainian," Steven Jobbitt notes the pleasure he derives from both taking and teaching Ukrainian dance classes. Although he is not Ukrainian by birth or heritage, he has been a longstanding member of a Ukrainian dance group in Thunder Bay. His story unabashedly refutes the criticisms of multiculturalism in the 1970s as creating superficial cultural silos by demonstrating how dance creates opportunities to learn about cultures beyond one's own heritage and foster community-building beyond the bounds of ethnicity.

In Chapter Eighteen, "Old Roads, New World: Exploring Collaboration through Kathak and Flamenco," Catalina Fellay concludes our collection by examining *Old Roads/New World* (1996) and *Firedance: Collected Stories* (1999), the collaborative choreographic works of Joanna De Souza, a specialist in Kathak dance, and Esmeralda Enrique, an expert in Flamenco. Fellay explores how these artists co-choreographed these dances in ways that value tradition while simultaneously facilitating pluralistic partnerships and choreographic innovation.

Although *Moving Together* contributes to the ongoing scholarly debate about pluralism in Canada, it does not presume to offer definitive conclusions.

Indeed, the volume will be most effective if it sparks new conversations and research that extend beyond its covers. To this end, readers are encouraged to pursue other examples of how dance contributes to the ongoing contestation and reconceptualization of pluralism, not only in Canada, but in transcultural contexts as well. That is, how does dance in Canada function as a conduit for practices that foster or curb cultural diversity in relation to dance activities in nations with similar immigration histories? Productive comparisons could also be made with countries that have differing histories and divergent understandings of immigration and pluralism.

The ultimate goal of *Moving Together* is to focus on experiences, problems, and aspirations as expressed in Canada. Through their methodological approaches and resulting analyses, our contributors demonstrate how dance can be used not only to contemplate the contours of pluralism in Canada, but also to offer models for change that combine pragmatism with optimism. Conversely, chapters that examine hurdles faced by dance artists due to the cultural illiteracy and prejudices of audiences, reviewers, administrators, or funders provide a necessary reminder that more work is needed before equality can be fully realized. In short, our contributors raise complex and often vexing issues while offering creative strategies that can be transposed into everyday opportunities as we move together to fulfill our potential as a country dedicated to the ideals of pluralism.

NOTES

1 Lloyd Wong and Shibao Guo, "Revisiting Multiculturalism in Canada: An Introduction," in *Revisiting Multlticulturalism in Canada; Theories, Policies and Debates*, eds. Shibao Guo and Lloyd Wong (Rotterdam: Sense Publishers, 2015), 1.

2 Ibid.

3 Right Hon. Justin Trudeau, Prime Minister of Canada, "Diversity Is Canada's Strength," London, United Kingdom, November 26, 2015, accessed September 27, 2019, http://pm.gc.ca/en/news/speeches/2015/11/26/diversity-canadas-strength. According to the 2016 nationwide census, Canadians reported over 250 ethnic origins compared to the approximately twenty ethnic groups that were counted in the 1871 census, the first to be held after Confederation. Statistics Canada, "Ethnic and Cultural Origins of Canadians: Portrait of a Rich Heritage," October 25, 2017, accessed September 6, 2019, http://www12.statcan.gc.ca/census-recensement/2016/as-sa/98-200-x/2016016/98-200-x2016016-eng.cfm.

4 Statistics Canada, "Table 35-10-0066-01, "Police-reported Hate Crime, by Type of Motivation, Canada (Selective Police Services)," accessed September 6, 2019, https://doi.org/10.25318/3510006601-eng.

5 Gloria Galloway, "Hate and Hope in Thunder Bay: A City Grapples with Racism Against Indigenous People," *Globe and Mail*, March 27, 2019, accessed September 9, 2019, https://www.theglobeandmail.com/canada/article-hate-and-hope-in-thunder-bay-a-city-grapples-with-racism-against/.

6 "School, City Condemn Neo-Nazi Posters Plastered in St. Clair West Area Park," CBC *News*, May 29, 2018, accessed September 9, 2019, http://www.cbc.ca/news/canada/toronto/neo-nazis-anti-semitic-posters-1.4682529. See also, "Truck of Former Reservist with Alleged Neo-Nazi Ties Found Near U.S.-Canada Border," CBC *News*, September 3, 2019, accessed September 9, 2019, http://www.cbc.ca/news/canada/manitoba/patrik-mathews-neo-nazi-group-recruitment-1.5268780.

7 For a more detailed discussion about the dance as a form of social activism, see Allana C. Lindgren, "Civil Rights Strategies in the United States: Franziska Boas's Activist Use of Dance, 1933-1965," *Dance Research Journal* 45, no. 2 (August 2013): 25–62.

8 For more details and commentary on the articulations of multiculturalism in Europe and accompanying critiques, see Raymond Taras, *Challenging Multiculturalism: European Models of Diversity* (Edinburgh: University of Edinburgh Press, 2013); Jonathan Laurence and Justin Vaïsse "The Dis-Integration of Europe," *Foreign Policy*, March 28, 2011, accessed August 26, 2019, http://foreignpolicy.com/2011/03/28/the-dis-integration-of-europe/; Kenan Malik, "The Failure of Multiculturalism: Community Versus Society in Europe," *Foreign Affairs* 94, no. 2 (March/April 2015): 21–32; Matthew Weaver, "Angela Merkel: German Multiculturalism has 'Utterly Failed'," *The Guardian*, October 17, 2010, accessed August 26, 2019, http://www.theguardian.com/world/2010/oct/17/angela-merkel-german-multiculturalism-failed; "Merkel Says German Multicultural Society Has Failed," BBC *News*, October 17, 2010, accessed August 26, 2019, http://www.bbc.com/news/world-europe-11559451. See also, Oliver Wright and Jerome Taylor, "Cameron: My War on Multiculturalism," *The Independent*, February 5, 2011, accessed August 26, 2019, https://www.independent.co.uk/news/uk/politics/cameron-my-war-on-multiculturalism-2205074.html; and John F. Burns, "Cameron Criticizes 'Multiculturalism' in Britain," *New York Times*, February 5, 2011, accessed August 26, 2019, http://www.nytimes.com/2011/02/06/world/europe/06britain.html. In addition, see Peggy Hollinger, "Sarkozy Joins Multiculturalism Attack," *Financial Times*, February 10, 2011, accessed August 26, 2019, http://www.ft.com/content/05baf22e-356c-11e0-aa6c-00144feabdc0.

9 For a detailed discussion of the various approaches to multiculturalism and their various proponents, see Michael Murphy, *Multiculturalism: A Critical Introduction* (London: Routledge, 2012).

10 Rita Dhamoon, *Identity/Difference Politics* (Vancouver: UBC Press, 2009), 3. Even within the context of liberal multiculturalism, there are a range of approaches,

including between Taylor and Kymlicka. For a detailed discussion of liberal multiculturalism, see Dhamoon, especially "Chapter One: The Problem with 'Culture.'"

11 Ibid., 8.

12 See, for example, Neil Bissoondath, *Selling Illusions: The Cult of Multiculturalism in Canada* (Toronto: Penguin, 1994).

13 This critique about multiculturalism has been made by many scholars. For a more detailed discussion, see, for example, Himani Bannerji, *The Dark Side of the Nation: Essays on Multiculturalism, Nationalism and Gender* (Toronto: Canadian Scholars' Press, 2000), 46–55.

14 David B. MacDonald, "Aboriginal Peoples and Multicultural Reform in Canada: Prospects for a New Binational Society," *Canadian Journal of Sociology* 39, no.1 (2014): 67.

15 Ric Knowles, *Performing the Intercultural City* (Ann Arbor: University of Michigan Press, 2017), 28.

16 Rustom Bharucha, *Theatre and the World: Performance and the Politics of Culture* (London: Routledge, [1990] 1993). See also Knowles, *Performing the Intercultural City*, 2, 127.

17 For a detailed critique, see Chapter Four, "Peter Brook's Mahabharata: A View from India," in *Theatre and the World: Performance and the Politics of Culture*, 69–88.

18 For an example that demonstrates this oversight, see Richard Schechner, "Foreword," in *Teaching Performance Studies, eds. Nathan Stucky and Cynthia Wimmer* (Carbondale, IL: Southern Illinois University Press, 2002), ix–xii.

19 Knowles, *Performing the Intercultural City*, 31.

20 Jacqueline Lo and Helen Gilbert, "Toward a Topography of Cross-Cultural Theatre Praxis," *TDR* 46, no. 3 175 (Fall 2002): 34.

21 Ibid.

22 Another term is "interweaving." As imagined by Erika Fischer-Lichte, the interweaving of "performance cultures can and quite often do provide an experimental framework for experiencing the utopian potential of culturally diverse and globalized societies by realizing an aesthetic which gives shape to unprecedented collaborative policies in society," (11). For further commentary, see Erika Fischer-Lichte, "Introduction: Interweaving Performance Cultures—Rethinking 'Intercultural Theatre': Toward an Experience and Theory of Performance beyond Postcolonialism," in *The Politics of Interweaving Performance Cultures: Beyond Postcolonialism*, eds. Erika Fischer-Lichte, Torsten Jost, and Saskya Iris Jain (New York and London: Routledge, 2014), 1-24.

23 For a more detailed discussion of this issue, see Knowles, *Performing the Intercultural City*, 2; and Bharucha, *Theatre and the World: Performance and the Politics of Culture*, 244. See also, Royona Mitra, *Akram Khan: Dancing New Interculturalism* (Basingstoke: Palgrave Macmillan, 2015), 15. For an overview of the debates about multiculturalism and interculturalism more generally, see Nasar Meer, Tariq Modood, and Ricard Zapata-Barrero, *Multiculturalism and*

Interculturalism: Debating the Dividing Lines (Edinburgh: Edinburgh University Press, 2016).

24 Following, in part, Knowles' bibliographical lead, see Bharucha, *Theatre and the World: Performance and the Politics of Culture*; Christopher Balme, *Decolonizing the Stage: Theatrical Syncreticism and Post-colonial Drama* (Oxford: Oxford University Press, 1999); and Helen Gilbert and Jacqueline Lo, *Performance and Cosmopolitics: Cross-Cultural Transactions in Australasia* (Basingstoke: Palgrave Macmillan, 2008).

25 Stéphane Dion, "Diversity Is a Fact; Inclusion Is a Choice," Keynote speech for the conference, Inclusive Societies? Canada and Belgium in the 21st Century, Palais des Académies, Brussels, September 22, 2017, accessed September 28, 2019, http://www.canadainternational.gc.ca/germany-allemagne/highlights-faits/2017/2017-09-26-diversity_fact-diversite_fait.aspx?lang=en#_ftnref19.

26 See McIvor's excellent "Introduction: New Directions?" for a nuanced overview of the contentiousness as well as the potential benefits of "new interculturalism": Charlotte McIvor, "Introduction: New Directions?" in *Interculturalism and Performance Now: New Directions?* eds. Charlotte McIvor and Jason King. (Basingstoke: Palgrave Macmillan, 2019), 1-26.

27 McIvor reviews the relevant literature, which focusing particularly on "Asian interculturalism." For more details, see McIvor, 6. For other strategies, see McIvor, 4.

28 The "Diversity Evaluation Tool" is a form that helps arts organizations to assess and communicate their level of engagement with diversity. See also Canada Council for the Arts, "Glossary," accessed August 29, 2019, https://canadacouncil.ca/glossary.

29 Ibid.

30 The phrase "cultural diversity" has additionally faced criticism from other quarters. Homi Bhabha, for instance, has suggested that "cultural difference" is less problematic than "cultural diversity":

> Although there is always an entertainment and encouragement of cultural diversity, there is always also a corresponding containment of it. A transparent norm is constituted, a norm given by the host society or dominant culture, which says that "these other cultures are fine, but we must be able to locate them within our own grid"...The difference of cultures cannot be something that can be accommodated within a universalist framework. Different cultures, the difference between cultural practices, the difference in the construction of cultures within different groups, very often set up among and between themselves an *incommensurability*. (Emphasis in original.)

See Homi Bhabha as quoted in Jonathan Rutherford, "Interview with Homi Bhabha," in *Identity: Community, Culture, Difference*, ed. Jonathan Rutherford (London: Lawrence & Wishart, 1990), 208, 209. See also Homi Bhabha, "Cultural Diversity and Cultural Differences," in *The Post-Colonial Studies Reader*, eds. Bill Ashcroft, Gareth Griffiths, and Helen Tiffin (London: Routledge, 2006), 155–56.

31 The term is used, for example, by Co.ERASGA, a dance company in Vancouver founded and led by Alvin Erasga Tolentino. (The company's website states that "Co.ERASGA has a distinguished international reputation with its vision of hybrid dance, diversity and collaboration with other artistic practices and multimedia.") See Co.ERASGA, accessed August 29, 2019, http://companyerasgadance.ca/about/. Hybridity is not without its critics. For a more detailed discussion of the term within the context of postcolonialism, see Amar Acheraïou, *Questioning Hybridity: Postcolonialism and Globalization* (Basingstoke: Palgrave Macmillan, 2011).

32 See Menaka Thakkar Dance, accessed August 29, 2019, http://www.menaka thakkardance.org/about-mtdc.html and http://www.menakathakkardance.org/about-menaka.html.

33 The Global Centre for Pluralism, accessed September 9, 2019, http://www.pluralism.ca/who-we-are/. "Pluralism," as defined by this organization, is "an ethic of respect for diversity. Whereas diversity is a fact, pluralism is a choice. Pluralism results from the daily decisions taken by state institutions, by civil society actors and associations and by individuals to recognize and value human differences." See the Global Centre for Pluralism, accessed September 9, 2019, http://www.pluralism.ca/what-we-do-2/.

34 For instance, see Library and Archives Canada, House of Commons, *Debates, 28th* Parliament, 3rd Session, Volume 8 (October 8, 1971): 8545; see also, Hédi Bouraoui, *The Canadian Alternative: Cultural Pluralism and Canadian Unity* (Downsview: ECW Press, 1980).

35 We would like to thank P. Megan Andrews for alerting us to the increased use of the term within the Canadian dance community.

36 The Cultural Pluralism in the Arts Movement Ontario "seeks to open opportunities for Indigenous and racialized professionals and organizations to build capacity through access and working relationships with cultural institutions across Ontario that will result in constructive relationships with Indigenous and racialized professionals and organizations." See Cultural Pluralism in the Arts Movement Ontario, accessed August 29, 2019, http://cpamo.org/what-cpamo-does/. The Canadian Dance Assembly, a national advocacy agency for professional dance in Canada, has similarly adopted the term. The University of Toronto Scarborough offers a "Cultural Pluralism in the Arts" program through its Department of Arts, Culture and Media.

37 Anthony Shay and Barbara Sellers-Young, eds., *The Oxford Handbook of Dance and Ethnicity* (Oxford: Oxford University Press, 2016), 13.

38 Susan A. Reed, *Dance and the Nation; Performance, Ritual, and Politics in Sri Lanka* (Madison, WI: University of Wisconsin Press, 2010), 4.

39 Ibid., 5.

40 Ibid., 4.

41 Yutian Wong, *Choreographing Asian America* (Middletown, CT: Wesleyan University Press, 2010), 10.

42 Susan Leigh Foster, "Worlding Dance—An Introduction," in *Worlding Dance*, ed. Susan Leigh Foster (Basingstoke: Palgrave Macmillan, 2009), 2.

43 Anthony Shay, *Choreographing Identities: Folk Dance, Ethnicity and Festival in the United States and Canada* (Jefferson, NC: McFarland & Company, 2006).

44 Janet O'Shea, *At Home in the World: Bharata Natyam on the Global Stage* (Middletown, CT: Wesleyan University Press, 2007), x.

45 Stephanie Nohelani Teves, *Defiant Indigeneity: The Politics of Hawaiian Performance* (Chapel Hill: The University of North Carolina Press, 2018), 4–5.

46 Emily Wilcox, *Revolutionary Bodies: Chinese Dance and the Socialist Legacy* (Oakland, CA: University of California Press, 2018), 7.

47 See, for instance, Thomas Bender, ed., *Rethinking American History in a Global Age* (Berkeley: University of California Press, 2002).

48 Susan Manning, "Dance History," in *The Bloomsbury Companion to Dance Studies*, ed. Sherril Dodds (London: Bloomsbury, 2019), 313. Also see the dance chapters in Stephen Ross and Allana C. Lindgren, *The Modernist World* (London: Routledge, 2015).

49 Jen Harvie, *Staging the UK* (Manchester: Manchester University Press, 2005), 2.

50 Ibid., 3.

51 Kevin A. Ormsby, "Between Generations: Towards Understanding the Difference in Realities and Aspirations of the First and Second Generation of Culturally Diverse Artists," in *Pluralism in the Arts in Canada: A Change is Gonna Come*, ed. Charles C. Smith (Ottawa: Canadian Centre for Policy Alternatives, 2012), 76. For a detailed discussion about "cross-cultural" reviewing that addresses dance practices from a wide range of cultural influences, including those beyond the critic's own demographic, see Samantha Mehra, "Dance, Culture and the Printed Word: A Call for the Cosmopolitan Dance Critic," *Forum for Modern Language Studies* 46, no. 4 (September 2010): 431–40.

52 Natasha Bakht, "Mere 'Song and Dance': Complicating the Multicultural Imperative in the Arts," in *Pluralism in the Arts in Canada: A Change is Gonna Come*, ed. Charles C. Smith (Ottawa: Canadian Centre for Policy Alternatives, 2012), 19–20.

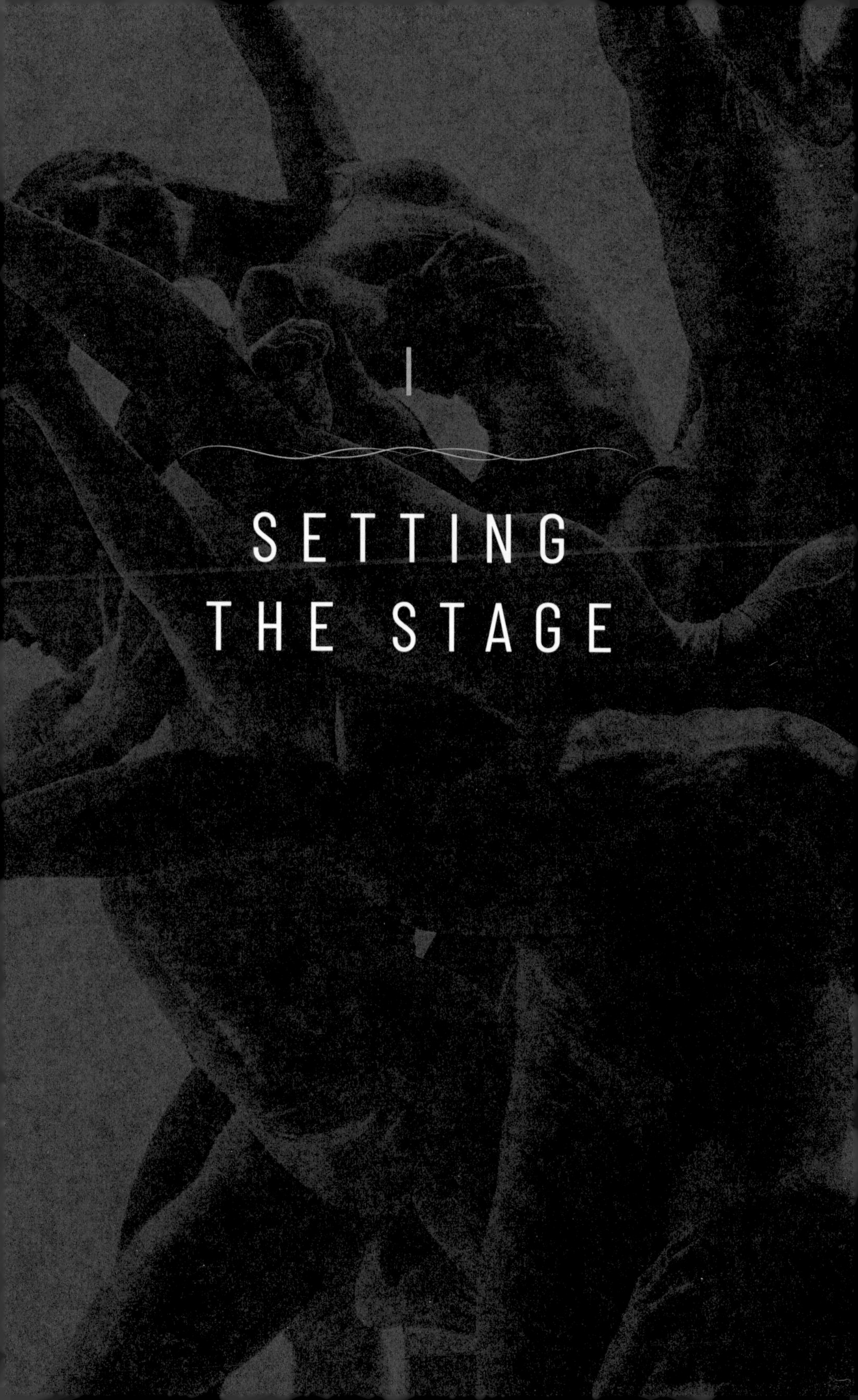

I

SETTING THE STAGE

ONE

DANCING PLURALISM IN CANADA

A BRIEF HISTORICAL OVERVIEW

Allana C. Lindgren

In 1909, Agnes Deans Cameron published *The New North: Being Some Account of a Woman's Journey through Canada to the Arctic*, a memoir of the Victoria-born woman's travels to the Arctic Ocean in the company of her niece, Jessie Cameron Brown.[1] Watching dancers at the wedding celebrations in a home in Northern Alberta, Cameron describes how babies were placed on benches along a wall while dogs peered through the windows into the crowded room where the air was thick with mosquitoes and tobacco smoke.[2] The atmosphere was festive as the first fiddler began to play, while two others waited to "relieve each other in turn, for fiddling, beating time with your moccasin on the earthen floor, and 'calling out,' is hard work for one man."[3] Dancing the Red River Jig likewise required intense energy. As Cameron observed, "Endurance is a sign of merit in the Red River Jig. A man or woman steps into the limelight and commences to jig, a dark form in moccasins slips in front of the dancer, and one jigs the other down, amid plaudits for the survivor and jeers for the quitter."[4]

It is uncertain if Cameron fully understood the complex hybrid origins of the Red River Jig as a Métis dance that integrates Indigenous, French, Scottish, and Irish influences.[5] Like the Métis themselves, the Red River Jig has culturally diverse roots. The style has drawn together different movement vocabularies to create a new tradition that pulsates with dynamism in performance. It is, in other words, an embodied affirmation of the power of pluralism in Canada.

At the same time, however, the Red River Jig also highlights discriminatory assumptions that have helped to perpetuate hierarchical social structures in Canada.[6] In 1928, only nineteen years after Cameron's eyewitness account of the Red River Jig appeared in print, Elizabeth B. Price wrote an article for the *Toronto Star Weekly* describing how two dance teachers in Calgary, Mrs. Angus McDonald and her daughter Marie, wanted to learn the Red River Jig in order to preserve it.[7] The article claims that the steps and music for the dance were no longer widely known, or as Price laments, "The only 'folk dance' of the west seemed to vanish."[8] The McDonalds, working with the Calgary Old Timers, an association that hosted banquets featuring historical dances, eventually found the Kiplings, a multigenerational family of Red River Jig dancers and musicians whom Price variously describes as a "pioneer family" and "native."[9] Readers are told that Willie Kipling, a fiddler, worked hours with Marie McDonald until she could play the music on the piano and that she was in the process of creating a piano score "so that anyone who reads music may play it."[10]

Price's article exemplifies the salvage ethnography trope that presumed the end of Indigenous societies and asserted the need for white settlers to preserve Indigenous cultural remnants.[11] To this end, Price paradoxically praises the McDonalds and Calgary Old Timers' preservation project while completely ignoring the fact that the Red River Jig *was* being preserved by families like the Kiplings, who corporeally archived the dance and passed it on from one generation to the next.[12] In other words, their embodied stewardship of Métis culture was neither recognized nor valued. Indeed, Price does not acknowledge the Red River Jig as a Métis dance and—equally as troubling—overlooks the Indigenous contribution to the movement style. Instead, she recasts the Red River Jig as European, writing, "Like the settlement of the west in those early days, it is a mix of new and old country nationals—an expression of a people far from their homes adapting themselves to a new country."[13]

Both Cameron's and Price's reactions to the Red River Jig demonstrate how dance can help to clarify how people in Canada have understood, practised, and contested pluralism. Dances, in other words, have their own histories that can supplement, enrich, and even complicate existing narratives about diversity in

Canada. To this end, this chapter begins by reviewing federal policies and laws related to immigration and multiculturalism before shifting to a dance perspective. This alternative history is by no means comprehensive, but instead offers an overview intended to contextualize the other chapters in this collection.

IMMIGRATION AND MULTICULTURALISM: POLICIES AND LAWS

Policies and laws are important repositories of attitudes towards race and ethnicity. Amendments to the Canadian Immigration Act, for instance, chart shifting perspectives about the desirability of diversity.[14] The Immigration Act of 1869, the first legislative statement on immigration enacted after Confederation, was relatively open, as it reflected the motivation of the federal government's desire to "settle" the West.[15] Conversely, the Chinese Immigration Act of 1885 was the first Canadian law to discriminate against prospective immigrants based on ethnic origin. Enacted in response to the influx of Chinese labourers hired to work on the Canadian Pacific Railway in the 1880s and the ensuing Royal Commission on Chinese Immigration (1885), the law levied a fifty-dollar duty on most people from China.[16]

This exclusionary view of immigration soon extended to applicants from countries beyond China. A goal to stem the increased immigration from Central, Eastern, and Southern Europe led to the Immigration Act of 1906, although labour needs appear to have mitigated the intended effect as immigration to Canada from countries like Italy and Ukraine, as well as Asian countries, actually continued to grow following this amendment.[17] A subsequent amendment in 1908 required immigrants to travel in a continuous journey from the countries in which they were born or of which they were citizens: a decree that particularly affected people from India and Japan, as there was no way at the time to travel directly from these countries to Canada. Further amendments in 1910 legalized the denial of entry to applicants considered "unsuited to the climate or requirements of Canada."[18] This phrase was used in an Order in Council the following year, which specifically prohibited "any immigrants belonging to the Negro race, which is deemed unsuitable to the climate and requirements of Canada."[19] In 1919, the Immigration Act was amended again to prohibit people viewed as enemy aliens because they came from countries that had fought against Canada and its allies during the First World War.

This targeted approach to immigration prevailed during the 1920s and 1930s. The 1922 Empire Settlement Act was a concerted attempt by the United Kingdom and the Dominions to expedite the migration of British subjects, while the Chinese Immigration Act of 1923 effectively halted emigration from China to Canada until the law was repealed in 1946. At the same time, however, immigration from previous banned European countries—except for Jewish applicants from these countries—was allowed in an attempt to address labour shortages in the agricultural sector.[20] The Depression years were accompanied by the strictest policies to curtail immigration that had been seen in the nation's history.[21] In 1931, only British and American citizens with demonstrated financial resources, farmers who had the ability to establish themselves, and spouses and offspring below the age of majority were allowed to relocate to Canada.

Efforts to achieve more inclusivity slowly began during the latter half of the twentieth century through the adoption of federal policies and the enactment of laws. Significant amendments were made to Canada's immigration policy in the early 1960s. As Ellen Fairclough, the Minister of Citizenship and Immigration at the time (and Canada's first female cabinet minister) stated, the new policy emphasized skills and promised to "provide for all applications to be dealt with on the basis of exactly the same criteria without discrimination on grounds of race, colour, ethnic origin or on any other grounds."[22] The result was an increase in the diversity of immigrants.

Also during the 1960s, the federal government initiated the Royal Commission on Bilingualism and Biculturalism (1963–1969). This initiative was prompted by a variety of factors, including the mounting frustration during the Quiet Revolution in Québec among French Canadians who wanted to protect their language and culture. The Commissioners, under the leadership of André Laurendeau and A. Davidson Dunton, were tasked with the following mandate:[23]

> To inquire into and report upon the existing state of bilingualism and biculturalism in Canada and to recommend what steps should be taken to develop the Canadian Confederation on the basis of an equal partnership between the two founding races, taking into account the contribution made by the other ethnic groups to the cultural enrichment of Canada and the measures that should be taken to safeguard that contribution....[24]

In addressing the contributions of immigrants, the Commissioners wrote in their final report that diversity was indeed important for the country:

> Canadian culture has been the richer for the knowledge, skills, and traditions which all the immigrant groups brought with them. Their many distinctive styles of life have gradually increased the range of experience, outlook, ideas, and talents which characterize the country. Cultural diversity has widened our horizons; it has also given opportunities—not always seized upon—for varied approaches to the solution of our problems. [25]

In the same vein, the Commissioners specifically noted the importance of pluralism to the arts in Canada:

> The coming together of diverse peoples in Canada also benefited our culture in the humanistic sense of the term. For a long time the frontier was not a rich soil for the arts and letters. Many of the frontiersmen had taken little part in the artistic life of their homeland, or if they had, they were forced to forgo such pursuits in the new country. As it matured, however, Canadian society turned to the search for grace and leisure, and the folk traditions preserved by the sons and daughters of the early settlers combined with the artistic sense, the talents, and the skills of later immigrants to add new dimensions to literature, music, and the plastic arts in Canada.[26]

Despite their apparent embracing of pluralism, the Commissioners took a less magnanimous stance towards Indigenous peoples. On the one hand, the final report urged "that everything possible must be done to help the native populations preserve their cultural heritage, which is an essential part of the patrimony of all Canadians."[27] On the other, they dismissed the idea that Indigenous peoples were part of the Royal Commission's mandate:

> We should point out here that the Commission will not examine the question of the Indians and the Eskimos. Our terms of reference contain no allusion to Canada's native populations. They speak of "two founding races," namely Canadians of British and French origin, and "other ethnic groups," but mention neither the Indians nor the Eskimos.[28]

In this way, the Royal Commission sidestepped both the issue of how Indigenous communities contributed to pluralism in Canada and any political implications of recognizing the presence of Indigenous people at the "founding" of Canada.

On October 8, 1971, the significance of plurality was prominently addressed in the House of Commons when Prime Minister Pierre Elliott Trudeau acknowledged that previously "substantial public support has been given largely to the arts and cultural institutions of English-speaking Canada" and that the Royal Commission on Bilingualism and Biculturalism had been a catalyst for "a conscious effort on the government's part to correct any bias against the French language and culture." He affirmed that funds were being channelled "to support cultural educational centres for native people."[29] The focus of his speech that day, however, was to announce that his government was responding to the Royal Commission on Bilingualism and Biculturalism Report by introducing a new policy intended to advance pluralism in Canada:

> A policy of multiculturalism within a bilingual framework commends itself to the government as the most suitable means of assuring the cultural freedom of Canadians. Such a policy should help to break down discriminatory attitudes and cultural jealousies. National unity if it is to mean anything in the deeply personal sense, must be founded on confidence in one's own individual identity; out of this can grow respect for that of others and a willingness to share ideas, attitudes and assumptions. A vigorous policy of multiculturalism will help to create this initial confidence. It can form the base of a society which is based on fair play for all.[30]

In years that followed, the federal government pursued its policy of multiculturalism through a range of initiatives.[31] In 1982, multiculturalism was enshrined in the newly created Canadian Charter of Rights and Freedoms in the Constitution, which asserted: "This Charter shall be interpreted in a manner consistent with the preservation and enhancement of the multicultural heritage of Canadians."[32] The Multiculturalism Act, passed in 1988 under the leadership of Prime Minister Brian Mulroney, declared that the federal government would "recognize and promote the understanding that multiculturalism reflects the cultural and racial diversity of Canadian society and acknowledges the freedom of all members of Canadian society to preserve, enhance and share their cultural heritage."[33] Of particular relevance to artists was the statement that the Government of Canada would "promote the understanding and creativity that arise from the interaction between individuals and communities of different origins."[34]

In assessing multiculturalism in terms of a governmental—if not strictly arts—context, it is worth noting that the programs the federal government has implemented over the years as a way to actualize the aspirational language in the Multiculturalism Act are not immobile. Multiculturalism as a governmental operating practice has not remained static since the 1970s and 1980s; it has modulated over the years in response to shifting social attitudes, political priorities, and in response to the needs and critiques of artists. In 1995, for instance, in reaction to criticism about multiculturalism, the government reviewed its various multicultural activities. Two years later, it implemented a new multicultural policy that focused on social justice, civic participation, and identity.[35] Indeed, in charting the trajectory of multiculturalism in Canada from the 1970s to the 1990s, Laurence Brosseau and Michael Dewing have underscored the adaptability of both the concept and practice of multiculturalism in Canada:

> Where early multicultural policies concentrated on cultural preservation and intercultural sharing through promotion of ethnic presses and festivals, the rejuvenated multiculturalism policy emphasized cross-cultural understanding and the attainment of social and economic integration through institutional change, affirmative action to equalize opportunity, and the removal of discrimination barriers.[36]

Further revisions of multicultural strategies and activities have followed. The policy was modified again in 2008 to recommend "support for the economic, social, and cultural integration of new Canadians and cultural communities" and to articulate a desire to facilitate programs that foster "mentorship, volunteerism, leadership, and civic education among at-risk youth of different cultural backgrounds" while also promoting "intercultural understanding and Canadian values (democracy, freedom, human rights and the rule of law) through community initiatives" intended to curtail "cultural social exclusion (parallel communities) and radicalization."[37] While terms like "integration" and "values" can be problematic if they equate with the assimilation of cultural difference, some scholars have conversely argued against using multiculturalism as a shield to import and perpetuate injurious and discriminatory cultural values and practices, particularly those that potentially devalue or restrict the liberty of women.[38]

More recent revisions to multicultural programs in Canada are articulated in the 2018 report titled, "Taking Action Against Systemic Racism and Religious Discrimination Including Islamophobia." This document lists several recommendations, including the following:

> Increase multiculturalism funding dedicated to eradicating systemic racism and religious discrimination and to promote greater intercultural understanding and awareness. In particular funding should be dedicated to groups whose statistics demonstrate are the most acutely affected by systemic racism and religious discrimination.[39]

Similarly, the government's report outlining its review of multiculturalism programs from 2011–2012 to 2016–2017 states: "Multiculturalism is not just about managing ethnic relations but it is also about producing desirable outcomes like inclusion, equality and equity. Accordingly, multiculturalism must constantly be 're/interpreted according to the times and spaces where the political, economic, social and cultural circumstances change.'"[40]

A HISTORY OF PLURALISM IN DANCE

While this brief history of immigration and multicultural policies and laws is instructive, it is not the only way to chart attitudes towards racial and ethnic diversity. A second, dance-focused narrative adds more nuance to how legislative, civic, and popular stances towards pluralism have fluctuated since Confederation. For example, one of the most conspicuous dance-related examples of how hierarchical social structures were reinforced through assimilationist legislation was aimed specifically at Indigenous peoples. The Indian Act, which was first enacted in 1876, introduced measures that were baldly intended to expedite the end of Indigenous traditional and cultural practices. As Duncan Campbell Scott, one of the "poets of Confederation" and the Deputy Superintendent of the Department of Indian Affairs from 1913 until 1932, stated in 1920:

> I want to get rid of the Indian problem. I do not think as a matter of fact, that this country ought to continuously protect a class of people who are able to stand alone. That is my whole point. Our objective is to continue until there is not a single Indian in Canada that has not been absorbed into the body politic, and there is no Indian question, and no Indian Department [...].[41]

The regulation of dance was one of the ways that the government attempted to divest itself of the "Indian problem." Beginning in 1884, provisions in the Indian Act prohibited certain Indigenous dance activities. Initially, participation in the potlatch, a Northwest Coast ceremony that involves dance, and the Tamanawas dance were deemed to be misdemeanours that could result in a two-to-six-month jail term. Even encouraging these activities could lead to the same penalty.[42] The following year, the legislation was extended to include "any celebration or dance of which the wounding or mutilation of the dead or living body" was a component: an amendment that banned the Plains Sun Dance.[43]

The result of further amendments in 1914 meant that Indigenous people had to obtain the consent of an Indian Agent to participate in dances held off their reserve. It was also not permissible to participate "in any show, exhibition, performance, stampede or pageant in aboriginal costume without the consent of the Superintendent General of Indian Affairs or his authorized Agent."[44] Likewise, there were potential legal consequences for encouraging or employing an Indigenous person for these purposes. The rationale was that these activities took Indigenous people away from agricultural duties while also "exposing them to temptation arising during the excitement of the celebrations."[45] The draft bill for these amendments paternalistically claimed that the Department of Indian Affairs was not trying to prevent Indigenous people from partaking in these events, but to ensure that only those "whose interests will not suffer" were granted permission.[46]

As time went on, the federal government continued to add regulations related to dance activities, increasing its reach to prohibit all non-ceremonial dance. A 1927 amendment allowed the Superintendent General to regulate dance halls, poolrooms, and other places of entertainment.[47] When the Indian Act was altered yet again in 1932–1933, the phrase "in aboriginal costume" in the section related to performing in exhibitions, stampedes, or pageants was removed, thereby extending the law to any Indigenous person who participated or potentially even attended these events.[48] While these revisions to the law signalled an attempt on the part of the federal government to tighten its control of Indigenous dance, by 1951, legislative perspectives and political priorities had shifted and all the sections regulating dance in the Indian Act were repealed.

These dance-related provisions of the Indian Act offer insight into both federal assimilationist goals and strategies, as well as evidence of Indigenous resistance to the attempted eradication of their dance activities as the federal government resorted to increasingly detailed and stringent legislation. Department of Indian Affairs correspondence during the period when regulations related to Indigenous dance were being enforced confirms that many Indigenous peoples continued to dance despite the legal penalties.[49] Indigenous leaders also appealed directly to the general public to state their case. In a story that appeared in the *Daily Province* on June 23, 1914, chiefs on Vancouver Island voiced their resistance to the amendment to the Indian Act that forced Indigenous people on reserves to obtain the permission of an Indian Agent in order to participate in dances on different reserves.[50] They argued that it was unfair that they were being obstructed as they attempted to partake in their celebrations. In the same way, they reasoned, it would be wrong to prevent white Christian people from celebrating Christmas.

In addition to resistance by Indigenous people, there are instances where non-Indigenous people similarly indicated their opposition to the restrictive laws. In 1913, for example, Archibald Glenlyon (Glen) Campbell, the Chief Inspector of Indian Affairs in Western Canada, wrote to his colleagues in Ottawa, describing a dance performed by the Pasqua First Nation people near Fort Qu'Appelle, Saskatchewan, asserting that the performance he witnessed was "as much the national dance of the Indians as is the Highland Fling of the Scotch, and in my opinion as harmless."[51] By the 1930s, Department of Indian Affairs correspondence indicates that public opinion did not support the rigorous application of the law. Two incidents support this view. In the summer of 1933, Reverend Charles Keith Kipling Prosser, rector of Alert Bay, British Columbia, caused consternation in the Department of Indian Affairs when he apparently donned Indigenous regalia and encouraged potlatch dances.[52] A 1936 "letter to the editor," which appeared in the *Daily Province* and had been written by missionaries, strenuously objected to a salacious description of the potlatch that had appeared in the Vancouver newspaper.[53] Wanting to correct the record, the writers, who had attended a potlatch ceremony, wrote: "All of the dances throughout were conducted with the utmost dignity and decorum and we spent a most enjoyable evening viewing the dances and the very elaborate costumes and masks."[54] They concluded by hoping that their comments would "bring about a better understanding with and about a people we are proud to call our friends."[55]

These historical examples help us to understand that the reactions to laws intended to assimilate Indigenous peoples through control of their bodies were varied and nuanced. So too were the responses to the dances performed by immigrants. One of the most assertive and active dance artists in Canada in the early twentieth century was Vasile Avramenko, a Ukrainian folk dancer and teacher who was fervent in his dedication to advocating for Ukraine's independence from Russia. Avramenko, who immigrated to Canada in 1925, quickly established multiple dance schools in Toronto and organized public performances, eventually touring and opening more studios in other cities across Canada.[56] The press reception to Avramenko's concerts disclosed an appreciation for his work among audience members within and beyond the Ukrainian émigré community. In response to a performance by Avramenko and his dancers in Winnipeg in 1927, the review in the *Manitoba Free Press* offered high praise:

> The event as intimated, brought to the Playhouse stage much that was artistic and beautiful in the realm of folk songs and folk dances. By presenting this imposing Ukrainian ballet last night and tonight the Playhouse management certainly provided for its patrons a veritable feast of song, colour, grace and rhythmic gorgeousness. Vasile Avramenko, the director of the ballet, is a past master in the training of students and of the native dances of the Ukraine and he seems peculiarly successful in instilling in his pupils all the sparkle, fire and symbolism of those very wonderful dances.[57]

Similarly, a review in the *Montreal Gazette* in 1929 explicitly voiced an appreciation for the value dance contributed to pluralism in Canada:

> The spontaneity of the dancers quickly infected the audience and the patter of applause was almost as continuous as the beat of the drum that marked the Slavic rhythm of the dances. New Canadians, like last night's dancers, who are keeping alive in their new home the beauty of the land from which they came, are making a very real contribution to the life of the country and thoroughly deserve the warm reception that was accorded them.[58]

Positive responses to the artistic contributions of immigrants were, however, more complicated than the newspaper reviews of Avramenko's dancers suggest. The promotion of diversity could, in fact, perpetuate established social hierarchies. Or, as Anne Flynn discusses in the opening chapter of this collection, the Canadian Pacific Railway (CPR) folk festivals simultaneously celebrated and controlled pluralism. J. Murray Gibbon, the CPR's publicity manager, initiated and oversaw the festivals in the 1920s and 1930s as a way to attract tourists to the CPR hotels and resorts that hosted them.[59] He also coined the phrase "Canadian mosaic" to describe how the diversity of cultures in Canada remained distinctive, but unified. Despite Gibbon's commitment to the use of folk and traditional arts as a way to foster understanding and respect, British culture was always privileged in the festivals.[60]

Interest in pluralism, in other words, did not always lead to actions of equity. The hierarchical positioning of cultures was often accompanied by the assumed right to "borrow" or co-opt iconography, narratives, and customs, particularly from Indigenous communities. In dance, in particular, there are numerous historical precedents of cultural appropriation, as the exoticized Other has long been a part of the theatrical choreographic imagination. In the early twentieth century, for example, choreographers like Amy Sternberg, a successful dance teacher in Toronto, featured stereotypical portraits of Indigenous people in productions including *Historical Pageant* (1927), which Sternberg choreographed as part of the Imperial Order of Daughters of the Empire celebrations for Canada's Diamond Jubilee.[61]

Modernists, including Boris Volkoff, Cynthia Barrett, and Janet Baldwin, among others, similarly constructed primitivist representations that glossed over the contentiousness of race relations in Canada.[62] In fact, the first time a group of dancers officially represented the country in an international context occurred in 1936 when Volkoff, a Toronto choreographer and teacher, and his students performed at the Internationale Tanzwettspiele, an event that preceded the Olympic Games in Berlin.[63] The group received positive media attention in Canada and Germany for their ersatz artistic interpretations of Indigenous cultural traditions, which Volkoff used to represent Canada's history and national character.

This desire to construct a Canadian identity through the arts intensified after the Second World War with the rise of cultural nationalism, though there were conflicting ideas about what that identity should be—a situation that underscored Canada's complicated history with colonialism. On the one hand, artists like Volkoff looked to the country's Indigenous peoples to define the nation. While some did so as a form of homage, their engagement in cultural appropriation perpetuated the presumed entitlement of settler cultures to co-opt and alter Indigenous traditions freely.

On the other hand, there were proponents of cultural nationalism who looked to Britain to set artistic standards. Vincent Massey, who had served as Canada's High Commissioner to the United Kingdom from 1935 to 1946 and became the first Canadian-born Governor General in 1952, was a vocal critic of the Americanization of Canadian culture who had strong Anglophile leanings. In 1949, Massey was appointed as the Chair of the Royal Commission on National Development in the Arts, Letters and Science (commonly known as the Massey Commission). Two years later, the Commission tabled its Report. Tasked with providing recommendations to guide the federal government's involvement with post-secondary and cultural institutions in Canada, the commissioners travelled the country hearing testimony and receiving submissions from interested individuals, associations, and communities.

The resulting Report acknowledges the significance of the folk arts and "Indian" arts, including dance, but focuses its advice on the promotion of "high art," particularly ballet, expressing surprise that ballet could succeed—and be acceptable—in Canada:[64]

> Ballet has been a late-comer among the arts in Canada, but in little more than ten years it has made astonishing progress. Rather to our surprise we have discovered, as was found in Great Britain, that classical ballet for so long thought exclusively indigenous to Russia, Italy and France, can be successfully transplanted; and, still somewhat self-consciously, with other English-speaking people, we are beginning to discern the fallacy in the ancient maxim, "no sober man ever dances", on which our attitude toward the dance has for so long been based.[65]

In expressing apparent astonishment that ballet could flourish in an Anglicized setting, the Report not only completely ignores the Québécois and other demographics of people in the country, but it also discloses its—and Massey's—preference for British models by suggesting that ballet in Canada follow a British example: "There is nothing to prevent the growth in

Canada of a national ballet comparable to that of Sadler's Wells, which beginning from almost nothing, in twenty years has become one of the world's great ballet companies."[66]

The Report's views on ballet are perhaps not surprising, given Massey's well-known affinity for Britain. Moreover, in preparing their Report, the Commissioners had spoken to some of the people who had consulted with Ninette de Valois, the Artistic Director of the Sadler's Wells Theatre Ballet, prior to the creation of National Ballet of Canada in 1951. This British influence extended to the choice of Celia Franca, a former dancer with the Sadler's Wells company, who became the company's founding Artistic Director.[67]

The success of ballet in Canada was paralleled by growing interest in the "folk arts," including dance, especially during the country's Centennial year. Les Feux-Follets, a dance company founded in 1952 under the direction of Michel Cartier, was arguably the most popular folk group during this period. Created as an ethnographic performance ensemble with the stated mandate to perform the traditional dances of Canada's founding peoples "authentically," the company obtained national and international stature through productions like *The Canadian Mosaic,* which it performed at Expo '67.[68]

Despite the success of Les Feux-Follets, there was some resistance to presenting folk dance on the same program as concert dance forms like ballet and modern dance, suggesting that divide between so-called "high" and "low" art was often delineated along ethnic lines. Notably, at the final Canadian Ballet Festival, which was held in Toronto in 1954, the program included eight concert dance groups and, for the first time, folk dance was represented alongside ballet and modern dance through the inclusion of five ensembles performing traditional dances from Finland, Denmark, Czechoslovakia, France, and Germany.[69] Herbert Whittaker, writing in the *Globe and Mail,* voiced his disapproval, arguing that ballet was an art form that demanded sustained study and exceptional skill. Folk dance was merely a form of recreation and should not be performed on the concert stage:

> The opening night of the Ballet Festival introduced a group of Finnish Folk Dancers, whose blond and scrubbed personalities made a strong contrast to the native ballet dancers. But folk dancing is more for the doing than the watching, and the stamping feet and repetition of the Finnish national dancers sat oddly in the evening.[70]

There were further divides in dance. Specifically, there has been criticism of ballet's recalcitrance in its continued lack of racial diversity.[71] Certainly, the dancers in the early years of all the ballet companies in Canada were overwhelmingly white.[72] Conversely, rare glimpses of self-determined racial diversity, which would become more valued towards the end of the twentieth century, could be found on television, including on the 1954 television program *Bamboula: A Day in the West Indies,* which was produced by CBUT, the CBC affiliate in Vancouver, and choreographed by African-Canadian Len Gibson.[73] The multiracial cast of *Bamboula* became a close-knit group and called themselves the "United Nations."[74] They quickly earned praise from local reviewers. One writer claimed: "This is what TV-viewers here have been waiting for—a show originated in Vancouver with local talent that tops anything done on television from Toronto and as good as musical programs of its kind from the US."[75] Another reviewer applauded Bamboula as "extremely well-produced, photographed and performed."[76] The racial diversity of the cast appears to have been referenced only once by a reviewer who described the performers as "clean as a whistle and colorful as a rainbow."[77] Notwithstanding the positive critical response, the program was cancelled after only three episodes, leaving some of the artists associated with the program to wonder if racism was a factor.[78]

In the 1960s, and especially during the 1970s, Canada participated in the dance boom that occurred in North America and Europe. Folk dance, as well as ballet and modern dance, attracted new participants and audiences as they "popularized" their productions. In 1969, Alan Lund, a performer and choreographer oriented towards musical theatre, replaced Michel Cartier as the Artistic Director of Les Feux-Follets. The company then became part of the Charlottetown Festival and shifted its ethnographic orientation, reinventing itself as a theatrical entertainment.[79] Similarly, in the 1970s, the Ukrainian Shumka Dancers, which was founded in Edmonton, Alberta, in 1959, decided use Ukrainian folk dance technique to interpret full-length stories with high production values.[80]

At the same time, and in step with the rise of multiculturalism as an official federal government policy in the 1970s, the Ontario Folk Dance Association was created in 1969 to promote and facilitate folk dancing in Ontario.[81] The Association presented dance concerts, dinners and dances, parties, and workshops that featured the dance traditions of a range of cultures, including, for example, Korean, Indian, Serbian, Scandinavian, and Croatian events in its early years. Folk dance groups in other parts of Canada were also formed in the 1970s, such as the Scandinavian Dancers of Vancouver (1971), Les Éclusiers de Lachine in Montréal (1975), and the Village Green English Dancers in Winnipeg (1976), among others.

Although the preservation of ethnic dance customs was—and remains—important to most of these groups, as both Suzanne Jaeger and Janelle Joseph assert in this collection, part of the attraction of dance is the opportunity it provides for the bonding between participants. New communities are created while performing traditional and/or popular dances from specific cultures. Indeed, as the Village Green English Dancers website states, newcomers are welcome: "just come and enjoy an evening filled with music, dancing, and laughter."[82] While this type of engagement has been criticized for perpetuating celebratory multiculturalism, which emphasizes cultural difference, contributes to the siloing of cultures, and ignores the ongoing racial and ethnic disparities in Canada, Steven Jobbitt adds nuance to the conversation by eloquently explaining in his chapter in this volume how folk dance groups can create liminal spaces where cultural respect and understanding are fostered.

Even in the 1970s and 1980s, dance artists were complicating critiques of multiculturalism by reaching out to colleagues from different racial and ethnic backgrounds to pursue educational opportunities and/or collaborative projects. One of the first was Rina Singha, a Kathak dance artist from Kolkata (formerly Calcutta) who, in 1965, arrived in Canada with her husband and children.[83] In 1977, she founded the Canadian Multicultural Dance Theatre to showcase intercultural projects in school and community settings.[84]

Menaka Thakkar was another early proponent of cross-cultural collaborations. Renowned for her expertise and artistry in Bharatanatyam and Odissi styles, Thakkar founded Nrtyakala, the Canadian Academy of Indian Dance, a highly respected school in Toronto, in 1975. Three years later, she established the Menaka Thakkar Dance Company. Thakkar was quick to initiate cross-cultural collaborations with other artists, working with Grant Strate (a charter member of the National Ballet of Canada and, at the time, the chair of the dance department at York University) to create *Blue Saturn* in 1983.[85] Other "fusion choreography" productions—to use Thakkar's preferred phrase—followed: *Moods of Morning* (1992) co-created with Robert Desrosiers; *Duality* (1997) co-created with Claudia Moore; *Farewell to Heaven* (1995) co-created Dana Luebke and Alex Pauk; and *Land of Cards*

(1998), which was co-created with Danny Grossman, Bengt Jörgen, William Lau, and Patrick Parsons.[86]

Moving Together is arguably the first collection to include research related to the economics of diversity in dance in Canada, even though access to funding is almost always a key concern for dance groups.[87] It was not until the 1980s, however, that arts councils began to rethink the exclusionary effects of their funding policies. While the Canada Council's Dance Section did not openly discriminate against dance companies that were rooted in non-European or American dance styles and/or techniques, the definition of "professional dance" used to determine eligibility for funding excluded all but the largest and most mainstream of companies. In order to be considered professional, a company had to meet the following criteria:

> A company directed by fully trained people, operating on a continuous basis, attempting to employ dancers full time (although it is recognized that dancers might still have to earn a significant portion of their income from other sources), administered by some permanent staff, incorporated as a non-profit organization, and assigned a charity number by Revenue Canada.[88]

Performance ensembles like the Menaka Thakkar Dance Company, which produced highly respected productions, did not meet the criteria and therefore did not qualify for funding from the Dance Section; instead, they had to seek support from the Arts Awards and Touring Offices.[89]

The Ontario Arts Council, which was established in 1963, had a similarly restrictive funding policy, though in the early 1980s, the Ontario Arts Council began to extend services and opportunities for Indigenous and other non-European dance artists.[90] In 1986, many of these initiatives were formalized into policy as the Ontario Arts Council launched the Multicultural/Folk Arts Dance Grant, which was replaced by the Culture Specific Dance grant in 1990.[91] As Katherine Cornell notes in her comprehensive overview of multicultural funding for dance, this latter grant was created to facilitate the transfer of artists "from the multicultural dance stream to mainstream acceptance."[92]

By 1990, however, many dance artists were distancing themselves from the term "multiculturalism."[93] Dissatisfaction with the term was evident in the Ontario Art Council's 1991 report "Consultations with Artists in a Culturally Diverse Society," which was written by Lina Fattah, the Council's first Multicultural Coordinator.[94] Based on her conversations with dance artists in Ontario, Fattah articulated the paradoxically restrictive consequences of language originally intended to signal and name diversity. As she wrote, many artists

> considered themselves Canadian artists practising Canadian art. They felt that labels such as "multicultural" or "ethnic" stereotyped them and excluded them from participation in the general stream of Canadian art. They believed that definitions of what was artistic needed to be broadened greatly. In general, participating artists wanted to access regular OAC programmes and not be slotted in "multicultural" slots.[95]

In tandem with changes at the Ontario Arts Council, and in response to shifting societal attitudes, the Canada Council implemented policy and program reforms in the 1990s. In 1991, for instance, the Canada Council published the report "Inventory of Dance: 'Other Forms.'"[96] This document indicated that artists were chaffing against the limited framing of dance and exclusionary criteria that equated professional dance only with ballet and modern dance.[97] As a result, the Canada Council modified its criteria and definitions of professional dance to allow for greater accessibility to its funding programs, which, in turn, provided funding opportunities to dance companies exploring techniques and styles beyond ballet and modern dance. Since the 1990s, respect for plurality has been a key factor influencing these funding agencies' priorities. (Yet, as P. Megan Andrews' interview with belly dancer Yasmina Ramzy suggests, there are still artists who feel frustrated by arts funding structures in Canada).

In 2011, the Canada Council and the Ontario Arts Council jointly initiated the Canada Dance Mapping Study, which was intended to provide an overview of dance activities in the country. The results documented the impressive diversity of dance styles practised in Canada. The inclusion of non-concert dance activities as well as an accompanying "Survey of the Social Impacts of Dance Organizations in Canada," which outlines the findings of the study, suggest that the arts councils are increasingly interested in dance forms—like many discussed in this collection—that seek to improve the lives of participants in areas including "education, civic engagement and sense of community belonging, sports and recreation, and multiculturalism."[98]

FINAL THOUGHTS

While *Moving Together* demonstrates that there is an effusion of dance activity from a broad range of racial and ethnic communities that continues into the twenty-first century, this collection is not comprehensive. More research is needed in all regions across Canada to keep pace with the abundance of dance. For instance, in the late twentieth and early twenty-first centuries, there has been a resurgence of Indigenous dance. The Aboriginal Dance Program (and now the Indigenous Dance Residency) at the Banff Centre for Arts and Creativity, the Dancers of Damelahamid on the West Coast, Toronto's Red Sky Performance, the Twilight Dancers in Pimicikamak Cree Nation, the b-girls and b-boys of the Clyde River Hip Hop dancers in Nunavut, and the numerous Powwows held each year are just a few examples of the wealth of Indigenous dance today.

V'ni Dansi, a Métis dance company founded in 2000 in Vancouver, is a particularly intriguing case study of contemporary Indigenous dance. Under the artistic direction of Yvonne Chartrand, a seventh-generation Métis woman, the company performs traditional Métis jigging as the Louis Riel Métis Dancers. Watching Chartrand jig, one begins to understand the rhythmic footwork and the vigour of the dance.[99] Her movements evoke the laughter, clapping, cheering, and laboured breath of the dancers Agnes Deans Cameron encountered at a crowded and spirited wedding party over one hundred years earlier. Seeing Chartrand perform excerpts from *Eagle Spirit* (2016), a V'ni Dansi contemporary dance solo she choreographed in response to the passing of her mother, the viewer is moved by her long-limbed fluidity.[100] As she holds feathers between her fingers, she stretches her arms open so that they look like the broad wingspan of an eagle, and as she slowly and resolutely flaps her arms/wings, the air whips through the feathers in sync with the sound of her exhalations. She is a bird in flight.

Chartrand's ability to perform a range of dances styles is a testament to her talent and the aesthetic flexibility of V'ni Dansi. It is also a reminder that dance can connect us to our ancestors while conveying our cultural experiences and identities to our contemporaries. Her dancing is a powerful example of how honouring one's heritage can productively inform present-day creativity. Or, as Chartrand has stated, "This one elder always told me, 'You know, you need to not only live in the traditional world, and not only in the contemporary world, but you need to live in both worlds.'"[101]

Chartrand and the other dancers included in this brief historical overview do indeed exemplify how it is possible to live in the traditional world and the contemporary world. They also provide access to the range of attitudes towards pluralism expressed throughout Canadian history and demonstrate how dance can function as an embodied mode of conceptualizing and enacting the possibilities and implications of plurality, not only for dancers, but for their audiences and critics, as well. In these ways, these dancers have made important contributions to the ongoing creation of Canada.

NOTES

1 Agnes Deans Cameron, *The New North: Being Some Account of a Woman's Journey through Canada to the Arctic* (New York: Appleton, 1909), 316–17.

2 Ibid., 316.

3 Ibid.

4 Ibid., 316–17.

5 For more information about the Red River Jig, see The Louis Riel Institute, accessed October 3, 2019, http://www.louisrielinstitute.com/music-a-dance.php. See also, "Interview with Yvonne [Chartrand] about Red River Jig," V'ni Dansi, accessed October 3, 2019, http://www.vnidansi.ca/company/interview-yvonne-about-red-river-jig. More generally see, Sarah Quick, "The Social Poetics of the Red River Jig in Albert and Beyond: Meaningful Heritage and Emerging Performance," *Ethnologies* 30, no. 1 (2008): 77–101.

6 It should be noted that *The New North* also contains comments that depict Indigenous people from a racist perspective.

7 Elizabeth B. Price, "Preserving the Red River Jig for Posterity," *Toronto Star Weekly*, April 7, 1928, 51. Sarah Quick discusses this example in her article about the Red River Jig. See Quick, "The Social Poetics," 80. For more information about the Calgary Old Timers, see "The Old Timers hold Their First Great Banquet in Calgary," *Calgary Daily Herald* (December 1, 1901), 1.

8 Price, "Preserving the Red River Jig for Posterity," 51.

9 Ibid.

10 Ibid.

11 It is important to acknowledge that recent debates about salvage ethnography are nuanced. Some critics have addressed Indigenous agency within salvage ethnographic activities. Others have examined the interpretative and reclamation power of subsequent Indigenous generations and the temporal implications of the "saved" artifacts. For more information, see Nick Yablon, "For the Future Viewer: Salvage Ethnography and Edward Curtis's 'The Oath—Apsaroke," *Journal of American Studies* (2019): 1–31.

12 For a more detailed study of embodied knowledge, see Diana Taylor, *The Archive and the Repertoire: Performing Cultural Memory in the Americas* (Durham: Duke University Press, 2003).

13 Price, "Preserving the Red River Jig for Posterity," 51.

14 For documentation related to history of immigration in Canada, see the Canadian Museum of Immigration at Pier 21, accessed September 27, 2019, http://pier21.ca/research/immigration-history/order-in-council-pc-1911-1324.

15 The legislation focused on the conditions of travel on ships from the United Kingdom, its Dominions, and ports in Europe instead of explicitly delineating desirable demographics. The Act set penalties for prospective immigrants that had physical and/or mental challenges or were financially destitute.

16 There were some exceptions: diplomats, tourists, and students, for instance, were exempt from the duty. For more details, see Ninette Kelley and Michael Trebilcock, *The Making of the Mosaic: A History of Canadian Immigration Policy*, 2nd ed. (Toronto: University of Toronto Press, 2010), 98.

17 K. Tony Hollihan, "'A Brake upon the Wheel': Frank Oliver and the Creation of the Immigration Act of 1906," *Past Imperfect* 1 (1992): 106–07.

18 Statutes of Canada, *An Act to Amend the Act Respecting Immigration and Immigrants, Revised Statutes of Canada 1906, ch. 19, Statutes of Canada 1910*, ch. 27, section 218.

19 For a more detailed discussion, see Barrington Walker, ed., *The African Canadian Legal Odyssey: Historical Essays* (Toronto: University of Toronto Press, 2012), 30, 45.

20 Kelley and Trebilcock, *The Making of the Mosaic*, 198–210.

21 Ibid., 220.

22 Ellen Fairclough, House of Commons Debates, June 9, 1960, 4711 as quoted in G. A. Rawlyk, "Canada's Immigration Policy, 1945–1962." *Dalhousie Review* 42, no. 3 (Autumn, 1962), 297. See also, Fairclough correspondence to Diefenbaker November 23, 1961, LAC, RG26, Vol. 100, file 3-15-1, part 8, as quoted in Mai Nguyen and Garth Stevenson, "Immigration Reform in Canada and the United States: A Comparative Analysis," presented at the annual meeting of the Canadian Political Science Association, Vancouver, British Columbia, June 4, 2008, 38, accessed September 26, 2019, http://www.cpsa-acsp.ca/papers-2008/Stevenson.pdf.

23 For more details about the work of the Commission and one example of how it was represented in the press, see Robert Fulford, "Can these Two Men Really Figure Out Canada?" *Maclean's* (May 16, 1964): 16–17, 57–58, 60.

24 Canada, *Report of the Royal Commission on Bilingualism and Biculturalism*, Book 1 (Ottawa: Queen's Printer, 1967), xxi. The Commission defined "race" as follows: "In our view the reference to the two 'founding races' or 'peoples who founded Confederation' is an allusion to the undisputed role played by Canadians of French and British origin in 1867, and long before Confederation. The word 'race' is used in an older meaning as referring to a national group, and carries no biological significance." (Ibid., xxii.)

25 Ibid., xxv.

26 Ibid., xxv–xxvi.

27 Ibid., xxvii.

28 Ibid., xxvi. The rationale offered was that "it is obvious that these two groups do not form part of the 'founding races,'" and that the term "other ethnic groups" referenced immigrants and not first inhabitants of this country. (Ibid., xxvi.)

29 Right Hon. Pierre Elliott Trudeau, Prime Minister of Canada, Speech, House of Commons, October 8, 1971, 8545, accessed September 22, 2019, http://parl.canadiana.ca/view/oop.debates_HOC2803_08/811?r=0&s=3.

30 Ibid.

31 For a thorough overview of the federal government's multicultural programs, see Laurence Brosseau and Michael Dewing, "Canadian Multiculturalism," Background Paper (revised) (Ottawa: Library of Parliament, [2009] 2018), accessed September 23, 2019, http://lop.parl.ca/staticfiles/PublicWebsite/Home/ResearchPublications/BackgroundPapers/PDF/2009-20-e.pdf. See also, Tamara Seiler, "Thirty Years Later: Reflections on the Evolution and Future Prospects of Multiculturalism," *Canadian Issues* (February 2002): 6–8.

32 Brosseau and Dewing, "Canadian Multiculturalism," 4. See also, *Canadian Charter of Rights and Freedoms,* section 27, Part 1 of the *Constitution Act,* 1982, being Schedule B to the *Canada Act 1982* (UK), 1982, c 11.

33 *Multiculturalism Act, Statutes of Canada 1988,* ch. 31, section 3.1.a.

34 Ibid., section 3.1.g.

35 Brosseau and Dewing, "Canadian Multiculturalism," 7.

36 Ibid., 5.

37 Ibid., 8.

38 Susan Moller Okin, ed., *Is Multiculturalism Bad for Women?* (Princeton, NJ: Princeton University Press, 1999).

39 House of Commons, Standing Committee on Canadian Heritage, "Taking Action Against Systemic Racism and Religious Discrimination Including Islamophobia," 1st Session, 42nd Parliament, February 2018, 4, accessed September 22, 2019, http://www.ourcommons.ca/Content/Committee/421/CHPC/Reports/RP9315686/chpcrp10/chpcrp10-e.pdf.

40 Canada, "Evaluation of Multicultural Program 2011-12 to 2016-17," accessed September 20, 2019, http://www.canada.ca/en/canadian-heritage/corporate/publications/evaluations/multiculturalism-program.html.

41 "Memorandum of the Six Nations and other Iroquois," March 30, 1920, LAC, RG10, Vol. 6810, file 470-2-3, part 7, as quoted in Brian Titley, *A Narrow Vision: Duncan Campbell Scott and the Administration of Indian Affairs in Canada* (Vancouver: UBC Press, 1986), 50. In 1920, Campbell appeared before a special parliamentary committee considering "Bill 14," which proposed granting the Department of Indian Affairs the power to enfranchise Indigenous people without their consent. (In 1857, the Province of Canada established a process by which Indigenous men could apply for enfranchisement. If successful, the applicant would receive a parcel of reserve

land, which would be taxed. Enfranchisement in this context did not mean the right to vote. The applicant, however, would be required to relinquish the right to live on the remaining reserve lands as well as other rights granted to Indigenous people living on reserves.) The issue of enfranchisement had been resisted by many Indigenous people since 1857, in part because it was seen as an attempt to disperse Indigenous land. The proposed 1920 amendment was similarly contested. As Duncan told the special parliamentary committee, Bill 14 would advance the government's assimilationist agenda, which he personally and fervently supported. For further information about Duncan's comments and their implications, see Wendy Moss and Elaine Gardner-O'Toole, "Aboriginal People: A History of Discriminatory Laws," Government of Canada ([1987] 1991), accessed September 8, 2019, http://publications.gc.ca/Collection-R/LoPBdP/BP/bp175-e.htm.

42 *An Act further to Amend "The Indian Act, 1880," Statutes of Canada 1884*, ch. 27, section 3. The 1886 amendments changed the wording slightly from the original 1884 version:

> Every Indian or other person who engages in or assists in celebrating the Indian festival known as the "Potlach" or the Indian dance known as the "Tamanawas" is guilty of a misdemeanor, and liable to imprisonment for a term exceeding six months and not less than two months:
>
> 2. Every Indian or person who encourages, either directly or indirectly, an Indian to get up such a festival or dance, or to celebrate the same, or who assists in the celebration of the same, is guilty of a like offence, and shall be liable to the same punishment.

The Indian Act, Revised Statutes of Canada 1886, ch. 43, section 114. See also, Sharon Helen Venne, *Indian Acts and Amendments 1868-1975, An Indexed Collection* (Saskatoon: University of Saskatchewan Native Law Centre, 1981), 157.

43 *The Indian Act, Revised Statutes of Canada 1886*, ch. 43, section 114. There were minor wording changes to the *Act* that were related to dance in 1906 and 1918. See Venne, *Indian Acts*, 158, 229.

44 *An Act to Amend The Indian Act, Revised Statutes of Canada 1906, ch. 81, Statutes of Canada 1914*, ch. 35, section 8. See also, Department of Indian and Northern Affairs, *The Historical Development of the Indian Act* (Ottawa: Department of Indian and Northern Affairs, 1975), 115, and Venne, *Indian Acts*, 230.

45 Draft Bill, 1914: PAC RG 10 B3, Vol. 6809: File 56,402, as cited in *The Historical Development of the Indian Act*, 115.

46 Ibid.

47 *An Act to Amend The Indian Act, Revised Statutes of Canada 1927, ch. 98, Statutes of Canada 1930*, ch. 25, section 16. See also, Venne, *Indian Acts*, 300.

48 *An Act to Amend The Indian Act, Revised Statutes of Canada 1927, ch. 98, Statutes of Canada 1932–1933*, ch. 42, section 10. See also, Venne, *Indian Acts*, 300.

49 See, for instance, D. D. MacKay, Indian Commissioner for British Columbia, letter to Secretary, Indian Affairs Branch, Department of Mines and Resources, February 22, 1938, LAC, RG10, C-II-2, Vol. 11297 [T-16110, 589–90].

50 "Indians Want Their Potlatches to Stand," *Daily Province*, 23 June 1914, n.p., LAC, RG 10, vol. 3826, file 60, 511-3 [C-10145, 102].

51 Archibald Glenlyon (Glen) Campbell, the Chief Inspector of Indian Affairs in Western Canada, letter to Secretary, Department of Indian Affairs, June 26, 1913, LAC, Indian Affairs, RG10, Vol. 3826, file 60, 511-4, part 1 [C-10145, 7–8].

52 Chas. C. Perry, Assistant Indian Commissioner for British Columbia, letter to the Secretary, Department of Indian Affairs, Ottawa, August 8, 1933, LAC, Indian Affairs, RG10, C-II-2, Vol. 11297, [T-16110, 768–70].

53 "Down with the Potlatch," *Daily Province*, February 18, 1936, LAC, Indian Affairs, RG10, C-II-2, Vol. 11297, [T-16110, 630-631] and Phyllis M. Arrowsmith and Amy Wakefield, letter to the editor, *Daily Province*, March 26, 1936, LAC, Indian Affairs, RG10, C-II-2, Vol. 11297, [T-16110, 633–34].

54 Ibid.

55 Ibid.

56 For more information about Avramenko, see Orest T. Martynowych's excellent biography of Vasile Avramenko: *The Showman and the Ukrainian Cause: Folk Dance, Film, and the Life of Vasile Avramenko* (Winnipeg: University of Manitoba Press, 2014) and Alexandra Pritz, "The Evolution of Ukrainian Dance in Canada," in *Visible Symbols: Cultural Expression Among Canada's Ukrainians*, ed. Manoly R. Lupul (Edmonton: Canadian Institute of Ukrainian Studies, 1984), 87–101. See also, Andriy Nahachewsky, "Conceptual Categories of Ethnic Dance: The Canadian Ukrainian Case," *Canadian Dance Studies* 2 (1997): 141. Many thanks to Selma Odom for sending a copy of Nahachewsky's article to the author.

57 *Manitoba Free Press*, June 4, 1927, as quoted in Martynowych, *The Showman and the Ukrainian Cause*, 34.

58 *Montreal Gazette*, April 15, 1929, as quoted in Martynowych, *The Showman and the Ukrainian Cause*, 43–44.

59 Gordana Lazarevich, "The Role of the Canadian Pacific Railway in Promoting Canadian Culture," *A Celebration of Canada's Arts 1930–1970*, eds. Glen Carruthers and Gordana Lazarevich (Toronto: Canadian Scholars' Press, 1996): 11. See also, John Murray Gibbon, *Canadian Mosaic: The Making of a Northern Nation* (Toronto: McClelland and Stewart, 1938).

60 Lazarevich, "The Role of the Canadian Pacific Railway," 11–12.

61 For more details, see Allana C. Lindgren, "Amy Sternberg's Historical Pageant (1927): The Performance of IODE Ideology during Canada's Diamond Jubilee," *Theatre Research in Canada* 32, no. 1 (2011): 1–29.

62 For instance, see Allana C. Lindgren, "Contextualizing Choreography: Cynthia Barrett's *Eskimo Dances* and National Identity in Post-War Canada," *The Dance Current* 8.2 (Summer 2005): 40–42.

63 For more details, see Allana C. Lindgren, "English-Canadian Ethnocentricity: The Case Study of Boris Volkoff at the 1936 Nazi Olympics," in *The Oxford Handbook of Dance and Ethnicity*, eds. Anthony Shay and Barbara Sellers-Young (Oxford: Oxford University Press, 2016): 412–37.

64 For more details, see Allana C. Lindgren, "Beyond Primary Sources: Using Dance Documentation to Examine Attitudes towards Diversity in the Massey Commission (1949–1951)," in *Canadian Performance Histories and Historiographies*, ed. Heather Davis-Fisch (Toronto: Playwrights Canada Press, 2017): 141–60.

65 Canada, Royal Commission on National Development in the Arts, Letters and Sciences, *Report* (Ottawa: King's Printer, 1951), 201.

66 Ibid., 202.

67 By the end of the 1950s, the country had three major ballet companies: the National Ballet of Canada in Toronto, along with the Royal Winnipeg Ballet (founded as the Winnipeg Ballet Club in 1939), and Montréal's Les Grands Ballets Canadiens (established in 1957).

68 Amy Bowring, "Les Feux-Follets: A Canadian Dance Enigma," *Dance Collection Danse Magazine* 60 (Fall 2005): 16–17. In many ways, Les Feux-Follets was representative of a particular moment in Canadian dance history. In 1967, Canadian Folk Art Council was established with special funds from the Centennial Commission. To celebrate one hundred years since Confederation, the Canadian Folk Art Council helped to arrange for hundreds of folk dance festivals throughout Canada. See Catherine Limbertie, "Diversity and Toronto: The Transformative Role of The Community Folk Art Council of Toronto" (Toronto: Community Folk Art Council of Toronto, n.d.): 1–5, accessed July 22, 2019, http://cfactoronto.com/wp-content/uploads/2015/05/The-Transformative-Role-of-The-Community-Folk-Art-Council-of-Toronto1.pdf.

69 "Folk Dances of Many Nations at Ballet Festival," *Globe and Mail*, April 28, 1954, 17.

70 Herbert Whittaker, "Showbusiness," *Globe and Mail*, May 4, 1954, 11.

71 See, for instance, Jennifer Fisher, "Ballet and Whiteness: Will Ballet Forever Be the Kingdom of the Pale?" in *The Oxford Handbook of Dance and Ethnicity*, eds. Anthony Shay and Barbara Sellers-Young (Oxford: Oxford University Press, 2016), 585–97.

72 For a more detailed discuss of this topic, see Allana C. Lindgren, "The National Ballet of Canada's Normative Bodies: Legitimizing and Popularizing Dance in Canada during the 1950s," in *Contesting Bodies and Nation in Canadian History, eds.* Patrizia Gentile and Jane Nicholas (Toronto: University of Toronto Press, 2013): 180–202.

73 A professional tap dancer from the age of five, Gibson had appeared on Vancouver stages with touring groups like The Eddie Cantor Show. In 1947, he had been a last-minute replacement in Katherine Dunham's company when the group needed a dancer during a Vancouver tour stop. His talent as a quick study earned him a scholarship to Dunham's New York school where Miles Davis's first wife, Frances Taylor, was often his partner. When he returned to Canada a year later, he won

standing ovations for his participation in the 1949 British Columbia provincial dance festival. For more information about *Bamboula*, see Allana C. Lindgren, "*Bamboula* Turns 50," *Dance Collection Danse Magazine* 58 (Fall 2004): 14–17. See also, Allana C. Lindgren, "Broadcasting Race in Canada: Len Gibson's *Bamboula* (1954)," *Proceedings of the Congress on Research in Dance (CORD) Spring 2005 Conference, Tallahassee, Florida, March 3-6, 2005* CORD, 2005: 159–65.

74 Beverley Barclay Craig, telephone interview with author, August 19, 2004.

75 Les Wedman, "Bamboula Bows in as Best-Yet Show," *Vancouver Province* (August 28, 1954): 8.

76 John Ray, "In TV Land," clipping, Gordi Moore Private Papers, Vancouver, British Columbia.

77 Ibid.

78 Wedman, "Bamboula Bows in as Best-Yet Show," 8.

79 Amy Bowring, "Les Feux-Follets: Popularizing Canadian History," *Dance Collection Danse Magazine* 61 (Spring 2006): 29. See also, Amy Bowring, "Theatrical Multiculturalism: Les Feux-Follets at the Charlottetown Festival," in *Renegade Bodies: Canadian Dance in the 1970s*, eds. Allana C. Lindgren and Kaija Pepper (Toronto: Dance Collection Danse Press/Presse, 2012), 83–108.

80 The most ambitious of these productions include *Shumka's Cinderella* (2000). More recently, the company also collaborated with the Running Thunder Cree Dancers to create *Ancestors and Elders* (2018). See the companion documentary, Leslie Sereda and Steven Glassman, dirs. *Dancing on Eggshells: The Making of Ancestors and Elders*, Edmonton, Alberta: Blue Toque Productions, 2019. For more details about Shumka's decision to move towards theatrical concert dance productions, see "Shumka Dancers on Whirlwind Tour," *Student* (February 1979): 4; and Victor Malarek, "Edmonton Troupe Marks 25th Anniversary," *Globe and Mail*, March 10, 1984, E3. For an overview of the company's history, see Alice Major, *Ukrainian Shumka Dancers: Tradition in Motion* (Edmonton: Reidmore Books, 1991). Shumka was not the only Ukrainian dance group in Canada. During the 1950s, 1960s, and 1970s, several performance groups were created across the country. For more details, see Alexandra Pritz, "The Evolution of Ukrainian Dance in Canada," in *Visible Symbols: Cultural Expression Among Canada's Ukrainians*, ed. Manoly R. Lupul (Edmonton: Canadian Institute of Ukrainian Studies, 1984), 89–91.

81 Marg Murphy, *The Ontario Folk Dance Association: Twenty-Five Years, 1969–1994* (Toronto: Ontario Folk Dance Association, 1994), 1.

82 Village Green English Dancers, "Welcome," accessed September 3, 2019, http://villagegreenenglishdancers.org/.

83 Nadine Saxton, "Rina Singha," *Encyclopedia of Theatre Dance in Canada*, ed. Susan McPherson (Toronto: Dance Collection Danse, 2000), 579.

84 Uma Parameswaran, "Rina Singha: Seventy Years and Still Dancing," *Dance Collection Danse Magazine* 64 (Fall 2007): 18; see also, "How Rina Singha FOUND her Feet in Canada," *Canada Bound Immigrant*, May 2, 2012, accessed

September 28, 2019, http://www.canadaboundimmigrant.com/successsnapshots/article.php?id=446. See also, Marg Murphy, *The Ontario Folk Dance Association: Twenty-Five Years, 1969–1994* (Toronto: Ontario Folk Dance Association, 1994), 12.

85 Saxton, "Rina Singha," 579.

86 Ibid.

87 The topic has also been investigated by dance scholars in other countries. Most notably, see Priya Srinivasan, *Sweating Saris: Indian Dance as Transnational Labor* (Philadelphia: Temple University Press, 2011).

88 Susan Macpherson, *Inventory of Dance: 'Other Forms'* (Ottawa: Dance Office, Canada Council, 1991): 4, as quoted in Katherine Cornell, "Dance Defined: An Examination of Canadian Cultural Policy on Multicultural Dance," in *Canadian Dance: Visions and Stories*, eds. Selma Landen Odom and Mary Jane Warner (Dance Collection Danse, 2004), 419.

89 Ibid., 418. See also, Katherine Cornell, "Dance Defined: An Examination of Canadian Cultural Policy on Multicultural Dance," in *Continents in Movement: Proceedings of the Meeting of Cultures in Dance History*, eds. by Daniel Tércio (Oeiras, Portugal: Edições FMH, 1998), 47.

90 Cornell, "Dance Defined" *Canadian Dance: Visions and Stories*, 416–17.

91 Ibid., 417.

92 Ibid.

93 Ibid.

94 Ibid.

95 Lina Fattah, as quoted in Cornell, 417.

96 Cornell, "Dance Defined," 418.

97 These findings aligned with the Canada Council's Racial Equity Advisory Committee's recommendation that each section of the Canada Council, including the Dance Section, create intern positions intended to address equity issues.

98 Ekos Research Associates, *Survey of the Social Impacts of Dance Organizations in Canada* (Ottawa: Canada Council for the Arts and the Ontario Arts Council, 2016), iv.

99 "Yvonne Chartrand," Artsayer, accessed October 3, 2019, http://www.youtube.com/watch?v=SQneXV9CWEU.

100 Yvonne Chartrand, *Eagle Dance*, excerpts from creation phase studio showing, accessed October 3, 2019, http://www.vnidansi.ca/media/videos.

101 "myVancouver: Compaigni V'ni Dansi," accessed October 3, 2019, http://www.youtube.com/watch?v=znjvfPCmAgs.

II

THE DISCOURSES OF PLURALISM

TWO

EMBODYING THE CANADIAN MOSAIC

THE GREAT WEST CANADIAN FOLK DANCE, FOLK SONG, AND HANDICRAFT FESTIVAL, 1930[1]

Anne Flynn

"Sprightly folkdance and quaint folksongs—Program at the Grand on Thursday was vastly entertaining: Many nations represented" was the headline of a review published in the *Calgary Albertan* on March 21, 1930.[2] The review continues, "Encouraging whoops were plentiful, many of the strenuous steps and figures were all performed with visible vigor, while the costumes added the final gay touch of color that reflected the holiday spirit."[3] One day later, another review in the same newspaper proclaims, "Flashing hither and thither over the stage, swinging with dizzying speed and carrying the air of joyous abandon of the real folk dance, performers in the presentation of the Ukrainian National Ballet brought the concert to a close with a performance that drew the well merited appreciation of the audience."[4]

This is a small sample of the written reviews commenting on the Great West Canadian Folk Dance, Folk Song, and Handicraft Festival, a four-day festival in Calgary, Alberta, orchestrated by the Canadian Pacific Railway (CPR) along with the Alberta branch of the Canadian Handicraft Guild, upon invitation by the premier of Alberta. Calgary's two daily papers—*Calgary Albertan* and the *Calgary Daily Herald*—provided extensive coverage of the event, beginning with previews and continuing with daily reviews of each performance and surrounding events, including luncheons and high tea.

Like dance scholar Jens R. Giersdorf, who has written about dance in East Germany, I am particularly "interested in a critical analysis of the potential employment of culture—and specifically dance—for the visionary rethinking and restructuring of societies more generally."[5] In this light, I focus on the 1930 festival—one of sixteen organized by the CPR in the years 1928 to 1931—as an example of the use of the concept of "folk" as a tool for nation building.[6] I will also examine how, through the lens of "folk" and all that the notion and practice of "folk" entailed at this particular historical moment, the dancing bodies of European "racial" groups attempted to transform formerly "undesirables" into desirable settlers and articulate a culturally diverse vision of Canada.[7] Following Cultural Studies and Dance Studies approaches that Jane Desmond has noted are oriented toward a "commitment to uncover ideological workings of representation, that is, how symbolic systems are imbued with issues of power," my analysis addresses a number of the elements that created the conditions for such enthusiastic promotion of folk dance performances across the country: whiteness, capitalism, and anti-modernism as expressed through tourism.[8] I also examine the powerful effect of individual agency demonstrated by CPR employee John Murray Gibbon, who initiated and promoted the festivals, and by the folk dancers themselves. My goal is to bring these dancing bodies into our imaginations and to contribute to the recording of their activities in Canada's social history.

USING THE FOLK: THE CPR AND JOHN MURRAY GIBBON

According to historian Douglas Francis, "one of the tenets behind the philosophy of railways was the belief that railroads not only revealed the greatness of the Anglo-Saxon race but also provided the physical means by which the virtues of British civilization could be brought to other parts of the world."[9] In the large-scale settlement of the West (once the CPR railroad was complete in 1885) by people of European heritage, the Canadian government relied on private companies like the CPR to engage in tourism as well as recruitment. The company aggressively advertised Canada abroad to both tourists and potential immigrants and built hotels in cities across the country.[10] In places like the Banff Springs Hotel in the heart of the Rocky Mountains, the company sold

Figure 2.1. This photo was used on the inside cover of the Great West Canadian Folk Dance, Folk Song, and Handicraft Festival in 1930 (Calgary). The caption read: "Russian Folkdancers of the Canadian West." The photo was taken at the CPR Regina festival in 1929 where the brothers performed. Left to right: Valentine, Christian, Conrad, and Michael Reich. Photograph courtesy of the Collection of Tim Reich.

"nature" to the tourists in the form of hiking, trail riding, and skiing. The CPR became involved in show business and tourism in order to generate cash and thus began "mining" Canada for its renewable cultural resources.

These tourist and theatrical initiatives were carried out by company executives and government representatives. One such executive was John Murray Gibbon, CPR publicity agent and one of Canada's most well-known cultural promoters for the first half of the twentieth century. Born in 1875, Gibbon grew up on a tea plantation in Ceylon, graduated from King's College and Oxford University where he studied the humanities and arts, and began working as a writer in London. His first encounter with Canada was hosting a group of British newspaper editors on a tour in 1907, which he would do numerous times before settling in Montréal and becoming the CPR publicity agent from 1913 to 1945.[11] Through controlling visual and print advertising abroad, and then becoming involved in orchestrating the actual animation of those images here in Canada, Gibbon was personally involved in diverse but related aspects of the company's promotion of Canada's national identity for over thirty years. From trail riding and hiking in the Rocky Mountains, to writing novels and folk songs, to producing major art festivals, to serving on boards of directors for arts organizations, Gibbon was everywhere.

Significantly, Gibbon believed, along with many of his contemporaries, that the "folk" as represented in music, dance, literature, and handicrafts could express the essential characteristics of any "racial" group.[12] Ian McKay includes Gibbon in a cluster of "urban cultural producers, pursuing their own interests and expressing their own view of things," who "constructed the Folk of the countryside as the romantic antithesis to everything they disliked about modern urban and industrial life."[13] Gibbon used his creative sensibilities to "produce" the Canada of his dreams and is credited with popularizing the concept of the "Canadian mosaic," which he described as "a decorated surface, bright with inlays of separate coloured pieces, not painted in colours blended with brush on palate.[14] The original background in which the inlays are set is still visible, but these inlays cover more space than that background, and so the ensemble may truly be called a mosaic."[15] While Canada proudly continues to refer to this image of the mosaic as representative of liberal multiculturalism, Stuart Henderson observes, "Gibbon's mosaic was a pluralism built upon a stable foundation, an immutable background of white Anglo-Celt (male) hegemony onto which he could manufacture his mosaic."[16] (In her chapter in this collection, Batia Boe Stolar notes that El Viento Flamenco, which was established in St. John's in the late 1990s, a full sixty years after Gibbon's "mosaic" image was popularized, was repeatedly characterized by the media as an exotic oddity in the region. In this way, the critical reception of El Viento Flamenco demonstrates the continuing power of this immutable white Anglo-Celt dominance in Canadian multiculturalism.)

DOING THE FOLK

Gibbon's program selections for the series of sixteen festivals he produced across Canada were custom tailored for each city based on his ideas of what that community needed to perform for itself.[17] In Toronto, the festival program consisted of English music; in Québec, it was French Canadian music; and in the West, it was "racial groups in picturesque costumes of their country of origin."[18] The Calgary festival included professional singers from Eastern Canada and "amateur" dance groups representing Scotland, England, Sweden, French Canada, France, Wales, Norway, Ukraine, Hungary, Denmark, Germany, Ireland, Poland, and Russia. According to Gordana Lazarevich, in the festival program, which Gibbon wrote, the description of the artists from the British Isles is the longest and is written as history with names, places, and dates.[19]

In contrast, and unaccompanied by a photograph, is the description of a Polish group, which was written by Polish-born actress Helen Modjeska: "Our peasants are almost all vegetarians by necessity. They are poor and can only very seldom afford the luxury of meat, yet they are strong, vigorous, always singing at work. The songs are for the most part improvisations, they are often witty and always melodious. These people can no more help singing than the birds."[20] The contrast in representation between the British program description and the Polish one is indicative of a racialized hierarchy. The immigrants are speaking for themselves about themselves but in terms that fit the colonial mind set, seeking admiration for peasant immigrants' natural, naïve expressivity while simultaneously emphasizing their unthreatening, uneducated status.

The Calgary festival program is filled with numerous other exaggerated descriptions extolling the virtues of the singing and dancing "peasants" of Europe.[21] The actual dancing that took place for four consecutive nights demonstrated the physical sturdiness and vigour of these immigrants. It is as though Gibbon was trying to show, via the dancing, that these new immigrants were healthy, strong, neuromuscularly fit for hard labour, and able to "control" themselves to perform the precise steps of the choreography. Their considerable physical prowess was "contained" by the choreography and then wrapped in elaborate costumes that revealed attentiveness to visual beauty and the skill of fine handwork. When we see them smile, see "their dances of the countryside... which are centuries old," and see their "charming and gay dresses designed and made by the country folk," as the festival program describes, we don't see a problem; we are not threatened or afraid. In other words, the festival packaged the new immigrants in an easily palatable form for Anglo audiences to digest, and it appears to have worked. Indeed, in *Canadian Mosaic*, Gibbons shares a story about how his friend Ralph Connor (author of the popular novel *The Foreigner*, 1909) was so moved by the professional quality and refinement of the Polish dancers at the Winnipeg festival in 1928 that he asked to meet them, and, after meeting them, confessed his remorse for having misjudged this ethnic group. No longer an undifferentiated group, Connor interacted with individual Polish people and had to rethink previous opinions.[22]

Another perhaps astonishing act of imaginative inclusion was the programming of British old-time dancers and Indigenous dancers at a high tea performance prior to the opening night of the Calgary festival. On March 21, 1930, the *Calgary Albertan* published this review: "The first of the three day series of program teas took place in the main dining room of the hotel, opening at 4 o'clock, and here old English folk dancing done with conscious grace and measured tread contrasted strongly with the pure abandon and rousing joyousness of the native Indian dances."[23] After decades of government sanctioned bans on dancing among "Indians" beginning in the 1870s,[24] the Calgary CPR festival underscores how corporate interests could make federalist assimilation policies flexible. The newspaper review continues,

> The men and women dressed in white danced the simple numbers of the country folk of England much as they were danced on the high days and holidays by a people of gentle yet imaginative minds. The dances are typical of the English people in their easy grace and conventionality. The Indians, on the other hand, danced with great exuberance, their vividly colored costumes suggesting something of the wild gaiety of the whole affair in the

> Rabbit dance, the Quadrille and the Breakdown, or the Duck Dance, and again in the Handkerchief dance which concluded the series, the spirit of fun and frolic which invested them seemed almost to be caught up by the audience. Wearing moccasins and bright costumes, their long black hair caught up into braids, the women were typical of their race…The Handkerchief dance was prettily done with continual toe dancing lasting for some time showing the strength as well as the grace these people possess.[25]

The sentiment in the review that commends the Indigenous dancers on their "strength" and "grace" at performing the difficult toe dancing suggests that the reviewer has placed these dancers on a professional stage where they are evaluated for their technical accomplishments based on a European aesthetic of movement difficulty, such as "toe dancing." Within the capitalist frameworks of show business and tourism, the "Indians" could now contribute the "pure abandon and rousing joyousness" needed to provide aesthetic balance in a variety-style live theatrical entertainment, while the English could take care of the "conscious grace." White audiences could feel totally safe coming to high tea because the English dancers were there to provide familiarity, recognition, and emotional connection to the British Empire, while the "Indian" dancers allowed the white audience to take a comfortable, temporary voyage, a diversion, into the embodied expressions of "primitive" culture.[26]

PRODUCING THE FOLK: IDEOLOGY, IMMIGRATION, AND TOURISM

As previous scholars have suggested, anti-modernism expresses an attachment to a time before industrialization caused rapid growth of cities and the dispersing of communities and their distinct "traditions" and is defined by its opposition to modernity by promoting an idealized versions of pre-modern time.[27] According to Ian McKay, "The Folk were the living antithesis of the class divisions, secularisms, and 'progress' of the urban, industrial work—that *Gesellschaft* of modernity, of contracts and class divisions, and of that scourge of the oral culture of the Folk, the printed word."[28] If so, the attempted alignment of the modern as represented by the CPR as a symbol of commercial travel and destination tourism with the seemingly anti-modernist pursuit of traditional folk dances might appear to be misguided. The CPR's use of folk dance, however, is more nuanced and can be viewed as enacting what Donald A. Wright has suggested is anti-modernism's ability "to make sense of modernity not through rejection but through the creation of a psychological retreat."[29] In this way, the CPR festivals provided the perfect conditions for dance to enter the arena of commerce as a repository of the folk.

Moreover, McKay, among others, suggests that, in addition to its work of erasing class divisions, the folk also performed the job of instilling national allegiance.[30] The practical economic needs of a growing nation forced a continual re-evaluation and revision of the categories of "us" and "them." As Canadian philosopher Will Kymlicka asserts, "The whole system of colonialism was premised on the assumption of a hierarchy of peoples, and this assumption was the explicit basis of both domestic policies and international law."[31] Legislation in Canada restricting the immigration and mobility of Asians, African Americans, First Nations Canadians, and Ukrainians was enacted based on the belief that certain "races" were better suited to citizenship than others.[32]

The choreography within the Calgary folk festival and the other CPR festivals exemplifies the normalcy of the hierarchal colonial formations that existed—a normalization that is reflected in Anne Glen Broder's 1930 review for the *Calgary Daily Herald*: "On such an occasion it was eminently fitting that those who had endured many hardships and made the path of progress easier for their successors should have pride of place together with a residue of aboriginal inhabitants in the first program presented at the Great West Canadian Festival."[33] Stuart Henderson observes in his analysis of Broder's description of the opening night performance, particularly the pageant *Old Timers' Tableaux*, "This lengthy excursus into the past seems less concerned with excavating Folk traditions than with reinforcing hegemonic power and control over the ownership of Western Canada."[34]

Broder's festival review, connecting past, present, and future, motored by dancing and the railroad's sponsorship, expresses the important job of "folk" at this historical moment, the important work of embodied practice as a form of generational transmission, and the value of corporate sponsorship of the arts. It set the tone for business, government, and arts partnerships, and it demonstrated to industry the rewards that could be gained from supporting the arts.

The enthusiasm expressed in Broder's quote speaks to the tremendous success of the festival with the opening night theme of "Western Canada" and its unproblematic theatrical display of the white settlers' narrative of populating of the prairies.

> Seventy-seven countries contribute to the population of the Dominion of today and from each country has been brought something of worth which may be worked into the "Canadian Mosaic" to make a strong and virile race, declared Premier J.E. Brownlee in addressing the luncheon sponsored by the Canadian Handicrafts Guild, Alberta branch, in the Palliser hotel, Wednesday. A friendly attitude towards the new settlers, that they might freely bring their offering of culture and wisdom to the moulding of a great nation was advocated by premier Brownlee in his address.[35]

Broder and Brownlee conveyed the same message to Calgarians about how the traditions of the new immigrant folk needed to be preserved, needed to be seen, admired, and appreciated, but also needed to be controlled by white producers who generate revenue for the corporation and government.

Aesthetic representations of people, portrayed as equal stars on a stage in festivals such as these, mask the inequities immigrant peoples experienced in their day-to-day lives. However, another more optimistic reading is possible—a reading that views their performance on a proscenium stage in Calgary's most elegant theatre as an attempt to acknowledge their presence in the community—to make them visible. Yes, these folk performers entered the theatre through the stage door as the workers, not through the front door as the consumers, but, nonetheless, they were inside the theatre building where they shared the backstage space and dressing rooms with the ruling class. Bodies of difference mingled during entrances and exits. The theatre became a mini version of cultural diversity in play where status was not economically stratified but existed in relation to the skill of the dancers. Admittedly, the circumstances of the theatre were—and are—temporary; the performance ended, and the dancers re-emerged into their racially coded society. Perhaps the dancers viewed themselves differently as they walked down city streets, and perhaps their co-citizens recognized them as dancers rather than immigrants. Perhaps, in the long run, these marginalized groups derived value from the staging of folk, concentrating all that muscular effort, sweat, vigour, and even joy to carve out a place in the Canadian mosaic despite the forces operating against such inclusion.

In the end, the Great West Canadian Folk Dance, Folk Song, and Handicraft Festival of 1930 demonstrates how an idealized and from-the-past-but-in-the-present performance of the folk permitted racism to dance hand-in-hand with inclusion. The folk dances in the festival were an embodiment of all this contradiction. The staging of mixed programs of folk dance, in other words, exemplifies how folk operated in nationalist terms and how dancing enabled both the mobility and entrenchment of racial categories.

ACKNOWLEDGEMENTS

Special thanks to research assistants Erin Wunker and Michelle Phipps, and to my co-investigator, Lisa Doolittle.

NOTES

1 Parts of this chapter appear in the journal *Discourses in Dance*. See Anne Flynn, "Embodying the Canadian Mosaic: The Great West Canadian Folk Dance, Folk Song and Handicraft Festival 1930," *Discourses in Dance* 5, no. 2 (2013): 53–72.

2 The Grand Theatre opened in 1912 and still exists today. It is two short blocks from the formerly owned CPR Palliser Hotel, where festival guests stayed and where the handicraft festival took place. For a comprehensive history of the Grand Theatre and the roster of famous entertainers who performed there, see Donald B. Smith, *Calgary's Grand Story* (Calgary: University of Calgary Press, 2005).

3 *Calgary Albertan*, March 21, 1930.

4 Ibid.

5 Jens R. Giersdorf, "Dancing, Marching, Fighting: Folk, the Dance Ensemble of the East German Armed Forces, and Other Choreographies of Nationhood," *Discourses in Dance 4, no. 2 (2008): 2. Linda Tomko's Dancing Class: Gender, Ethnicity, and Social Divides in American Dance, 1890–1920* (Bloomington and Indianapolis: Indiana University Press, 1999) was also an important resource for this chapter, helping me to understand the role of folk dance in American settlement houses.

6 For a cultural studies perspective of the three prairie festivals that provided tremendous insight for this chapter, see Stuart Henderson, "'While there is still time…': J. Murray Gibbon and the Spectacle of Difference in Three CPR Folk Festivals, 1928–1931," *Journal of Canadian Studies* 39, no. 1 (Winter 2005): 139–67.

7 For a dance studies overview of folk dance festivals in the United States and Canada, see Anthony Shay's *Choreographing Identities: Folk Dance, Ethnicity and Festival in the United States and Canada* (Jefferson, NC, and London: McFarland, 2006).

8 Jane Desmond, "Terra Incognita: Mapping New Territory in Dance and 'Cultural Studies,'" *Dance Research Journal* 32, no. 1 (2000): 43.

9 Douglas Francis, "The Philosophy of Railways: The Transcontinental Railway Idea in British North America," review of *The Philosophy of Railways: The Transcontinental Railway Idea in British North America*, by A. A. den Otter, *Canadian Historical Review* 79, no. 3 (September 1998): 583.

10 As E. J. Hart writes, "Alexander Begg's Emigration Department had launched its campaign to sell CPR lands in western Canada as early as 1881 with the distribution of the settlement guide *The Great Prairie Provinces of Manitoba and the Northwest Territories*. Soon afterwards it began to distribute tens of thousands of maps, folders, and pamphlets in ten languages to agencies all over Britain and continental Europe. Coordinating its activities out of its London office, the department published ads regularly in 167 British and 147 continental journals and newspapers." See E. J. Hart, *The Selling of Canada: The CPR and the Beginning of Canadian Tourism* (Banff: Altitude Publishing, 1983), 22. The brochures and advertisements most often relied on scenery and wildlife imagery in order to convey the abundance that awaited both settlers and tourists in Canada. Hart suggests that the production of all the tourist brochures, posters, and magazine ads fostered a distinct identity for Canadian visual artists calling it "the railway school" (1983, 31).

11 Hart, *Selling of Canada*, 81.

12 Henderson, "'While there is still time…': J. Murray Gibbon and the Spectacle of Difference in Three CPR Folk Festivals, 1928–1931," 140. For a thorough examination of British and US influences on Canada's construction of the "folk," see Ian McKay's first chapter "The Idea of the Folk" in *The Quest of the Folk* (Montréal and Kingston: McGill-Queen's University Press, 1994): 3–42.

13 McKay, *The Quest of the Folk*, 12–13.

14 Gibbon won the Governor General's award for his book *Canadian Mosaic* when it was published in 1938, indicating the value ascribed to his work by the government of Canada.

15 John Murray Gibbon, *Canadian Mosaic: The Making of a Northern Nation* (Toronto: McClelland and Stewart, 1938), viii.

16 Henderson, "Gibbon and the Spectacle of Difference," 40.

17 Ibid., 142.

18 Poster copy for the Great West Canadian Folk Dance, Folk Song, and Handicraft Festival, Regina 1929, in Hart, *Selling of Canada*, 109.

19 Gordana Lazarevich, "The Role of the Canadian Pacific Railway in Promoting Canadian Culture," in *A Celebration of Canada's Arts 1930–1970*, eds. G. Carruthers and G. Lazarevich (Toronto: Canadian Scholar's Press, 1996): 3–13.

20 From "Memories and Impressions of Helen Modjeska," published in the official program for the Third Great West Canadian Folk Dance, Folk Song, and Handicraft Festival, Calgary, March 19–22, 1930, page 6.

21 A seminal analysis of class and culture of origin in Canada is John A. Porter's *The Vertical Mosaic: An Analysis of Social Class and Power in Canada* (Toronto: University of Toronto Press, 1965).

22 Gibbon, 277–78.
23 *Calgary Albertan*, March 21, 1930.
24 Just eight years after the proclamation of the Indian Act in 1876, a section was added that expressly forbade the cultural practice known as potlatching, a give-away type of ceremony, which included dancing. In 1894, the prohibition was extended to dances of the Plains Indians. Again, in 1913, the act was amended to prohibit any dancing outside Indigenous reserves. These laws proved extremely difficult to enforce, but many dancers were still imprisoned or forced to perform hard labour. Please see Christopher Bracken's *The Potlach Papers: A Colonial Case History* (Chicago: University of Chicago Press, 1997) for a study of Britain's colonial activities on the West Coast.
25 *Calgary Albertan*, March 21, 1930.
26 See Marianna Torgovnick, *Gone Primitive: Savage Intellects, Modern Lives* (Chicago: University of Chicago Press, 1990), chapter one.
27 Donald A. Wright, "W. D. Lighthall and David Ross McCord: Antimodernism and English-Canadian Imperialism, 1880s–1918," *Journal of Canadian Studies* 32, no. 2 (1997): 135.
28 McKay, 12–13.
29 Wright, 135.
30 McKay, 12–13.
31 Will Kymlicka, *Multicultural Odysseys: Navigating the New International Politics of Diversity* (New York: Oxford University Press, 2007), 89.
32 Franca Iacovetta, Paula Draper, and Robert Ventresca, eds., *A Nation of Immigrants: Women, Workers and Communities in Canadian History, 1840s–1960s* (Toronto: University of Toronto Press, 1998), ix–x. See also, "Order-in-Council PC 1931-695, 1931," Canadian Museum of Immigration at Pier 21, https://pier21.ca/research/immigration-history/order-in-council-pc-1931-695-1931, and the "Canada Yearbook 1939," Statistics Canada, https://www66.statcan.gc.ca/eng/1939-eng.htm, which states: "Therefore, the Government, on Aug. 14, 1930, passed an Order in Council whereby immigrants, except Britishers coming from the Mother Country or self-governing Dominions, and United States citizens coming from the United States, were allowed to come in only if they belonged to one of two classes—(a) wives and unmarried children under eighteen years of age, joining family heads established in Canada and in a position to look after their dependents; (6) [*sic*] agriculturists with sufficient money to begin farming in Canada" (154); and "Canadians prefer that settlers should be of a readily assimilable type, already identified by race or language with one or other of the two great races now inhabiting this country and prepared for the duties of Canadian citizenship. Since the French are not, to any great extent, an emigrating people, this means in practice that the great bulk of the preferable settlers are those who speak the English language—those coming from the United Kingdom or the United States. Next in order of readiness of assimilation are the Scandinavians, Dutch, and Germans, who readily learn English and are already

acquainted with the working of democratic institutions. Settlers from Southern and Eastern Europe, however desirable from a purely economic point of view, are less readily assimilated, and the Canadianizing of the people who have come to Canada from these regions in the present century is a problem both in the agricultural Prairie Provinces and in the cities of the East. Less assimilable still, are those who come to Canada from the Orient." (158)

33 *Calgary Daily Herald*, March 20, 1930. Most of what we know about the CPR festivals and how they were viewed by the general public comes from local newspaper writers, and as Batia Boe Stolar points out in her chapter in this collection, newspaper reviews continue to provide (seventy years later) "a window into the cultural Canadian (un)conscious."

34 Henderson, "Gibbon and the Spectacle of Difference," 157.

35 *Calgary Albertan*, March 20, 1930.

Figure 3.1. El Viento Flamenco at the St. John's Arts and Culture Centre, 1998. Photograph by Greg Locke, Stray Light Media Inc.

THREE

OLÉ, EH?

CANADIAN MULTICULTURAL DISCOURSES AND ATLANTIC CANADIAN FLAMENCO

Batia Boe Stolar

When El Viento Flamenco emerged in the cultural scene of St. John's, Newfoundland, in 1996, the response was a mixture of fascination and incredulity: Flamenco in St. John's? Reviewing a performance in 1999 for *The Muse* (Memorial University's student paper), Hans Rollmann wrote, "Spanish cheers, gypsy music, and flamenco dancers may not be what most Newfoundlanders have in mind when they talk about the St. John's music scene, but they're rapidly becoming a sought-after staple of downtown culture."[1] Similar reviews regularly celebrated the company's performances and public appeal,[2] but they did so largely by emphasizing the company's oddity. As the title of Michelle Macafee's 1999 review illustrates, the incongruity stems from the characterization of Flamenco and Newfoundland as polar opposites: "Flamenco…On the Rock: Evelyne Benais Took Spain's *Hottest* Dance and Brought It to the *Cold* North Atlantic."[3] Embedded in the reviews, which span just over a decade, is a dualist machinery that stereotypically associates Flamenco with heat—exoticism, passion, colour, and sensuality—and Newfoundland with coldness—bleakness, starkness, whiteness, and remoteness.

This binary is not only reductive, but it also ignores the historical Iberian-Newfoundland connection that remains visible in place names like Cape Spear, Cape Race, Cape Fogo, Spaniard's Bay, and Spanish Room; in statues of explorers like Gaspar Corte-Real; and in traditional songs like "Spanish Main."[4] These references speak to the early presence of Basque, Portuguese, and Spanish explorers, fishermen, and sailors on the island. By the mid-twentieth century, the Iberian connection had reached legendary status with the famed Portuguese White Fleet and the integration of sailors who fished the Grand Banks into the daily fabric of St. John's, as they often divided their time between Portugal and Newfoundland, in many cases supporting two separate families. Given these historical connections, the absence of Flamenco in Newfoundland should be more incongruous than its potential presence, especially to those reviewers well versed in Newfoundland's history.

The insistence on polarization and difference tells us more about how Canadian multiculturalism operates at a national discursive level, and how it in turn seeps into a distinct, regional culture (in this case, Newfoundland's): the import is celebrated for its exotic Otherness as a way of naturalizing the Nordic character of the nation-state—coldness fits the North Atlantic climate and alludes more conventionally not only to the Canadian winters, but also to social constructions of whiteness that characterize Nordic settler Canadians as emotionally reserved, orderly, and polite. The dualist machinery thus reinforces ideas of national identity that tend to homogenize regionalisms in favour of national myths and therefore neglect to acknowledge that Flamenco (as a stand-in for Andalusia) and Newfoundland are already sites of what theorists like Pnina Werbner and Jonathan Friedman might term "cultural hybridity."[5] For instance, Andalusia, according to William Washabaugh, is a space that informs the "flamenco forms," the "rhythmically distinct varieties of flamenco" cante and dance: "Flamenco forms like *Soleá, Alegría, Bulería, Fandango, Malagueña, Tango, Rumba,* etc. are derived from Andalusian peoples, including Muslims, Jews, Gitanos[,] ... and from Latin American influences."[6] Similarly, musicologist Glenn Colton notes, "Newfoundland's vibrant art music scene has ... been the site of an array of creative synergies rooted in aspects of culture and place."[7] For example, Colton describes a collaboration between Kelly Russell, Peter Gardner, and the Newfoundland Symphony Orchestra that resulted in "a locally inspired fiddle concerto" he states could be described as "Vivaldi meets Émile Benoît."[8] For Colton, the fusion between different cultural styles and traditions of classical music and folk, like Pamela Morgan's "folk opera," *A Nobleman's Wedding*, and Brian Sexton's narrated symphony, *The Newfie Bullet*, is compelling and speaks to a sense of place.[9] More specifically, he describes the Sound Symposium as a "provocative... sonic landscape" and "an international celebration of new music that epitomizes the spirit of stylistic eclecticism and experimentation characteristic of the [contemporary] Newfoundland music scene.... In the symposium's signature event, the Harbour Symphony, music and place merge into one as ship's [*sic*] horns are transformed into a mammoth nautical 'orchestra.'"[10] Colton thus argues that "culture" and "place" are and have been sites of cross-pollination: "Newfoundland popular musicians today can trace their musical roots to a myriad of creative pathways and international contexts as part of a global discourse fuelled by the accelerated growth of new media.... As folklorist Cory Thorne reminds us, 'Newfoundland music is not just jigs and reels.'"[11]

Cultural hybridity, Werbner argues, has the potential to challenge essentialist and integrationist tendencies and practices. Emphasizing hybridity of both Flamenco and Newfoundland thus serves to question the essentializing of each category within a reductive binarism. However, as Werbner argues, once hybridity becomes "routine in the context of globalizing trends," there is the potential for rendering "even the notion of strangerhood meaningless," and therefore powerless.[12]

As the case of El Viento Flamenco illustrates, reviewers continuously negotiate intersecting lines between oddity (strangeness), fascination (exoticism), and familiarity (banality). In this chapter, I analyze how the discourses of Canadian cultural diversity, evident in the reviews of El Viento Flamenco's performances, initially work to solidify "Flamenco" and "Newfoundland" as seemingly fixed, opposite categories, which are used in a dualist machine to cement essentialist national myths. Following the trajectory of the company's evolvement, the binary breaks down and, as the reviews near the end of the company's lifespan illustrate, resonates with a current national myth that is more in keeping with cultural hybridity: the production of a home-grown Atlantic Canadian flamenco.

Contemporaneous to the troupe's performances, the reviews provide a window into the cultural Canadian (un)conscious of the late 1990s, to the lay attitudes and beliefs in Newfoundland and the mainland about multiculturalism. Although the reviewers do not use the word "multiculturalism" directly in their texts, the ways in which they describe the performances and the company's genesis, as well as the members' experiences and artistic vision, betray hegemonic ideologies about multiculturalism in Canada more generally. It is therefore important to look closely and critically at the language they use in their texts, as analyzing metaphors, similes, and diction allows us to glean more insight into the ways in which multiculturalism serves to fix and stabilize national identity. Characterizing the multicultural as an exotic, visible Other, for instance, is one of the ways in which multicultural discourses unify and solidify the often-elusive category of Canadian identity. In this way, Canadian identity is defined by what it is not. The performance reviews are also useful when considering who authors them. Written by academics, members of the audience, and journalists with expertise in the arts, these social commentaries reflect the populace while actively shaping how the populace will (or should) think by writing *to* them (how to interpret, how to think, how to see, etc.) about Flamenco (explicitly) and multiculturalism (implicitly).[13] As my analysis of El Viento Flamenco illustrates, multiculturalism, while said to be a celebration of national diversity within the nation, at first uses the ethnic Other to reinforce federalist ideals by drawing on national stereotypes that homogenize regional differences; in other words, multiculturalism resists the very inclusivity premised in its ideal. However, by the end of the troupe's lifespan, a shift in how pluralism appears is evident, celebrating cultural hybridity as distinctly Canadian.

EL VIENTO FLAMENCO: A BRIEF HISTORY

In its inaugural year, El Viento Flamenco consisted of three members: its founder, dancer Evelyne Benais (Lemelin), guitarist Bob Sutherby, and vocalist Sean Harris. During its lifespan (1996–2007), the troupe drew on the local talent of musicians and dancers, including guitarist Alex Schwartz, percussionist Adam Staple, Costa Rican singer Eylem Rodriguez, and dancer Jill Dreddy (one of Benais's students). In 1999, percussionist Tony Tucker became a permanent addition, making the move with Benais, Sutherby, and Harris to Halifax in 2001. Once relocated to Nova Scotia, the troupe continued to draw on local talent, regularly featuring those of Benais's students who "really enjoy[ed] performing."[14] Two of her students eventually formally joined the troupe: Marak Perk (as vocalist and dancer) and Megan Matheson, who went on to found her own company, Compañía Azul, effectively replacing El Viento Flamenco and its school of dance.[15]

El Viento Flamenco garnished recognition, winning the East Coast Music Award for Best Roots/Traditional Group recording in 2007 and the Lieutenant Governor's Award of Excellence.[16] Their website provides information about the troupe's members, including select videos of their performances, an online archive of the company's reviews, as well as a link to the website of the Compañía Azul, which is "under the artistic direction of Megan Matheson with Bob, Sean, and Tony of El Viento Flamenco."[17] Supported by provincial and federal grants,[18] Matheson's troupe continues to be active, featuring dancers Matheson ("La Azulita") and Sandra Tziporah, guitarists Sutherby ("El Tortuga") and Daniel MacNeil, percussionist Ian MacMillan, and Harris on vocals. Neither website offers an update on Benais's current work.[19] However, her legacy—bringing Flamenco to Atlantic Canada where it now thrives—remains.[20]

CRITICAL RECEPTION: TEXTUAL ANALYSIS OF MULTICULTURAL DISCOURSES

Writing for the Halifax *Chronicle Herald*, Stephen Pedersen rhetorically asks, "Can a traditional ethnic dance form survive with any kind of vitality thousands of miles from its geographical origin, and in an entirely different and even opposite climate?"[21] There are numerous assumptions here, ranging from the use of the words "ethnic" and "traditional" to the adherence to the hot/cold binary that evokes early immigration debates and fears about immigrants' (in)ability—or willingness—to assimilate into the Canadian geocultural landscape. In the context of Atlantic Canada, Scottish highland dancing has survived and thrived "thousands of miles from its geographical origin." The root of the question thus has less to do with the transplantation of dance and more with who qualifies as "ethnic," as well as the differences between Atlantic Canada and Andalusia, which are exacerbated here by the "opposite climate." While the weather may seem a neutral and benign topic of conversation, its discursive roots can be traced to its use to discriminate against those deemed "undesirable" immigrants: the Immigration Act of 1910, for instance, effectively barred immigrants "belonging to any race deemed unsuited to the climate or requirements of Canada."[22] Taking into account the historical allusions implicit in Pedersen's statement, the use of the word "traditional" promotes thinking about ethnicity as a form of authenticity. Yet, as Marcia B. Siegel notes, "Although ethnic shows may want us to believe we're seeing some 'pure' essence of a people, we know that culture and cultural forms don't remain static. Tribal groups migrate and mix; their dances get suppressed or exploited; technology adds its enhancements. Politics often pays the piper and calls the tune."[23]

In the context of 1990s Spain, Flamenco, Timothy Dewaal Malefyt argues, increasingly became a commercial, mainstream commodity with a global appeal, leaving local aficionados in Andalusia holding onto "tradition" and mobilizing "to localize and preserve flamenco 'art' in private peña clubs, apart from commercialization."[24] To the aficionados, "flamenco song is an art form that imparts cultural heritage in its capacity to transmit the collective sentiments of Andalusian suffering."[25] The discrepancy between the commercialized version and the traditional version works to reinforce tensions between the local and global while reaffirming the illusion that dance, like a people, is rooted in a geographical place. Its product is proliferated by the media, which shapes as it retells these kinds of stories in what urban theorist Edward Soja has termed "glocal" contexts.[26] The illusion of authenticity is maintained in multiple reviews of El Viento Flamenco's performances. We see the same discourse evoked in various reviews of performances in Newfoundland and the mainland, in which the Andalusian character transforms the provincial stages in similar ways. Gail Lethbridge, for instance, describes her experience of watching Benais dance in Halifax as follows: "That performance took place on a cold November night in Halifax, but when Evelyne clicked her heels and twirled her red skirts, it might as well have been a hot night in Andalucia."[27] Put this way, it is the venue and the audience, rather than the dance, which is temporarily transplanted to an exotic locale.

Such transplantations, however, are enabled by the repetition of the hot/cold binary, as Richard Boisvert's review illustrates: "On aurait pu difficilement imaginer un contraste plus total que celui de la bise glaciale qui soufflait vendredi soir sur Québec avec la chaleur apportée sur la scène de Louis-Fréchette par El Viento Flamenco." (It would be difficult to imagine a more complete contrast than that of the glacial wind that was blowing across Québec on

Friday night, and the heat brought onto the Louis-Fréchette stage by El Viento Flamenco.)[28] Here again the binary opposition between the "heat" of the exotic Other and the "cold" of the Canadian host appears. The multicultural discourses cut across regional divisions to suggest an authentic national character united by geography and a shared climate. Relying on the hot/cold binary unifies distinct provinces (Newfoundland, Québec, and Nova Scotia in these examples) and emphasizes Flamenco's influence (heat) on the otherwise cold Canadian scene/stage. In this vein, the exotic Other is embraced and welcomed as a desirable, consumable commodity. As such, it fits more with what Stanley Fish described in 1997 as "boutique multiculturalism... the multiculturalism of ethnic restaurants, weekend festivals,"[29]—and "ethnic" dance. For Fish, the boutique multiculturalist presumes there is a universal humanness underneath the superficial difference marked by ethnic food, dress, and culture, but "a boutique multiculturalist does not and cannot take seriously the core values of the cultures he tolerates."[30] This kind of multiculturalism reduces the Other to a consumable product while reinforcing assimilationist ideals. In the Canadian context, multicultural differences can be voiced through ethnic celebrations (like dance) so long as multicultural groups assimilate to a Canadian way of life of shared values.

Paradoxically, however, as Lethbridge's review suggests, Flamenco's heat is celebrated for its ability to transform a Canadian audience by transplanting, however ephemerally, Canadians into an Andalusian landscape. While this can take the form of cultural tourism, the language used to describe the performance also emphasizes the transformative qualities of the ethnic product that carries the potential to assimilate the average Canadian. The reviews thus point to a continuing debate within immigration and multicultural discourses that render the foreign(er) simultaneously desirable and threatening, but nevertheless foreign. This becomes more evident in stories about Benais. In addition to being characterized as "the sexiest person" in St. John's,[31] she is described as "an exotic creature" in Newfoundland:[32] reviewers point out that "Benais is not Spanish, nor is she a gypsy,"[33] but nonetheless refer to her "raven hair and olive skin."[34] Her exotic factor is twofold, due in part to her being "the daughter of French immigrants from France and Tunisia in North Africa,"[35] and in part to her being a Flamenco dancer in Newfoundland. Notably, once Perk joins the troupe in Halifax, the lure of exoticism shifts to her. In Benais's words, Perk is "half Turkish, half-Armenian and brings a knowledge of folklore and the pop music of those cultures into the mix."[36] In her review of a performance at Laurentian University in Sudbury, Ontario, Nadine Visschedyk focuses almost exclusively on Perk's "soaring voice that is clear and exotic. She brings her Armenian background and her Turkish culture to Flamenco dancing, adding just one more way that El Viento Flamenco individualized this already highly interesting art."[37] The failure to recognize that Flamenco is already a culturally hybridized site renders Perk's inclusion and influence an oddity that works to characterize El Viento Flamenco as original and distinct; "individualized" here nods to the pluralism within the group that refracts Canadian ideals of multiculturalism more generally.

Focusing mostly on binaries and the exotic, the reviewers rarely mention what forms of Flamenco are performed. While they frequently refer to Benais's spectacular footwork, they do not use Flamenco terms like taconeos, nor do they mention her muñecas and flores to describe her hand movements or braceo for arms. Rarely do they mention her continuously performing—and in fact leading—each dance en compás. When they refer to her commanding figure on stage, they do not refer to her as a Maja who accentuates individual dances with gólpes and pellizcos.[38] Instead, the reviewers consistently focus on the "heat" of her technical prowess. Tim Boudreau, for instance, notes that her "dancing added the heat" with "her fiery dance steps."[39] Similarly, Janet French describes how the "crowd was dazzled by the frantic footwork of dancer Evelyne Benais" with the "reverberating clicking of [her] shoes,"[40] and Nicole Underhay describes "the awe-inspiring Evelyne" as follows: "She makes it seem like moving your feet rhythmically at approximately 3000 km/hr is a natural thing."[41] Denise Williams calls attention to Benais's commanding presence on stage, noting that, "when her heels were stomping so fast that even her cheeks were shaking, she never lost that rigidly dignified composure...Benais was a regal beauty with thunder in her heels."[42] Just as Lethbridge's review suggests the possibility of the Canadian assimilation to the ethnic import, these reviews maintain the ethnic Other's difference as a desirable commodity that is sexualized and racialized.

The insistence on the "hot" import detracts from the implicit similarities between Flamenco and Anglo-Irish dance—similarities that could have been just as easily expounded. Contextually, Roger Saint-Fleur describes the cultural scene in St. John's during the 1990s as follows: "Saint-Jean vibrait jusqu'à present au rythme de la musique irlandaise, celtique, ecossaise ou terre-neuvienne." (St. John's presently vibrates to the rhythm of Irish, Celtic, Scottish or Newfoundland music.)[43] While Saint-Fleur asserts that "le flamenco [est] un art populaire andalous synonyme de passion et de chaleur" (Flamenco is a popular Andalusian art synonymous with passion and heat), it should be noted that Irish, Scottish, and Celtic forms of dancing, with their energetic and demanding footwork, are not lacking passion or heat.[44] Michael Flatley's 1990s spectacles, *Lord of the Dance* and *Riverdance,* were received as ardent international sensations that brought fast and furious step dancing to many Canadian stages.[45] When reviewers comment on Benais's footwork, their descriptions of her stomping and quick footwork are informed by such styles. Elissa Barnard is most explicit in comparing the two when she writes of "the fiery passion of Newfoundland flamenco dancer Evelyne Lemelin" precisely in such terms: "she cut up the floor in a storm of stepdance more exciting than Riverdance" with the "dazzling stomp[s] [of] her lightning feet."[46] Hence, while "fire" conforms to the "hot" import, "thunder" and "lightning" are more closely related to the tempestuous North Atlantic, suggesting, as Mark Vaughan-Jackson implicitly does when he describes the troupe's performances as "melting the thousands of miles separating Seville and St. John's,"[47] that there is a melding taking place—a melding that is not unlike that of an assimilationist model of the American melting pot.

In her chapter in this collection, Anne Flynn similarly examines how writings about dance at the 1930 "folk" festival in Calgary, whether performance reviews or descriptions in the festival's program, make visible ideological stances on such issues as immigration and national identity. She notes there are numerous "exaggerated descriptions extolling the virtues of the singing and dancing 'peasants' of Europe.... It's as though [John Murray] Gibbon was trying to show, via the dancing, that these new immigrants were healthy, strong, neuromuscularly fit for hard labour, and able to 'control' themselves to perform the precise steps of the choreography."[48] Sixty years later in Atlantic Canada, reviews and descriptions about the performances of El Viento Flamenco continue to illustrate how reviews about dance are a vehicle to voicing ideological stances on cultural diversity in Canada. The contested line between assimilation and respect of cultural differences, which marks a shift in Canadian attitudes toward cultural diversity, becomes increasingly evident in the reviews once El Viento Flamenco gains prominence. Past its point of novelty, reviewers shift their focus; the exoticism of the company remains, but instead of focusing on the foreign element (Benais or Andalusia), the exotic is more directly linked to the strangeness of the home-grown product. For instance, Merill Rasmussen, an audience member in Halifax, states, "I kept thinking it's so odd that these people are from Newfoundland."[49] For Pedersen, it is precisely this oddity that informs the company's exoticism; as he puts it, "Benais' flamenco dance company is an exotic Mediterranean flower not just growing, but thrusting its roots down and thriving in rocky, windy Newfoundland."[50] On the one hand, what is celebrated here is the transplantation of the exotic onto Canadian soil (or rock); on the other, the exotic has less to do with the "hot" import and more to do with the seemingly incongruous pairing. It is a site of conjunction that gives the troupe its name: "El Viento Flamenco" literally translates as "A Flamenco Wind"—wind being a defining characteristic of Newfoundland. Hence, the "melting" that Vaughan-Jackson alludes to reinforces the idea of a Newfoundland-made Flamenco that is unique *because* it incorporates elements of both Andalusia and Newfoundland. This oddity further differentiates the troupe from the more established Canadian Flamenco companies in other parts of the country, like Compañia Carmen Romero in Toronto, where Benais first apprenticed and performed before starting her own troupe.[51]

The genesis of the troupe was premised on the financial viability of Benais having received a grant from the Newfoundland and Labrador Arts Council that allowed her to pursue a career as a Flamenco dancer (over that of a French literary scholar) and to apprentice with Carmen Romero in Toronto before settling in St. John's to begin a troupe of her own.[52] It was then that she applied for and received a Canada Council grant to bring Flamenco guitarist Patricio Tito to train and work intensively with Sutherby for a month.[53] Supported by provincial and federal grants, Benais's multicultural enterprise—bringing Flamenco to a region in Canada that had none—is hinged on the troupe's proficiency—or *legitimacy*—in Flamenco. This is reflected in the story of how Harris came to join the troupe, a story that is retold multiple times.[54] With Benais and Sutherby sufficiently trained, the duo required someone "to handle the 'cante'—the singing that is at the heart of Flamenco."[55] Benais recounts that Tito, attending a concert of the Gravel Pit Campers,[56] suggested Harris, assuring her, "He can learn Spanish later. Listen to how powerful a voice he has, the rhythm he has, and also how much he gives of himself on stage. He's not up there trying to look cool, putting on airs. He's just singing his heart out and that's what you need for a flamenco singer."[57] In this story, the "authentic"

Flamenco voice, Tito's, legitimizes not only who can be a Flamenco singer, but also *what* a Flamenco singer is.[58]

We see this kind of legitimization again when reviewers mention that Benais, and later the whole troupe, train repeatedly in Spain. Linda Rimsay, for instance, comments that "Evelyne Lemelin recently returned from further studies in Spain and, as in the past, with each return to St. John's brings new depth and understanding to the art form."[59] These annual visits to Spain to train are also emphasized on the bios of the troupe's members.[60] While Romero is credited for the start of Benais's career, little is mentioned of the "beginner Spanish dance classes" she took with Sandra Blackmore in St. John's.[61] Thus, in spite of there being a genuine Flamenco presence in Canada that has yielded such artists like Romero and Esmeralda Enrique, reviewers emphasize Benais's connection to Flamenco as developing separately and more directly in contact with the *authentic* place.

By the end of the troupe's lifespan, Benais was quoted as speaking more authoritatively and knowledgeably about the Flamenco scene in Spain, and how El Viento Flamenco measured in relation to that scene rather than Toronto's. In 2005, she tells Nemetz, "Age is appreciated in the south of Spain in general and the greatest dancers today are all in their 40s and 50s and still packing the theatres. They have a devoted public. It's not about being cute or pretty, but about being sincere, authentic, expressive."[62] The use of the words "sincere" and "authentic" are not coincidental. The troupe's website builds on these concepts to legitimize the troupe's claim to/on Flamenco, as well as to differentiate themselves from any other Flamenco troupe.

As early as 1997, Saint-Fleur identified Benais's choice of dancing as "la forme la plus rarement dansée, la Siguiriya" (the rarest style of dance, the Siguiriya).[63] One of the oldest forms of Flamenco, the siguiriya is, as Donn E. Pohren notes, "probably the most difficult of the jondo dances to dance well, due to its character and necessarily slow-paced compás. The dancer must be able to captivate solely by an exceptional personality and dance of the upper torso, for any type of theatricalism or artificiality, including prolonged speeding up of the compás to 'relieve the boredom', immediately and thoroughly destroys the essence of the siguiriyas."[64] After relocating to Nova Scotia and incorporating Perk and Matheson, the troupe's repertoire included tangos flamencos, which Pohren notes are differentiated by their toque: "driving and rhythmical, [the tango] is straightforward and exciting."[65] If there is a difference in the technical difficulty of the dances in the evolvement of the company, it is largely grounded on the talents and backgrounds of each of its members. The change in direction of the dances correlates with the promotion of the company as an authentic Flamenco troupe. Drawing on their blues and gospel music background, the troupe is described as follows: "Just as Blues purist Eric Clapton sings the blues without trying to reproduce the sound of the Delta note for note, El Viento Flamenco is in love with the tradition, but also brings its own voice to the genre."[66] Attention is called to the cultural, linguistic, and musical diversity of its members, celebrating these as assets integral to the troupe's unique style: "El Viento Flamenco brings its own, very distinct voice to the art form."[67] Harris's voice, similarly, is hailed as "perhaps the most defining element of El Viento Flamenco's sound" insofar as "he has developed a unique style and clear timbre which sets El Viento Flamenco apart from other Flamenco troupes around the world."[68] Celebrating the diverse contributions of each of its members, the promotional website concludes, "in its own way, El Viento Flamenco is fiercely authentic."[69]

It is at this juncture in the troupe's lifespan that we see cultural hybridity at work most explicitly. As Homi K. Bhabha argues, "For hybridity, empowerment is about the achievement of agency and authority, rather than the fulfillment of the 'authenticity' of identity—however mixed, however 'multi', however intersective or intercultural."[70] While Bhabha does not deny "the obvious importance of forms of civic registration or political recognition—passports, visas, papers, citizenship—that entitle subjects to exercise cultural choice and political agency," he argues that it is precisely in "relation to these 'ordering' principles that hybridity derives its agency by activating liminal and ambivalent positions *in-between forms of identification that may be asymmetrical, disjunctive and contradictory."*[71] For Benais, the concept of authenticity is best understood in terms of what she calls "sincerity," as she explains to Angelique Binet: "La danseuse doit avant tout être sincere. 'Quand le chant touché, la tristesse transparâit naturellemnt [*sic*] sur mon visage et dans mes gestes,' expliqué-t-elle." (The dancer must above all be sincere. "When the song is touching, the sadness is naturally evident on my face and in my gestures," she explains.)[72] And, as she elaborates on the versatility of styles that range in tone and feeling, she states, "it's very important to be a natural, authentic, spontaneous and sincere performer, whether it's the cheerful or the darker, more dramatic pieces."[73] Notably, Benais's attitude toward Flamenco at this point positions El Viento Flamenco as an authoritative Flamenco company because it "is a unique St. John's creation."[74] The evolvement of the company and the multicultural discourses evident in the reviews of the troupe's lifespan suggest that competing ideas about what multiculturalism is, should, or could be continue to inform the very cultural products it produces and promotes, often in troubling and contradictory terms. The reviews also show that, despite how multiculturalism is officially or conceptually articulated, its underpinnings betray ways of thinking about ethnicity, the Other, and Canadian identity that may be at odds with the ideals multiculturalism espouses. As the case of El Viento Flamenco illustrates, multiculturalism in Canada, like dance, is continuously evolving and adapting.

NOTES

1 Hans Rollmann, "Dance—Like You've Never Danced Before," *The Muse*, October 1, 1999. Reviewers most often refer to "gypsies" instead of "the Romany people" when writing about flamenco, perhaps in part because the term is translated from the Spanish "Gitano," commonly used in Andalusia and in Flamenco circles. This chapter uses the term "Romany people," and only uses the terms "gypsy" and "gypsies" when these terms are part of a quotation.

2 All reviews cited in this chapter were found on El Viento Flamenco's archive of reviews, "Reviews and Articles," El Viento Flamenco, accessed July 10, 2016, http://www.elvientoflamenco.com/reviews/reviews.htm.

3 Michelle Macafee, "Flamenco…On the Rock: Evelyne Benais Took Spain's Hottest Dance and Brought It to the Cold North Atlantic," *The Canadian Press*, October 2, 1999; emphasis is the author's.

4 See William B. Hamilton, *Place Names of Atlantic Canada* (Toronto: University of Toronto Press, 1996), 8.

5 See their work in *Debating Cultural Hybridity: Multicultural Identities and the Politics of Anti-Racism*, eds. Pnina Werbner and Tariq Modood (London: Zed Books, 2015).

6 William Washabaugh, "The Flamenco Body," *Popular Music* 13, no. 1 (January 1994): 75.

7 Glenn David Colton, *Newfoundland Rhapsody: Frederick R. Emerson and the Musical Culture of the Island* (Montréal: McGill-Queen's University Press, 2014), 16.

8 Ibid., 16.

9 Ibid., 16.

10 Ibid., 16.

11 Ibid., 16.

12 Pnina Werbner, "Introduction: The Dialectics of Cultural Hybridity," in *Debating Cultural Hybridity: Multicultural Identities and the Politics of Anti-Racism*, eds. Pnina Werbner and Tariq Modood (London: Zed Books, 2015), 1–2.

13 In her chapter in this collection, "Embodying the Canadian Mosaic: The Great West Canadian Folk Dance, Folk Song, and Handicraft Festival, 1930," Anne Flynn similarly draws on reviews of the Canadian Pacific Rail's folk festival in Calgary, Alberta, as she examines how "the concept of 'folk' [is used] as a tool for nation building" in Canada.

14 Andrea Nemetz, "Spanish Flavour," *Halifax Chronicle Herald*, May 25, 2005.

15 See "El Viento Flamenco School of Dance," El Viento Flamenco, accessed July 10, 2016, http://www.elvientoflamenco.com/school.

16 See their home page, El Viento Flamenco, accessed July 10, 2016, http://www.elvientoflamenco.com; see also, "About El Viento Flamenco," El Viento Flamenco, accessed July 10, 2016, http://www.elvientoflamenco.com/about.htm.

17 "About El Viento Flamenco," accessed July 10, 2016, http://www.elvientoflamenco.com/about.htm.

18 El Viento Flamenco's website acknowledges the support of the Nova Scotia Department of Communities, Culture and Heritage, Arts Nova Scotia, and the Canada Council; see "Awards and Sponsors," El Viento Flamenco, accessed July 10, 2016, http://www.elvientoflamenco.com/awards.htm.

19 In an interview with Dan Carlinsky, Benais indicates that she relocated to Paris in 2008, where she continues to teach Flamenco and performs occasionally. See Dan Carlinsky, "Flamenco Dancer: At the Crossroads between Academia and the Life of a Dancer, Evelyne Benaïs-Lemelin Chose Her Passion," *U of T Magazine*, Summer 2015, accessed July 10, 2016, http://magazine.utoronto.ca/cool-jobs/flamenco-dancer-evelyne-benais-lenelin-cool-jobs.

20 The local scene has grown considerably and hosts the Atlantic Flamenco Festival, supported by Matheson's company and school of dance as well as the Maria Osende Flamenco Company, which promotes Flamenco by bringing in talent from Spain.

21 Stephen Pedersen, "Flamenco Group Dances with Attitude," *Halifax Chronicle Herald*, February 11, 2000.

22 Statutes of Canada, *An Act Respecting Immigration, 1919, Statutes of Canada 9-10 Edward II*, ch. 27, section 38.

23 Marcia B. Siegel, "Multicult: The Show," *The Hudson Review* 49, no. 3 (Autumn 1996): 463.

24 Timothy Dewaal Malefyt, "'Inside' and 'Outside' Spanish Flamenco: Gender Constructions in Andalusian Concepts of Flamenco Tradition," *Anthropological Quarterly* 71, no. 2 (April 1998): 63.

25 Ibid.

26 See Edward W. Soja, "On the Concept of Global City Regions," *ART-e-FACT: Strategies of Resistance* 4, accessed July 10, 2016, http://artefact.mi2.hr/_a04/lang_en/theory_soja_en.htm.

27 Gail Lethbridge, "Flamenco in Frogrante Delicto. Ribbit, er, Olé," *Halifax Chronicle Herald*, April 2004.

28 Richard Boisvert, "El Viento Flamenco et l'OSQ: rythme, chaleur et jeu de jambe," *Le Soleil*, November 17, 2007; translation by El Viento Flamenco.

29 Stanley Fish, "Boutique Multiculturalism, or Why Liberals Are Incapable of Thinking about Hate Speech," *Inquiry* 23, no. 2 (Winter 1997): 378.

30 Ibid., 379.

31 Nicole Underhay, "Livin' La Vida Flamenca," *Current*, February 2000.

32 Marilyn Smulders, "Flamenco Dancer from the Rock," *The Daily News*, February 10, 2000.

33 Kathleen Lippa, "Spanish Lady," *The Express*, January 28, 2001; Pedersen, "Flamenco Group Dances with Attitude."

34 Nemetz, "Spanish Flavour."

35 Smulders, "Flamenco Dancer from the Rock."

36 Quoted in Nemetz, "Spanish Flavour."

37 Nadine Visschedyk, "El Viento Flamenco Performs to a Packed House," *Lambda*, October 2006.

38 "Gólpes" means stamping the floor with the entire foot, and "pellizcos" literally means "pinching," referring to small, spontaneous gestures that can also be defined as playful and flirtatious movements.

39 Tim Boudreau, "Olé, This Is Hot!" *The Journal*, February 16, 2000.

40 Janet French, "Dancin' Round the World," *Dalhousie Gazette*, February 1999.

41 Underhay, "Livin' La Vida Flamenca."

42 Denise Williams, "World Dance at Live Art New Dance Festival," reprinted in "Reviews and Articles—Excerpts," El Viento Flamenco, accessed July 10, 2016, http://www.elvientoflamenco.com/reviews/reviews-excerpts.htm#williams.

43 Roger Saint-Fleur, "Portrait: Evelyne Lemelin," *La Gaboteur*, February 10. 1997.

44 Within an Anglo context, Irish, Scottish, and Celtic cultures have also been Othered.

45 In 1998, Canadian ice dancers Shae-Lynn Bourne and Victor Kraatz chose *Riverdance* for their Olympic free dance in Nagano; they finished fourth in a controversial ice dance competition. Amy Shipley writes: "The Canadians, Bourne and Kraatz, leave here with nothing to show for their performance, other than the satisfaction of tonight's crowd-pleasing 'Riverdance' program, which lead Riverdance dancer Colin Dunn helped develop. They finished third in the free dance, but it wasn't enough to lift them out of fourth overall"; Amy Shipley, "Grishuk, Platov Repeat as Olympic Champions," *Washington Post*, February 17, 1998.

46 Elissa Barnard, "Dance Fest Offers Eclectic Mix," *Halifax Chronicle Herald*, February 8, 1999.

47 Mark Vaughan-Jackson, "A Spanish Wind: Newfoundland Flamenco Troupe Takes Flight for Mainland Canada and Spain," *St. John's Telegram*, January 8, 1999, 11.

48 Flynn, "Embodying the Canadian Mosaic."

49 Kim Garritty, "Flamenco Captures Halifax," *Nova News Net*, February 15, 2000.

50 Pedersen, "Flamenco Group Dances with Attitude."

51 Garritty, "Flamenco Captures Halifax."

52 Ibid.

53 Vaughan-Jackson, "A Spanish Wind."

54 In 1998, the author attended a performance of El Viento Flamenco at the LSPU Hall in St. John's. As a Mexican Canadian, the only part of the performance that was dissonant for the author was Harris's voice, not in emotion, but in hearing him sing phonetically.

55 Vaughan-Jackson, "A Spanish Wind."

56 The name of this local band refers to the once popular "gravel pit camping" in Newfoundland, which was eventually made illegal by the province due to instances of littering, leaving fires unattended, etc.

57 Garritty, "Flamenco Captures Halifax."

58 None of the reviewers take issue with Harris's voice, and for many, his singing in Spanish was impeccable.

59 Linda L. Rimsay, "Festival of New Dance a Celebration of Talented Newfoundlanders," *St. John's Telegram*, Summer 1998.

60 "Member Bios," El Viento Flamenco, accessed July 10, 2016, http://elvientoflamenco.com/bios.htm.

61 Lippa, "Spanish Lady."

62 Nemetz, "Spanish Flavour."

63 Saint-Fleur, "Portrait: Evelyne Lemelin."

64 D. E. Pohren, *The Art of Flamenco*, 43rd anniversary ed. (Westport, CT: Bold Strummer, 2005), 240.

65 Ibid., 250.

66 "About El Viento Flamenco," El Viento Flamenco, accessed July 10, 2016, http://www.elvientoflamenco.com/about.htm.

67 Ibid.

68 Ibid.

69 Ibid.

70 Homi K. Bhabha, foreword to *Debating Cultural Hybridity: Multicultural Identities and the Politics of Anti-Racism*, eds. Pnina Werbner and Tariq Modood (London: Zed Books, 2015), xii.

71 Ibid.

72 Angelique Binet, "Le Flamenco est en ville," *Le Courrier de la Nouvelle Ecosse*, February 18, 2000.

73 Skana Gee, "Gypsy Time," *Daily News*, May 25, 2004, 19.

74 Lippa, "Spanish Lady."

FOUR

ILLUMINATING A DISPARATE DIASPORA

FIJIAN DANCE IN CANADA[1]

Evadne Kelly

GROWING UP ON VANCOUVER ISLAND, BRITISH COLUMBIA, AS the daughter of a Fiji-born Australian, I developed a love and appreciation for all things Fijian, so much so that I became interested in researching how, when, and why people identify with the "traditional"[2] Fijian song-dance genre called meke. However, I soon realized that meke is not simply an expression of Fijian culture and identity as it conveys some of the tensions of Fiji's colonial history. This history was front and centre as I conducted my fieldwork and archival research in Western Canada and Viti Levu, Fiji, between the summer of 2011 and the fall of 2012, causing certain questions to linger in my mind. Why, for instance, does meke provoke political anxieties for some Fijians living in Canada? And how is an essentialist notion of the ethnic group—the notion that members from a particular geopolitically bounded nation share a harmonious and homogenous culture, tradition, or heritage, even though they no longer live in that nation—both transcended and sustained in relation to the notion of cultural diversity in Canada?

The term "diaspora" typically refers to tangible, quantifiable, and bounded groups that are culturally homogenous and organized around common issues and concerns.[3] Conversely, Fiji's Canadian diaspora offers an alternative understanding, which is characterized by practices that expose diverse political realities and concerns related to various forms of "difference." Indeed, when I returned from my fieldwork, I realized that I had encountered what I now call a "disparate diaspora" in relation to meke. A disparate diaspora refers to nonexclusive articulations of community, politics, and cultural difference.[4] Within Fiji's Canadian diaspora, such articulations do not have a foundation in kinship or geographic origin. Instead, Fijian Canadians, who have differing histories of dispossession, displacement, and marginalization, articulate identifications with Fiji in divergent ways that are, nevertheless, entangled with one another. This meke-invoked disparate diaspora is made visible through dancing bodies that reveal the tensions within the Fijian community in British Columbia. I argue, ultimately, that the visibility of these tensions shows how ethnic groups are not simply homogenous, harmonious, fixed, and bounded.

The disparate diaspora is evident in two separate and competing Fiji Day festivals;[5] it is also evident in a Christian meke for a church fundraiser. All three events complicate assumptions of ethnic group homogeneity and boundedness as they foreground a pre-existing and divisive tension between Fijians of Indian descent and iTaukei[6] (Indigenous "people of the land"[7]) descent that relates to Fiji's tumultuous independence[8] involving four coups d'état since 1987.

A DISPARATE DIASPORA

The Fijian diaspora in Canada is multifarious, with individuals of varying cultural backgrounds including Indian, American, Samoan, and Tongan. Fiji's Vancouver-based diaspora is not culturally homogenous, nor do those who identify as Fijian necessarily share in the same cultural traits and practices that are tied to a specific geopolitical territory.[9] This is due in part to Fiji's political history. From the early years of British colonial rule until 1916, Indian indentured workers were brought to Fiji and their labour exploited by the Colonial Sugar Refinery,[10] a company that was a lynchpin for the economic survival of the colony.[11] Due to this importation of labour, by the 1940s, Indians and Fijians of Indian descent outnumbered iTaukei. However, for the most part, only those native to Fiji could own land, an enduring policy that has continued to impact land ownership.[12] Today, the vast majority of Fiji's land continues to be reserved for permanent communal ownership by iTaukei.[13] It is this colonial history and the demand for social and political equality by the indentured and post-indentured Fijians of Indian descent that informs the current divisive and tumultuous Fijian political landscape.[14] Due to the rising tensions between Fijians of iTaukei descent—who were afraid of losing their land, which is, for many, an integral part of their identification with culture and heritage and subsistence living— and Fijians of Indian descent—who wanted equality with iTaukei—the two military coups in 1987 and a third coup in 2000 resulted in increased prejudice against Fijians of Indian descent, destruction of their property, and harassment leading to massive emigration to other countries, including Canada.[15] While current national discourses in Fiji espouse multiracialism and equality for all citizens of Fiji regardless of race, the hegemonic position of the iTaukei remains.[16]

Despite these tensions, British Columbia's immigrants from Fiji simply label themselves as "Fijian."[17] This is in keeping with the popular and widely familiar discourses of Canadian multiculturalism, whereby people who hail from the same nation are lumped into one ethnic group category and are assumed to share a culture and identity.[18] This approach perpetuates stereotypes of the "ethnic" and homogenous Other rooted in the past,[19] as culture becomes nominalized as a thing that exists and is bounded, fixed, and unchanging. As Catalina Fellay articulates in her chapter on Kathak and Flamenco, such discourses fail to appreciate cultural performance traditions as sites for innovative cultural blending, and they result in a failure to acknowledge the differences within, rather than simply between, ethnic groups—in other words, a failure to recognize the ongoing machinations of a disparate diaspora, which I discuss further below.

TWO FIJI DAYS

In Vancouver, the tensions within the Fijian diaspora are not always obvious. On the surface, the idea that all Fijians in Canada identify with their "Fijianness" is echoed by many of my research participants: "In Canada," one interviewee states, "everything is good, we are all just Fijians."[20] Many of those with whom I conversed explain that, in Canada, Fijians leave their politically divisive issues behind and that, with multiculturalism, everyone is allowed to have the same rights. On a deeper level, however, this proclaimed harmony is belied by the presence of a recently added second Fiji Day festival in Vancouver, which provides evidence that the politically divisive ethnic groupings established during British colonial rule in Fiji, and which are explosive in post-Independence nationalist politics, continue to haunt Fijian migrants in Canada. I am told, for example, by one research participant, not to talk to two iTaukei Fijian men about their withdrawal from performing meke at the older of the annual Fiji Day festivals, which has been an annual event for over ten years. The festival aims, in its own way, to connect with multicultural discourses in Vancouver by opening with an international parade of people representing different countries of the world and their associated cultures through costumes and music statically associated with the cultures being represented. A primary organizer of the festival spent time showing me his comprehensive video coverage and promotional materials for the 2009 and 2010 festivals. Footage of the festivals reveals primarily Fijian Indian programming with a Fijian audience of predominantly Indian descent. The iTaukei Fijian programming is minimal in comparison, reduced to a brief kava ceremony and a few meke dances performed by one dance group, created and led by iTaukei Fijians based in Vancouver. When I ask the organizer, who is a self-identified Indo-Fijian, about this meke group performing, he tells me that iTaukei Fijians from this group have been critical of his Fiji Day festival, have since withdrawn from it, and have started their own festival with primarily iTaukei Fijian programming.[21] This comment speaks to ethnic divisiveness that rubs away at the earlier sentiment of "we are all just Fijians in Canada."

I then interview members of the meke group who are the source of the most recently added annual Fiji Day festival, who are also on my list of interviewees. They focus their festivities on rugby and Indigenous Fijian music (by bringing to Vancouver a popular Fijian musical group that mixes iTaukei music and dance with popular Western music). Interviewing members of this iTaukei Fijian group becomes particularly important after I am told explicitly not to speak with them by my Indo-Fijian research participant who is involved with the organization of the older annual Fiji Day festival.

These tensions are further made evident when I ask members of the meke group who have organized the newer of the festivals what is different about the two Fiji Day festivals. They answer that mostly Fijians of Indian descent go to the older Fiji Day festival. I ask why this is the case, and they suggest that it has to do with the organizers being of Indian descent. They add that their festival, being organized by iTaukei Fijians, attracts more iTaukei Fijians. The two Fiji festivals both attempt to connect with the wider Vancouver communities and want to express their love of Fiji; both, however, also perpetuate a particular divide, with one geared towards stressing Fijian identity in Canada as Fijian of iTaukei descent, and the other geared towards stressing Fijian identity in Canada as Fijian of Indian descent.

While these two groups underline how Fiji's tense political history is present in Vancouver, they also highlight one of the main problems with Canadian multiculturalism. The discourse of multiculturalism implicitly promotes the idea that people from a particular geopolitically bounded nation—Fiji, in this case—share a harmonious and homogenous culture, tradition, or heritage. Canadian multiculturalism starts with the premise that immigrants arrive from nations that are culturally homogenous and thereby constitute a clearly defined ahistorical ethnic group. As Marcia Ostashewski and Steven Jobbitt have demonstrated in their chapters on theatrical Ukrainian dance, cultural dance practices in Canada expose tensions between positive, community-building articulations of diaspora, as well as negative articulations of racial hierarchy, heteronormativity, exclusivism, and other antagonisms within groups. The categorization of people upon which multiculturalism rests "erases the differences between immigrants from the same nation, thereby erasing any of the political, historical, economic, social, and religious differences between them."[22] The discourse of multiculturalism does not leave much room to address more nuanced notions of culture, the impact of colonization, and situations where the immigrants have their own culturally particular and variant experiences.[23] Clearly, the two Fijian festivals organized and carried out in Vancouver are tied to Fiji's colonial past and to present independence realities. The festivals, taken together, show how differing approaches to identifying as "Fijian" in Canada coexist and complicate the ethnic group typology that underlines Canadian multicultural discourses.

A CHRISTIAN MEKE FOR A VANCOUVER-BASED FIJIAN PENTECOSTAL CHURCH FUNDRAISER

In the following example of a Christian meke for a Pentecostal church fundraiser, meke deployed as a "traditional" dance speaks, once again, to the tensions embedded in Vancouver's Fijian diaspora. The event was designed to raise funds to send to Fiji. It featured an evening of Fijian culture intended to be shared with a wider Vancouver audience. The meke performed for the event demonstrates how one's sense of cultural identity and belonging is shaped by past experiences, and how these are complexly expressed within discourses of Canadian multiculturalism. Yet, it also highlights how an essentialist notion of ethnicity, so dominant and divisive in Fiji's postcolonial reality, is both transcended and sustained through the deployment of the concept of "tradition."

> Wearing *masi*[24] print shirts with long, ankle-length brown skirts and plastic red Hibiscus flowers behind their ears, the dancers sit with their legs crossed on the stage and pulse a rhythm with their knees. They connect with the earth as they pound it with their hands and then their fingers spring upwards from their mouths towards the sky to demonstrate they are not heathens worshipping Fiji's devils or demons but Christians. The phrasing of their movements and rhythms are framed with *cobo*—a hand clap that, on its own, carries historical weight and meaning expressed through its rhythm-motion-based affects. Their hand movements are not graceful or soft, but strong, geometric, and patterned. Their eyes watch their hands to give the movements life,[25] all the while creating accents with their heads, softly (but not fluidly) and with ease, tipping back and forth. Their movements and accents connect their feelings and their bodies to the past, to their Christian faith, and to a shared nostalgia for Fiji.[26]

In some ways, this Canadian-Christian meke transcends an essentialist notion of ethnicity by allowing people of dominant and non-dominant cultures and identities to give a corporeal expression to Fijianness. To explicate, participants who self-identify as being from varying backgrounds of descent congregate out of a love and nostalgia for Fiji to raise money for disaster relief in Fijian villages. Notably, the movements for this meke come together from a number of different sources including Fiji, and from other countries of Oceania, such as Samoa, Tonga, and Wallis and Futuna. The meke combines what is considered "traditional" meke movements with new movements inspired by the Christian performers who self-identify as being from a wide range of backgrounds, including Fijians of iTaukei descent, Fijians of Indian descent, and Canadians of Irish descent. Such combinations highlight the ways in which ethnicity may be fluid and changeable, and full of tension. They also reveal how people selectively draw from the past for present needs and future desires. In the Christian meke, for example, the cobo (pronounced THAWM-boe), a particular way of cup clapping the hands, is used throughout the performance. Cobo, as a movement, relates to what research participants referred to as "traditional iTaukei" customs that are thought to have emerged out of rituals, such as meke ni yaqona (a sacred ritual performed for a high chief, whereby meaning is ignited by movement, lyrics, cobo, and the gathering of people to witness the sacred performance),[27] that were once part of the worship of pre-/Christian ancestor spirits. In these customs, the rhythm, movement, and depth of sound of cobo is still of great importance in communicating a physiological feeling/emotion of deep gratitude, energy, and respect, or vinaka vaka levu.[28] These deeper cultural and historical meanings of cobo give strength to this Vancouver meke and, in that strength, a feeling of iTaukei legitimacy. On the one hand, then, the Christian meke puts forth a sense of harmony—a coming together in the spirit of helping Fijians in Fiji—among a diverse group of people in Vancouver; on the other hand, the use of the rhythms, affects, and movement of cobo supports a notion of Fijianness in Canada that is distinctively iTaukei, recalling the past and present colonial distinctions in Fiji. Today, 99 percent of iTaukei in Fiji identify themselves and their traditions as Christian,[29] the result of early Wesleyan Methodist missionaries interweaving Christianity with Indigenous customs, beliefs, and practices.[30] The power of this connection between Methodism and Fijian custom supported a hegemonic hierarchy; colonial administrators and primarily Methodist chiefs held positions of power, and the chiefs were installed by the colonial administration as a form of indirect rule. For iTaukei, then, the homogenizing influence of Christianity became centred on the land. The land is believed to be sacred because iTaukei believe it to have been given to them by God.[31]

The focus on cobo here and its significance for Fijianness is, in addition, also in tension with the meanings associated with how Christianity—a legacy of Fiji's colonial history—is incorporated into the movements of the meke performance. A series of newly created gestures where the fingers of the meke dancers spring upwards from their mouths, alternating hands, is a case in point. These are not gestures that were learned from Fijian elders. Rather, the participants of the meke group have chosen these gestures in order to align with the words of the song to which they are dancing that mean "word of God." The dancers use these light, springy, joyful, and quick movements to express feelings associated with their Christian beliefs and values. These particular movements demonstrate a clear reverence to their Christian God and thereby distance this meke from the pre-Christian meke that the iTaukei dancers in this group associate with "devil worship." But their physical demonstration of Christian faith also distances this dance from the dances of Fijians of Indian descent, who are primarily Hindu.[32] Thus, not only is this Christian meke religious, it is also political, as it exacerbates the dissonance between Christians and Hindus, in this case in the context of the Fijian and Fijian-Canadian diaspora populations. This meke expresses a God-given right to land ownership in Fiji, driving right to the heart of a conservative Fijian national politics and the source of the coups in Fiji[33] aimed at keeping the power in the hands of the Christian iTaukei and out of the hands of Fijians of Indian descent.[34]

Through the meke for a church fundraiser, self-identified Fijians of iTaukei descent reach towards inclusion, belonging, and recognition as an "ethnocultural" group in Canada by performing a "traditional" and Indigenous Fijianness that aligns with the policies and practices of Canadian multiculturalism. The Canadian Multiculturalism Act and its policies treat culture as bounded with ethnically homogenous "communities" with singular geographic origins.[35] In this approach to pluralism, cultures are not continuously transforming and responding to social, political, religious, etc., forces, but are instead treated as bounded substances that live side by side in a mosaic.[36] In order to situate themselves into this multicultural mosaic, the dancers perform Fijianness as "traditional," iTaukei, Christian, homogenous, and cohesive. In doing this, although not necessarily with intention, they reify a separation between Fijians in Canada, making iTaukei a legitimate source of Fijian identity. The meke performs not the varied and complex cultural realities of Fiji and Fiji's Canadian diasporic populations, but rather a Fijianness that reasserts the power and dominance of Christian iTaukei for new purposes of inclusion and recognition in Canada's multicultural mosaic.

CONCLUSION

Meke performances and movements underline how colonial and postcolonial tensions enter bodies and become part of them. In her chapter "Being a Body in a Cultural Way," Sally Ness examines how current culturally focused dance research explores how past histories and memories, imaginings, and future potentials can be expressed in the body through dance movement.[37] These insights guide this chapter in that they ask questions about how bodies, by and through dance performances, may serve to disrupt notions of ethnicity as bounded, homogenous, and harmonious. I suggest that the two Fiji Day celebrations and the Christian meke push against the Canadian discourse of multiculturalism, which erases tensions and differences and contradictions within so-called ethnic groups. For what is clear is that the political, social, and religious differences among the Fijians living in Vancouver underline a disparate diaspora that offers a critique of Canadian multiculturalism by demonstrating the multifariousness of one of Canada's so-called ethnocultural groups.

NOTES

1 My chapter for *Moving Together* has informed portions of my book, though the writing and arguments are different. See *Dancing Spirit, Love, and War: Performing the Translocal Realities of Contemporary Fiji* (Madison, University of Wisconsin Press, 2019).

2 Instead of using the term "tradition" as it is often used to legitimize an act as authentic and original, I view tradition as sustaining an engagement with the past through selective or constructed continuity with past practices. My usage of "tradition" comes from concepts of tradition that have been critically analyzed by Theresa Jill Buckland, "Dance, History, and Ethnography: Frameworks, Sources, and Identities of Past and Present," in *Dancing from Past to Present: Nation, Culture, Identities*, edited by Theresa Jill Buckland (University of Wisconsin Press, 2006: 3–24); Janet O'Shea, *At Home in the World: Bharata natyam on the Global Stage* (Middletown, CT: Wesleyan University Press, 2007); Eric Hobsbawm, "The Nation as Invented Tradition," in *Nationalism*, edited by Anthony Smith and John Hutchinson (Oxford University Press, 1994: 198–205); and Nicholas Thomas, *In Oceania: Visions, Artifacts, Histories* (Durham: Duke University Press, 1997).

3 Khachig Tölölyan, "Rethinking Diaspora(s): Stateless Power in the Transnational Movement," *Diaspora* 5, no. 1 (1996): 4; Rogers Brubaker, "The 'Diaspora' Diaspora," *Ethnic and Racial Studies* 28, no. 2 (January 2005): 1–19.

4 I am building on concepts and characterizations of diaspora outlined by James Clifford. See James Clifford, "Diasporas," *Cultural Anthropology* 9, no. 3 (1994): 302–38.

5 Once celebrating cession to the United Kingdom (1874), Fiji Day now celebrates its independence (gained in 1970).

6 "Fijian Affairs (Amendment) Decree 2010" states that "Indigenous" Fijians be referred to as "iTaukei" in all official laws and documentation. Accessed August 27, 2018. https://countrysafeguardsystems.net/sites/default/files/Fiji%20Fijian%20Affairs%20Amdmt%20Decree%20iTaukei%202010.pdf. However, many of the Fiji immigrants I have spoken with in Vancouver identify themselves generally as "Fijian" and more specifically in relation to each other as being of Indian descent or Indo-Fijian, and of "native" Fijian descent. To address these differences in preference (and the complex political implications of each), I use terms as outlined in the 2010 decree except when drawing directly from field experiences, at which time I refer to Fijians in Vancouver in the ways individuals identified themselves and each other.

7 Martha Kaplan, *Neither Cargo nor Cult: Ritual Politics and the Colonial Imagination in Fiji* (Durham: Duke University Press, 1995).

8 John D. Kelly and Martha Kaplan, *Represented Communities: Fiji and World Decolonization* (Chicago: University of Chicago Press, 2001).

9 Khachig Tölölyan, "Rethinking Diaspora(s): Stateless Power in the Transnational Movement," *Diaspora* 5, no. 1 (1996): 4.

10 Claudia Knapman, *White Women in Fiji, 1835–1930: The Ruin of Empire?* (Sydney: Allen and Unwin, 1986).

11 Kelly and Kaplan, *Represented Communities*, 162.

12 Ibid.

13 Ibid., 162.

14 Ibid. In 2013, Fiji adopted a new constitution in preparation for the first democratic election since military takeover in 2006, which was held in 2014. The new constitution promises to improve on the social and legal inequities that Fijians of Indian descent have faced in Fiji. However, at the time of writing this chapter, it is too early to know if the new constitution is reducing inequities.

15 Matt Tomlinson, *In God's Image: The Metaculture of Fijian Christianity* (Berkeley: University of California Press, 2009), 8. See too, Brij V. Lal, "Fiji Islands: From Immigration to Emigration," *Migration Policy Institute* (April 1, 2003), accessed March 11, 2014, http://www.migrationpolicy.org/article/fiji-islands-immigration-emigration.

16 Ibid., 47.

17 In my British Columbia interviews, Fijians of iTaukei and Indian descent referred to themselves as "Fijian."

18 *Canadian Multiculturalism Act, Revised Statutes of Canada* 1985, c. 24, accessed June 19, 2014, http://laws-lois.justice.gc.ca/eng/acts/C-18.7/FullText.html. The Act states: "Whereas the Government of Canada recognizes the diversity of Canadians

as regards race, national or ethnic origin, colour and religion as a fundamental characteristic of Canadian society"; section 3 (1) (d) "Multiculturalism Policy of Canada" aims to "recognize the existence of communities whose members share a common origin"; and, in "Implementation of the Multiculturalism Policy of Canada," section 5 (1) (g), to "assist ethno-cultural minority communities to conduct activities with a view to overcoming any discriminatory barrier and, in particular, discrimination based on race or national or ethnic origin."

19 This critical view is exemplified by an example in the news of former BC Liberal premier Christy Clark's multicultural outreach plan, designed and implemented by her minister of multiculturalism, focusing on "quick wins" or ways of getting the "ethnic vote," such as public apologies for past Canadian atrocities rooted in racism. Individuals were upset at being treated as homogenous "ethnic" groups without complexity and having their histories used by the Liberal government in what was termed "ethnic manipulation" in order to gain voter support. "BC Liberals Ethnic Vote Scandal Costs Multiculturalism Minister His Job," *Beacon News*, March 5, 2013, accessed March 10, 2013, http://beaconnews.ca/blog/2013/03/bc-liberals-ethnic-vote-scandal-costs-multiculturalism-minister-his-job/.

20 At the time of my interview, choosing to identify as "Fijian" did not seem to be the result of the 2010 Fiji government decree that all Fiji citizens be referred to as "Fijian" but a choice to demonstrate moving on from the "ethnic" tensions experienced in Fiji.

21 Patel ([pseudonym] Fiji festival organizer), in conversation with the author, Vancouver, Canada, August 2011.

22 Bonnie Urciuoli, "Producing Multiculturalism in Higher Education: Who's Producing What and for Whom?" *International Journal of Qualitative Studies in Education* 12, no. 3 (1999): 295.

23 Ibid., 294.

24 Fijian bark cloth often covered with patterns and motifs.

25 A movement technique described by Lavonne Gucake Donu, the meke choreographer, in conversation with the author, Vancouver, January 2012.

26 This description of a meke came from observing a recorded performance of the dance, learning the dance myself, and then discussing the movement with Lavonne Gucake Donu, the iTaukei choreographer, Vancouver, January 2012.

27 Damiano Logaivau (*daunivucu* [meke composer/choreographer]) in email correspondence with the author, July 2013.

28 Damiano Logaivau (*daunivucu*) in conversation with the author, Pacific Harbour, Fiji, July 2012.

29 Tomlinson, *In God's Image*, 3.

30 Thomas, *In Oceania*, 198.

31 Tomlinson, *In God's Image*, 23, 3.

32 Fiji Bureau of Statistics, "Population by Religion and Province," *2007 Census of Population and Housing*, accessed June 17, 2014, http://www.statsfiji.gov.fj/index.php/2007-census-of-population.

33 Fiji's most recent coup in 2006—which was seen by some in Fiji as a way to return Fiji to democracy, or as a coup "in the name of multiculturalism"—is an exception to this trend. Lynda Newland, "Religion and Politics: The Christian Churches and the 2006 Coup in Fiji," in *The 2006 Military Takeover in Fiji: A Coup to End All Coups?*, eds. Jon Fraenkel, Stewart Firth, and Brij V. Lal (Canberra: Australian National University Press, 2009), 193.

34 Kelly and Kaplan, *Represented Communities*, 133.

35 *Canadian Multiculturalism Act*. This underlying assumption is expressed in the Act, its interpretation (for example, section 3 [1] [d]), and policies (for example, section 5 [1] [g]), http://laws-lois.justice.gc.ca/eng/acts/C-18.7/FullText.html (accessed June 19, 2014).

36 A. Marguerite Cassin, Tamara Krawchenko, and Madine VanderPlaat, *Racism and Discrimination in Canada Laws, Policies and Practices* (Halifax: Atlantic Metropolis Centre, 2007), 8–9.

37 Sally Ann Ness, "Being a Body in a Cultural Way: Understanding the Cultural in the Embodiment of Dance," in *Cultural Bodies: Ethnography of Theory*, eds. Helen Thomas and Jamilah Ahmed (Malden and Oxford: Blackwell Publishing, 2004: 121–44).

FIVE

UKRAINIAN THEATRICAL DANCE ON THE ISLAND

SPEAKING BACK TO NATIONAL AND PROVINCIAL IMAGES OF MULTICULTURAL CAPE BRETON

Marcia Ostashewski

On a stunning summer day in Sydney, Nova Scotia, on the August 2013 long weekend, the local community gathered at Open Hearth Park for its much-anticipated and nationally touted grand opening event, Stronger Than Steel. Formerly the site of a steel plant that had drawn immigrants and employed Cape Bretoners of diverse origins for decades, it is now a beautifully manicured green space, which holds playgrounds, sculptures, game fields, running tracks, and biking trails. A large stage was erected for the park's opening event, where revellers could enjoy continuous concerts. Among the performers were Sydney's Ukrainian dancers. Although the performance was requested outside the dance group's regular rehearsal period, the children and their parents and teachers rearranged their summer holidays so that the dancers could rehearse and perform. After the concert, CBC Cape

Breton host and celebrations MC Wendy Bergfeldt remarked on the outpouring of the audience's delight at the young Ukrainian dancers' colourful costumes and vibrant performance. In addition to the Open Hearth Park kickoff, the dancers had also been invited to perform at the centenary celebrations of St. Mary's Polish Parish that summer.

These dancers were following a long-standing inclusion of Ukrainian cultural traditions at public celebrations in Nova Scotia. An earlier generation of the dancers, for instance, performed for the Canada Games in 1980, hosted at Sydney's university campus; and these same dancers were asked to welcome British royalty to Halifax in 1986. The creative cultural activities of Cape Breton's Ukrainians—including award-winning parade floats in the early 1900s, theatrical performances and choral concerts in the 1950s and 1960s, and dancing on stages since at least the 1930s—have long been valued as part of local community events.

Despite their contributions to the region and their inclusion and visibility within the greater community, Cape Breton Ukrainians and their civic activities are rarely acknowledged in official representations of Cape Breton culture; indeed, the official representation of Cape Breton's culture tends to, rather stereotypically, spotlight the music, dance, and language of the Scottish Gaels, Acadians, or Mi'kmaq. The contributions of Ukrainians, cultural and otherwise,[1] have largely been overlooked by tourism, education, and cultural policy. Yet, if they are properly recognized, they nuance the history, culture, communities, and development of Cape Breton, and challenge official government-supported and entrenched stereotypes of the Atlantic Canadian region, as well as Canada as a whole.

At the advent of the twentieth century, Cape Breton Island was at the centre of North American industrial development, particularly with respect to economic development, and therefore was a desirable place to settle for newly arrived immigrants. Writing at the outset of the 1900s, historian C. W. Vernon remarked, "At the beginning of the twentieth century the eyes of the world have been directed towards Cape Breton as a result of the important developments which have taken place in the coal, iron and steel industries and in the vicinity of the Sydneys [Sydney, North Sydney, Sydney Mines]."[2] A major conduit for increasingly mobile people and goods, and a nexus of economic, political, and cultural activities, the island had already been home to Indigenous peoples for millennia. French settlers had been established there as early as the 1630s, and immigrants from the British Isles, including Scottish settlers, began to colonize the region in the late eighteenth century.[3] While these ethnic groups dominate the historical records, the early 1900s saw the large-scale immigration of many more diverse groups to Cape Breton Island, facilitated by new immigration policies intended to encourage economic development in the new Dominion of Canada.[4] The island soon became home to Central and Eastern Europeans and people from the West Indies who immigrated there seeking work in the coal mines and steel plants—the industries that underpinned the region's then-booming economy.

Ukrainians began to settle in the area in the late 1800s and early 1900s, around the same time as they arrived on the Prairies. They contributed to the economic development of Cape Breton as labourers, merchants, and farmers; they also helped to create and establish a rich community life maintained through religious, cultural, educational, and political institutions.[5] It is in this context that I focus my discussion on Ukrainian theatrical dance practices in Cape Breton. As an integral part of the vibrant and diverse cultural landscape and history of the island, Ukrainian theatrical dance continues to be practised in Cape Breton—a fact that is largely ignored in scholarly work.

UKRAINIAN HERITAGE AND CULTURAL PRODUCTION IN CANADA

While histories of Ukrainians in Canada largely address communities from the western part of the country, oral narratives and historical evidence in Cape Breton support similar experiences, community dynamics, and developments. Public Canadian attitudes about the earliest wave of Ukrainian immigration to Canada, beginning in the 1890s, were frequently potently negative.[6] Examples in the anglophone conservative press referred to these newcomers as being from "degraded races." They were further described as "poor and filthy" and of "disgustingly low moral standard"; "the most unfit of the scum of the lowest civilizations of Europe."[7] Buoyant and determined, however, the Ukrainian immigrants to Canada rejected such labels and refused to let go of their cultural practices. Even prior to the construction of community halls and churches, a multitude of plays and concerts—including choirs, orchestras, and dance performances—were staged in the homes of Ukrainians in Canada at least as early as 1904.[8] Soon after, Ukrainian immigrants began to establish community halls that quickly became centres of cultural education and performance activities, including lending libraries, reading rooms, and spaces to foster the production and performance of plays, dance, and music. Such support for creative and cultural educational activities in community halls had likewise been common practice in their European homeland.[9]

In Canada, a number of sociopolitical organizations were established during the period of interwar migration. Some organizations had religious connections; others grew out of non-religious revolutionary and nationalist sensibilities.[10] Many Ukrainians joined community organizations more for their program of cultural activities—language classes, theatre, music, and dance—than as a result of their associated ideological aspirations.[11] This is not to suggest that Ukrainian communities across Canada—nor even within regions—are unified, ideologically homogenous, or held together primarily by religious belief.[12] Ukrainians, like many other ethnically identified groups in Canada, have produced a variety of antagonistic factions,[13] particularly between religious conservatives and progressive labour-farmer socialist politics.[14] Although sometimes the values of religious and secular groups conflicted, all of these groups and their halls supported a diversity of Ukrainian cultural education and national cultural practices, most specifically theatrical dance.[15] These halls facilitated the bourgeoning of amateur theatrical and dance groups, choirs, and orchestras. Local Ukrainian performance groups toured among Ukrainian communities in Canada along a transregional circuit between the Prairies and Ontario.[16] Research participants in Cape Breton tell us that their Ukrainian drama, dance, and music groups toured on the island, performing in theatres and community halls of nearby towns. Moreover, these venues showcased and promoted Ukrainian dance in Canada to non-Ukrainians. By the mid-twentieth century, in contrast to earlier derisive publications about Ukrainian immigrants, the English-language press began to celebrate Ukrainian cultural performance in Canada.

One of Canada's most significant assertions of a pluralistic nationhood began in the 1960s with the establishment of the Royal Commission on Bilingualism and Biculturalism (1963–1969); on its heels came multiculturalism. The resulting policies and acts were taken up by the federal and provincial governments. The involvement of Canadian Ukrainians in the institutionalization of multiculturalism was due to an expressed interest in gaining recognition for all peoples who have contributed to the development and progress of Canada beyond the "founding" French and English. Among the most prominent Canadian Ukrainians invested in this development were Canadian Senator Paul Yuzyk and Manoly Lupul, the latter man an academic dedicated to the study of Ukrainian Canadians. Lupul referred to this process as "the dignification of ethnicity."[17] Senator Yuzyk's first speech in the Senate was dedicated to multiculturalism; he is credited, at least by other senators, as "the first to initiate the movement to have Canada recognized as multicultural," which was eventually adopted by the Canadian government in a 1971 policy.[18] Notwithstanding the conspicuous absence of Indigenous peoples from the "founding" groups, the symbol of Canada's nationhood became the "mosaic"—not one homogeneous culture, but one culture made up of fragments of many. It is within this concept that Ukrainian culture, especially Ukrainian dance, became more visible within the Canadian imaginary. It is no coincidence that, in the late 1960s and early 1970s, Ukrainian dance companies like Shumka and Cheremosh, and, soon after, the Vegreville and Dauphin festivals, arose. However, the ways in which the various fragments of the mosaic are (re)presented locally, regionally, nationally, and internationally is informed by a complex cultural politics; it is not arbitrarily chosen.[19] In Cape Breton, where the focus of official discourse on culture and communities is on Scottish, Acadian, and Mi'kmaq groups, official politics have worked against promoting awareness of the Ukrainian contributions to the island. Yet, no critical attention has been paid to Ukrainian dance in Cape Breton; this chapter is the first such publication.[20]

HISTORICAL CONTEXTS OF UKRAINIAN DANCE IN CAPE BRETON

Ukrainian theatrical dance practices in Canada are generally believed to exhibit a continuity with centuries-old ethnocultural Ukrainian practices and to have arisen in the context of a rurally based, peasant lifestyle. According to historian Frances Swyripa, the first wave of immigrants and their children built "on the folk culture introduced by the peasant pioneers, selectively reinforced by two subsequent immigrations, often as art, and frequently transformed into something uniquely 'Ukrainian Canadian,' particularly on the prairies."[21] Swyripa describes Ukrainianness in Canada as strongly located in the Prairies—distant from, but drawing selectively upon, the agriculturally based experiences of immigrants who came decades ago from what is now Ukraine. While some aspects of Ukrainian culture may be shared across the country, Cape Breton's Ukrainians feel that there are other aspects that are distinct, most particularly in connection with dance. Many of Cape Breton's Ukrainians have noted their isolation in relation to other Ukrainian Canadian communities. Where the sharing of Ukrainian performance across western and central Canadian regions was, and continues to be, commonplace, such interregional and community exchange does not appear with the same frequency in Cape Breton. There are a few exceptions. Pavlo Yavorsky, who came originally from Western Canada, gave classes in Sydney's Whitney Pier and the nearby town of Dominion. He had been a student of Vasile Avramenko,[22] who popularized Ukrainian theatrical dance in Cape Breton when he arrived there to teach dance in the late 1930s. Although Yavorsky was of Ukrainian Orthodox faith, he was welcomed to teach at the Ukrainian Catholic parish hall in Whitney Pier. While the embracing of religious differences is not uncommon nowadays, it was so in Yavorsky's time, even between Ukrainian religious groups. However, given their isolation, Ukrainians in Cape Breton came together in support of cultural education through dance, regardless of fractious religious boundaries.

Moreover, non-parishioners came to dance at the Ukrainian Catholic parish, signalling, perhaps, a willingness on the part of Cape Bretoners to engage in multiculturalism decades before it was officially part of the Canadian imagination. Collaborations between Sydney's Ukrainian dancers and local non-Ukrainians were not unknown. The very first major instance of this was in 1940 and sprung from the losses of the Second World War. In that year, "ballet master" Yavorsky organized a concert of the Ukrainian dancers in support of the Canadian Red Cross. The dancers were accompanied by a local Croatian tamburitza orchestra—a small orchestra of traditional string instruments. Furthermore, on May 19, 1941, Yavorsky directed the dancers at the Cape Breton Festival of Music and Elocution at the Lyceum Theatre in downtown Sydney. The dancers were featured alongside a variety of performers, including singers of folk songs from the British Isles, piano soloists playing Brahms, and the tamburitza orchestra performing arrangements of concert music from the Croatian opera *Zrinski*. Yet other concerts in the area featured the two groups among other cultural performers, as is evident in this program for the "Fourth Annual Concert of the Kennington Girls' Chorus." These cross-cultural alliances appear to be unique in Canada at the time.

Programme

FIRST PART

O CANADA.

CHILDREN'S SONG .... Kipling
Ruth Mackley

OUR NATIVE LAND .... Anon

NOW IS THE TIME OF YEAR .... Brahms
WHERE THE POOLS .... Brahms
Senior Class

DOLL SONG AND DRILL

MINUET IN G .... Beethoven
Joan Pue Gilchrist

THE LITTLE PINK ROSE .... Jacobs-Bond
Shirley Townsend

ON WINGS OF SONG .... Mendelssohn
MERRY THE TIME .... Schumann
Senior Class

OTHER PEOPLE'S BABIES ....
Annie Routledge

LITTLE BUTTERCUP (Pinafore) .... Sullivan
Margaret Livingstone

THE CONSCRIPT
THE QUEST
TO THE GARDEN } .... Folk Songs
Junior Class

BELINDA GOES A SHOPPING ....
Group of Girls

SECOND PART

BLOW MY BULLY BOYS
HAUL AWAY, JOE } .... Sea Shanties

SAILOR'S HORNPIPE ....
Eileen McAdam and Kathleen McGillivary

SLUMBER BOAT .... Nevin
Diana Darrow

BOY CRAZY .... Ryerson Clements
Louise Cusack

THREE LITTLE MAIDS (Mikado) .... Sullivan
Zelma Rolls, Vivian Smith and Nan Wilson

THE GYPSIES
THE CUCKOO } .... English Folk Songs
Senior Class

"ARMY SCENES" from Opera Zrinski,arr.by Ivan pl Zajc
Croation Tamburitza String Orchestra

UKRAINIAN SOLO COASSCK DANCE "TCHUMAK"
John Huk

ALL THROUGH THE NIGHT .... Welsh Folk Song

THE SANDMAN .... Brahms

THE NATIONAL ANTHEM

'Tis the Songs you sing an[illegible] he Smiles you wear
That make the Sun[illegible] everywhere.

Figure 5.1. Kennington Girls' Chorus program, ca. 1940. Reprinted from John Huk Collection, MG 21.13. Photograph courtesy of the Beaton Institute, Cape Breton University.

In other locations where Ukrainians settled in large numbers, and thus where the presence of Ukrainian musicians was more than likely readily available, collaborations with non-Ukrainians might not have been necessary. In light of Cape Breton's relative isolation from other Ukrainian communities, Sydney's Ukrainian dancers remember those occasions for which they have travelled off-island to interact with other Ukrainian communities. For example, Kenny Horechuk recalls visiting the National Ukrainian Festival in Dauphin, Manitoba, as a teenager in 1974. In an emotional interview, Horechuk told me of the strong impression the experience made on him; he was deeply affected by being part of such a large and vibrant Ukrainian community. To be among several thousand other Ukrainian Canadians in Dauphin—as opposed to the few hundred, at most, who might gather at an event in Cape Breton—was positively overwhelming. Supported by a small government grant, Sydney's Ukrainian dance group was able to travel to this well-known Ukrainian festival under the instruction of John Huk (himself a previous dancer under Yavorsky). That year, the dancers from Cape Breton won their competition. More than thirty years later, when I met John Huk in 2008, he very proudly showed me the plaque awarded to the group that summer in Dauphin. At that time, "authenticity" was a prime concern for competition judges—and Sydney's Ukrainian dancers performed Avramenko choreographies that Huk remembered learning as a child from Yavorsky. The performance would no doubt have seemed to come from a different era to Western Canadian judges and dancers, who were no longer performing in Avramenko's style. Many of the dances performed even today by Sydney's Ukrainian dancers continue to echo Avramenko's choreography.

Inspired by the strong impression that had been made upon Kenny Horechuk as a dancer in 1974, Sydney's Ukrainian dancers made a second visit to the Dauphin festival in the mid-1980s, with Horechuk as instructor; by this time, innovative choreography, stemming from Ukraine, was increasingly emphasized in Ukrainian dance. Dancers in the rest of Canada, most especially in the Prairies, had developed their practice through years of intense competition and innovations, whereas Sydney's dancers, who did not enjoy similar levels of government support, were not able to do likewise. As a result, perhaps, they did not fare so well in competition this time. Although the dancers have said little to me about this visit to Dauphin, in the contexts of research interviews or otherwise, they have remarked that participating in such an event was a valued experience.

While the Dauphin festival took Sydney's dancers from Cape Breton to other parts of Canada, there have also been a few occasions in which Ukrainians from other parts of Canada visited Cape Breton and shared their expertise. Such off-island influences include dance instructors who, like Yavorsky, "came from away."[23] One such instructor was Daria Stechishin (later Stefura) who arrived in Sydney in the mid-1980s. Horechuk hired this Alberta-born and Ontario-based instructor on behalf of the dance group; Horechuk received a small government grant that facilitated this off-island connection. Stechishin was employed to create new choreography in preparation for the Canada Games, hosted on the local university campus. A recording of Sydney's Ukrainian dancers' performance at the Canada Games shows strikingly different dance material from their previous performances. This new choreography integrated novel movement sequences, music, costumes, and choreography that worked in tandem with the multilevel and temporary surround stage that was built specifically for the opening Games event.

Other pieces of the choreography created by Stechishin included a boys' Cossack dance and a lyrical girls' dance that incorporated flowered branches. The Cossack dance—a long-time favourite in many Ukrainian communities—was full of bravado and athletic tricks and involved barrels as robust and spectacular props.[24] While Cossack dances had been part of Sydney's Ukrainian dance repertoire since at least as early as the Yavorsky years—they had been part of the choreography introduced in the 1920s by Avramenko and his cadre of student teachers—this new Cossack choreography was akin to the dances being performed in Western Canada at the time and was considered new to Sydney's dancers. Moreover, it is also a dance typically performed only by boys or men. However, where in the 1980s about half of the approximately sixteen dancers were young men, today most of the dancers are young women. A "sword dance" variant based on the new Cossack dance continues to be a favourite among Sydney's audiences and young dancers. The Cossack costume, which all dancers wear for this dance, has a strong nationalist and masculine association. The girls shirk their traditional skirts and flowered wreaths for boys' pants and hats that cover their braided hair. Skirts would be impractical in light of the many squatting, jumping, and kicking segments in which the underdress of dancers would be revealed to the audience. This gender inversion is not unique to Cape Breton, as the numbers of male dancers are dwindling nationwide.[25] While most of my conversations on the history of Ukrainian dance have occurred with Huk and Horechuk, both men, many members of the community, including women, still speak fondly and frequently of a beautiful flower dance that was also introduced to Cape Breton by Stechishin, among them Kenny Horechuk's sister, Cathy Horechuk, who was a teenage dancer in the 1980s.[26] For many years afterward, the flower dance continues to be performed in the community, as does the Cossack sword dance—now adopted into the repertoire of "old dances" (as it is referred to among the dancers and instructors) in Cape Breton. These are in addition to specific dance choreographies such as Chumak that were part of the Avramenko-based canon of dances first taught in the community by Yavorsky and continued by Huk and Horechuk.

CONTEMPORARY ISSUES

Despite their comparatively limited support and cultural visibility, Cape Breton's Ukrainians have worked together to find ways to keep their Ukrainian heritage vital. Because Ukrainian theatrical dance is valued and celebrated locally by both residents of Ukrainian ancestry and the general populace, the Ukrainian Canadian community has mobilized their efforts to sustain it as a component of local culture. This is despite their historical marginalization from official discourse.[27] For example, Cape Breton's Ukrainian dancers continue to be active. There are a variety of classes, from a class for toddlers to an adult dance group composed of eight women ranging in age from seventeen to seventy-six. The women in the group are committed and enthusiastic, stating that they enjoy the "camaraderie" the activity allows and value the opportunity to foster their cultural legacy.[28] This aligns, too, with historian Frances Swyripa's assertion that it has been the women of Ukrainian descent in Canada who have played the largest role in continuing the practice of cultural traditions;[29] certainly, all Ukrainian dancers I have spoken with across the country have noted the overwhelming majority of female dancers in their groups. However, in the case of Cape Breton's Ukrainian dancers, until recently, men played the role of instructor. Although some classes today are still led by Kenny Horechuk, who has been teaching since as early as the 1980s, more recently, classes are also led by his younger sister, Cathy Horechuk. Kenny Horechuk continues to play a supportive role now that age and injury have restricted his physical ability to teach.[30]

The collaborative and emergent model for this group is different than that of Ukrainian dance groups across the rest of the country. In conventional groups, a local dance organization hires an individual to create and teach choreography for any given group. This model dates back to as early as the 1920s, when Vasile Avramenko trained dancers and dance teachers—many of whom established similar schools. Conventional Ukrainian theatrical dance groups also emphasize competition. Since at least the 1970s, dozens of competition festivals have arisen in Western Canada. Young dancers across the country strive to be acclaimed for originality and excellence. In Cape Breton Ukrainian dance, however, there seems to be less of an emphasis on technical excellence or innovation. Sydney's Ukrainian dancers, the region's only dance group, foster community and celebrate culture through dance.[31]

When I moved to Cape Breton in 2013, I was asked to introduce new material into the region's Ukrainian dance practice and to establish an adult performance group. This modification to the current practice did cause some concern: could such an innovation undermine the current group's sense of community? It was immediately obvious that most of the choreography was based on repertoire that the community recognized and had cherished for decades. While non-local choreographers had introduced some new material in the mid-1970s and mid-1980s, most of the dances arose from material that had been performed since the 1930s. This underscores the region's emphasis on community.

Why do the region's Ukrainian dancers cherish this older material? At least part of the answer lies in the island's relative isolation. There simply have not been many occasions for interaction with or exposure to Ukrainian dance groups from off-island communities. As such, Cape Breton's Ukrainians have retained older styles and choreography. Another reason is the lack of access to government programs, tourism, and educational initiatives.[32] Different from Ukrainians in Western Canada, Cape Breton's Ukrainians have not enjoyed an influx of resources that would support intense innovation and development. This is not to downplay the important contribution and innovation of some locals (e.g. Kenny Horechuk); rather, it is to note and investigate the differences that have arisen in a particular context. Perhaps especially because they feel they have had little external support, Ukrainian dancers in Cape Breton feel compelled to look after one another and their shared cultural practice. Because of this, they have grown to value community-building and cultural maintenance over technical excellence and innovation.

THE POLITICS OF CONSTRUCTING REGIONAL HISTORY

Looking to Cape Breton and seeing only Scottish, Acadian, or Mi'kmaq cultures limits the potential for understanding the region's diversity of cultures, communities, and human experience. On the one hand, a multicultural

Canadian discourse created a particular space for, and encouraged innovation in, Ukrainian theatrical dance in Canada. On the other, the dominant narratives about Ukrainian Canadians and, in Cape Breton, about the Scots, Acadians, and Mi'kmaq, have made it difficult to consider Ukrainian communities in regions of Canada other than the Prairies, and even more challenging to investigate the diverse cultural practices, communities, and experiences of the Ukrainian Canadians in Cape Breton.[33] Conventional understandings of what it means to be Ukrainian in Canada, and what it means to be a Cape Bretoner, do not overlap at the national or provincial levels.[34] This is not surprising given the long history of promoting the province, and Cape Breton, specifically, as Scottish or Celtic from within official government offices and institutions. Cape Breton has been "tartanized"—or "made Scottish"—through cultural, economic, and tourism policy.[35]

These activities in Nova Scotia may be understood as part of broader anti-modernist efforts that were begun in the early 1900s by "cultural foot soldiers" like Canadian Pacific Railway employee John Murray Gibbon, as discussed by Anne Flynn in this edited collection. Gibbon created concert programs across the country "based on his ideas of what [each] community needed to perform for itself":[36] in Toronto, English music; in Québec, French Canadian music. In Nova Scotia and Cape Breton, public performances have been largely Scottish and Celtic. Flynn argues such anti-modernist efforts—whether on the part of Gibbon or others in Nova Scotia—may largely be about "reinforcing hegemonic power" (Broder quoted in Flynn), in this case, the place of settlers from the British Isles as the first "true people".[37] A further discussion about the history of Gaelic-speaking Cape Bretoners, who were themselves once marginalized within Nova Scotia, is needed here, with critical consideration of major issues such as anti-modernism and whiteness (Flynn makes reference to these issues, as well). It bears noting, though, that while an Office of Gaelic Affairs exists within the Nova Scotia provincial government, no government office exists specifically to support Ukrainian culture—not even on the Prairies, where Ukrainians have arguably the strongest public presence. In this context, public recognition of Ukrainian (and other marginalized ethnocultural groups) in Nova Scotia may thus be understood as politically disruptive, particularly when dance is understood as a mobilizing action.[38]

Ukrainian theatrical dance is varied and thriving; its contribution to Canadian cultural landscapes is now indisputable. It flourishes in western regions—particularly Alberta—and, in different ways, in other parts of the country, as in Sydney on Cape Breton Island. Economic, social, cultural, and political institutions have greatly advanced the development of Ukrainian theatrical dance in Alberta, especially in the Edmonton area. The West has a long history of capitalizing on Ukrainian culture, and Ukrainian cultural elites and institutions are strongly established in this region. By contrast, in Cape Breton, Ukrainian theatrical dance has historically had very little in the way of political or other infrastructural support, even though it has had tremendous support in its home parish community.[39]

Despite its marginalization, the vibrant history of Ukrainian cultural practices in general—and dance in particular—could be invigorated in much the same manner. This chapter speaks back to the national and provincial image of Cape Breton by offering up a few historical and contemporary details about Ukrainians on the island and their past and continuing efforts to maintain and express their culture through dance. In doing so, it underlines and expands upon other aspects of the island's rich cultural history—aspects that deserve to be duly recognized as an integral part of cultural diversity in Cape Breton, part of the history of Ukrainian Canadians, and part of the diverse cultural landscape of Canada.

NOTES

1 The author is currently leading a team of emerging scholars who are collaboratively investigating the contributions of those of Ukrainian origin and heritage to Cape Breton's history and culture. The team's studies are focusing on labour and religion, among other aspects of the Ukrainians' contributions to the region.

2 Charles William Vernon, *Cape Breton, Canada, at the Beginning of the Twentieth Century: A Treatise of Natural Resources and Development* (Toronto: Nation Publishing, 1903), 3.

3 D. A. Muise, "Cape Breton Island," in *The Canadian Encyclopedia* (Toronto: Historica Canada, 2006), accessed January 26, 2015, http://www.thecanadianencyclopedia.ca/en/article/cape-breton-island/.

4 Patrick A. Dunae, "Promoting the Dominion: Records and the Canadian Immigration Campaign," *Archivaria* 19 (1984–1985): 73–93; Vernon, Cape Breton.

5 A prominent Cape Breton archivist, Jane Arnold (Beaton Institute), recently remarked that while the island may currently be best known for its Gaelic and French immigrants, "in the early 1900s, Cape Breton may have been the most culturally diverse of all regions of Canada" (personal communication, November 12, 2014).

6 Ukrainian immigration to Canada is represented in histories as having occurred in three waves: the 1890s to the outbreak of the First World War, the interwar years, and post-Second World War. A fourth wave—or a more constant "trickle"—of immigrants has been coming to Canada since the glasnost era of the late 1980s.

7 These quotes are from several issues of the *Winnipeg Telegram* from the year 1899. See Peter Melnycky, "Political Reaction to Ukrainian Immigrants: The 1899 Election in Manitoba," in *New Soil—Old Roots: The Ukrainian Experience in Canada*, ed. Jaroslav Rozumnyj (Winnipeg: Ukrainian Academy of Arts and Sciences in Canada, 1983), 21–22.

8 Peter Krawchuk, *Our History: The Ukrainian Labour-Farmer Movement in Canada, 1907–1991* (Toronto: Lugus Publications, 1996), 331.

9 William Noll, "Musical Institutions and National Consciousness among Polish and Ukrainian Peasants," in *Ethnomusicology and Modern Music History*, eds. Stephen Blum, Philip Vilas Bohlman, and Daniel M. Neuman (Urbana: University of Illinois Press, 1991), 139–58; William Noll, "Economics of Music Patronage among Polish and Ukrainian Peasants to 1939," in *Ethnomusicology* 35, no. 3 (1991): 349–79.

10 Frances A. Swyripa, "Ukrainian Canadians," in *The Canadian Encyclopedia* (Historica Canada, 2012), accessed November 2, 2015, http://www.thecanadianencyclopedia.ca/en/article/ukrainian-canadians/.

11 Nelson Wiseman, "Ukrainian-Canadian Politics," in *Canada's Ukrainians: Negotiating an Identity*, eds. Lubomyr Y. Luciuk and Stella Hryniuk (Toronto: University of Toronto Press, 1991), 353.

12 Evadne Kelly makes this same point regarding Fijian diaspora in Canada in her chapter in this collection.

13 Wiseman, "Ukrainian-Canadian Politics," 352.

14 Krawchuk, *Our History*, v. The hundredth anniversary of Ukrainians in Canada was celebrated in 1991. It is noteworthy that three histories of Ukrainians in Canada were published around that time, all referring to largely the same periods: Krawchuk's *Our History* (1996), published by the Association of United Ukrainian Canadians; Swyripa's history of Ukrainian-Canadian women from 1891–1991, entitled *Wedded to the Cause* (1993); and the third, *Canada's Ukrainians: Changing Perspectives, 1891–1991*, by Luciuk and Hryniuk (1991). Steven Jobbitt, in his contribution to this collection, makes a similar point about the layers of politics within the Ontario Ukrainian dance scene and the challenges they pose for newcomers and non-Ukrainians.

15 Oleh Gerus, "Consolidating the Community: The Ukrainian Self-Reliance League," in *Canada's Ukrainians: Negotiating an Identity*, eds. L. Luciuk and S. Hryniuk (Toronto: University of Toronto Press, 1991), 169–70.

16 Marcia Ostashewski, "Performing Heritage: Ukrainian Festival, Dance and Music in Vegreville, Alberta" (PhD diss., York University, 2009), 241.

17 Manoly R. Lupul writes of the deep personal significance of this political process in his memoir, *The Politics of Multiculturalism: A Ukrainian-Canadian Memoir* (Edmonton: Canadian Institute of Ukrainian Studies Press, 2005), v:

"Multiculturalism—the dignification of ethnicity—was to me much more than political sloganeering."

18 Rhéal Bélisle, *Honorable Senator Paul Yuzyk: In the Footsteps of Nationbuilders*, accessed October 30, 2007, http://www.yuzyk.com.

19 Beverley Diamond, introduction to *Canadian Music: Issues of Hegemony and Identity*, eds. Beverley Diamond and Robert Witmer (Toronto: Canadian Scholars' Press, 1994), 1–22; Augie Fleras and Jean Leonard Elliot, *Engaging Diversity: Multiculturalism in Canada*, 2nd ed. (Toronto: Nelson, 2002).

20 The author began community-based research with Ukrainians in Cape Breton in 2008, and followed up through a postdoctoral research program from 2010 to 2012. This research led to a position as Canada Research Chair (CRC) in Communities and Cultures at Cape Breton University, and one focus of this CRC's mandate is the cultural production of Ukrainians and other communities that have, until now, in large part, not been attended to in the region's discourse and representation, whether academic or public. In 2009, together with the local community, the author curated a gallery exhibit on Ukrainian dance in Cape Breton (for a slideshow of the exhibit opening, see http://culture.cbu.ca/ccbs/Ukrainian_Exhibit.html). This book chapter arises from the ensuing research, which, due to the nature of such deeply collaborative and community-based practice, has necessarily taken time to publish. Other publications and digital resources are forthcoming.

21 Frances Swyripa, "Ukrainians," in *The Encyclopedia of Canada's Peoples*, ed. Paul Robert Magocsi (Toronto: University of Toronto Press, 1999), 1310.

22 See Orest T. Martynowych, *The Showman and the Ukrainian Cause: Folk Dance, Film, and the Life of Vasile Avramenko* (Winnipeg: University of Manitoba Press, 2014) for a more detailed historical treatment of Avramenko and his important role in the development and widespread popularization of Ukrainian theatrical dance in Canada.

23 A customary Cape Breton expression referring to people not born on or from the island.

24 See my discussion of Ukrainian Cossack dancing in Canada and masculinities in Marcia Ostashewski, "A Song and Dance of (Hyper)masculinity: Performing Ukrainian Cossacks in Canada," in "Music, Dance and Masculinities," eds. Marcia Ostashewski and Sydney Hutchinson, special issue, *World of Music*, 3 no. 2 (2014): 15–38.

25 The author performed a Cossack dance in a boy's costume as a teenager growing up in a small Alberta town in the 1980s.

26 Kenny Horechuk maintains a friendship with Stechishin and has visited Ontario. The parish was also provided a grant to invite Stechishin's Ontario dance company to perform at the church's centenary concert in 2012.

27 See "Fun at Open Hearth Park," for example. At the event that day, the concert MC, local CBC producer and host Wendy Bergfeldt, told me that she thought the audience cheered the loudest for the Ukrainian dancers, and that "the crowd loves to see the kids in their colourful costumes and really enjoys their dancing!" (Bergfeldt,

personal communication, August 2013). In a more recent email conversation on the topic, Bergfeldt elaborated further: "The Ukrainian dancers were the 'Hometown' favourites. They were certainly one of only a couple of groups that came from the [Whitney] Pier. That might have accounted for the welcome too… I think that mattered a lot that day and probably had a lot to do with the reception they got. It was the Pier community reflected back at an audience that probably had roots there. Other performance pieces onstage that day were 'of the island' for sure, and there were a couple of younger groups from the African Nova Scotian community that the audiences got really enthusiastic about too. But the [Ukrainian] dancers were kids [whose]… grandpas came from the steel working community around [Open Hearth] park… I think the context matters here" (Bergfeldt, email message to author, February 13, 2015).

28 This is based on many conversations with the dancers and teachers in the new adult group, 2013–present: Darlene Baggio, Shalynn Bates, Mary Best, Rose Marie Best, Leslie Donovan, Cathy Horechuk, Ken Horechuk, Diane Jamieson, Stephanie Sawka, and Theresa Serwatuk.

29 Frances Swyripa, *Wedded to the Cause: Ukrainian-Canadian Women and Ethnic Identity, 1891–1991* (Toronto: University of Toronto Press, 1993).

30 To be sure, this raises a wider gender-related issue that has yet to be documented or studied in great detail for Ukrainian dance across Canada. Such a study, however, is beyond the scope of this chapter.

31 Even the name of the new adult dance group, suggested by a lifelong community member, is Razom, which means "together."

32 An important exception to this is the very recent funding that supported upgrades and renovations to the Ukrainian Hall in Whitney Pier, ahead of the parish's centenary in 2012. Indeed, a discourse of cultural diversity is beginning to grow in Cape Breton and, as part of this, Ukrainians are beginning to garner some attention. The author's Canada Research Chair may be understood to be a part of this recent development.

33 This point relates to a research presentation the author delivered at a Canadian prairie university in 2010. A Ukrainian studies scholar challenged the importance of the existence of Ukrainians in Cape Breton, arguing that, considering there were so few Ukrainians there relative to the number in other communities in Canada, they were not important as a focus of study. But the entire population of Cape Breton is small relative to most other regions of the country. In Cape Breton, particularly the Sydney and Glace Bay areas, the histories and continuing contributions of Ukrainians are significant.

34 As Batia Boe Stolar describes in her chapter in this collection, regional stereotypes are not merely exclusionary. When a strong regional narrative exists, it usually diminishes the national narrative in the region. In this case, where the strong regional narrative of Scottish or Celtic heritage exists in Cape Breton, national multicultural narratives that might be more inclusive of diverse cultural groups and stories of cultural hybridities are less apparent.

35 Adrian Ivakhiv, "Colouring Cape Breton 'Celtic': Topographies of Culture and Identity in Cape Breton Island," in *Ethnologies* 27 no. 2: 107–36, doi: 10.7202/014043ar. 2005; Ian McKay and Robin Bates, *In the Province of History: The Making of the Public Past in Twentieth-Century Nova Scotia* (Montréal and Kingston: McGill-Queen's University Press, 2010).

36 From Anne Flynn's chapter in this collection, "Embodying the Canadian Mosaic: The Great West Canadian Folk Dance, Folk Song, and Handicraft Festival, 1930."

37 Ibid.

38 Ibid.

39 Recall Yavorsky's popularization of Ukrainian dance in Cape Breton. Additionally, there was, fleetingly, an Orthodox parish and a Labour Temple in Sydney and a community hall (with yet undocumented origins) in the nearby town of Dominion. However, the Holy Ghost Ukrainian Catholic parish has been the one active and supporting Ukrainian religious institution (and the only Ukrainian church east of Montréal). It was also home to after-school and weekend Ukrainian school from the early 1900s until approximately the 1950s. Grants to Sydney's Ukrainian dance group have been scarce. And while Ukrainian language newspapers once circulated in Cape Breton from other parts of the country, few subscribe any longer. Moreover, no local Ukrainian press has existed (except in cases where the Labour Temple might have circulated material prior to the Second World War).

SIX

ZAB MABOUNGOU

TRANCE AND LOCATING THE OTHER*

Bridget E. Cauthery

CULTURAL DIVERSITY, AS A GOAL, AIMS TO REPRESENT ALL ETHnicities equally and fully, without partiality or prejudice. In Canada, cultural diversity has become intrinsically linked to social policies of multiculturalism that, in theory, intend to fulfill this goal through programs, incentives, and a persistent ideology that pervades the Canadian social imaginary. In practice, however, multiculturalism frequently fails to realize its reflexive stance by containing people labelled as "visible minorities" in time, space, and place. New Canadians are often asked to perform their identities in both public and private spaces in ways that do not reflect their status as evolving, contemporary beings. To quote Batia Boe Stolar in this volume, "the insistence on polarization and difference" that characterizes how "multiculturalism operates at a national discursive level" in this country is in direct opposition to what arts funding policies and demonstrations of inclusivity seek to

* This paper was first presented at the twenty-eighth annual Society of Dance History Scholars Conference at Northwestern University, Evanston, Illinois (June 9–12, 2005).

accomplish.[1] As an example of these inconsistencies, this chapter engages with performances of multiculturalism wherein the minority subject "speaks back," refusing to be delimited and subverting both the homogenizing gaze and constructed narratives that seek to contain her and the art she creates.

I was first introduced to Zab Maboungou, a Franco-Congolese dancer and choreographer based in Montréal, Québec, when I was asked to moderate a panel on dance and diaspora at the Canada Dance Festival in Ottawa in 2004. After that encounter, Maboungou's career and her experiences as an artist of colour within multiculturalist policies became the subject of the first of four case studies in my doctoral research. Of particular interest was how Maboungou's relationship with trance simultaneously indulged and resisted colonialist constructions of Other bodies and how these constructions are reinforced both performatively and discursively.

My interest in trance stems from my belief that the stories ballet and contemporary dancers tell about their performance experiences—descriptions of out-of-body, flow, or zone-like physiological experiences that can occur on stage or in the studio—should be regarded as instances of trance states. The reason these events are not regarded as instances of trance is that trance, as a subject of anthropology, rave culture, neopaganism, or other subculture groups, is an attribute of the Other. By otherizing trance, its appearance in Western practices—such as ballet and contemporary dance, which represent and embody notions of the Self—goes unacknowledged.

Ethnographers studying trance relate a range of alterations in their subject's qualitative functioning, which include, but are not limited to, a disturbed sense of time, changes in body image, a sense of the ineffable, feelings of rejuvenation, increased motor skills, and the deferral of pain[2]—qualities that have likewise been expressed by dancers after especially evocative performances.[3] While American anthropologist Erika Bourguignon, the founder of the anthropology of consciousness, maintains that the attainment of trance states is a universal human capacity, the majority of people born and raised in the West—including dancers and anthropologists—refuse to consider, let alone acknowledge, that trance exists "in their own backyards."[4]

With this blind spot in mind, it became apparent that, in dialectic terms, one could construct a paradigm of trance experience that problematizes the practice and application of trance occurrence and the research it attracts based on which side of the West/non-West divide subjects happen to reside. This proposition led me to propose that trance research has been directed exclusively at what, in postcolonial theory, has been termed the Other, and that, by extension, the accumulated knowledge and data about trance is implicitly colonialist. As a means of redressing this imbalance, I propose that trance is an attribute or characteristic of the Self, as exemplified by dancers engaged in Western dance practices. In suggesting that trance has been miscast, I am endeavouring to unravel the cultural history of trance in the West in the pursuit of ascertaining the degree to which it can be a meaningful construct within the cultural analysis of ballet and contemporary dance performance when, as a culture, the West does not acknowledge trance as natively occurring within its imagined borders—let alone as a universal practice.

My research owes much to the work of anthropologist James Clifford—in particular, his theories in "On Collecting Art and Culture" (1988). In this article, Clifford analyzes the West's preoccupation with collecting, and how the value of collections or items within a collection either ameliorate or decrease in value according to shifts in aesthetic taste, political trends, or beliefs about authenticity. The act of collecting either material or immaterial commodities, Clifford argues, plays a role in "Western identity formation." As such, collecting is simultaneously a means of validating the West's revered image of Self as owner, and of distinguishing, in geopolitical terms, "us" from "them" and, in historical terms, "now" from "then." Collecting in this manner finds equal expression in, for example: Margaret Mead's stated aims, in her career as an anthropologist, to "complete" a culture; in a settler museum installation of Native American or Canadian Indigenous art taken from Indigenous people; and even in the jars of shells and beach glass collected and displayed after a summer holiday. Each collection is intended to be representational in-and-of-itself without recourse to temporal or historical contexts, entitlement, or provenance.[5] While Clifford speaks mainly of physical artifacts—such as works of art, Indigenous crafts, and tourist knick-knacks—his theorization of collecting holds true for intangible objects, as well. With this in mind, I argue that trance is an artifact—a cultural "thing" or relic that has been observed, collected, displayed, and coveted for its exotic Otherliness.[6] And whether the subject of a film such as *Divine Horsemen: The Living Gods of Haiti* by Maya Deren, an account of the !Kung people of the Kalahari, or a conversation between acquaintances after "happening" upon a whirling dervish ceremony on a recent trip Istanbul, trance continues to be collected, categorized, and labelled to effectively delineate the Self from the

Other—a delineation based on an assessment of those who trance, and those who do not.

This exercise in thinking critically about how the West constructs and maintains ethnocentric categories of practice has been aided within dance studies by the work of Joann Kealiinohomoku.[7] In proposing that ballet is an ethnic dance form, Kealiinohomoku opened the possibility that ballet, and by extension contemporary dance, could be subject to the same kinds of critical paradigms that have been applied to ethnic dance. More recently, Canadian anthropologist Michael Lambek, who directly questions the absence of trance in the West, has influenced my research. According to Lambek:

> With the significant exception of certain subcultures (or "peripheral cults"), the West of the present day is quite unusual by world standards in radically devaluing the trance state, providing few, if any, control mechanisms, positive models, or integrated symbolic structures with which to organize it... The occurrence of trance in other societies is considered exotic, crying out for "rational explanation." But in point of fact, the unusual society in this case is the West...The question for the West becomes one of understanding why trance has been so rigidly excluded or ignored.[8]

So with this sense of trance as an artifact that plays a part in the West's identity formation, Lambek's perceptive comment becomes another avenue by which I examine the trance-as-Other paradigm. Yet it was not simply a matter of investigating why trance has been excluded or ignored; I also needed to be mindful of where and to what end trance may have been *included* in the West. This line of inquiry led me to Zab Maboungou.

As I have mentioned, in June 2004 I was invited to moderate a panel discussion with Canadian dance artist Maboungou and her collaborators following a performance of Maboungou's work Nsamu at the Canada Dance Festival at the National Art Centre in Ottawa. During a lull in the exchange between artists and audience, I asked Maboungou about a quote in her press package. The quote, excerpted from a review of one of her performances by critic Philip Szporer, states that "Zab Maboungou performed in a trance-like altered state of consciousness that was mesmerizing to watch." The quote is from a review written by Szporer for a Montréal weekly, but the exact date of publication is unclear. The quote appears on a page titled "Press Quotes" that includes extracts from Canadian and international presses variously summarizing, highlighting, and praising Maboungou's performances and artistry. Szporer's is not the only quote on the Press Quotes page that mentioned trance; Donald Huters from *Dance Magazine* describes Maboungou's drumming accompaniment as "trance-inducing." Interestingly, in another quote from a review published by *Dance Connection*, Szporer describes that what "is most striking" about Maboungou's performance is her "sense of 'groundedness.'"[9]

At issue here is not whether a single critic can express multiple—or, in this case, conflicting—opinions of the same artist (albeit in different performances), but to problematize both the choice Szporer made in describing Maboungou's performance as trance-like, and Maboungou's choice to include that particular quote in her press kit. The reality that a single sentence or phrase, isolated from both the much larger piece of writing and from the work itself, can stand for the artist and the artist's oeuvre is interesting in and of itself. However, in this instance, the use of the quote resonates at a deeper level when one considers the incongruities and conflicting agendas at play in Maboungou's practice in relation to trance.

When I brought the quote to Maboungou's attention during the panel, I asked her whether Szporer's response to her performance was accurate, and whether she in fact performs in a "trance-like" state or attained an altered state of consciousness on stage. Her response was quick and decisive: she does not allow herself to enter a trance or trance-like state in performance because it is disingenuous to both her onstage collaborators and to her audience. She describes her work as "tightly choreographed," so to allow herself to enter such an altered state of consciousness could jeopardize the integrity of the performance.[10]

In May 2005, I met with Maboungou in her studio in Montréal and in a one-on-one interview reminded her of our exchange. I asked if she still stood by her answer. She restated her position and did not waver from the answer she had given eleven months before. In fact, she added, she had "allowed" herself to enter a trance only once in her performance career and was "shamed" by an African elder for forgetting "her place."[11] It had never happened again. So I asked, "Why use the quote? Why endorse through the medium of her press kit a description that is in sharp contrast to the tenets of her practice and to the respect she embodies for her art form?" In response, Maboungou told me the story of her life.

Maboungou describes herself as a "child of colonialism."[12] The daughter of a Congolese father and French mother, she was born in Brazzaville, the capital of what is today Congo-Brazzaville, the former French colony of the Moyen-Congo (Middle Congo) straddling the equator in sub-Saharan West Africa. Born prior to its independence from France, Maboungou came of age in Congo-Brazzaville during a period when postcolonial unrest led to an artistic and cultural renaissance that placed an emphasis on African identity. She believes that she was drawn to dance, and by the age of thirteen understood that dance would be her vocation. Despite secession, Congo-Brazzaville, like

Figure 6.1. Zab Maboungou in her own work, *Wamunzo*. Photograph by Kevin Calixte.

many former colonies, continued to be influenced by France's education policies with regards to assimilation, and, being a bright student, Maboungou was encouraged to study in the "mother country." In 1969, like her father before her, Maboungou went to Paris to study philosophy. There she met other children of African colonization, and together they began sharing their knowledge of traditional African music and dance. Social gatherings formalized into dance clubs organized by African student associations that sponsored students' activities to recreate and reconnect to their lost heritages.

It would perhaps be useful here to take a moment to discuss the term "African dance." It is not a term that I am particularly comfortable with—is it not too generalist? Too impersonal? But Maboungou is firm in her claim to be a practitioner of *African* dance. When questioned—usually by Europeans keen to fix her to a certain place and time—she complies and describes herself as a practitioner of *Congolese* dance. But this, she explains, is a fabrication. The Indigenous peoples living in what is today's Congo-Brazzaville did not always live there—it is not their traditional homeland. By virtue of forced settlement or displacement by European colonizers, the people living within the borders imposed by the Congo Act, which gave France control of the region, became "Congolese." Thus, to speak of Congolese dance is meaningless; there are dances performed by the Kongo people, but these dances are not performed strictly within the geographical territory defined as the Congo. So African dance, encompassing a range of regional traditional dances within a global diaspora, shared between generations within the Congo but also recreated in the colonial mother countries and in other former colonies, conveys a richness of solidarity within the fractured African identity.

In Paris and later in Canada, Maboungou continued to study the traditional music and dance of the Middle Congo, but also undertook studies in the traditional dances of Mali, Ivory Coast, Senegal, Guinea, Nigeria, and Zimbabwe. Similarly to dancer/choreographer Hari Krishnan who, in this volume, states that he was reluctant to be only perceived as a practitioner of *Indian* dance, Maboungou likewise does not wish to be defined or confined to just one form or style of West African dance.[13] Such positioning not only misrepresents her artistic goals, but the history of Africa as a site of colonial conflict, as well. In refusing to allow herself to be associated with only one geocultural area, Maboungou dissolves boundaries between forms—for, in fact, colonizers imposed those boundaries. Like Krishnan, Maboungou is a *global* artist wherein African dance accommodates a depth and breadth of interpretation and innovation within the contemporary period that suits Maboungou's goals for herself and her company.

In 1973, Maboungou emigrated from Paris to Montréal. Like the Congo, the history of Québec is rooted in colonization: Québec's first inhabitants were Indigenous and Inuit peoples, but the paradise of the New World was soon transgressed by Norse explorers, Basque whalers and cod fishermen. Commissioned by France's François I, the French explorer Jacques Cartier landed in the Gaspé in 1534. Cartier claimed possession of the immense territory for France, establishing a European presence and the creation of New France. The territory remained in the hands of the French for more than two hundred years, and it was eventually annexed by the British following France's defeat at the Battle of the Plains of Abraham in 1759. Four years later, under the Treaty of Paris, the King of France granted to "His Royal Majesty, King George II, the sole ownership of Canada and all its dependencies." This transfer of power and territory from France to England sparked a flood of new colonists from England, Ireland, and Scotland. The Canadian Constitution Act of 1791 established two provinces: Upper Canada (primarily English-speaking Ontario), and Lower Canada (primarily French-speaking Québec) with Québec City as its capital. By 1830, Montréal—the "Paris of the North"—had become Canada's major industrial centre, welcoming waves of European immigrants fleeing war and hardship in their homelands. But the original French colonists of Québec resisted British rule, leading to the Québec Patriot Rebellion of 1837–38. The rebellion was crushed, and fearing further reprisals, the British united Upper and Lower Canada in the Act of Union in 1841 to solidify its authority. In 1867, the signing of the British North America Act established the Confederation of Canadian Provinces, which included Québec, Ontario, New Brunswick, and Nova Scotia.[14]

At the time of Maboungou's immigration, shortly after the "Quiet Revolution," debates over the supremacy of the French language were crystallizing in Québec.[15] Issues such as sovereignty and Québec's independence from the rest of English-speaking Canada were current. Although two referendums to secede from Canada were narrowly defeated, the preservation of French as the official language of schools and of commerce, autonomy regarding immigration, and the recognition of a separate and distinct Québécois culture were established. Cultivating a separate and unique Québécois identity was also expressed in terms of support for the arts. Explicitly aligning themselves with a "European model," the province of Québec, at the time, provided more arts funding than any other province in Canada, and the thriving dance community it supported was perceived by the rest of the country to be more "European," with strong ties to the French and Belgian dance scenes.[16]

Yet despite generous support for the arts in Québec, Maboungou's career stalled. Though small numbers of French-speaking Africans had been immigrating to Québec since the demise of colonial rule in the decades following the Second World War, Maboungou was something of an oddity. Two years prior, in 1971, the federal government of Canada had drafted its official policy of multiculturalism, and cultural groups performing traditional African dance as part of cultural arts festivals and nationalist celebrations such as Canada Day were common and encouraged under the new policies.[17] But a woman of African descent purporting to create *modern* African was incomprehensible to the funding bodies and arts councils of the 1970s and 1980s, which were white, elitist, and proud of the province's ballet and contemporary dance companies. Maboungou was a square peg trying to fit into a round hole.

Outspoken to the point of being considered "radical," Maboungou continued to create and advocate for her work despite the arts councils' cool reception, self-producing and cultivating her own steadfast community through performances and workshops within Canada and abroad.[18] Her perseverance was eventually rewarded: in 1990, Maboungou had the distinction of being the first African Canadian choreographer to receive funding from the Canada Council for the Arts and the *Conseil des arts et des lettres du Québec*. Foreign Affairs Canada, whose mandate is to "support Canadians abroad, work towards a more peaceful and secure world, and promote [Canadian] culture and values internationally," features Maboungou in their 2002 Canada World View publication in an article titled "African-Canadian Sights and Sounds." Here she is described as "one of the many talented African artists who have come to Canada in search of a new life and made outstanding contributions to Canadian culture."[19] With support from an arts development grant from Heritage Canada, Maboungou inaugurated a special program in the study and teachings of African dance in Québec in 2003. She has published a book on her teachings and philosophy of African dance and runs Compagnie Danse Nyata Nyata, a school and centre for dance creation.

The change in perception of Maboungou's creative output and her rise to multicultural poster child parallels the journey that, according to James

Clifford, certain artifacts take when their relative value changes. Clifford's adaptation of Fredric Jameson's semiotic square (1990) illustrates how cultural artifacts and works of art change in value according to aesthetic trends or sociopolitical precedents.[20] A reputed masterpiece falls out of favour when it is revealed to be a fake; a piece of roadside pottery purchased on a holiday is revealed to be priceless Etruscan earthenware. Yet Clifford is not only concerned with changes in value according to perceived authenticity. What is also of interest is when cultural artifacts become high art as a result of shifts in societal views. In Canada, the paintings and soapstone carvings of the Inuit are examples of once-devalued tourist *tchotchkes* transformed into priceless artworks as the perception of the cultural worth of the Inuit people and their threatened way of life has changed. But again, artifacts need not be tangible; Maboungou's work has likewise experienced an increase in its aesthetic value. Initially, Maboungou's creative output was regarded as traditional and folkloric, and when Maboungou resisted these classifications, the councils were dumbfounded. Her work only became valuable to the establishment when it was perceived to reinforce both Canadian—pluralist, multicultural—and Québécois—distinctly French-Canadian—identity. As the policy of multiculturalism gradually became practice, the creative output of multicultural artists expanded to include innovation within a traditional framework—immigrants could be more than transported vessels of their cultural heritage, and they could also be *modern* Canadians. Here, their creative output became valued as high art and eligible for governmental support.

It was during this latter phase of Maboungou's career that she came to the attention of American dance scholar Ann Cooper Albright. Albright was moved to write about Maboungou after seeing her perform as part of Off-FIND, an extension of the *Festival international de nouvelle danse* in Montréal (FIND) in 1995.[21] Her treatment of the artist appeared in her groundbreaking 1997 work *Choreographing Difference*. In the first chapter titled "Mining the Dancefield," Albright describes what she calls slippages and double representation. In the act of witnessing (that is, active engagement as opposed to passive consuming), the viewer is aware of and/or engaging with double representations of the dancer. The viewer is aware of both the dancer's cultural and somatic identities ("how one's body renders meaning in society" and "the experience of one's physicality," respectively).[22] These identities are constantly in a state of relational flux, converging and diverging at different points in the performance moment. The viewer is engaged in contending with these modes of representation, and within that contention, Albright perceives slippages—moments where, for the viewer, the dancer is neither wholly fused with either identity but slips between them. In slipping between, a viewer perceives and creates new or tangential identities. As Albright describes, in Maboungou's work *Nsamu*, the viewer is aware of the artist as a petite woman of African descent, with a short afro, dancing barefoot and dressed in a costume derived from Africanist elements. These characteristics combine to form Maboungou's cultural identity in the eyes of the viewer and her appearance on stage, dancing to African drums, constructing an image of Maboungou as a traditional African dancer. Yet with regard to her somatic identity, Maboungou's presence on stage—how she dances, how she responds to the music, and how she constructs her performance—contrasts with what Western audiences have typically come to associate with traditional African dance. Witnessing and reconciling the double representation allows for slippages to occur that exempt Maboungou from being categorized based solely on her appearance and the associations that her appearance creates.[23]

Within Albright's analysis of the negotiation of identities, I wish to add the caveat that the act of witnessing and recognizing slippages changes according to the audience member's degree of engagement with the work, and that the degree of engagement depends on the viewer's relative familiarity and knowledge. The more informed the viewer is of the work and the performer, the more aware he/she will be of these slippages. This seems perhaps an obvious point, but I believe it is important to distinguish between Albright's capacity to witness and the capacity of another viewer who is less informed. Likewise, it is important to recognize that a learning curve pertains when a viewer progresses from a novice witness to an informed witness and how that process of education alters the breadth or the frequency with which slippages are acknowledged.

This point becomes slightly more complex when the viewer is a critic and that critic has enacted their own learning curve, moving from a novice to an informed viewer as they become more familiar with the artist's body of work. Yet at the same time, the critic must still mediate that performance for a diverse readership. The critic as mediator must reconcile their own response to the work with what an audience may or may not know about the work and/or the performer. The critic aims to provide a description that appeals to a range of readers, taking into consideration both the lowest and the highest degree of knowledge of the work and performer under review.

I would argue that such a learning curve and sense of responsibility to one's audience played a part in Philip Szporer's decision to invoke trance in describing Maboungou's performance. At the time the review was written Szporer was an experienced dance critic, but he was also new to Maboungou's work. He remembers being impressed by Maboungou's presence on stage, by her integrity, and by her state of both total engagement and total disengagement or transcendence in her performance.[24] To convey this unusual but highly compelling quality to his readers, Szporer described Maboungou as performing in a trance-like altered state of consciousness. In retrospect, Szporer maintains that his statement accurately reflects the performance he saw but adds that, at the time, it was the only turn of phrase he could come up with to describe what he had seen that would also be intelligible to his readers.[25] Szporer acknowledges that the use of trance was predictable, but he believes that it was not entirely inappropriate. Was he reacting to Maboungou's intensity? Or was he himself en-tranced by her performance? Szporer is unsure. Today he continues to review Maboungou's work, and in the intervening years has acquired a more discerning eye and inclusive vocabulary with which to promote her performances to his readership. His capacity to witness has expanded with continued exposure to Maboungou's work and that of other African performers, and he admits that, today, he is more aware of the Eurocentric bias with which the majority of North American audiences view non-Western dance.[26]

While Szporer, in this instance, may be guilty of Eurocentrism, Albright argues that, in performance, Maboungou actively resists the "colonial gaze." According to Albright, Maboungou does this by: a) not presenting her work in a "recreated" manner in contrast to other performers of African-derived dance that perform in a "celebratory" manner in a "traditional village" setting; b) by neither denying her ethnicity nor suggesting that she or her work is representative—hers is a very personal performance; c) by actively engaging in double representation through movement, minimalist choreography, lighting, and staging conventions that do not allow her to be fixed but in a state of actively performing her identities; d) by being engaged in her own experience; e) by emphasizing/engaging a process of "becoming"; and f) by fracturing the power dynamic in traditional gazes where the object of sight is there for the viewer's pleasure, not the dancer's.[27]

Yet the attribution of trance changes this assessment. If trance is a trait, an element, and/or a product of the colonial encounter, then the attribution of

Figure 6.2. Performers (left to right): Elli Miller-Maboungou, Adama Daou, Karla Etienne, Gabriella Parson, Luis Cabanzo, and Raphaelle Perreault in Maboungou's *Monzongi*. Photograph by Kevin Calixte.

trance to her performances places Maboungou family within the colonialist gaze. Or does it?

Maboungou is acutely aware of the dichotomy with which she is engaging in accepting and channelling the attribution of trance. She is consciously manipulating the trance-equals-Other equation—playing the colonizer's game by his rules because she seeks to capitalize on the West's fascination with trance. In marketing her performances as opportunities to witness trance, she invites the public to add her to their collection. In a political climate where, even in Québec, funding for the arts is decreasing, full houses ensure continued success. Maboungou perceives that as a Black African artist working within a European-dominated culture, trance is both unavoidable and potentially profitable. Maboungou seeks to lure her audience with trance, but with the intention of initiating them in an alternative construction of African dance. But it leads one to question both the degree to which a viewer who anticipates trance can shed their preconceived notions upon entering the performance space, and the degree to which Maboungou is likewise invested in trance for its exotic appeal. In a classic reactionary move, Maboungou engages in self-exotification, appropriating the means by which she has been exoticized by the colonizers. In doing so, she attempts to subvert the colonial gaze.

Here too, then, Albright's slippages between double representations come into play: the artist as trance-producing artifact to be consumed; and as free agent actively seeking to contradict and/or sustain that impression in performance depending upon who is witnessing and what is at stake. Maboungou is a practitioner of *African* dance, so named in response to the defacing effects of colonialism, and within that, an exponent of *modern* African dance: a necessary modifier to deny those who wish to keep the formerly colonized in the past. Maboungou's work is an artifact that has been elevated to the rank of high art by the arts councils. As a favoured artist, the Canadian government collects and exhibits her as a model of multiculturalism. As a purveyor of trance, Maboungou responds by offering her work to be collected, and then *withdraws* that offer by projecting alternate identities in performance. In addition, Maboungou's personal history has conspired to create multiple double representations where she is simultaneously from the West (i.e., Canadian) and from the non-West (i.e., Congolese); a practitioner of modern dance (Western) and of African dance (non-Western); and of white European and Black African descent. Who she is and what she does—her cultural and somatic identities—fall somewhere in between these two poles.

Maboungou insists that it is European audiences that question her modern aesthetic, insist that she fix her ethnicity to a particular geography, and attribute trance to her performances. In the end, trance may itself be a slippage between states, the key to seeing the in-between of performance identities that exist to challenge notions of resistance and conformity. Recognizing the potential for trance to be a meaningful construct in the cultural analysis of ballet and contemporary dance does not require that dancers from either side of the West/non-West divide be exoticized or engage in self-exotification; it requires that trance be de-Othered, not in an attempt to universalize or naturalize the phenomenon, but to move forward with the reflexive commitment made not only by Canada, but also by dance studies, to embrace cultural diversity and to see *all* dance forms as ethnic.

NOTES

1 See Batia Boe Stolar's chapter, "Olé, eh?: Canadian Multicultural Discourses and Atlantic Canadian Flamenco," in this volume.

2 See Harold Courlander (1972); Margaret Kartomi (1973); Margaret Thompson Drewal (1975); Teri Knoll (1979–1980); Anita F. Newman (1979–1980); Michael

Lambek (1981); Kathy Foley (1985); Faith Simpson (1997); Irit Averbuch (1998); Kevin Stuart and Jun Hu (1998); Eva Zorilla Tessler (1998); Bettina E. Schmidt and Lucy Huskinson (2010); Keith E. McNeal (2011); and Anne Harrington (2016).

3 See Erik Bruhn in John Gruen (1986); Twyla Tharp (1993); Eric Franklin (1996a and 1996b); Russell Maliphant in Malve Gradinger (1996); Deborah Hay (1994); Sheila Hughes (1998); and Angel Corella in Judy Kinberg and Jodee Nimerichter (2004).

4 See Erika Bourguignon, *Religion, Altered States of Consciousness, and Social Change* (Columbus: Ohio State University Press, 1973), and also her essay "Trance and Ecstatic Dance" in Ann Dils and Ann Cooper Albright's *Moving Histories/Dancing Cultures* (Durham: Wesleyan Press, 2001), 97–102.

5 James Clifford, "On Collecting Art and Culture," in *The Predicament of Culture: Twentieth Century Ethnography, Literature and Art* (Cambridge: Harvard University Press, 1988), 59–60, 66.

6 This idea of trance as an artifact is explored in depth in "Vincent Sekwati Mantsoe: Trance as a Cultural Commodity" in Dena Davida's volume *Fields in Motion: Ethnography in the Worlds of Dance* (Waterloo, ON: Wilfrid Laurier University Press, 2011), 319–38.

7 Joann Kealiinohomoku, "An Anthropologist Looks at Ballet as a Form of Ethnic Dance," in *Impulse Magazine* (San Francisco: Impulse Publications, 1969–1970): 24–33.

8 Michael Lambek, *Human Spirits: A Cultural Account of Trance in Mayotte* (Cambridge: Cambridge University Press, 1981), 7.

9 Philip Szporer, *Dance Connection* (year, volume, and issue unknown), accessed September 22, 2018, http://www.nyatanyata.org/anciensite/eng/reviews.html.

10 Zab Maboungou, Canada Dance Festival, The National Arts Centre (June 11, 2004). Public panel.

11 Zab Maboungou, personal interview with the author, Compagnie Danse Nyata Nyata studio, Montréal, May 12, 2005.

12 Ibid.

13 See Hari Krishnan's chapter, "A Contemporary Global Artist's Perspective," in this volume.

14 See Catriona Misfeldt, et al., *Early Contact and Settlement in New France* (Vancouver: The Critical Thinking Consortium and Ministry of Education, British Columbia, 2002); John A. Dickinson and Brian Young, *A Short History of Quebec*, 4th ed. (Montréal/Kingston: McGill-Queen's University Press, 2008); and André Vachon, *Dreams of Empire: Canada before 1700* (Ottawa: Canadian Government Publication Centre, 1982).

15 Québec's "Quiet Revolution" was a period from roughly 1960 to 1970 marked by a resurgence of pride in Québec's French cultural heritage, a lessening of the influence of the Catholic Church in state affairs, and a determination to assert Québec's place as a modern and distinct society.

16 Michael Crabb, "Joining the Circuit," *International Arts Manager* (May 2005): 3–4.

17 Right Hon. P. E. Trudeau (Prime Minister), addressing the House of Commons in response to the Royal Commission on Bilingualism and Biculturalism on October 8, 1971, stated: "It was the view of the royal commission, shared by the government and, I am sure, by all Canadians, that there cannot be one cultural policy for Canadians of British and French origin, another for the original peoples and yet a third for all others. For although there are two official languages, there is no official culture, nor does any ethnic group take precedence over any other. No citizen or group of citizens is other than Canadian, and all should be treated fairly… A policy of multiculturalism within a bilingual framework commends itself to the government as the most suitable means of assuring the cultural freedom of Canadians. Such a policy should help break down discriminatory attitudes and cultural jealousies. National unity if it is to mean anything in the deeply personal sense, must be founded on confidence in one's own individual identity; out of this can grow respect for that of others and a willingness to share ideas, attitudes and assumptions. A vigorous policy of multiculturalism will help create this initial confidence. It can form the base of a society which is based on fair play for all." "Pierre Elliot Trudeau: Multiculturalism," *Canadian History,* accessed September 23, 2018, http://www.canadahistory.com/sections/documents/Primeministers/trudeau/docs-onmulticulturalism.htm.

18 Philip Szporer, personal interview with the author, Café du Nouveau Monde, Montréal, May 13, 2005.

19 Department of Foreign Affairs and International Trade, "African Canadian Sights and Sounds," in *Canada World View 16* (Summer 2002): 20–22, accessed December 11, 2018, http://publications.gc.ca/collections/collection_2011/aecic-faitc/E12-15-2002-16-eng.pdf.

20 Clifford, "On Collecting Art and Culture," 65.

21 The first FIND festival took place in 1985 after a period of renewal within the Canadian dance community that began in the late 1970s. In the fifteen years that FIND existed, the festival earned praise, respect, and support from the international dance community, yet within Canada, FIND has been criticized for failing to fully represent the Canadian dance community by seldom programming dance artists and companies from outside of Québec.

22 Ann Cooper Albright, *Choreographing Difference: The Body and Identity in Contemporary Dance* (Hanover: Wesleyan University Press, 1997), xxiii, 4.

23 Albright, *Choreographing Difference,* 21–27.

24 Szporer, personal interview, 2005.

25 Ibid.

26 Ibid.

27 Albright, *Choreographing Difference,* 25–27.

III

IDENTITY FORMATION AND ARTISTIC AGENCY

SEVEN

A CONTEMPORARY GLOBAL ARTIST'S PERSPECTIVE

Hari Krishnan

The following reflection is an edited excerpt from the transcript of a recorded conversation between Hari Krishnan and Allana C. Lindgren that occurred on May 19, 2014, in Toronto. Krishnan's dance company, inDANCE, presents both original choreography using Bharatanatyam technique and contemporary works that draw on a range of dance influences to explore a diverse range of themes. In particular, Krishnan has used Bharatanatyam and contemporary dance to explore the intersections between race and gender. The company has been invited to perform around the world, including at the Jacob's Pillow Dance Festival (Berkshires, MA), the Mondavi Arts Centre (Davis, California), Sutra Dance Theatre (Kuala Lumpur), La MaMa Experimental Theatre and Asia Society (New York City), Canada Dance Festival (Ottawa), Maison des Cultures du Monde (Paris, France), and the NAFA Lee Theatre (Singapore).

Figure 7.1. INDANCE's *Tiger by the Tail* (2016). Performed by Hari Krishnan (dancer/choreographer) and Kajan Pararasasegaram (percussion). Photo by Christopher Duggan; photo design by John Elmore. Jacob's Pillow Dance Festival–Inside/Out on July 6, 2016. Photograph courtesy of Nicole Tomasofsky, Jacob's Pillow Dance Festival.

I WAS BORN AND RAISED IN SINGAPORE, A COSMOPOLITAN AND diverse country. It has a large, rich cross-cultural history, which has become a deep part of the people's DNA, thanks to both colonialism and the advent of immigrant transmigration. It was this hybrid culture in which I was studying classical Bharatanatyam (south Indian classical dance), Ottan Thullal (a "folk" art from Kerala), and dabbling in classical ballet. In addition to this, I was also involved with Singapore's first children's theatre company, act 3, as a teen actor for many years. This experience ignited my love and passion for performing and the stage as a young child.

Without my realizing it, the Bharatanatyam I was learning in Singapore was very modern. The Kalakshetra school—which is known for resuscitating Bharatanatyam, but, most importantly, for restructuring the technique based on influences of people like Anna Pavlova as well as the Bolshoi Ballet—was imprinted on me. A major part of the problem—in addition to the severely problematic caste and class issues that plagued this modern version of Bharatanatyam—was its heavily gendered nature. The boys would dance a certain way, and the girls would dance a certain way. I wasn't happy with that. Maybe it was my latent queerness; I wasn't out to myself at that point. There was something very uncomfortable. Why did I have to move a certain way? Why did I have to play princes and kings in all these dance dramas when I was growing up?

I chose to come to Canada in my late teens because, at that time, the University of Manitoba was not charging a differential fee for foreign students. My undergraduate degree was in linguistics and Asian studies. I specifically studied linguistics because I saw commonalities between choreography and constructing language. Less than six months after I came, I discovered Rachel Browne, the founder of Winnipeg's Contemporary Dancers, which is Canada's oldest modern dance company. I went to see Winnipeg's Contemporary Dancers at the Gas Station Theatre, and I saw Rachel Browne's *Dancing Toward the Light*. That work changed my entire perception of dance forever! Along with my exposure to Rachel and Winnipeg's Contemporary Dancers, I attended performances by the Royal Winnipeg Ballet. In addition, Ruth Cansfield, another modern dancer in Winnipeg, was making amazing, interesting work. I also followed Tedd Robinson's and Tom Stroud's work.

I moved to Toronto around 1998 to pursue a career in dance and to pursue my master's degree in dance at York University. I knew at that time I wanted to devote myself to dance. I wanted to be a full-time artist in addition to being a scholarly dancer! In Toronto, I would see all the companies that would come to the city. I also really liked Serge Bennathan's choreography when he was the Artistic Director at Dancemakers. His *Sable/Sand*—his contemporary dance choreography—had Middle Eastern accents that were incorporated into the soundscape, which further influenced my eclectic conception of contemporary dance from a global perspective. I was already influenced by a panoramic, global imagining of the potential of dance ever since I was a child in Singapore, and moving to Toronto solidified these experiences. This, coupled with my travels to New York City, and various parts of Asia and Europe, enabled me to experience a range of performances and performance styles by various dance artists and companies. I was motivated to continue creating original work, inspired by contemporary dance from global perspectives.

Along with contemporary dance, at the time I was also researching multiple critical readings of Bharatanatyam because I wasn't happy with the popular narratives of this style and how gender was enacted within the form. Then, as my academic education progressed—I took a variety of courses in critical history and theory—I continued to explore the complex traditions of courtesans, who were, in an earlier period, the sole performers of Bharatanatyam. Beginning in the early 1990s, during summer and winter breaks, I travelled to India. I went to remote villages in search of dance teachers from the hereditary courtesan dance communities. It was there, in the village of Tanjavur, South India, I met my dance master, the iconic K.P. Kittappa Pillai (1913–1999) who would transform my entire life. Courtesan dance was banned in 1947 because of sociopolitical factors, most importantly because the courtesan herself was misconstrued as immoral within the context of a colonial, patriarchal India. They were misfits in a colonial, emergent right-wing Hindu, upper-caste, misogynistic Indian society. Their presence represented one of a few instances in Indian history in which a small group of women had access to various forms of education and were relatively financially independent. The women also usually had the ability to choose their non-conjugal partners, and they danced about eroticism and sexuality. It is important to remember that the essence of this dance is an unapologetic performance of love songs deeply couched in eroticism and sexuality that were eradicated in the early twentieth century. This of course stands in striking contrast to the elite reconstructions of Bharatanatyam in the early twentieth century, when the dance was recast in the language of Hindu religion and nationalism. I was intentionally reclaiming these older representations through deep and ethically informed research, intense documentation, and a complex enterprise of making these repertoires accessible for the contemporary stage, infusing it with my original voice.

I found that exciting. I remembered Rachel Browne's *Dancing Toward the Light*. What Rachel did, and what I learned from my courtesan teachers, was, for me, similar in terms of physical intimacy, honesty, and authenticity. This was coupled with my own exposure to other iconic practitioners of European contemporary dance—such as Pina Bausch, Anne Teresa De Keersmaeker, and Wayne McGregor—whose work I was seeing extensively. That is, all these aesthetics came from an organic place of creative practice, improvisation, sincere practice, and deep understanding of the body and form. But it took me a while to make that connection. That's why I see myself as a contemporary dance artist working from global perspectives. I also felt the primal need to express myself as a sexual, erotic, and "thinking" being. I found that realization to be a coming-of-age, "eureka" milestone moment in my life that integrated completely into my identity, and into my search for gender neutrality and androgyny, and my desire to ask larger questions, including: what does gender really mean? I eventually completed my PhD in dance at Texas Woman's University, where my research was on dance and film. This provided an additional site for me to explore issues of intermediality and intersectionality in my work.

In 2000, I formed inDANCE, an umbrella to incorporate all my various activities: teaching, choreography, collaboration, research, and most importantly, sociopolitical engagement through community outreach. inDANCE is being "in dance"—in the dance profession—but the name also plays with the phrase "Indian dance" by turning Indian dance on its head. This playfulness was very appealing to me.

From very early on, I did not want to be defined as solely an Indian choreographer. While Indian dance is one of the colours in my choreographic palette, my work is so much more than that. I wanted—and continue to want—to be defined as a choreographer who is informed by Indian dance in addition to other dance styles, aesthetics, and sensibilities. This is very important for me, but I faced a lot of pushback twenty years ago, especially from members of the South Asian community who thought this choice was sacrilege, and members of the modern dance community who thought my work was (and should remain) Indian! This was a display of soft racism and provided me more resolve to continue forging my authentic path of creating work representative of my twenty-first-century complex reality. That was when I totally embraced my queerness, and this became an important part of my identity and a significant hallmark of all my work. We're all complex beings. And I think acknowledging that complexity is really important. That is why I am particular that the diverse array of dancers, designers, musicians, and scholars I choose to collaborate with are complex, nuanced, and progressive in addition to being uber-skilled in what they do. My collaborators always continue to inspire me to grow, both as an artist and thinker.

Part of that growth, and one of the main hallmarks in my work, is subverting clichés and stereotypes, because I fight these burdens every day of my life. This can mean fighting heteronormative gender archetypes, or fighting ideas of what it means to function in an ambiguous dance space in which you are influenced by everything and yet you are not duplicating anything you see around you. "Subversion" for me means creating a personal choreographic and personal voice by using whatever skills and tools you have available to you to foster a much more enriching, meaningful, open, and larger dance discourse.

For me, it's been a long struggle of always being recognized and defined by my skin colour, my ethnicity, and my dance, as if Indian dance is all I do. There's a particular box in which, for a long time, presenters, press, audiences, and people defined me. Happily, things have changed over the years. It's much more empowering, and I have worked very hard. I'm fortunate to work with an amazing pool of dancers, musicians, designers, and scholars who support my vision of a transnational way of looking at the world—a much larger and complex way of looking at the world.

At this point, I must acknowledge my partner, Rex, who is the love of my life. He's also a visual designer, so we often collaborate. He's also Indian, but has had a different trajectory—he lived in New York City for many years, and we met in India when I was working on a project. We've been together since 1997. He and I see eye-to-eye in terms of the larger worldview, and we never want to be in an ethnic, community-based, compartmentalized box. We continue to resist every day, wherever we are in the world, refusing to pander to racial and heteronormative stereotypes. I acknowledge my Indianness. I acknowledge my Singaporeness. I acknowledge my Canadianness. And I live in Canada. That's who I am. And I'm queer, I am an artist, I am a thinker. I am complex!

In 2001, through a series of divine coincidences—I use the word "divine" tongue in cheek, of course—I was offered a job at Wesleyan University, initially to be an artist-in-residence (and now I am Chair and fully tenured professor in the Department of Dance with a concurrent appointment as Professor of Feminist, Gender, and Sexuality Studies). When I was initially offered the job, I had to make a decision. Do I pack up and move to Middletown, Connecticut, and say goodbye to whatever Canada has given me? Or do I say "no" to the position? Canada was/is still my home. Because of Canada, I'm the kind of dance artist I am, the thinker I am... I decided to try shuttling for six months. Six months has turned into seventeen years now. Wesleyan is a very progressive university with a history of global dance and music—a hallowed university where great artists made work and taught, including John Cage and Merce Cunningham, creating some of their early collaborative experimentations, and where the iconic courtesan Bharatanatyam dancer, T. Balasaraswati, and her family members taught dance and music. I was honoured and humbled to continue this legacy with my skills and experiences, working in an extremely progressive and cordial dance department with some amazing colleagues. The variety of courses I teach at Wesleyan include multiple approaches to Bharatanatyam, contemporary dance techniques, dance and film courses, and LGBTQ perspectives and dance courses, along with hybrid courses exploring global contemporary dance courses. My pedagogy is not presented from just one perspective; it is intentionally rooted in multiple perspectives. So the idea of multiplicity continues to inform my life. It's a combination of being hybrid, acknowledging my hybridity, and being passionate and steadfast in this "confused" state. And to acknowledging multiple influences constantly seeping through me, and engaging through me—that's what Wesleyan has given me, and what Canada has given me. These are my two eyes; how can I give up either? I need to see. I need both my eyes to see multiple complex visions that have "conversations" with each other—a kind of interoccularity. Which is why I've decided each of those worlds nurture each other. I continue to bring inDANCE to Wesleyan and vice versa. And I bring Wesleyan students to Canada to perform with my company. Both my worlds continue to integrate, nourish, nurture, and inform each other.

I've managed—knock on wood—so far, to integrate both my worlds together. Because what I don't want to be is someone who sees the world in a polarized way. I don't want to be someone who sees the world as binary—either this or that. East or West. Contemporary or Indian dance. Or Wesleyan or Toronto. I'm much more complex—life is complex. We don't live binary, compartmentalized lives. We live much more integrated, cohesive, complex, and confused lives. Let's celebrate the confusion, and let me acknowledge the confusion, and let me partake.

What undergirds the confusion, however, is a very critical discourse and inquiry, in whatever I do. For instance, some presenters try to put me in a box and straightjacket me. In 2013, I created a piece called *I, Cyclops*. The concept of the Greek mythological Cyclops allowed me to explore multiple cultures, because I used the idea of Cyclops as the all-seeing eye—as well as the idea of the Hindu god Shiva, who has the third eye—and added these factors to my fascination with pop culture, particularly the X-Men character, Cyclops, in the X-Men movies. That combination of sources of inspiration resulted in *I, Cyclops* with dancers from Singapore and Canada. It was very well received. We premiered at a prestigious dance festival. Unfortunately, the Artistic Director of the festival wanted a more traditional work, even though all my publicity material featured my contemporary work. It was an absolutely ill-informed perspective, because it contradicted the program notes, which promoted the cultivation of the plurality of old and new ideas. Why did this happen? Because my name is Hari Krishnan. I'm brown-skinned and my initial training is in Bharatanatyam. Straitjacketed. The journey continues, and I am even more resolute about embracing a wide range of work in which representations of fluid sexuality, critical readings of dance history, and pop culture all find space in my choreographic universe.

This is just one recent example that really upset me, but also empowered me to say, "No, I'm going to continue breaking walls, and continue breaking boundaries, and continue being the artist I want to be." No one has the right to dictate what an artist should do and shouldn't do. And no one has the right to arrogate—to dictate—what is "tradition" and what is "modern" given today's messed-up global world. And I will scream this message from the tallest building!

Ultimately, however, I prefer to focus on the positive. All of these worlds I inhabit criss-cross constantly. When they collide, I feel great harmony. I don't feel anxious; I feel great harmony and an excitement—an insane excitement. Dance is still an amazing art form for me. It's a lifelong love affair for me, the dancing body. The more flexible the mind and the body are, the more interested I am in working in this craft.

EIGHT

RE-IMAGINING THE MULTICULTURAL CITIZEN

"FOLK" AS STRATEGY IN THE JAPANESE CANADIANS' 1977 CENTENNIAL NATIONAL ODORI CONCERT[1]

Lisa Doolittle

IN THE SUMMER OF 1977, THIRTY YOUNG JAPANESE CANADIAN girls, the Nikka Festival Dancers, along with a large cohort of parent technicians, wardrobe assistants, makeup artists, stagehands, chaperones, and an assortment of kimonos, wigs, instruments, props, and backdrops, embarked on a six-city tour of Canada with an unprecedented, evening-long production of Odori (Japanese dance). Charged with depicting the one hundred years since people of Japanese ancestry first arrived in Canada, the production was the flagship event of the Japanese Canadian community's centennial celebration.[2] The program stated:

> The National Odori Concert will portray to the public-at-large the rich cultural heritage of the Japanese Canadians. Demonstration of this graceful art form by these youthful Canadians is a reminder that this country's culture will be enriched by the contributions of their fathers and forefathers.[3]

Figure 8.1. Local Japanese Canadian women and girls in rehearsal for Odori Centennial Dance Variety Concert in May 1977, Lethbridge, Alberta, part of the cross-Canada community participation initiatives connected to the National Odori Concert. Photograph courtesy Andrew Chernevych, Galt Museum and Archives.

The National Odori Concert was unprecedented because of its scale,[4] its mixture of Japanese dance forms, and its broad-ranging strategic objectives.

In the 1970s, many Japanese Canadian citizens were at least three generations removed from being native Japanese. This community, characterized as a potential enemy collaborator during the Second World War, suffered enormous trauma and loss through forced displacement, seizure and resale of its members' assets, and family breakup. The Canadian government uprooted what had been tightly knit West Coast enclaves, isolated Japanese Canadian citizens in remote mountainous camps or sent them to exile in war-torn Japan, extracted labour for wartime road construction and farming, and ensured, through post-war travel and settlement restrictions, that the community would remain scattered across Canada.[5] Quietly assimilating through intermarriage,[6] it became and remains the most assimilated ethnic group in Canada with one of the country's highest rates of intercultural marriage.[7] The community was not unified in quiet acceptance of its oppression, however. The National Japanese Canadian Citizens' Association, a highly political organization at the end of the war, sued the government.[8] This organization became the vehicle for uniting Japanese Canadian communities across Canada for the Japanese-Canadian centennial celebrations in 1977.

There are different ways to read the National Odori Concert. For many in the Japanese Canadian community, the performance of dance in a centennial concert, although endorsed by a politicized citizen's organization, might have been viewed merely as a celebration of the community's ethnoracial heritage within the greater context of Canadian cultural diversity and therefore seemingly inconsequential. A non-Japanese Canadian audience would have likely also read any dance repertory performed by ethnic "others," whether based on folk or classical Japanese traditions, as "folkloric." Critics of Canada's early multicultural policies argue that "folk" performances—the celebration through dance, diet, and dress of ethnic differences—in the context of multiculturalism's problematic racialized positioning of ethnic others in the national imaginary are frivolous, backward-looking, and politically inefficacious.[9] The lower class, rural, backward connotations of "folk" seem to allow ethnic difference to remain hierarchized, opening up the possibilities for the hegemonic, white colonial groups to continue to assert superiority even while they embrace ethnic difference in the name of multicultural universality.[10] In this scenario, the Canadian multicultural embrace of "folk" seems doomed only to participate in the delegitimization of the Other. As such, the concert project could be interpreted as signalling aestheticized acquiescence,[11] and contributing to, rather than breaking down, the continuation of racialized social hierarchies.[12] This chapter suggests instead that the making and touring of the dance concert helped connect the then-fractured Japanese Canadian community and contributed to success in obtaining redress for human rights violations during the Second World War.

Drawing upon dance studies theories of embodiment, performance, and agency,[13] and critiques of nationalism and diaspora[14] to explore the "folk" in the dancing, the case of the National Odori Concert suggests a different analysis of the effects of "folk"oriented multicultural policies on perceptions of ethnic, racial, and national identity in general, and on the Japanese Canadian community in particular. The Japanese Canadian Centennial Committee promoted the public representation of Japanese "folk" tropes from long ago and far away (among other types of dance and cultural content) and appropriated government and corporate resources[15] dedicated to the preservation and dissemination of "folk" cultures with the goal of creating a turning point in their own community. As an attempt to radically reconfigure the place of Japanese Canadians in the here and now, the concert and its ancillary activities challenged racist attitudes of Canadians and contributed to the growing resistance to the erasure of the injustices this community had suffered. More specifically, I suggest that it was the creative mobilization of "folk" tropes throughout the concert project that destabilized dichotomies entrenched in nationalist conceptions of ethnicity and racial identity—dichotomies of us and them, primitive and contemporary, national and foreign. While the concert presented an unusual combination of Japanese folk, classical and contemporary dance choreographies, the performance was created in the Canadian multicultural context of the presentation of "folk" dancing as an expression of cultural identities. The perception of "folk" dance as benign and uncontroversial allowed organizers access to valuable resources, venues, and publics in support of their project of reuniting their communities and combatting social delegitimization. Considerable thought was given by the choreographer and director as to how best to represent classical traditions in classically influenced choreography, to include Japanese regional origins of immigrants in regional folk dances, and to appeal to younger generations of Japanese Canadians as well as non-Japanese Canadians. As a result, the National Odori Concert's innovative and hybrid approach to choreography allowed participants and their audiences to perceive Japanese Canadian identity in new and potentially transformative ways.

To support a rethinking of "folk" as more than just multicultural celebration, I will first describe how Japanese Canadian dance functioned within the discourses of Canadian pluralism in the 1970s. Second, I will look at the nature of the dancing, the biographies of the concert's director and choreographer, the scope and kind of media attention it received, and the ways in which the concert was received by both Japanese Canadian audiences and by the general Canadian public. With the concert thus contextualized, I will explore issues of agency, and the extent to which this embodied danced event empowered its participants and mobilized broader social change.

CANADIAN MULTICULTURALISM POLICY AND "FOLK"

Who, or what "folk" was in Canadian society became a pivotal question in the 1970s. Liberal prime minister Pierre Elliot Trudeau and his government forged a new vision of the nation through official multiculturalism—ideas of an idealized egalitarian pluralistic utopia that were first proposed in a multiculturalism policy in 1971 and became law in the Canadian Multiculturalism Act, 1985. More pragmatically, this government saw ethnic "folk" as a kind of ballast population that would help divert the menace of separation fermenting between the "founding" colonial cultures of France (Québec) and England (the rest of Canada).[16] New policies on multiculturalism and on immigration sought to weave together the threads of a nation that francophone-anglophone political, economic, and linguistic disparity threatened to unravel. Further, the 1970s marked a new stage in the ways the Canadian government articulated immigration policies with multiculturalism policies.[17] Canada was, for the first time, receiving much larger waves of what is now referred to as "visible minority" immigrants: immigrants from the Caribbean and Asia—a trend that created new anxieties for some Canadians and elicited new strategies and policies for the management of those anxieties. Anthropologist Eva Mackey explains that, in multicultural Canada, "the bid for dominance... [is a] process not [of] the erasure of cultural difference but the proper management of cultures—a hierarchy of cultures—within a *unified project*" (italics in original).[18]

One of the ideological means by which diverse cultures are managed into hierarchical order is the deployment of "folk" tropes. According to Mackey, official multiculturalism, while seeming to welcome non-colonial ethnicities (i.e., not French and English), tended to erase the centuries-long history of immigrants' and Indigenous peoples' lives in Canada by turning ethnic communities' present into an eternal unchanging "folk" past. In contrast, sociologists Augie Fleras and Jean Leonard Elliott propose that multiculturalism did not focus exclusively on cultural preservation "but on fostering involvement and institutional participation as well as individual mobility and freedom of choice through elimination of 'cultural jealousies' and 'discriminatory attitudes.'"[19] The Japanese Canadians' centennial initiatives were imagined and executed in the midst of both the call to present an unchanging past and to foster institutional participation—and the cultural fusion and transculturalism that results from institutional participation—within the geopolitical confines of Canada. The organizations, performers, and audiences of the Odori concert were caught within these manoeuvres concerning immigration, ethnicity, race, and Canadian nationalism.

THE 1977 NATIONAL ODORI CONCERT[20]

In front of the curtain, in a spotlight, the shakuhachi (flute) soloist breathes present emotion into old melodies. A disembodied, young female voice wafts above the charged pauses in the musical phrasing: "I am a Japanese Canadian. My heritage of ceremony, simplicity, grace, all this beauty I offer to you." The curtain rises to reveal a cherry tree in bloom with pink blossoms drifting down from above to animate a scene where dancers, two young women dressed in kimonos as male and female, are immobilized in a picture of an idealized bucolic past as the familiar and nostalgic strains of a traditional instrumental version of the Sakura song begins. The dancers gracefully pivot, rise and sink, and open fans, their bodies responding to their spiralling and rotating of their fans. The dancers pause in shapes that communicate graceful control of oppositional forces, only to immediately adjust, making an understated gesture of the head, a subtle shift in posture. They mirror each other, shadow each other. Indicating a journey together, they join hands and take three solemn crossing steps towards stage right, with eyes and upper bodies yearning diagonally upward. As the koto (harp) notes begin to multiply and cascade, two younger girls enter, moving much faster and covering much more territory, until finally they, too, take that slow, side-stepping, upward-yearning journey and then quickly exit. Left alone again, the original couple, one standing and one kneeling, heads tilting and rotating almost imperceptibly in a three-point gesture characteristic of Japanese classical dance, fans folded, hands retracted inside their sleeves, gaze at the audience through the pink snowfall of blossoms as the curtain lowers.

To an audience uneducated in the many complexities of Japanese dance forms, the choreography might appear to be an evocation of timeless Japaneseness. But deliberate choreographic choices in this classical dance-influenced staging of the traditional song evoke many of the centennial themes and objectives. This *Sakura* choreography connected Japanese Canadian audiences to the journey of the Issei, the first generation of immigrants, full of hope for the future in the new country and regret for the rupture from the homeland. This *Sakura* staged a vision of two generations and their contrasting emotional states and histories, the constrained movement of the older Nisei—the second generation—strongly rooted in Japanese culture and contrasting with the energy and freedom to move of the Sansei, the third generation, with a connection across generations poignantly suggested in the repetition of the "journey" motif.

The concert proceeded with *Sanbasso*, a Noh-based ritual dance where firm footwork, punctuated hand gestures, and clear linear pathways replaced the sinuousness of the previous dance. Here, ancient Japanese dance traditions evoked not the nostalgia and longing ignited in the opening number, *Sakura*, but rather strength and endurance.

Proceeding to *Harusame*, a love story and the next piece performed in the concert, the more fluid choreographic pattern of pause/pose and adjust, settle and shift, settle and shift was apparent. To my outsider's eye, this interplay of stillness and motion, typical in the classical dance genres of Japan, is particularly apt as an embodiment of the Japanese community's history of oppression, exile, and quiet adaptation. This reading is surely a post-hoc outsider's view, not at all supported by organizers' comments about the dance in their interviews with me. Yet, evidence for connecting the classical dance ethos directly to the centennial objectives of community reunification are apparent in the choreographer's remarks about "ma" in classical dance, ma being a space you leave between the poses, the pauses: "In that 'ma,'... you create that deep expression. Also to keep harmony with people, you need a proper ma."[21] Is ma in dance a movement metaphor for interracial harmony in society?

These three dances comprising the first section of the concert functioned to evoke venerable high-art cultural traditions and to raise the status of Japanese immigrants to Canada by referencing classical dance. Production director Sadayo, sister to choreographer Chiyoko (Tatsumi Yoshikiyo), notes that the concert was not intended to offer absolutely authentic classical Japanese dance choreography: "I wanted people to understand that dancing is an expression of character. We are not trying to be Japanese—we really are Japanese Canadian."[22] That said, the production respected classical Japanese dance's demand for adherence to choreographic rules and technical virtuosity. Choreographer Chiyoko sought permission from her sensei in Japan for making modifications to the set classical choreography, and in the end, she and her Japan-based sensei "edited" the dance together.[23] As Sadayo explains, the classical dances were refracted and modified both for the emerging skills of the teenaged dancers, and for the objectives of this performance.

In the subsequent *Minyo* section, "folk" traditions revealing particular characteristics of each region were foregrounded and performed in front of a backdrop of the map of Japan. This section of the Odori concert represented the many ethnicities within Japan, acknowledging the rich diversity within that country.[24] Elsewhere in this collection, Evadne Kelly uses the term "disparate diaspora" in her exploration of how dance's embodiments of diasporic diversity in Fijian Canadian communities reveal tensions and contest essentialist notions of any ethnic group. The *Minyo* section in the National Odori Concert, in representing the diversity of the origins of Japanese immigrants in Canada, may also be read as a way to contest essentialist and reductive attitudes about Japanese Canadian immigrants.

Immediately following (and in contrast to) the *Minyo* section was an experimental music and dance interlude that fused traditional Japanese dance, Western classical music (i.e., a Bach largo played on koto, shakuhachi, and stand-up bass), and contemporary abstract movement, performed by a trio of dancers in austere, modernist powder blue kimonos. In the Odori concert, choreographers sought specifically to address the issue of acculturation in this then-contemporary hybrid music/dance choreography. As stated in their mandate for the concert, they wished to assert the legitimate presence of Japanese Canadians in Canada, and to suggest the potential—both artistic and social—of a combination of cultures.

Responses to the cross-culturally hybrid dance in the National Odori Concert were mixed. In Edmonton, newspaper reviewer Liz Oscroft viewed this piece as an era-hopping artistic innovation: "Largo played on a *shakuhachi* and *koto*? Bach would never have dreamt it, but Friday night at the Citadel theatre, he did his bit for Canadian multiculturalism."[25] Vancouver's Lloyd Dykk found the Bach one of the most appealing pieces on the program, drawing attention to the commentary that informed the audience "unpretentiously of the paradoxical need for change in traditions in order that they might be passed on meaningfully."[26] The *Toronto Star* newspaper's prestigious theatre critic, William Littler, could not, however, reconcile what he saw as the traditional, preservationist goals of the concert with the updated *Minyo* section: "It was a mistake to have the Nikka trio…play Bach. The instruments were inappropriate and so was the context."[27]

These reactions display competing visions of the purpose of "folk" in Canadian pluralism: to enable both the preservation and fusion of cultures, and to enable transculturalism. The Odori concert's expansive vision was emphasized throughout the concert with a taped audio commentary inserted in between each number, which provided interpretive guideposts that directed audiences towards a reception of the dancing bodies as an embodiment of the underlying transgenerational—as well as transcultural—goals of the whole project. This approach was also carefully emphasized within the Japanese Canadian community, and in advertising about the concert to general audiences and funders. The fact that so much could get lost in translation speaks to the pervasiveness of the "folk"-driven vision of the ethnic other in Canada at this time in history.

The program concluded with a finale called *Wonderful Canada*. Here, "Japanese" and "Canadian" cultural attitudes were deliberately combined and updated in the choreographed qualities of movement. Manipulating a cherry blossom in one hand and a maple leaf branch in the other, dancers delivered Japanese tradition in the choreographic structure of a Bon Odori[28] dance, with "Japanese Canadian" movement qualities choreographed as upwardness, spatial expansiveness, and lightness, connoting optimism and freedom. The choreographer, teachers, and participants who perform this dance, which continues to be re-enacted in Southern Alberta summer Odori festivals, all called these movement qualities "Canadian" in contrast to "Japanese" dance qualities of containment and rootedness. Or, according to Sadayo, "The movements were very kind of uplifting and more bubbly, more Japanese Canadian.... there's no way you could say this was Japanese, because [while] we are utilizing Japanese costumes, and Japanese music, we are expressing in our own ways."[29] The movements thus signified successful Canadian acculturation, and seized an opportunity to link generations within the community while representing their community's past and potential contributions to Canadian society.

Despite the stated mandate to depict one hundred years of the experiences of Japanese immigrants in Canada, the concert did not show the internment period, nor the racial tensions that were rife prior to or after the war. Given the opportunity to "tell their story," it is difficult for this writer to understand the omission of these indelible historical experiences. A description of the disrupted lives and transcultural experience of the Nisei-generation creators of the concert sheds some light on this gap in the Odori concert's timeline. Parents tended to protect Nisei children from the full brunt of the tragedies of the internment and exile, taking an attitude of shikata ganai (nothing can be done about it).

While eagerly assimilating into Canadian society, the Nisei were nonetheless deeply rooted in Japanese culture, in large part because of wartime experiences. For example, the Canadian-born director Sadayo, her sister, choreographer Chiyoko, and many of their Vancouver-based family members were first interned in Greenwood, a remote mountain town in the interior of British Columbia. Then, after the war, forbidden to return to their coastal homes and despite being Canadian citizens, they evacuated to Japan to live with grandparents they had never met and who did not speak their language, Canadian English. Sadayo was seven years old, Chiyoko five. In war-torn Japan, their mother sold her wedding kimonos and homemade soap to pay for daily Odori lessons at a Wakayagi school. She was sure they would all end up back in Canada, and she wanted her girls to get the best Japanese cultural education possible. After six years of impoverished exile, the family returned to Canada. Chiyoko continued her Odori training with annual trips to work with her sensei—trips she was able to make as an employee of Canadian Pacific Airlines, the company that later helped to sponsor the cross-Canada travel of the National Odori Concert company. Chiyoko established an Odori school in Richmond, British Columbia, and the high quality of her students' dance performances caught the eye of the national committee who appointed Chiyoko choreographer and her sister Sadayo director in 1976. Impressively coordinating the project from opposite ends of the country, their commitment embodies the community unification that the concert was meant to enact. These sisters, and the concert they conceived and produced, embraced multiculturalism's offer of belonging; but an explicit depiction of their history of violent racist exclusion was never considered.

In the 1970s, as a result of the Nisei shikata ganai (nothing can be done) approach, cross-generational discussion of internment stories and embodied experiences of internment was limited, and pro-assimilation attitudes were prevalent within the Japanese Canadian community. This earlier climate is difficult to imagine from the vantage point of the late twentieth and early twenty-first centuries, where official Canadian acknowledgements and apologies for wrongdoing towards multiple ethnic minorities were/are more common. Nevertheless, the concert was presented at a pivotal moment when attitudes within and outside the Japanese Canadian community were shifting dramatically.

Director Sadayo reveals only a very subtle politicization in the concert content, explaining that the inclusion of so much Japanese dance in the centennial concert actually reflected "a lot of political concern ... [as] the Japanese

Canadians were not really considered Canadian for seventy-five of their hundred years [of immigration to Canada]. So the first three-quarters of the program was highly influenced by Japanese culture."[30] The content of the show, like the logo for the centennial—a maple leaf surrounded by a larger cherry blossom, and emblazoned on kimonos worn by centennial community Odori groups across the country—asserted Canadianness, but within an enveloping Japaneseness. The *Wonderful Canada* dance finale, combining traditional Japanese dance with movement qualities promoted as "Canadian," deliberately avoided direct political overtones. Instead, the lyrics for the music accompanying this finale perform a particularly forgetful version of historical events, as exemplified in this excerpt:

> From many corners of the earth,
> They came, our fathers came
> In search of wealth, in search of happiness, in search of friends,
> And in the end, they all became new Canadians.
> *(chorus)*
> This shining land, this utopia.
> Canada is wonderful, wonderful Canada.

How could this innocuous and ephemeral concert, performed by teenage girls, have contributed to the community's actual social and political betterment?

AGENCY AND "FOLK" ON STAGE

Dance scholar Susan Leigh Foster argues that, traditionally, the impact of dance performances is too narrowly conceived, seldom allowing "that moving bodies have agency, and often emphasizing individual genius over the rehearsal process and the social networks and institutional frameworks that enable the production of the dance … privileging the thrill of the vanished performance over the enduring impact of the choreographic intent."[31] The choreographic intent of the National Odori Concert, through its juxtaposition of contrasting movement forms, positioned the Japanese Canadians as simultaneously authentic (folk dances showing deep connections to regions in Japan), cultured (evocations of a classical dance heritage that rivalled ballet), and contemporary (movement abstraction, musical and danced cultural fusion, and youthfulness). Not peasant-like "folks" to be relegated to the sidelines, nor threateningly alien enemies, the performers depicted rather more complex folks, to whom the Canadian nation owed an apology.

Judith Butler's theory about gender as performative rather than a biological given prompts the question: "To what extent, then, is ethnicity performative?"[32] Did the National Odori Concert enable participants to embody a new vision of their place in the nation by allowing them to form a critical relationship to cultural and social norms that defined them in ethnically and/or ethnoracially negative terms? The Sansei, those teenage Japanese Canadian girls, were felt to be a better choice to perform than the more accomplished older dancers because their Canadian-born-and-bred bodies had absorbed Canadian experiences; their performance of the traditional dances would be better inflected with Canadianness. They symbolized the community's hopes for the future—the continuation of Japanese Canadian culture and the securing of its place in the national imaginary. For most of these girls, the involvement in dance turned out to be temporary, but their connection to the community through dance was not. The Odori concert gave history back to these young women and to other young people in the audience. Embodying both Japaneseness and Canadianness, the Sansei performers invoked the past in order to make new history—a deep, slow, political activism, made up of an accumulation of dozens of public performances, and countless encounters with their older relatives, with the larger national organization, and with their own bodies and selves in hours of practice and repetition. Empowerment happened not only for participants as they performed their ethnicity differently. The performers and choreographer could also, as Sara Wolf has suggested about the performative power of gender, "rewrite the contract with their audience, shifting how the dance event and the dancers themselves are perceived." The potential for undoing ethnic stereotypes consists "in the audience's labor to look differently, to engage what might be called renegade perception."[33]

PERCEIVING AND RECEIVING THE "FOLK"

Choreographer Chiyoko's following observation captures the emotional reaction of audience members:

Figure 8.2. Local Japanese Canadian women and girls in rehearsal for Odori Centennial Dance Variety Concert in May 1977, Lethbridge, Alberta, part of the cross-Canada community participation initiatives connected to the National Odori Concert. Photograph courtesy Andrew Chernevych, Galt Museum and Archives.

> The older people were in tears watching the show, because it brought Japan back to them.... Even the kids who wanted to [move] away from the Japanese community couldn't believe the beauty of... their own culture... it brought the community closer. As well they don't have to feel shame about how they were treated during the war.[34]

The apparent positive reception within the community created an immediate, powerful, affective connection for many Japanese Canadians. This embodied emotional power was mobilized further through the community-based mandate and enormous scale of the project. Beyond the elite concert tour, the committee established a cross-country network of local teaching and performing events. Seven dance workshops were conducted across Canada, upgrading the level of teaching and dancing nationally.

As a result, hundreds of women and girls performed *Wonderful Canada* along with touring dancers in locations across Canada. These activities mobilized local community leaders (many of them women), involved hundreds of grassroots volunteers, and built participation among youth and across generations, making it an exercise in actual, not only symbolic, community reconstruction.

Extensive coverage in all available media was crucial to the concert's enduring power. The scope of dissemination is rather staggering. The festival dancers and local dance groups participated in a total of twenty-six events with a combined audience estimated at over 65,000 people. The concert, presented in Toronto, Hamilton, Edmonton, Calgary, Vancouver, and Ottawa, was performed mostly in major regional playhouses. Sold out in Calgary and Vancouver, hundreds were turned away, unable to see the performance. The project's final report estimates that media coverage of the concert tour through newspaper articles and reviews, television, and radio coverage reached 1,695,000 people.[35]

AGENCY, "FOLK," AND ACTION

It is no coincidence that a decade after the centennial, Japanese Canadians were the first ethnic community in Canada to receive an official apology from the federal government, along with the most generous package of financial reparations ever paid.[36] Roger Obata, the president of the centennial committee responsible for organizing the concert, went on to figure very prominently in human rights in Canada and was at the centre of the successful redress movement. While few of the Sansei performers are still dancing, their assertion of a Japanese identity through dancing that was part of a high-profile event arguably caused perceptual shifts in Japanese Canadians' identification of themselves. It was largely the Sansei generation, often informed about wartime injustices through contacts made during the centennial year, which spearheaded the drive throughout the 1980s to secure an apology and reparations. While wartime governments had choreographed a scattering and breakup of the community, the centennial projects staged a gathering and reuniting around the retrieval of cultural heritage, bringing a once-reviled cultural identity back to many sites of deliberately "forgotten" trauma and communities where Japanese Canadian citizens who had been most affected by the internment now lived.[37]

The National Odori Concert consciously and strategically mobilized "folk" to forge community cohesion, cross-cultural comprehension, and more fully enfranchised citizenship for Japanese Canadians. My analysis contests notions still prevalent that mark performances commonly labelled as "folk" as a negative force when it comes to the achievement of multicultural equity. The gathering of women in dance was an exercise in actual, not only symbolic, community reconstruction, which helped to trigger political and personal consequences. Further, an examination of "folk" as deployed in the National Odori Concert provides a glimpse of "folk" as a tactic of resistance rather than acquiescence.[38] Staging themselves as Canadian *and* Japanese, the National Odori Concert ostensibly embraced the goals of pluralist nationalism that the official multicultural policies sought to enact through folk dance promotion. Simultaneously, the concert's avoidance of representations of the community's oppression in the internment period also reveals the forgetting of violence that was essential to the project of post-war nation-building and the making of citizens.[39] Yet somehow, in the process of performance creation and dissemination, the innocuous-seeming "folk" connection became a lever that helped to pry open the unacknowledged history of wartime injustices. The National Odori Concert, including its participatory and community-initiated events, helped to foster connections to tradition, communication across generations, and the embodiment of new identities. Furthermore, along with other centennial events, the concert project was part of the momentum necessary for Japanese Canadians to collectively denounce wartime human rights violations and ultimately secure an apology and financial redress and reparations, which subsequently allowed this community to live within the country of their birth while maintaining rather than erasing difference. The connection was affective; this reinvention of "folk" mobilized emotion. As Dipesh Chakrabarty has suggested, "no invention of tradition is effective without a simultaneous invocation of affect, of sentiments, emotions and other embodied practices."[40]

In the end, the Japanese Canadian centennial initiatives demonstrate the significance of individual and community agency in cultural production, made all the more meaningful "in light of the unrelenting efforts of conservative social forces to monopolize the invention of tradition."[41] The centennial Odori concert's inventive reimagining of tradition serves as a challenge to all Canadians to remember the silences and dislocations of oppression, to witness the struggle for justice, and to acknowledge the resilience of a community that included "folk" when it chose to dance its inclusion.

ACKNOWLEDGEMENTS

My deepest thanks to all members of the Momiji Dance Group in Lethbridge with whom I danced for five years and whose stories inspired this research; to Mary Ohara, Chiyoko Hirano, Sadayo Hayashi, and Kay and Denise Fujiwara; to my patient senseis (teachers) Tatsumi Yoshikiyo and Aya Hironaka; to research assistants Erin Wunker, Afra Foroud, Naomi Brand, Catherine Gannon, Judith Lopez-Damian, and Lily Marquez. This essay is part of a multi-year research project funded by the Social Sciences and Humanities Research Council of Canada and the University of Lethbridge Research Fund.

NOTES

1 Parts of this essay appear in *Discourses in Dance*, where a comprehensive analysis further explores "folk" as a keyword for dance, as well as Doolittle and Anne Flynn's multiculturalism and dance research. Lisa Doolittle, "Re-imagining the Multicultural Citizen: 'Folk' as Strategy in the Japanese Canadians' 1977 Centennial National Odori Concert," *Discourses in Dance* 5, no. 2 (2013): 73–91.

2 While the author did not investigate pre- or post-war Japanese dance training institutions or performances in Canada prior to the centennial concert project, interviewees (mostly former residents of coastal BC communities) spoke about their pre-war and pre-internment childhood dance experiences, in both lessons and informal concerts, primarily, it seems, in folk dance forms. It is also likely that during internment, dance teaching and presenting continued. For example, at the museum in New Denver, BC, the author saw photographic evidence of large groups of kimono-clad women dancing in front of the local TB sanatorium. Given the circumstances, which the author discusses, of the Japanese Canadian dispersal during the internment and the cultural erasure, which many in the community practised after the war, it is unlikely that large-scale public performances were considered.

3 Introduction, commemorative concert program, 1977.

4 The Odori concert was by far the largest budget item in the list of centennial activities. Organizers "were under tremendous pressure to compromise on quality for the sake of greater involvement ... but the National Centennial Committee did endorse the concept of a high quality concert in spite of these costs because of the prestige and the public relations value [we hope to] achieve by such a show. It will certainly advance our cultural contribution to Canada." Roger Obata, "Japanese Canadian Citizen Association (JCCA) Minutes," Roger Obata Fonds, R9332, 1:5 (1976), Library and Archives Canada.

5 Arthur Miki, *The Japanese Canadian Redress Legacy: A Community Revitalized* (Altona, MB: National Association of Japanese Canadians, 2003).

6 Tomoko Makebe, "Intermarriage: Dream Becomes Reality for a Visible Minority," *Canadian Ethnic Studies* 37, no. 1 (2005): 121–26.

7 Some internees who were interviewed believe that the breakup of exclusively Japanese Canadian pre-war communities had positive repercussions. They feel it is better to have entered mainstream Canadian society than to have remained linguistically and culturally separate.

8 Miki, *The Japanese Canadian Redress Legacy*, 12–13.

9 See, for example, Valerie Knowles, *Strangers at Our Gates: Canadian Immigration Policy, 1540–2007* (Toronto: Dundurn, 2007): "Even some members of the ethnic communities themselves have rejected the [multiculturalism] policies, claiming that they accentuate the differences between various ethnic groups, ignore the tougher issues of racism and bigotry and prevent 'ethnics' from moving into mainstream society... No longer is it correct to identify official multiculturalism with just the three Ds (dress, diet and dance). In fact, for years multiculturalism has moved beyond the song-and-dance approach to fighting discrimination and integrating immigrants into the evolving mainstream of Canadian society" (271).

Smaro Kamboureli argues (in *Scandalous Bodies: Diasporic Literature in English Canada*, Don Mills: Oxford University Press, 2000): "The emphasis is placed on reproducible and therefore reductive heritage images, precisely because they are seen as reflecting a past irrelevant to Canada's and therefore of little, if any, political pertinence to Canadian culture. Such displays of difference promote a fetishization of ethnic imaginaries: they cast minority Canadians as objects of national voyeurism by keeping them, as it were, under surveillance" (110). See also, Natasha Bakht, "Mere 'Song and Dance': Complicating the Multicultural Imperative in the Arts," in *Home and Native Land: Unsettling Multiculturalism in Canada*, eds. May Chazan, Lisa Helps, Anna Stanley, and Sonali Thakker (Toronto: Between the Lines, 2011), 175–83. Bakht argues for a nuanced discussion of the critiques regarding dance and multicultural arts policies and attitudes.

10 David Theo Goldberg, *Racist Culture: Philosophy and the Politics of Meaning* (Oxford and Cambridge: Blackwell, 1993).

11 Lisa Lowe, *Immigrant Acts* (Durham and London: Duke University Press, 1996); A. Kobayashi, *Women, Work, and Place* (Montréal: McGill-Queen's University Press, 1994).

12 John A. Porter, *The Vertical Mosaic: An Analysis of Social Class and Power in Canada* (Toronto: University of Toronto Press, 1965); Eva Mackey, *The House of Difference: Cultural Politics and National Identity in Canada* (London and New York: Routledge, 1999).

13 Susan Leigh Foster, "Introduction," in *Choreographing History*, ed. Susan Leigh Foster (Bloomington and Indianapolis: Indiana University Press, 1995), 3–21; Susan Leigh Foster, "Choreographies of Protest," *Theatre Journal* 55, no. 3 (2003): 395–412; Jane Desmond, ed., *Meaning in Motion: New Cultural Studies of Dance,* (Durham and London: Duke University Press, 1997); Sara Wolf, "Renegade Gender: Theorizing

the Female Body in Extreme Motion," in *Proceedings, Society of Dance History Scholars Conference* (Paris, June 21–24, 2007): 54–58; Emily Colburn-Roxworthy, "'Manzanar, the Eyes of the World Are upon You': Performance and Archival Ambivalence at a Japanese American Internment Camp," *Theatre Journal* 59 (2007): 189–214.

14 Benedict Anderson, *Imagined Communities: Reflections on the Origin and Spread of Nationalism* (London: Verso, 1983); James Clifford, "Diasporas," *Cultural Anthropology* 9, no. 3 (1994): 302–38; Eric Hobsbawm, "Introduction: Inventing Traditions," in *The Invention of Tradition*, eds. Eric Hobsbawm and Terence Ranger (Cambridge: Cambridge University Press, 1983), 1–14.

15 Funding for the project came from Wintario (a provincial government lottery fund), the Secretary of State (federal government), the Alberta Department of Culture (provincial government), the Prince Hotel (Toronto), and Canadian Pacific (CP) Air, along with considerable fundraising from within the community.

16 "Multiculturalism arose in the aftermath of the publication of the report of the Royal Commission on Bilingualism and Biculturalism in 1969." Augie Fleras and Jean Leonard Elliott, eds., *Unequal Relations: An Introduction to Race, Ethnic, and Aboriginal Dynamics in Canada*, 3rd ed. (Scarborough, Ontario: Prentice Hall Allyn and Bacon Canada, 1999), 301.

17 The 1976 Immigration Act that replaced the earlier policy, a "taps on taps off" response to labour demands, was a vision of immigration as a more "integral component of a sustainable economic growth policy." Fleras and Elliott, *Unequal Relations*, 262–63. This new conception of immigration surely influenced the attitudes and actions of the Japanese Canadian internees.

18 Mackey, *The House of Difference*, 150.

19 Fleras and Elliott, *Unequal Relations*, 301.

20 All dance descriptions and script transcriptions are taken from the VHS video of the Edmonton concert as filmed by ACCESS TV, the province of Alberta's educational TV station.

21 Chiyoko Hirano, interview with author, Richmond, BC, 2006.

22 Sadayo Hayashi, interview with author, Oakville, ON, 2005.

23 Chiyoko Hirano, interview with author, 2005.

24 See Evadne Kelly, "Illuminating a Disparate Diaspora: Fijian Dance in Canada," in this volume.

25 Liz Oscroft, "Dance Melds East, West," *Edmonton Journal*, August 6, 1977.

26 Lloyd Dykk, "Exercise in Excellence," *Vancouver Sun*, n.d., 1977.

27 William Littler, "Japanese Dances Worth Preserving," *Toronto Star*, section F, June 22, 1977.

28 Bon Odori is a Japanese Buddhist folk dance performed outdoors as part of a major summertime memorial festival in Japan and by the Japanese diaspora; it is a time to remember and honour ancestors and to recognize the continuation of their influence on the present.

29 Sadayo Hayashi, interview with author, 2005.

30 Ibid.

31 Foster, "Introduction," 15.

32 See Katrin Sieg, *Ethnic Drag: Performing Race, Nation, Sexuality in West Germany* (University of Michigan Press, 2002) for an examination of the complex relationships between performances of ethnicity and ethnicity's collective construction in specific historical and social contexts.

33 Wolf, *Renegade Gender*, 57.

34 Chiyoko Hirano, interview with author, 2006.

35 See the centennial project's final report. Roger Obata, "Final Report of the Centennial Committee," Obata fonds 3:1 (1979), Library and Archives Canada.

36 Miki, *The Japanese Canadian Redress Legacy*, 12.

37 The gathering and reuniting effect of the centennial concert project included moves that strengthened ties to Japan. Contracts with composers and designers and purchasing costuming and music elements had to be negotiated there, and permissions to innovate classical works had to be sought from Japanese dance experts. Clifford points to such transnational connections as further evidence of resistance: "Association with another nation ... region or continent, or world historical force (such as Islam) gives added weight to claims against an oppressive national hegemony." Clifford, "Diasporas," 311.

38 See Clifford, "Diasporas," 308.

39 See Mona Oikawa's "Cartographies of Violence" for an insightful examination of the effects of the legislated spatial separation of Japanese Canadian families and the role of the erasure of the actual internment camp sites in the forgetting of violence. Mona Oikawa, "Cartographies of Violence, in *Race, Space, and the Law: Unmapping a White Settler Society*, ed. S. H. Razack (Toronto: Between the Lines, 2002), 73–98.

40 Dipesh Chakrabarty, quoted in Stephen Vlastos, ed., *Mirror of Modernity: Invented Traditions of Modern Japan* (Berkeley: University of California Press, 1998), 294.

41 Vlastos, *Mirror of Modernity*, 19.

NINE

DANCE AS A CURATORIAL PRACTICE

PERFORMING MOVING DRAGON'S *KOONG* AT THE ROYAL ONTARIO MUSEUM[1]

Allana C. Lindgren

"Any museum or exhibition is, in effect, a statement of position. It is a theory: a suggested way of seeing the world."[2]

—Sharon Macdonald

FROM MAY 7 TO 9, 2010, VISITORS WANDERING THROUGH THE Gallery of Chinese Architecture in the Royal Ontario Museum (ROM) in Toronto might have seen Chengxin Wei standing in front of a large reproduction of an early twentieth-century photograph of three Chinese men standing in front of a large stone gateway.[3] Wei's stance and the direction of his gaze echoed those of the figures in the photograph; his pose created a visual parallel between himself and the men. Telescoping time and space, the juxtaposition symbolically blurred the boundaries between the past and the present, the image and the gallery. At the same time, however, just a few metres away from where Wei was standing, was a stone gateway—the same gateway that appears in the photograph. The actual presence of this gateway, coupled with the corporeality of Wei, arguably contrasted and therefore emphasized the physical absence of the trio despite their "remnant" existence in the photograph. As a result, the seemingly unremarkable instance of a person standing in front of a reproduction of a photograph in a museum implicitly asked observers to think about the similarities and differences between the men in the picture and Wei.

Curious visitors might have paused in the Gallery of Chinese Architecture long enough to discover that Wei's stance was from the opening of *Koong*, a fifteen-minute choreographic duet. Created and performed by Wei and his wife Jessica Jone, who is also his artistic collaborator and co-founder of the Vancouver-based dance company Moving Dragon, the piece was set to a score by composer Michael Vincent and performed by the TorQ Percussion Quartet as one of four dances presented in different parts of the ROM during the 2010 CanAsian International Dance Festival.[4]

As a site-specific choreographic work by two dance artists who self-identify as Chinese Canadian,[5] *Koong* can be situated in a larger and ongoing conversation about museums and cultural diversity. Charting debates about the politics of curating, museum studies scholars Kylie Message and Andrea Witcomb have noted that "while the new museology, sometimes also called 'critical museology,' might have emerged out of the concern to show how museums were embedded within a network of power relations that supported dominant interests, it has often also been employed by researchers wanting to counteract or challenge the image of museums as governmental apparatuses."[6] In the oscillation between these scholarly perspectives, researchers have noted "the increasing practice of representing and collaborating with culturally and ethnically diverse groups."[7] As James Clifford has asserted, this growing trend of incorporating diversity into museum programming is largely indicative of a wish to implement "active collaboration and a sharing of authority" with source communities traditionally marginalized in the institutionalization and interpretation of their own material culture.[8] One strategy to fulfill this agenda is to invite artists into museums to advise administrators and/or to provide commentary by engaging with artifacts and patrons. This approach has proven so popular that its novelty has long since faded. Or, as Anthony Alan Shelton, the director of the Museum of Anthropology at the University of British Columbia, has stated, "Artistic interventions in ethnographic museums to expose their paradoxes, contradictions, and parodies have ... become almost commonplace."[9]

While the phenomenon of artists in museums is not new, the implications of site-specific dance performances in settings like the ROM are worthy of further consideration. Most of the scholarship about choreographic performances in museums focuses on art museums, often addressing the relationship between dance and the visual arts.[10] Research related to dance in anthropological or ethnographic museums has tended to coalesce around issues pertaining to power imbalances and Indigeneity, post-colonialism, national identities, or the ownership of intangible heritage.[11]

Koong shifts the conversation to the more basic and methodological interest in how meaning or "narratives" are constructed in museum exhibitions. In so doing, it augments the work of previous scholars who have examined how museums create and convey meaning through inherently choreographic techniques: the configuration of exhibition space physically guides visitors, often subtly prescribing their experiences according to institutional values and priorities.[12] Notably, sociologist and museum theorist Tony Bennett has critiqued the political dimensions of exhibition configurations, arguing that chronologically linear displays often facilitate evolutionary narratives. "Organized walking," according to Bennett, becomes the embodiment of "an itinerary in the form of an order of things which reveals itself only to those who, step by step, retrace its evolutionary development."[13]

Bennett's observation is helpful in thinking about the ideological implications of how Wei and Jone traverse the ROM's Gallery of Chinese Architecture. Just as curators' choices privilege some narratives over others, choreographic choices in site-specific dances focus viewers' attention and, in so doing, emphasize certain aspects of the museum environment over others.[14] Yet, as this chapter asserts, *Koong* does not reinforce an evolutionary narrative. Instead, distilled to their essence, the dancers' movements through the gallery symbolize the potential for visitors to create their own paths—literally and conceptually—through the exhibition. As Wei and Jone dance, they engage with the artifacts on display, creating new narratives and demonstrating what Nicholas Thomas, the director of the Museum of Archaeology and Anthropology at the University of Cambridge, has termed "the mutability of things in recontextualization."[15]

When *Koong* is examined from this perspective, the choreography constructs new narratives about the cultural continuities, disruptions, and priorities in the Gallery of Chinese Architecture. More specifically, Wei and Jone model and aestheticize a desire for cultural interactivity that reaches across time when considering what having Chinese ancestry means in a contemporary Canadian context. In this light, dance can be a curatorial practice, helping the viewer to see and understand the displays in new ways and to think about the plurality inherent in terms like "China," "Canada," and "Chinese Canadian."

The rest of this chapter broaches these issues by first exploring how the artifacts in the Gallery of Chinese Architecture can be examined without reference to *Koong*. In particular, this section investigates how the historical contexts of the artifacts, as well as the story of their acquisition by the ROM, generate meaning that cannot be separated from the objects on display. To demonstrate how dance infuses new interpretive possibilities into the exhibition, the chapter then focuses on three additional narratives made possible by Wei and Jone's performance. I have categorized these new readings as internalized interculturalism, temporal collaboration, and refocusing the cultural gaze.

READING THE ROM

The Gallery of Chinese Architecture is a fitting performance venue for a dance whose title is a Chinese character meaning "emptiness" or "blankness," and which, in Taoism, references the concepts of "openness" and "vastness."[16] The voluminous exhibition space, which is several stories high, dwarfs anyone and everything in it. Large shafts of natural light falling from glass panes in the ceiling create an atmosphere that encourages enlightened tranquility and meditation.

The objects on display balance the capacious scale of the gallery. These artifacts represent Chinese architecture and related items from the Han to Qing dynasties—over 2,000 years of history.[17] Throughout *Koong*, the dancers interact with these artifacts, including the "Ming Tomb," a funeral mound created for General Zu Dashou, an important general in the late Ming dynasty, who died in 1656 during the early years of the Qing dynasty.[18] For Wei and Jone, the Ming Tomb aligns well with the themes suggested by the title they chose for their site-specific choreographic work because it reflects "the emptiness and vastness of the time and history" and provides the opportunity to explore several closely related themes: "the passage of time, the briefness of a lifetime in the context of history, the history of the artifact and the person that was memorialized, and the contrast between the coldness of the stone artifacts and our living, breathing movements that animated it."[19]

In addition to the Ming Tomb, the exhibition at the ROM features two gateways (including the one in the photograph Wei stands in front of at the beginning of *Koong*), a stone altar, and the tumulus, which is engraved with symbols of eternal life.[20] Carved figures of a civic official holding a writing tablet and a military figure with a segmented flail have been placed nearby. There are also stone statues of two reclining camels. Not all of these objects were constructed specifically for General Zu's tomb. One of the gates, for instance, belongs to an earlier tomb.[21] Nevertheless, these artifacts are surrogates for those that would have been originally arranged to create an avenue known as a spirit path, which led to the entrance of the cemetery and protected the souls of the general and his family.[22]

Even without the presence of the dancers, the artifacts can be read in a number of ways. These multiple narratives are both explicit and implicit, depending on the viewer's knowledge of the exhibition and its historical context. Most obviously, the objects have been gathered and displayed to make the ritualization of death and mourning tangible. The craftsmanship and construction techniques of Chinese ancestor worship are also on display. In this way, the aggregate effect of the exhibition invites visitors to consider the materiality, aesthetics, and functionality of funereal objects from the late Ming and early Qing dynasties.

Beyond their association with the funereal, these objects also tell us a lot about beliefs at the ROM and in Canadian society more generally; they serve as conduits for shifting cultural values. Part of the motivation to obtain and show these objects, for instance, was educational. The ROM Act was passed by the Ontario Legislature on April 16, 1912, and legislates the ROM's mandate to illustrate "the history of man in all ages"[23]—a directive Charles Trick Currelly, the first director of the Royal Museum of Archaeology (one of the initial divisions of the ROM), later stressed when discussing the Chinese collection:

> It looked as if we had the opportunity of obtaining a fairly good Chinese collection, and it seemed to me that as the Japanese and Chinese are our next-door neighbours, and Pacific trade might in future become as important as the Atlantic trade, and as, moreover, it is unlikely that our people will

> ever become familiar with Chinese or Japanese literature, a comprehensive collection of the art of these two great countries would enable our people to grasp something of their greatness.[24]

While Currelly was presumably sincere in his assertion that the Chinese collection would foster Canadian respect for Asian cultures, he was clearly aware that it also bestowed cultural prestige on the museum and the city of Toronto, proclaiming that the Chinese artifacts elevated the ROM "to the position of one of the world's great museums."[25]

The importance of donors is another narrative thread present in the Gallery of Chinese Architecture. Visitors reading the accompanying didactic panels carefully would note that most of the artifacts are part of the George Crofts Collection. Crofts, a fur merchant who also dealt in Chinese antiquities, secured most of the objects in the gallery for the ROM.[26] The gallery also features two large reproductions of photographs that were taken in China by Crofts. The first image is of the three men that Wei references in his opening pose. In this photograph, which I will call the "trio photograph," Crofts's Chinese antiquities dealer stands in front of the stone gateway accompanied by two Chinese workers. The second photograph, which I call the "solo photograph," hangs near the funeral mound and is very similar to the other photograph, except that the antiquities dealer stands by himself in front of the stone gateway.

The Crofts Collection dates back to the early years of the ROM when Crofts donated and sold numerous Chinese artifacts to the ROM at below-market prices, thereby allowing what was then a small regional museum to amass a sizable and valuable collection. In recognition of his centrality to the establishment of the ROM's Chinese collection, Crofts was awarded an honorary degree from the University of Toronto in 1922.[27]

All of these factors generate meaning that resonates in the gallery and position it as a repository for the material history of Ming and Qing cultural practices; an educational space; and the marker of individual, institutional, municipal, and regional importance. *Koong* does not necessarily challenge these readings but instead opens the narrative potential of the Gallery of Chinese Architecture or "re-curates" the room. What emerges through this process are new ways of understanding both the ROM and the significance of having Chinese heritage while living in twenty-first-century Canada.

INTERNALIZED INTERCULTURALISM

At first glance, the Ming Tomb exhibition appears to convey a relatively straightforward approach to categorization: the objects in the Gallery of Chinese Architecture are from China and therefore can be understood as representative of different periods in Chinese culture. Once Wei and Jone enter the gallery, however, the focus shifts away from China exclusively and leads to an investigation of the contours of transnational engagement—or, more accurately, the artistic implications of internalized interculturalism. That is, *Koong* does not educate the viewer about Chinese history, but rather redirects the spectator's attention to how individual dancing bodies can become sites for interculturalism, a term theatre scholar Ric Knowles has defined as "the continuing renegotiation of cultural values and the reconstitution of individual and community identities and subject positions"—processes that occur when different cultures intersect.[28] In other words, whereas interculturalism usually involves two or more groups of people from different cultures interacting with each other, internalized interculturalism is about how different cultures can be actively present in a single person.

Wei and Jone each epitomize the creative potential and plurality of internalized interculturalism. Although both artists are of Chinese heritage, their formative experiences that can be attributed to Chinese cultural influences are different—a point best demonstrated by how each trained in dance. When Wei was eleven years old, he was one of only twelve boys and twelve girls chosen from across China to study at the Beijing Dance Academy. After he graduated, he performed for three years as a principal dancer with the Guangdong Provincial Dance Theatre. He came to Canada in 2000 and has performed for numerous dance companies in Vancouver, including Joe Ink, Wen Wei Dance, and EDAM (Experimental Dance and Music). In addition, he was a member of Ballet BC for six years.

Jone first studied dance with her mother, Lorita Leung, at the Lorita Leung Dance Academy in Richmond, British Columbia. She continued her professional training in Chinese classical and folk dance at the Beijing Dance Academy, as well as at the Guangdong Dance School. She earned a degree from the contemporary dance program at Simon Fraser University. Her success as a dancer and as a choreographer has been recognized in both

China and Canada, as Jone was the recipient of the Chairman's Award at the Fourth Peach and Plum Dance Competition in Beijing and the recipient of two awards for best choreography at the North American Chinese Dance Competition.[29]

Despite the differences in their dance training, Jone and Wei discovered their artistic sensibilities were compatible. In 2004, the couple—who met in China, but now make Vancouver their home—performed as part of Moving Dragon, a mixed-program concert presented by the Lorita Leung Dance Association at the Roundhouse Community Arts and Recreation Centre. The first half of the evening featured traditional Chinese dance.[30] The second half showcased more contemporary work. The positive responses they received for their own work inspired them to create a dance company, Moving Dragon. At the time, the choreography they performed was strongly influenced by Chinese classical and folk dance. Yet, from the start, their impulse was to resist strict cultural demarcations and instead embrace artistic syncretism. As Wei remembers, "You wouldn't say 'That's Chinese dance,' because of the different concepts, and the different formations, using different pathways, and all the different toolboxes we used from the contemporary dance choreography. So that's when we started questioning the East and West [divide], and after that show, we started Moving Dragon."[31] Accordingly, they define their company's aesthetic as a "cross-cultural fusion" between classical Chinese dance and contemporary Western styles.[32] As Jone says, she and Wei consider Moving Dragon to be "a contemporary dance company with a Chinese influence, because of who we are as individuals, and our backgrounds and history."[33]

The mixture of influences in *Koong* invites the audience to think about how interculturalism can be a conversation that takes place at the corporeal level. That is, our bodies adopt and enact the multiplicity of cultures we encounter. As gongs and bells fill the air at one point in the dance, Wei steps forward in slow motion, angling his body, twisting with a beautiful fluidity like he is moving through water, like he is practicing tai chi, like his body is kinetic calligraphy. Wei specifically attributes this movement quality of fluidity to his training in traditional Chinese dance.[34] The ballet training he received in China is also evident in his performance, particularly in moments where the verticality of his torso is accentuated, in his effortless pirouettes, and in the ballet positions apparent in his port de bras. Furthermore, *Koong* incorporates everyday gestures and actions, like walking. At different moments in the piece, Wei's movements are also inflected with paradoxically elastic isolations reminiscent of Canadian choreographer Crystal Pite's unusual choreographic vocabulary—a real kinetic echo, since Wei has worked as a dancer for Pite.

This multiplicity of influences or internalized interculturalism is not surprising. When Wei first arrived in Canada, he was eager to assimilate into Western culture and dance. Yet, as he settled into his new life and home, he began to think about his identity and how he might bridge the two cultures. The establishment of Moving Dragon allowed him the opportunity to do so:

> We decided to start our Moving Dragon company because, as an immigrant, I think I was trying to find my identity. When I just moved to Vancouver, I danced with the ballet company for however many years, and at that time I wanted to eliminate, or get rid of, my Chinese training. I wanted to assimilate into the Western culture. Because—I think that, most immigrants have this struggle—when you go into a new place, and you want to just to fit into the new culture, and the new place. You think that's what you want to do. That's what you have to do. I started to train in ballet classes, and to want to be in the culture, and learn all the culture. I literally, I really struggled with a lot, the first few years. I think most immigrants have the same experience.[35]

Eventually, however, he began to reconsider this quest to reinvent himself: "I started to question myself about why I wanted to throw away, get rid of my roots. Because I think that's me. That's in my blood. And I can't really get rid of it. And in fact, that's me, and that's why I'm different."[36] Moving from self-imposed assimilation to an embrace of his own cultural pluralism, Wei realized he wanted to see how he could artistically reconcile the two cultures: "I started to rethink who I am, and to start thinking about my identity. I started to create works, and I started thinking: I have my Chinese background. And now I have the new training from the Western dance forms... How can I fit them together to merge, to bridge the two cultures together?"[37] When this internalized interculturalism was performed at the ROM in 2010 via Moving Dragon's *Koong*, it turned the Gallery of Chinese Architecture into a supportive space for polyglot dance.[38]

TEMPORAL COLLABORATION

As part of the process of exploring cultural pluralism, the issue of time enters the equation. The past and present coexist in *Koong,* as the traditional Chinese dance and the contemporary dance Wei and Jone studied in Canada are simultaneously present in the bodies of the dancers and in the choreography they perform.[39] Yet, *Koong* helps us to examine the issue in more depth. For instance, the dancers' costumes complicate the sense of identification and belonging that seemingly make knowing one's cultural history and ancestry both attractive and comforting. Wei wears a yellow shirt over a grey tank top and purple pants. Jone's costume similarly references contemporary street clothes, as she wears a red shirt over a multicoloured tank top and purple pants. Both dancers perform in running shoes. Their Western street clothes costumes contrast sharply with the traditional Chinese attire worn by the men in the photographs. According to Jone, "We chose the costumes because we wanted to juxtapose the modern against this historic backdrop... we wanted to represent our time in this space."[40] The effect of this choice is that *Koong* can be read as advancing the view that there is an incompatibility created by temporal distance. This contrast between the past and present asks viewers to consider if cultural changes over time render ancestors as ultimately unknowable because social contexts shift so dramatically.

Koong introduces another narrative—one that rethinks the relationship of the past and present in collaborative terms. That is, although the costumes clearly stress the differences between 2010 and the Ming and Qing dynasties, or even the 1920s when Crofts took the photographs of his Chinese antiquities dealer and workmen, *Koong* contains moments when the past and present converge. In the last section of *Koong,* for example, Jone and Wei run through the gallery. They dance in unison, revisiting movement phrases, including pirouetting on one knee. These "street" movements—running and the allusion to breakdance spinning—remind the viewer of the juxtaposition of present and past that regularly occurs in the museum as visitors wander through the exhibitions. Moreover, the blending of dance training and performance styles, as well as musical instruments and influences in *Koong,* reject any past/present binary. This simultaneity is another conscious choice for Jone and Wei. As Wei notes, "We saw the gate as a kind of passage into another time. We were inspired by the notion of past, present and future all meeting in this room."[41]

The artists were also attentive to the fleetingness of time—a brevity that quickly transposes the present into the past. Or, as Jone states,

> We find the entire concept fascinating; here's this Chinese tomb for a general who's long gone, it's totally out of context in downtown Toronto. And our dance has been created specifically for this unique space—it will be performed and then it will be gone. We've been touched by the artifacts, the room will be touched by us, and then it will all be over. It's completely ephemeral.[42]

In this light, at its most elemental, the dancers' interaction with the artifacts is a creative collaboration between the present and past. The past is a dance partner, inspiring and, at times, literally supporting Wei and Jone as they lean against the objects in the Gallery of Chinese Architecture. For instance, at one point in the dance, Jone stands with her back to the Ming Tomb. Her head is tilted up and away. She moves in slow motion, curling down to the bottom of the tomb, her cheek presses the cold stone before she rotates back to standing position and then melts into a backbend as she clings to the tomb. At another moment, near the middle of the piece, Jone is seated on the floor facing the tomb. She pauses before rising to her feet as Wei tumbles into the same space. This is the first time they are close to each other. They slowly roll and twist around the altar, making their way to the gate, which Jone uses to balance briefly in an arabesque before she sinks into deep lunges while Wei arches his back with his head pressed against the gate. Both the altar and the gateway support the dancers' movements and are the focus of them—static stone dance partners in choreography that transgresses the traditional exhibition taboo of "do not touch."

Through these types of choreographed phrases, *Koong* turns the Gallery of Chinese Architecture's focus on Chinese history into a venue where viewers are asked to think about how contemporary artists can pay homage to their cultural heritage while still pursuing their own creative agency. In so doing, the dance queries whether the past is sacred. By focusing on the flesh-and-blood bodies performing around, through, and with the historical objects, *Koong* supplants the concept of the museum as a place where the past is protected by glass cases and velvet partition ropes with a more collaborative approach between cultures. Creation, not conservation, is on display. As a result, the past does not simply inspire contemporary artistic expression, but is critical to its genesis and expression.

REFOCUSING THE CULTURAL GAZE

In addition to adding new narrative possibilities involving internalized interculturalism and temporal collaboration, *Koong* reinforces a narrative already present in the Gallery of Chinese Architecture by foregrounding the two photographs that Crofts took at the time that the gateway was being transported to Canada. The inclusion of these photographs in the display contextualizes the Ming Tomb exhibition; Wei and Jone recontextualize the photographs.

In both black-and-white photographs, there is rubble around the gateway, which is the solitary structure. It provides entry to nowhere. Tellingly, at the time of the ROM's acquisition of the tomb in the early 1920s, the land the gateway occupied was being developed. Most of the related funereal statues had been relocated or demolished, and General Zu's grave chamber had been ransacked except for a small stone altar.[43] The inclusion of both photographs in the exhibition can be understood as acknowledging the sensitive issue of the removal of cultural heritage as well as the labour, the commodification of historical objects, and the commercial transactions underpinning the creation of cultural capital. The self-assured assessment of the altruistic and educational benefits of displaying Chinese artifacts in Canada—a view articulated by Currelly, the former ROM director of Archaeology—can be read in tandem with Crofts's continued relationship with the ROM to suggest that the acquisition of the artifacts was welcomed and used to leverage further financial support. Subsequent assessments of the trade in cultural antiquities, however, have become more complex. In particular, the Chinese collection brought status to the ROM and Toronto, connoting an early twentieth-century cosmopolitanism that, as scholar Dennis Duffy has argued, validated the trade in antiquities in untroubled terms: "in this system, the dissolution of civility in one culture enables another to embody within a single building the myth of a continuous and universalist ('the arts of mankind') past whose centre now lodges in Toronto."[44] Regardless of the motivation for their inclusion in the exhibition, the effect of the enlarged reproductions of Crofts's photographs is to make the process of the objects' acquisition apparent and ever-present in the Gallery of Chinese Architecture.

In *Koong*, the dancers repeatedly call attention to the trio photograph—the image of Crofts's Chinese antiquities dealer and his workers. The choreography they perform functions like a camera lens to refocus the viewer's eye. For instance, at one point in the dance, as the music fades into a softly chopping staccato rhythm, Wei kicks to pivot himself so that he is facing this photograph. He ends his movement phrase seated on the floor. His stillness is a pause that is visually filled by his only action: looking at the image. Moving back to a standing position, he pauses again to glance at the trio photograph before surveying the rest of the gallery and moving toward the gateway. Jone, meanwhile, stands in front of one section of the audience. She backs away as her head follows a serpentine movement she makes with her right hand. As she does so, Wei backs away from the gateway, returning to the performance space. He kneels in front of the trio photograph, his gaze once more fixed on the image. Further into the dance, Jone is standing upstage looking at the same photograph. Once again, the dancers redirect the viewer's gaze to the documentary evidence of prior human contact with the material objects on display. Near the end of the piece, as the percussive beat intensifies, Jone runs to the photograph while Wei hurries to the tomb. They both pause, their breathing laboured from their exertion. This repose is fleeting as they begin their duet again. As the pulsing music recedes into a softer and more sustained sound like a choir holding a low note, the dancers' energy dissipates as Wei lowers himself to the floor and Jone walks slowly away from him. Jone gazes up at the gateway, pressing her palm gently against it as she walks through the archway. Slowly, she reaches out to the altar and then pivots back to the gate. A sense of wonder pervades. As *Koong* concludes, Jone walks slowly back to Wei, who is still seated. She stands behind him as they both look at the trio photograph of the unnamed men, who gaze back at them.

Wei and Jone's repeated references to the trio photograph possibly elicit politicized narratives for viewers conversant in the complex history of racism and exploitation that accompanied Chinese immigration to Canada, and was exemplified through the harsh and openly discriminatory working and living conditions faced by Chinese labourers working on the Canadian Pacific Railway (CPR); the federal head tax, which was first implemented in 1885, the same year the CPR was completed; and the *Chinese Immigration Act* (1923), which was enacted shortly after the Ming Tomb arrived in Canada and effectively put a moratorium on further emigration from China. The photographs—and the watchfulness of Wei and Jone—arguably remind visitors that real people's lives and livelihoods were involved in the transnational trade in cultural heritage at a time when Canadian laws enabled race-based discrimination. Without these images and eyes, this troubling history would be absent from the Gallery of Chinese Architecture. Instead, there would be an unquestioned narrative that emphasized the desirability and acceptance of Chinese culture in Canada—a narrative that would create an unspoken paradox: Chinese objects were venerated; Chinese immigrants vilified. Stated another way, without *Koong*, Crofts's photographs are easy to overlook as atmospheric wallpaper. Wei and Jone bring these images and the complex history of labour and race relations that they represent to the fore of the exhibition in the Gallery of Chinese Architecture. Their choreography insists that the present contemplate the past.

ETHICAL QUERIES AND OTHER FINAL THOUGHTS

Accompanying the question of what *Koong* can tell us about the role of Chinese ancestry in a contemporary Canadian context is the interest in finding the outer parameters of dance as a curatorial practice. Can Moving Dragon's approach serve as a model for other choreographers? At first glance, and given the proliferation of artistic interventions into museum settings noted at the beginning of this chapter by Anthony Alan Shelton, the most obvious answer is "yes." Yet, as a curatorial practice that refocuses and introduces new narratives into culturally specific exhibitions, *Koong* raises some old, but persistent, concerns about ownership and exploitation. Namely, Wei and Jone denounce cultural appropriation and the misuse of movement traditions based on cultural ignorance, suggesting that it is problematic for people from a specific culture to claim to represent their heritage through dance without significant training in that movement tradition.[45] They also are keenly aware of the power politics involved when an artist from a culturally dominant heritage interprets dance genres generated by counterparts from cultures that have been historically marginalized and/or that continue to struggle for more agency within Canada.

At the same time, however, the performance by Wei and Jone at the ROM could be seen as an example of exploitation in the name of cultural sensitivity. Clare Bishop, a professor of contemporary art, has raised the concern that dance is misused by cultural institutions: "Live dance seems to exist in a different time zone to that of history: it is usually deployed by the museum as presentist spectacle—a way to enliven its mausoleal atmosphere and play into the demands of an experience economy."[46] Extending this line of thinking to race, one might argue that inviting dancers of Asian heritage into a museum to perform is an economical way for a Western cultural organization to position itself as "progressive" without having to alter its collections or policies, while simultaneously disseminating a message of institutional openness. The point being made here is not that the ROM intended to capitalize on the political correctness of hosting performers associated with the 2010 CanAsian International Dance Festival, but rather that concerns about exploitation in museums—by and of dance artists—needs constant monitoring.

Finally, although this chapter has explored a range of issues raised by Moving Dragon's performance of *Koong* in the Gallery of Chinese Architecture, it is worth noting that other narratives are possible. For instance, although the theme of cultural continuity was already present in the gallery through the objects representing the lineage of Chinese dynasties, *Koong* personalized the theme. According to Wei, *Koong* "is one of our favourite pieces. It is special to Jessica, too, because she decided it would be her last project before focusing on starting a family."[47] This decision, presumably known only by Wei and Jone at the time, nevertheless would have informed their performance. As a "secret" narrative, it shifts the connotative possibility of the large and rounded funeral mound from a symbol of death to the shape of a rounded pregnant belly, turning the Gallery of Chinese Architecture into a space not just for indexing the past, but one that promises the perpetuation of familial lines and is full of hope for the future.

In their totality, the narratives discussed in this chapter indicate that using the metaphor and concept of curating to understand how choreography can augment, highlight, or refocus attention on different aspects of museum exhibitions, generates new meanings and offers new perspectives on diversity. Specifically, in *Koong*, Wei and Jone enhance the interpretive possibilities of the Gallery of Chinese Architecture at the ROM by introducing opportunities to consider how internalized interculturalism, temporal collaboration, and refocusing the cultural gaze might enrich our appreciation of the artifacts on display and deepen our understanding of how Chinese Canadians are curating their own subjectivity through dance.

NOTES

1 The author would like to thank Chengxin Wei and Jessica Jone for generously sharing their time and experiences. The author also greatly appreciate Carolyne

Clare's research assistance for this project. This article was written with the financial support of the Social Sciences and Humanities Research Council of Canada.

2 Sharon Macdonald, introduction to *Theorizing Museums*, eds. Sharon Macdonald and Gordon Fyfe (Oxford: Blackwell Publishers, 1996), 14.

3 The analysis in this chapter is based on an archival video of the production provided by Chengxin Wei and Jessica Jone.

4 The other choreographic works were by Natasha Bakht, Soojung Kwon, and the hip-hop collective F.A.M. For more information about the festival, see Paula Citron, "Fresh Moves in the Museum: A New Dance Production Makes Dramatic Use of the ROM Galleries," *Globe and Mail*, May 11, 2010, accessed October 4, 2015, http://www.theglobeandmail.com/arts/theatre-and-performance/fresh-moves-in-the-museum/article4318459/.

5 Chengxin Wei, email message to author, September 28, 2015.

6 Kylie Message and Andrea Witcomb, "Introduction: Museum Theory, An Expanded Field," in *The International Handbooks of Museum Studies*, vol. 1, *Museum Theory*, general eds. Sharon Macdonald and Helen Rees Leahy (Chichester, West Sussex: John Wiley & Sons, 2015), xxxvii. See also, Peggy Levitt, *Artifacts and Allegiances: How Museums Put the Nation and the World on Display* (Oakland, CA: University of California Press, 2015), 7–8.

7 Message and Witcomb, "Introduction," li, liii.

8 James Clifford, *Routes: Travel and Translation in the Late Twentieth Century* (Cambridge, MA: Harvard University Press, 1997), 210.

9 Anthony Alan Shelton, "Museums and Anthropologies: Practices and Narratives," in *A Companion to Museum Studies*, ed. Sharon Macdonald (Chichester, West Sussex: John Wiley & Sons, 2011), 78.

10 In addition to serving as muses and artistic subjects, dancers—including Isadora Duncan, Ruth St. Denis, Maud Allan, Mata Hari, Alexander Sakharoff, and Vaslav Nijinsky—have found inspiration and sometimes performance opportunities in art galleries and museums. Later dance artists such as Merce Cunningham, Trisha Brown, Robert Morris, and Donya Feuer, among others, have found art museums to be receptive supporters of their kinetic experimentation and innovations. For more thorough discussions of these and other artists, see Gabrielle Brandstetter, *Poetics of Dance*, trans. Elena Polzer with Mark Franko (Oxford: Oxford University Press, 2015); Roger Copeland, *Merce Cunningham: The Modernizing of Modern Dance* (New York and Abingdon: Routledge, 2004), 172–73; Mark Franko and André Lepecki, "Editor's Note: Dance in the Museum," *Dance Research Journal* 46, no. 3 (December 2014): 4; Erin Brannigan, "Dance and the Gallery: Curation as Revision," *Dance Research Journal* 47, no. 1 (April 2015): 5–25; and Juliet Bellow and Nell Andrew, "Inventing Abstraction? Modernist Dance in Europe," in *The Modernist World*, eds. Stephen Ross and Allana C. Lindgren (Abingdon: Routledge, 2015): 329–38.

Dance artists in Canada have also participated in this phenomenon. Most notably, scandal resulted in 1980 when Québécoise choreographer and dancer Marie

Chouinard performed her two-minute *La petite danse sans nom* at the Art Gallery of Ontario. Chouinard paced the stage in a beautiful long dress while carrying an aluminum bucket, drank a glass of water, and then, as she pliéd deeply in second position over the pot, she peed and then left the stage. Some viewers found the absurdity of the moment amusing: it is physiologically impossible for water to travel so quickly through a person's body. The ridiculousness was augmented by Chouinard's mock gravitas, which contrasted with the augustness of the AGO. Chouinard's performance of this usually private act—amplified and emphasized by the noisiness of the stream of urine falling into a metal pail—apparently was offensive to some audience members. Chouinard was banned from the AGO. As dance scholar Iro Tembeck later noted, the significance of this infamous event extended beyond the artistic to underscore differences in senses of humour and decorum in French and English Canada. For more information, see Iro Tembeck, "Dancing in Montreal: Seeds of a Choreographic History," *Studies in Dance History* 5, no. 2 (Fall 1994): 101–2.

11 For example, see Susanne Franco, "Reenacting Heritage at Bomas of Kenya: Dancing the Postcolony," *Dance Research Journal* 47, no. 2 (August 2015): 3–22. See also, Tone Erlien, "Methods of Disseminating Dance in European Museums," *Acta Ethnographica Hungarica* 60, no. 1 (2015): 93–101. Santee Smith's *Kaha:wi*, which was performed at the National Museum of the American Indian, is one case study that offers a defiantly Indigenous perspective that celebrates a First Nations' worldview. The production prompted dance scholar Jacqueline Shea Murphy to write, "*Kaha:wi*, as a Haudenosaunee dance presented in a museum theater, uses the tools of dance—movement vocabulary, spatial orientations, narrative, bodies trained and attuned to physical ways of knowing—to shift understandings of what constitutes knowledge production and collection." Jacqueline Shea Murphy, "Mobilizing (in) the Archive: Santee Smith's *Kaha:wi*," in *Worlding Dance*, ed. Susan Leigh Foster (Basingstoke: Palgrave Macmillan, 2009), 32–52 at 38.

12 For instance, see Helen Rees Leahy, *Museum Bodies* (Farnham, Surrey: Ashgate, 2012). See also, Heidi Overhill, "Design as Choreography: Information in Action," *Curator: The Museum Journal* 58, no. 1 (January 2015): 5–15.

13 Tony Bennett, *The Birth of the Museum: History, Theory, Politics* (London: Routledge, 1995), 44; 43.

14 Similar ideas have been broached by commentators addressing the effect of dance in art museums. The brochure for the Musée de la danse at the Tate Modern asserts: "By entering the public spaces and galleries of Tate Modern, Musée de la danse dramatises questions about how art might be perceived, displayed and shared from a danced and choreographed perspective." See *If Tate Modern Was Musée de la danse?* (London: BMW Tate Live, 2015), 2. Accessed November 28, 2018, https://www.tate.org.uk/download/file/fid/48353. Dance scholar André Lepecki suggests that dance is "a practice able to provide the necessary tools for rearticulating social-political dimensions of the aesthetic." See André Lepecki, "Zones of Resonance: Mutual

Formations in Dance and the Visual Arts since the 1960s," in *Move, Choreographing You: Art and Dance since the 1960s*, ed. Stephanie Rosenthal (Manchester: Cornerhouse Publications, 2011), 155.

15 Nicholas Thomas, *Entangled Objects: Exchange, Material Culture, and Colonialism in the Pacific* (Cambridge, MA: Harvard University Press, 1991), 28.

16 Chengxin Wei, email message to author, August 6, 2015.

17 Klaas Ruitenbeek, "The Gallery of Chinese Architecture," *Orientations: The Magazine for Collectors and Connoisseurs of Asian Art*, April 2006, 52.

18 Barry Till, "A Chinese General's Tomb: Identification of the 'Ming Tomb'," *The Rotunda: The Bulletin of the ROM* 14, no. 1 (1981): 10. James Hsu states that the general died in 1654. See James Hsu, "The Ming Tomb Gallery," *The Rotunda: The Bulletin of the ROM* 16, no. 1 (1983): 22.

19 Chengxin Wei, email message to author, August 6, 2015.

20 Till, "A Chinese General's Tomb," 7.

21 Charles Trick Currelly, *I Brought the Ages Home* (Toronto: The Ryerson Press, 1956), 247.

22 George Pawlick, "The Ming Tomb: Causes of Deterioration in Stone," *The Rotunda: The Bulletin of the ROM* 11, no. 3 (1978): 30–31.

23 *Royal Ontario Museum Act, Statutes of Ontario 1912*, c. 80, s. 4(b).

24 Currelly, *I Brought the Ages Home*, 184, 245.

25 Ibid., 244.

26 Ibid., 243.

27 Lovat Dickson, *The Museum Makers: The Story of the Royal Ontario Museum* (Toronto: Royal Ontario Museum, 1986), 46.

28 Ric Knowles, *Theatre and Interculturalism* (Basingstoke, Hampshire: Palgrave Macmillan, 2010), 4–5.

29 For more biographical information about Wei and Jone, please see http://www.chinesedance.ca/index.php?option=com_content&view=category&id=2&Itemid=5&lang=en.

30 Kaija Pepper, "View from Vancouver," *Dance International* 33, no. 2 (Summer 2004): 23.

31 Chengxin Wei and Jessica Jone, interview by Allana C. Lindgren, December 18, 2014.

32 Ibid.

33 Ibid. While Wei and Jone are clear about how they characterize their own work, they are less certain about how their dance colleagues in Vancouver view their choreography. Or, as Jone notes, "In the contemporary dance scene in Vancouver, I'm not quite sure where we fit in because it's a very varied community. And so, perhaps many would consider us to still be cultural dance, instead of contemporary dance."

34 Ibid.

35 Ibid.

36 Ibid.

37 Ibid.

38 This example demonstrates an intersectional shift from a binary understanding of identity to the kind of relational thinking explored in Patricia Hill Collins and Sirma Bilge, *Intersectionality* (Cambridge: Polity Press, 2016).

39 In this way, *Koong* resonates with the imbrication of classical Japanese dance, traditional folk dance, and contemporary choreography and training that Lisa Doolittle explores in her chapter in this collection. When read in tandem, this examination of *Koong* and Doolittle's chapter invite the reader to consider how the past and present concurrently exert influence on dancing bodies.

40 Christopher Jones, "ROM Artifacts Inspire Museum Dances," *TO Live with Culture*, accessed October 7, 2015, http://www.livewithculture.ca/dance/rom-artifacts-inspire-canasian-museum-dances/. [In possession of the author.]

41 Ibid.

42 Ibid.

43 Pawlick, "The Ming Tomb," 31.

44 Dennis Duffy, "Triangulating the ROM," *Journal of Canadian Studies* 40, no. 1 (Winter 2006): 174.

45 Wei and Jone, interview.

46 Clare Bishop, "The Perils and Possibilities of Dance in the Museum: Tate, MoMA, and Whitney," *Dance Research Journal* 46, no. 3 (December 2014): 72.

47 Chengxin Wei, email message to author, August 6, 2015.

TEN

KINETIC CROSSROADS

CHOUINARD, SINHA, AND CASTELLO*

Dena Davida

"We need an unlimited view of beauty that encompasses all of human experience."

—Deepti Gupta, choreographer

LIKE SO MANY DENSE URBAN CENTRES THESE DAYS, IN 1994 Montréal is fostering a new group of dance interculturalists. We occidental choreographers have long drawn inspiration from dance traditions other than our own. In the history of Euro-American Modern Dance, for instance, borrowing from abroad usually took on the character of reverent homage to an imagined "primitive" past, or even romantic musings about exotica from distant lands. But the recent political climate has begun to position our classical and contemporary dances on more equal footing, in terms of sophistication and cultural value, with the larger world of dances.

* Initially published as "*Croisements cinétiques: Marie Chouinard, Roger Sinha et Maria Castello.*" *Les cahiers de théâtre* JEU 72.3 (1994): 83-90 in a French translation by Michel Vaïs.

Now we only need travel a few métro stops to find dances from virtually everywhere. This proximity has encouraged an intermingling between the dominant contemporary dance, and especially its creed of experimentation, with traditional dance forms that have become strongly rooted in Québec (certain Spanish, African, South American, and East Indian dances, for example). The current interculturalist practice is still limited to a small group of Montréal choreographers—but the basis for exchange has changed completely. It is now common for contemporary dancers to study another culture or style of dance in depth, as if acquiring a second language in which to communicate. As for choreographers from other dance traditions who have more recently immigrated, it may be the ethos of artistic freedom that has compelled them to invent dances that represent their present-day lives in Montréal.

MARIE CHOUINARD: MOVING TOWARDS A TRANSCULTURAL DANCE

The curtain opens at Place des Arts on Marie Chouinard's tribal ode *Trous de ciel*. This is Montréal's mecca for the theatrical dance avant-garde, the Festival international de nouvelle danse, of which I was co-founder, in September 1992.

Seven dancers are aligned shoulder-to-shoulder in a deep squat à la seconde with hands joined above their heads in a triangular configuration. Their torsos are wrapped in loose-fitting beige bodysuits knotted at the pubis; wild hair tumbles from scalps and armpits; light glints off metallic bits of teeth and eyelids. The dance begins with a percussive, collective "ah!" from the dancers, amplified by sophisticated wireless microphones attached to their skulls like vestigial jawbones. A symbolic sun is rising on the upstage cyclorama.

Is this a fictional allegory from the past or a speculative future? We know (from the program notes) that the narrative framework is inspired by an Inuit folk tale from Chouinard's northern travels. She has always struck me as a kind of choreographic archaeologist, cataloguing ancient actions from around the world by excavating deep into the "soul, spirit and organic aspect of the body," as she has put it, in search of a kinetic collective unconscious.[1] Each new dancer becomes a site for spiritual discovery.

The dance progresses as if it is an urgent ritual, the dancers enacting a series of inevitable and cathartic events in the life of a fictional community.

Figure 10.1. Les trous du ciel (1991). Choreography by Marie Chouinard. Dancers (from left to right): Marie Josée Paradis, Daniel Éthier, Andrew Harwood, Dominique Porte, and Heather Mah. Photograph by Cylla Von Tiedemann.

Embedded in the movement phrases are images from Chouinard's journeys to Bali and Nepal, as well as glimpses of dance gestures from Spain, South America, and India. Voices and bodies act and react simultaneously as if motion and sound are inseparable, regenerated in the diaphragm. The calls and exclamations emanating from the dancers are reminiscent of a minimalist sound score for a mixed species animal chorus. Breath is expelled with a sharp sigh, the body shrinks and condenses; a percussive "ping!" springs the spine into extension, jerking limbs upwards. A bird-like strut incorporates the sinuous rising hands of Flamenco and later the outstretched arms of Bharatanatyam. This fantastic flock, often moving in unison, seems a curious species of wildlife that has assimilated behaviours from some of Homo sapiens sapiens' most highly refined dance forms.

Marie Chouinard is a home-grown Québécoise of French heritage, and has always been an iconoclast among her choreographic peers. She formed her first artistic alliances with performance artists in the seventies. It took nearly a decade for the dance milieu in Montréal to embrace her vision of a primal, almost pre-social, body. The style and content of her dancing fell completely outside the kind of expressionistic danse théâtre that has characterized contemporary Québec dance since the 1948 social revolution, the Refus Global.

As Chouinard dances into the Global Village, she positions herself at the centre of a heated North American debate on cultural appropriation that has particularly affected the fragile, fragmented artistic dance community in Canada. As Daryl Chin has written, "To deploy elements from the symbol system of another culture is a very delicate matter... when does that usage act as cultural imperialism?"[2]

For over a decade, I had perceived the integrative cultural mix in her work as a humanist quest for some biological common ground. And so, I was taken by surprise at the reaction of US presenters at the 1985 National Performance Network (NPN) meeting as I screened a videotaped excerpt of *Trous de ciel.* "How dare she steal an Inuit story," they raged.

In this current view of racism, artists of the majority Caucasian culture (though "white" Québécois ironically perceive themselves as a disenfranchised group within the Canadian context) are admonished not to use images from minority cultures in their artworks. This argument has arisen, I believe, in response to the changing demography of North America, and especially within its large urban centres, where repeated waves of immigrants have dramatically diversified the cultural character of society. At the epicentre of this public debate on the dynamics of power lie political questions of artistic freedom, censorship, and copyright. In terms of choreography, for instance, is it desirable or even possible for one culture (or choreographer!) to "own" a certain set of movements? Are the codes of classical ballet, modern, and postmodern dance the only allowable sources of movement inspiration for "white" Euro-American dancers? As for "non-white" creators, do they betray their cultural specificity when they reach into the "mainstream" for form and content? To what extent should a dance-maker acknowledge their sources of inspiration, however distant and subconscious? While musicians have pressed far ahead towards the concept of a world music based on a common pulsebeat, dance conservationists and innovators argue over the integrity of traditional dances as if they were endangered species (as many of them were under communist dictatorships).

The current danse d'auteur model requires that each choreographer reinvent the dance by devising an original, coherent choreographic universe.[3] As transnationalism increases and questions of culture push further into centre stage, a multitude of dance forms and styles is capturing the artistic imagination; and I wonder if the breakdown of stylistic purity is a natural outcome of the project of modern and postmodern dancers to free the body from rigidified classical codes. The 1948 Refus Global manifesto from Québec's mid-century révolution tranquille, a sociopolitical movement that determined to define the character of Québécois society, contained a key declaration of the local automatiste artistic ethos from choreographer Françoise Sullivan: "Above all the dance is a reflex, a spontaneous and vividly felt emotion." And in 1972, Yvonne Rainer declared all movements of equal interest to dancers in her American minimalist dance *Trio A*. Do we really want to create an e(s)th(et)ic of racial segregation in the dance studio?

ROGER SINHA: CHOREOGRAPHING RACISM

When Roger Sinha created his autobiographical solo *Burning Skin* in 1991, he presented Montréal's first dance essay on racism. This seasoned dancer describes himself as an Indo-Armenian-Canadian. His physical skills include the mastery of several modern dance styles, karate (black belt), and Bharatanatyam, which he fuses into a single movement style.

It is March, 1992. The *Ascendanse* series is occurring at Espace Tangente, for which I am the Artistic Director, a platform for contemporary dances influenced by traditional practices. The narrow stage can barely contain Sinha's explosive energy. At the core of his dance lies a childhood story of a Black boy who plunged into boiling water believing it would bleach him white. Sinha enters the stage like a whirlwind, extending the elegant Indian mudras into

stabbing and slashing motions. Into the mix he adds a voluminous red robe and trailing headdress. His body sweeps through space and freely recombines the traditional gestures, playing with variations on pathways and dynamic phrasing. At some point, this prelude becomes a karate-tinged parody of classical ballet clichés and we leap literally into the Western colonialist world.

Next comes a prim but messy parody of English high tea. As an oval constellation of electric teakettles begin to boil, Sinha steps into the steaming halo, assuming the well-known Krishna pose. Boiling water is poured into a pan with ritualistic care. More dancing ensues as Sinha strips down to black pleated pants and a naked torso. He begins a monologue—memories of racial incidents from grade school—as he retrieves a hot wet shirt and tie out of the boiling water and pulls them painfully onto his bare skin. An electric guitarist accentuates the increasing agitation. The performance art finale is raw and disturbing.

Sinha was born and raised in a cultural mixture of East Indian, Armenian, British, and English-Canadian identities. He entered directly and deliberately into the mainstream of Montréal nouvelle danse several years ago, quickly gaining recognition for his athletic dancing. His fiery temperament proved well suited to the expressionistic aesthetic of the Québécois dance community. While continuing to dance, he began creating choreographic studies.

His first impulses remained within the occidental conventions of contemporary dance. Then one day, a kind of cultural autobiography called *Burning Skin,* described above, emerged from his psyche to become a signature piece. Into this intense self-portrait Sinha reinvested his interest in text, symbolic objects, athleticism, and psychodrama. This potent mix has already won him invitations to perform at both contemporary arts venues in the Occident and dance festivals in India.

There appear to be literally hundreds of artists in North America working in this mixed genre. The politics of marginalization, living in diaspora, cultural fusion, ethnic and sexual identity have become favoured content, and the talking dancer[4] a familiar performance form. But *Burning Skin* is still a curiosity in Montréal where contemporary dancers have narrowly focused for more than fifty years on constructing a distinctly Québécois dance identity. Apart from its emotional intensity, Sinha's piece cannot be placed inside what French

OPPOSITE: *Figure 10.2.* Choreographer and dancer Roger Sinha performing his autobiographical solo *Burning Skin* in 1991 at Tangente in Montréal. Photograph by Steven Hues.

dance philosopher Laurence Louppe has reverently identified as the "Québec school of contemporary dance."[5] An interesting historical note: la nouvelle danse québécoise, like the "new dance" (postmodern) styles in other occidental countries, can itself be considered as arising out of the intercultural ferment of both the American and Central European strains of early Modern Dance, which included a flirtation with Asian cultures.

Sinha is also an anomaly for many of his traditionalist Indian colleagues. I attended a gathering of this international dance community in Toronto in 1993, the Kalanidhi Festival and conference, *New Directions in Indian Dance*. It soon became clear that this highly educated group of dance practitioners was deeply divided over the issue of preservation vs. innovation, as if the two were mutually exclusive. Most first-generation immigrants (to Canada and elsewhere) seem to be teaching their children with missionary reverence, trying to keep the cultural memory alive for future generations of Indo-Canadians. Others were engaged in adapting their dances in an effort to gain knowledge and support from their new fellow citizens. And some have been seized by the freedom to experiment, as Toronto choreographer Menaka Thakkar suggested, to be creative and to play with the dance. So the performance of *Burning Skin* was perceived by one side as taking outrageous liberties with classical form, and for the other (often younger) Indian dancers, Sinha was a model of success. So far, Sinha seems to be flourishing inside his multiple cultural identities, which he pulls firmly together into the single vocational identity of choreographer.

MARIA CASTELLO: THE MEETING OF NORTHERN AND SOUTHERN BODIES

Montréaler Maria Castello, born and raised in Argentina, created a minor disturbance among local choreographers at the *Ascendanse* series last year when she wove Latin-American folk dances and North American modern dance aesthetics into a series of tableaux drawn from legends. While the public-at-large and the local Latin community loved it, "serious" contemporary choreographers bemoaned its folkloric character in the context of a professional dance theatre.

In our various cultural ministries in Canada and Québec, we cling to our notion of the "professional" artist as criteria for providing state support. We still maintain our cherished high art/low art paradigm like some kind of artistic class system. Most folk dancers here do not yet fall within the model of the full-time vocational artist, and folk dancing is generally considered a recreational activity. This has recently caused confusion at the Canada Council for the Arts, as the Dance Office begins to open its doors to "all forms of professional dancing," inclusive of First Nations dancers. These dancers, of course, have very different aesthetic criteria than the Council had ever before encountered.

There is no doubt that Castello is treading on unfamiliar ground, for Montréalers at least, as she navigates choreographic compositions that lie between popular and high art dancing. For Castello, this process is intuitive. Her body has assimilated every kind of dancing with which it has come into contact, from ballroom to Bartenieff Fundamentals. She also takes particular delight in the movement possibilities of musicians as they play, as well as those of non-dancers.

Salgo a caminar was the result of a commission proposed to Castello by the contemporary dance presenter Tangente and Baru, a Panamanian dance association in Montréal with a pan-Latin mandate. Castello was the likely Montréal artist to bridge the two dance communities. Her first challenge was to gain the confidence of her folkdance-trained dancers who began rehearsals with trepidation ("Modern dance? Isn't that where everyone gets naked and has water thrown on them?"). Once a stable group was established, she began searching for a style and structure that could sustain her interest in weaving together the common threads of disparate dances from Latin-American cultures. The final choreography is reminiscent, to my mind, of the Caribbean-infused modern dances of US dance-maker Katherine Dunham. But Castello was born more than half a century later and has the postmodernist's love for collage and pastiche, creating a choreographic territory where unlikely dance combinations and fusions can coexist.

For *Salgo a caminar*, the black box stage becomes illuminated with a panorama of danced legends and myths, pulled together through seamless transitions as if a single continuing story. One movement motif seems to run throughout, which is the alteration between sensual pulsating motions and sharply percussive thrusting actions.

The story begins with a gyrating woman in a full skirt surrounded by four Indigenous men beating time in unison.[6] Ceremonial hopping, stamping, and spinning patterns accelerate. The dancers finally collapse, and into the tranquil

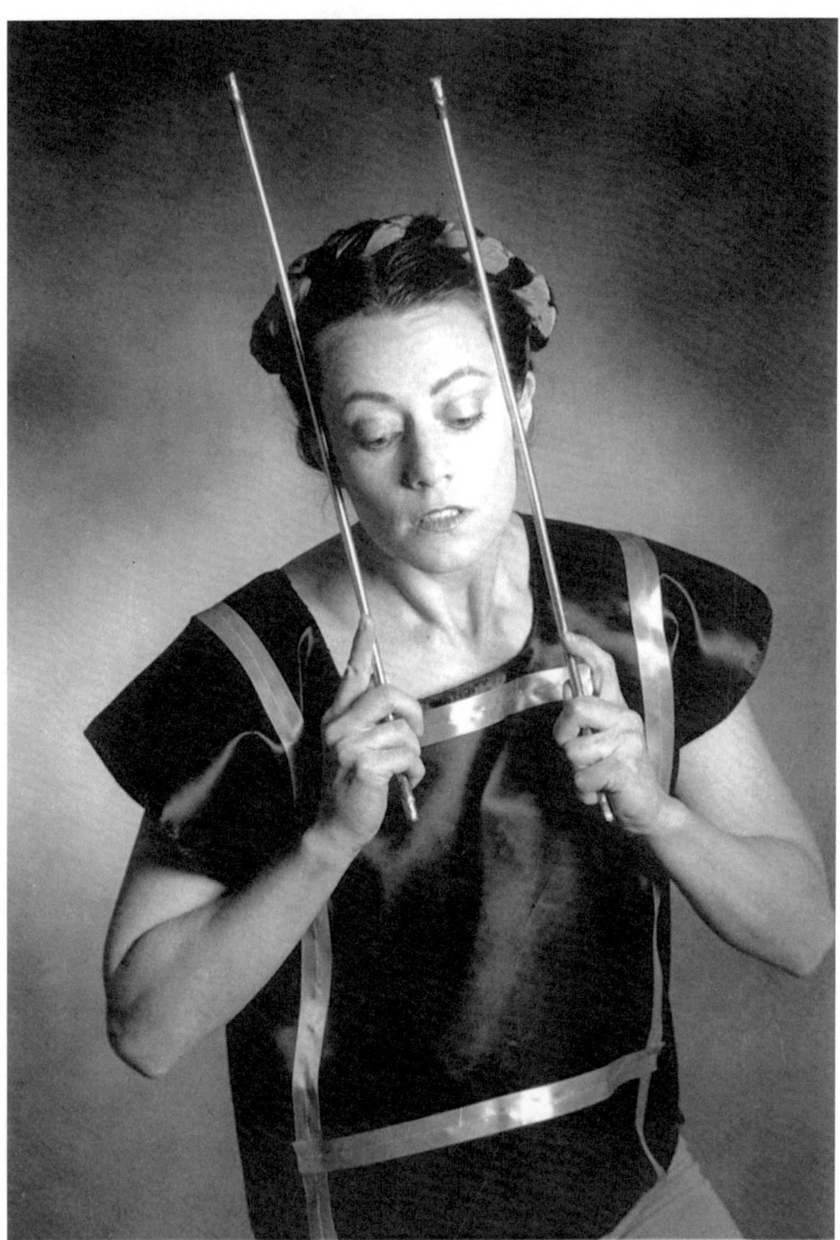

Figure 10.3. Choreographer and dancer Maria Castello performing a solo from her group work *Xóchitl*, presented in Montréal within Tangente's *Ascendance* series in 1993. Photograph by Alain Comtois.

landscape two percussionists enter and energize the choreography with bravura drum-and-foot beating. A wonderful male solo of swooping and diving phrases ensues: a prelude to a flirtatious sextet. Three women are spun onstage as they are unwound, by male partners, from trailing blue sarongs that stream behind them like waves. The effect lies somewhere between the organic beauty of art nouveau and the ebb-and-flow of contact improvisation. Castello (who also dances in her piece) then develops a spiralling contact duet in a playful "you catch me and I'll catch you" structure; and a second couple recreates a social dance of seduction through a dialogue of pulsating hips. A sparring male duo, inspired by contact improvisation, completes this ritualistic courtship section. The last series of tableaux begins with Castello's solo inspired by Mexican artist Frida Kahlo. She distills the tragic biography into a series of symbolic phrases, while her folkdance skirt transforms into mantilla and shroud. Stripped down to a body suit garnished with two metallic sticks, she becomes the hunted deer in one of Latin America's most popular legends. The finale is the iconic dance of death, which Castello has choreographed as an ominous hooded quintet.

At the end of the forty dense minutes of *Salgo a caminar*, I had the sense of having experienced an abridged survey of Latin themes and dance styles as viewed by a contemporary choreographer-cum-anthropologist. With a humanistic outlook, much like that of Chouinard, Castello is also seeking the ties that bind—in this case, those of her Latin-American compatriots. As a neo-Québécoise, she is not fearful of cultural assimilation and remains self-assured in the face of her hybrid acculturation. Much like other "multi-choreographic" dancers (who have mastered several dance forms and styles), at the core of her research lies the belief in a trans-dance essence that grounds her practice and gives her a clear sense of choreographic mission. It is this sensing of an essence that appears to allow traditional dancers here to venture out into contemporary experimentation with no sense of losing their past. In works like Salgo a caminar, tradition and innovation not only coexist but even fuse into a single purpose.

A NEW EPILOGUE: RETHINKING "KINETIC CROSSROADS" (2018)

With the invitation to contribute this essay to a new anthology twenty-five years after its inception, there is the rare opportunity to think through this set of ideas within current-day debates, and also to finally compose the conclusion that was never written. I have left the original text above intact as a vintage artifact of the 1990s, imposing only the light copy editing, which I had never done, for the English version was conceived as an informal conference paper.

Much has changed here since 1994. Montréal is now replete with intercultural choreographers. The combining and modernizing of dance forms and styles have become predominant, and these staged performances sourced in folk, street, and traditional dances are now (almost) fully embraced by audiences, critics, and funding bodies. A large number of choreographers have adopted dances from cultures other than their own as their life's work, dedicating themselves to deep and sustained study even as traditional dancers emigrating from abroad have embraced the freedoms of open-ended aesthetic experimentation in the local contemporary dance community.

At the 1996 conference of the Congress on Research in Dance (now the Dance Studies Association) in Ohio, we discussed deeply and intensely how and where we might move beyond questions of authenticity and appropriation in the dance world (the conference's overarching theme). It is interesting to note, as I have discovered through curatorial conversations with artists, that the imperative to be authentic, to representing one's "true inner self," is quite prominent at the moment in the discourse of Montréal choreographers. At the same time, the interest of combining ideas and materials from disparate geographies and cultures that characterizes postmodern art has completely transformed dance training and choreography into hybrid practices. Even our identities are now considered as complex combinations of the biological characteristics we have inherited and the beliefs of the social and cultural groups to which we choose to belong.

In this age of postcolonialist aspirations, one of the compelling central questions in so many democratic countries is how we might decolonize our worldviews, communities, and institutions to better promote diversity and democratization, and so to give agency to the disenfranchised. It is, as always, a matter of the dynamics of power. In a 2018 critique of the *Mobile Worlds* exhibit curated by Roger M. Buergel in the Museum für Kunst und Gewerbe, Jason Farago presses the debate yet further when he declares, "It's not enough just to call for 'decolonization,' a recent watchword in European museum studies; the whole fiction of cultural purity has to go, too."[7] In Montréal, the concept of cultural appropriation continues to be debated in the heated discussions currently pervading our dance community. But from all evidence there is one thing, I believe, that remains certain: choreographers will continue to make their work at "kinetic crossroads" by way of mixing and recombining, borrowing and transferring, translating and transforming the various forms, ideas, and phenomena that surround them as they move, ever so expressively, through the globalizing village.

NOTES

1 This is a paraphrase inspired by the text in the catalogue of the 1992 Festival international de nouvelle danse. See Chantal Pontbriand, "Marie Chouinard," in *Festival international de nouvelle danse* (Montréal: Éditions Parachute), 50–53.

2 Daryl Chin, "Interculturalism, Postmodernism, Pluralism," in *Interculturalism and Performance: Writings from PAJ*, eds. Bonnie Marranca and Gautam Dasgupta (New York: PAJ Publications, 1991), 94.

3 The source and character of this European concept was clarified for the author an article by Leonetta Bentivoglio, "Danse d'auteur." *Ballet International/Tanz Aktuell* 12, no. 4 (April 1989): 16–20.

4 Lucy Lippard used "talking dancer" to describe this kind of performer, and she elaborated a vivid critique of the intercultural phenomenon in the US in *Mixed Blessings: New Art in a Multicultural America* (New York: Pantheon Books, 1990).

5 Laurence Louppe, "Québec New Dance," program for the *Festival international de nouvelle danse* (Montréal, QC: Éditions Parachute, 1992).

6 The vintage edition of the essay read "native." Standardized to "Indigenous" for this anthology.

7 Jason Farago, "A New Type of Museum for an Age of Migration," *New York Times*, July 11, 2018.

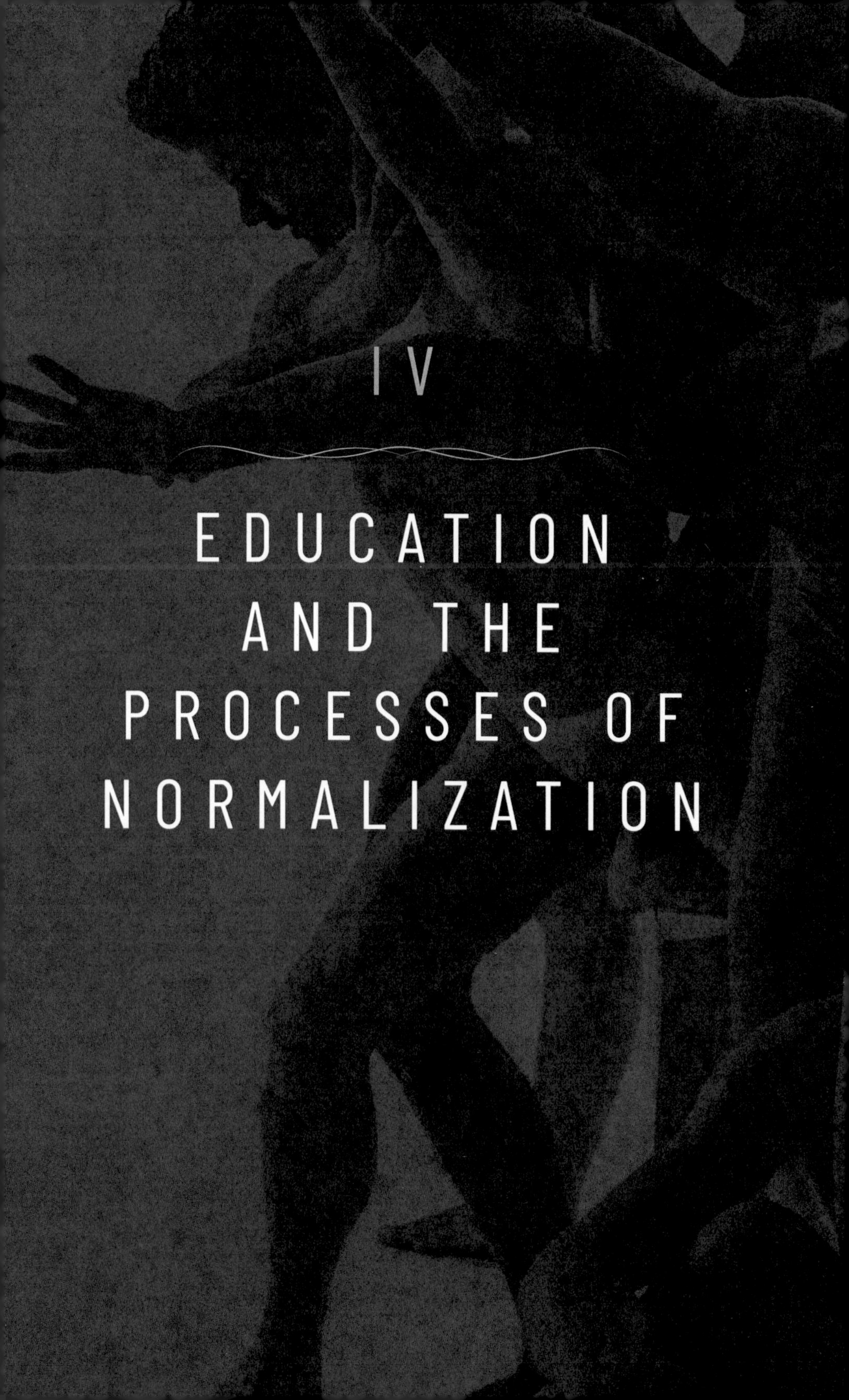

IV

EDUCATION AND THE PROCESSES OF NORMALIZATION

ELEVEN

FROM INCLUSION TO INTEGRATION

INTERCULTURAL DIALOGUE AND CONTEMPORARY UNIVERSITY DANCE EDUCATION[1*]

Danielle Robinson and Eloisa Domenici

THE IDEAS PRESENTED HERE GREW OUT OF A DIALOGUE BETWEEN two dance professors working in different hemispheres who share similar questions about university dance education. Although we were from geographically distant worlds, we quickly found that we struggled in similar ways with diversity issues in each of our modern dance-focused programs;[2] and so began an ongoing conversation about the causes of the marginality of Other dance forms within our institutions—and others like them, since our programs are not unusual—and possible strategies for their integration

* Reprinted with permission from Danielle Robinson and Eloisa Domenici, "From Inclusion to Integration: Intercultural Dialogue and Contemporary University Dance Education," *Research in Dance Education*, 11, no. 3 (2010): 213–21, doi: 10.1080/14647893.2010.527324.

into curricula. Not surprisingly, we soon discovered long-standing boundaries between so-called high and low art as well as the West and the rest, and we realized that this was only the beginning of our challenges. Eurocentrism emerged as the chief obstacle keeping diverse dance forms outside of universities.

We are not the first dance scholars to grapple with these issues. Peggy Schwartz and Judith Lynne Hanna have discussed the importance of diversifying dance curricula, while Naima Prevots, Suzan Moss, and Pegge Vissicaro have written about specific classes that they were able to re-vision in more culturally diverse ways.[3] In particular, over the past few decades much attention has been given to ways in which African-influenced concert dance forms can be included within our conceptualization of Western theatrical dance.[4] No one, to our knowledge, though, has written about *how* we might go about updating our university dance departments at the level of curriculum in a practical way. This is the challenge we have taken up in this chapter.

Despite the self-proclaimed multiculturalism of the locations of our programs in Canada and Brazil, neither has found a way to adequately *integrate* Other dance forms.[5] For us, "integration" refers to much more than the simple inclusion of a new dance technique class here and there. Rather, it refers to the interweaving of different dance forms at all levels of the dance curriculum—including technique, composition, pedagogy, and history. Here we draw on the ideas of educational theorist James Banks, whose notion of "content integration" stresses that teachers should aim to move beyond the mere inclusion of diverse "cultural" perspectives towards a more "transformational" approach that consistently draws upon multiple perspectives in order to illustrate core curricular concepts.[6]

By discussing the ideological foundations of existing university dance programs, we seek to imagine a more inclusive vision for dance education in our increasingly globalized local contexts. We argue that *contemporary* dance education must be rooted in an intercultural dialogue—a method we discovered through our own research and teaching collaborations. For us, the word "intercultural" emphasizes the relationships between cultures and goes beyond the mere inclusion implied by the word "multicultural."

To begin, we articulate what we consider to be the enduring modern dance myths that implicitly guide our decisions within university dance programs. Then we explain the protective justifications that we have seen frequently offered in defence of the Western focus of dance programs when they are faced with occasional criticisms. Finally, we discuss the three powerful assumptions about ourselves, our students, and the history of dance in education that often permeate discussions of multiculturalism and interculturalism in dance departments and at dance conferences. All of these ideas quietly undergird and protect the centrism of European and Euro-American values within academic dance programs. As a result, they have likely led to the exclusion of other dance forms, perhaps without that being an explicit intention. In the final section of this chapter, we discuss the model for intercultural dance education that we have developed together in the course of our own multiyear conversation across hemispheres.

ENDURING MODERN DANCE MYTHS

1. *Modern dance is a lingua franca, a universal language understandable within all cultures.* This myth is related in some ways to the often-abstract nature of modern dance technique and ignores the cultural specificity of all languages—bodily or otherwise. It is also related to the vision of several modern dance pioneers, like Martha Graham, who explored what they thought were universals through their choreography.[7]

2. *Modern dance is at the centre of our programs because it is the best, most complex, and intelligent dance form.* This self-perpetuating myth disseminates the idea that "ethnic dance" is suitable for entertainment but not for the serious training of dancers. It is supported by the fact that most of the scholarly literature on dance this century has focused on modern dance—its analysis, composition, and history. Given that modern dance has been cultivated within university environs since the 1920s, it is true that its discourses are exceptionally well-suited for academia, which renders it the most intelligible[8] practice at this time.[9]

3. *If modern dance is no longer at the centre of our programs, then they will lack cohesion and necessarily fall apart.* Many people find comfort in unity, control, and linearity, but that doesn't mean these features produce the best-prepared students. We further suggest that

single-centred programs provide only the illusion of control, because faculty and students alike come from diverse dance backgrounds, of which they must divest themselves as part of their conversion to modern dance. Alternatively, dance programs could respect and value difference and thus be powerfully united by their shared commitment to global dance studies, not just one kind of dance.

PROTECTIVE JUSTIFICATIONS FOR EUROCENTRIC DANCE PROGRAMS

1. *The inclusion of non-Western forms as part of the core curriculum is a rejection of the European and European-influenced practices that were formerly at the centre.*[10] This justification assumes a hegemonic model in which a single practice must always be at the centre and elevated above the rest. Decentring may feel like rejection to those formerly in power, but it really means sharing the stage with Others as equals.[11]

2. *Students should only study one technique in order to become well trained.*[12] This justification begs the question, are we training or educating dancers within academia? Owing to its fostering of skills in comparative analysis, deep training in more than one practice (or "cross-training," to borrow a Nike term) improves students' abilities in criticism, creation, teaching, and performance—not to mention their ability to engage in cross-cultural work.[13]

3. *The simple inclusion of different dance practices is enough.* Inclusion is not integration, and as a form of ghettoization, it can reinforce the marginalization of non-modern dance. Instead, integration[14] has to do with creating connections, exploring combinations, and comparing the internal logics of different dance forms.

4. *The incorporation of a new dance practice must lead to the loss of an existing one.* This zero-sum game turns integration into an overly dramatic tragedy in which a much-beloved teacher or practice has to be removed from the program.[15] Transformation of any academic program

is decades in the making and requires careful strategizing about new hires (in terms of desired background, expertise, training, and/or breadth of knowledge) as well as expanding the horizons of existing faculty. Such hiring will necessitate us self-consciously and bravely moving outside our comfort zone of familiarity, however. It is crucial to remember that we have much to gain, not lose, in re-visioning our programs. First and foremost, we have an opportunity to no longer be among the whitest departments on our campuses—both in terms of faculty and student demographics.

POWERFUL ASSUMPTIONS THAT PREVENT INTERCULTURALISM IN DANCE EDUCATION

1. *Students want a modern dance-focused education, and that is what they need in order to succeed professionally.* A recent internal survey at York, one of the largest dance departments in North America, showed that over 50 percent of students wanted to know more about and have more experiences with dance forms besides modern. In addition, dance scenes worldwide are now tremendously diverse. Cross-cultural collaborations between artists are common. As educators, we have a responsibility to prepare our students to work in this world, not in a homogeneous dance profession that doesn't exist.

2. *There is nothing else the faculty can teach besides modern dance, its theories, composition, and history.* In other words, we are limited to the strengths of existing faculty members—as if we never hire new faculty, accept talented graduate students with a wide range of abilities, or have the ability to learn after leaving graduate school. Interculturalism can begin with just an openness to learning about new forms of dance and grow from there.

3. *Our programs were always centred on modern dance and must stay this way in order to be true to our history.* Interestingly enough, before modern dance took over in the 1920s, the first academic dance programs included folk and ballroom dance.[16] Furthermore, modern

> dance's pioneering choreographers were inspired by and appropriated from African, Indigenous, and Asian cultures.[17] Appropriation is not the same as collaboration, of course, the latter of which is the ideal; nonetheless, if we do need to be true to our histories, then we should embrace our pioneers' cross-cultural intention to embrace different dance forms.

Clearly, the issues we have brought forward are not just dance issues. These myths, justifications, and assumptions are the epistemological foundations of many departments and universities; just replace "modern dance" with "Western classical music" or "English literature," for example. In fact, it might be wise for dance departments to look at how other disciplines, such as music, have dealt with these issues, both successfully and unsuccessfully, as we endeavour to make our programs more contemporary than modern in scope.[18]

Fears of the Other as well as of our own obsolescence can fuel strong reactions to these issues as they continue to emerge and re-emerge in educational settings and beyond. Cultural theorist John Jervis has argued that the Western fear of the Other is rooted in modernity's strategies of exclusion. He writes,

> [a] lot of the dynamism of modernity, its drive as a form of life, has derived from the ability to image and denigrate what is set up as contrast, even as this contrast is thereby constituted as internal to modernity itself, as an image of its own unacceptable face.[19]

Perhaps, in a similar fashion, "modern" dance as a concept is dependent on hierarchical relationships between the West and its cultural Others. The presence and power of cultural difference, however, will only increase in the future. If we don't quickly find a way to move beyond Western-focused models, the education we offer students *will* become increasingly irrelevant and obsolete.

Here, we hope to move beyond ideology and offer concrete suggestions that might help dance programs end their implied Eurocentrism, which excludes or marginalizes difference, and also beyond naive multiculturalism, which tends to entail the simple inclusion of difference. We are proposing a polycentric model that is rooted in the principle of *dialogue*. We want to reimagine hierarchical structures, invest in polycentric curricula, and search for more democratic and respectful ways of educating our students that draw upon and expand their expertise. One of our inspirations in this regard has been Brazilian educational theorist Paulo Freire,[20] whose work on critical pedagogy has revolutionized contemporary educational practices by insisting teachers account for and directly address the power dynamics operating implicitly within classrooms and curricula. He suggests that a "dialogic" approach is crucial to undoing the oppression inherent in the "banking system" of education, which renders learners passive receptacles of knowledge. For Freire, dialogue establishes respectful exchange, facilitates discovery, and enables transformation—for students and teachers alike.

BUILDING INTERCULTURAL DANCE PROGRAMS

Intercultural dance programs will look different in each instance because of the influence of local epistemologies and histories as well as departmental priorities and resources. For example, in "multiculturalist" Canada, our challenge is to work towards greater cross-cultural integration and to experiment more with cultural mixture.[21] In "mestizo" Brazil, on the other hand, cultural mixing is long established.[22] In both countries, however, we need to pay attention to the sociopolitical contexts of mixing.

No matter where it is located, an intercultural dance program would provide deep training in multiple techniques, and not just theatrical ones. Cross-cultural technique classes could be complemented by the study of multiple culturally specific creation strategies that would enable students to locate the theoretical underpinnings of the practices.[23] Creation labs might provide students with opportunities to experiment with the development of cross-cultural composition and improvisation practices as well as engage in comparative analysis. For instance, modern dance and Bharatanatyam's compositional strategies could be taught alongside contact improvisation and samba's improvisational strategies—such a class will likely need to be team-taught or incorporate guest artists to be most effective.

Studies classes would present dance as an intertwining of histories and cultures. They could discuss primarily the techniques taught within the curriculum and provide broader themes through which to understand them.[24] If possible, the technical training with which students walk into our programs should be included in such classes as a way of validating and engaging their backgrounds in dance.[25] Attention would be given, in such courses, to creation strategies and points of cross-cultural influence, with particular focus on histories of appropriation. Western dance traditions, along with Asian and African diasporic dance traditions, should be put in dialogue, with rich connections being made within a particular moment in time: between ragtime, Isadora Duncan, Rukmini Devi, and Eleo Pomare; or mambo, Katherine Dunham, Kazuo Ohno, and Martha Graham, for example. Ideally, Indigenous dance practices, local to the program, would be integrated as well.

In terms of performance opportunities, student performance groups should not be segregated by genre. If this were necessary, the department would need to support the different performance groups equally and present their work in appropriate settings. For example, a traditional Ghanaian performance group might be better suited to a theatre-in-the-round situation, whereas a traditional ballet group would need a proscenium setting. Guest artists, who are already working between cultures, perhaps in both popular and theatrical forms, should be invited to teach and talk about their professional and creative practices as well as set choreography on students. In short, we need to let the diverse world of professional dance-making into our programs in profound ways.

Finally, and perhaps most importantly, ongoing critical discussions within the studio and classroom should be generated around the cultural and political nature of all dance, as well as its potential to engender relationships between cultures. Comparisons between dance forms should remain analytical and interpretive, but not judgmental. Even if a dance program's curriculum was redesigned to be more intercultural, if faculty members continue to talk about dance in a universalizing and Eurocentric way, students will learn that limited point of view and not receive all the benefits of a contemporary dance education.[26]

Surprisingly, such programs do not necessarily cost more than traditional modern-focused dance programs. Interculturalism is about strategic choices, more so than simple additions—it is a long-term project that is worked towards gradually and deliberately, guided by a shared departmental vision. The university dance programs that have been among the most successful in implementing an intercultural approach thus far—University of Surrey in Guildford, University of Hawai'i at Manoa, and Arizona State University in Tempe—have actually been small and at public institutions, where financial restrictions can be felt more deeply than at private ones. Money is not a legitimate reason to let our programs remain segregated.

CONCLUSIONS

In these ways, our intercultural dance programs would adapt the art-based conservatory model that has fostered and protected modern dance since its inception, rendering our programs truly contemporary, no longer modern, and more connected to the rest of academia and our diverse communities and dance scenes. The conservatory model dedicated to the formation of professional dancers already exists and thrives. University dance programs, on the other hand, need to prepare students for a variety of professions; for this reason, they cannot and should not focus exclusively on technical training and performance, especially in just one technique.

All dance forms have something to offer our students. For example, ragtime dance could teach methods for rhythmic play; hip-hop teaches impulse and acrobatic virtuosity; samba can teach students about dynamic equilibrium and instability; and capoeira teaches exciting ways of relating to music as well as inversion strategies. At the same time, modern dance has much to offer students of other dance forms through its use of embodied abstraction and theatrically oriented choreographic practices.

Intercultural dialogue is the goal as well as the means of achieving it. It will enable us to dismantle the hierarchies that segregate dance practices within university dance education and within our students' minds. Yet, nothing less than a total epistemological shift is needed for interculturalism to be possible, which we recognize takes time, commitment, and teamwork—as well as a bit of fearlessness.

ACKNOWLEDGEMENTS

The authors would like to express gratitude to York graduate student Jennifer Taylor for her meticulous research assistance, ethnomusicologist Jeff Packman for his unparalleled scholarly generosity, and, most importantly, our students and former teachers for their ongoing inspiration.

NOTES

1 This chapter first came into being as a bilingual, joint conference presentation in 2007. Since then it was translated, adapted, revised, and shortened by the first author, initially for journal publication and now for this collection with the second author's permission. For this reason, the first author has retained the use of "we" to indicate the collaborative process that generated the ideas in this chapter.

2 The authors use the term "modern" here deliberately in order to emphasize an older model for conceptualizing dance, so that later in the chapter they can suggest "contemporary" as a term that might be strategically used to signal a more inclusive model. Although some programs in Europe and North America have begun to use the term "contemporary" to describe the dancing they teach, in most cases the dancing is modern in origin and not necessarily aimed towards an inclusive approach. Thus, describing these programs as "modern" works best within the framework of this chapter.

3 Peggy Schwartz, "Multicultural Dance Education in Today's Curriculum," *Journal of Physical Education, Recreation and Dance* 62, no. 2 (1991): 45–48; Judith Lynne Hanna, *Partnering Dance and Education: Intelligent Moves for Changing Times* (Champaign, IL: Human Kinetics, 1999); Naima Prevots, "The Role of Dance in Multicultural Education," *Journal of Physical Education, Recreation and Dance* 62, no. 2 (1991): 34–35, 48; Suzan Moss, "Learning from Latina Students: Modern Dance Meets Salsa and Merengue," *Journal of Physical Education, Recreation and Dance* 71, no. 3 (2000): 39–42; Pegge Vissicaro, *Studying Dance Cultures around the World* (Dubuque, IA: Kendall/Hunt, 2004).

4 Thomas DeFrantz, ed., *Dancing Many Drums: Excavations in African American Dance* (Madison, WI: University of Wisconsin Press, 2002); Brenda Dixon Gottschild, *Digging the Africanist Presence in American Performance* (Westport, CT: Praeger, 1998); Karen W. Hubbard, "Ethnic Dance, the Origins of Jazz: A Curriculum Design for Dance," *Journal of Physical Education, Recreation and Dance* 50, no. 5 (1988): 57–61; Karen W. Hubbard and Pamela A. Sofras, "Strategies for Including African and African-American Culture in an Historically Euro-Centric Dance Curriculum," *Journal of Physical Education, Recreation and Dance* 69, no. 2 (1998): 77–82; Julie Kerr-Berry, "Afrocentric Forms in 20th Century American Dance History: Transforming Course Content and the Curriculum," in *Focus on Dance XII: Dance in Higher Education*, ed. Wendy Oliver (Washington, DC: American Association for Health, Physical Education, and Recreation, 1992), 53–63; Julie Kerr-Berry, "African Dance: Enhancing the Curriculum," *Journal of Physical Education, Recreation and Dance* 65, no. 5 (1994): 25–47.

5 There are also a few dance programs that in recent years have tried to incorporate a more global perspective on dancing: University of Surrey, University of Hawai'i, UCLA's World Arts and Cultures program, Arizona State University, University of Wisconsin-Milwaukee, and UC Riverside. Some of these have been more successful than others, especially regarding the integration of multiple dance perspectives

at all levels of the curriculum, not just technique. They should all be lauded, nonetheless, for their courage, creativity, and commitment to putting into action the very principles many of us hope to teach our students: equality, diversity, cultural relativism, social justice, etc.

6 James Banks, "Multicultural Education: Historical Development, Dimensions, and Practice," in *Handbook of Research on Multicultural Education*, eds. James A. Banks and Cherry A. McKee Banks (New York: Macmillan Publishing Company, 1995), 3–24.

7 Mark Franko, *Dancing Modernism/Performing Politics* (Bloomington, IN: Indiana University Press, 1995).

8 Michel de Certeau, *The Practice of Everyday Life* (Berkeley, CA: University of California Press, 1988), 42.

9 Thomas K. Hagood, *A History of Dance in American Higher Education: Dance and the American University* (Lewistown, NY: Mellan Press, 2000); Janice Ross, *Moving Lessons: Margaret H'Doubler and the Beginning of Dance in American Education* (Madison, WI: University of Wisconsin Press, 2000).

10 See Greg Tanaka's "Dysgenesis and White Culture," in *Measured Lies: The Bell Curve Examined*, eds. Joe Kincheloe, Shirley Steinberg, and Aaron Gresson III (New York: St. Martin's Griffin, 1996), 304–14 for a fascinating discussion of what happens to students and faculty of European descent when a Western-focused arts department becomes an international arts department. His research suggests that the experience stripped them of feelings of racial superiority, which was good, but left them without any ethnic identity at all—which means no identity in the American context. The author indicates that future such curricular transformations should also aim to provide "white" participants with opportunities for the creation of new cultural identities that are not based on racial superiority.

11 This perspective also assumes that modern dance is wholly European derived, which Brenda Dixon Gottschild's *Digging the Africanist Presence in American Performance* already did much to disprove. This groundbreaking text points to the appropriations and resulting hybridities that have made American dance what it is today. Looked at from this perspective, modern dance is actually decentred in terms of content and could function as a decentring force in our programs if discussed with its complex and diverse history intact.

12 Jeff Packman, "Signifyin(G) Salvador: Professional Musicians and the Sound of Flexibility in Bahia, Brazil's Popular Music Scenes," *Black Music Research Journal* 29, no. 1 (2009): 83–126.

13 David Theo Goldberg, ed., *Multiculturalism: A Critical Reader* (Malden, MA: Blackwell, 1994); Moss, "Learning from Latina Students."

14 Banks, "Multicultural Education."

15 Tanaka, "Dysgenesis and White Culture."

16 Joseph E. Marks III, *America Learns to Dance: A Historical Study of Dance Education in America before 1800* (New York: Dance Horizons, 1957); Hagood, *A History of Dance in American Higher Education.*

17 Jane Desmond, "Dancing Out the Difference: Cultural Imperialism and Ruth St. Denis's 'Radha' of 1906," *Signs: Journal of Women in Culture and Society* 17, no. 1 (1991): 28–49; Susan Manning, *Modern Dance/Negro Dance: Race in Motion* (Minneapolis, MI: University of Minnesota Press, 2004); Jacqueline Shea Murphy, *The People Have Never Stopped Dancing* (Minneapolis, MI: University of Minnesota Press, 2007).

18 Patricia Shehan Campbell, *Lessons from the World: A Cross-Cultural Guide to Music Teaching and Learning* (New York: Macmillan, 1991); Patricia Shehan Campbell, *Teaching Music Globally: Experiencing Music, Expressing Culture* (New York: Oxford University Press, 2004); Terese M. Volk, *Music, Education and Multiculturalism: Foundations and Principles* (New York: Oxford University Press, 1998).

19 John Jervis, *Transgressing the Modern: Explorations in the Western Experience of Otherness* (Oxford: Blackwell, 1999), 1.

20 Paulo Freire, *Pedagogy of the Oppressed* (London: Continuum, 1970).

21 Sheenagh Pietrobruno, *Salsa and Its Transnational Moves* (Lanham, MD: Lexington Books, 2006). See also the chapters by Heather Fitzsimmons Frey and Janelle Joseph in this collection for a rich discussion of how dance can function as a form of embodied education that can promote cultural diversity.

22 Livio Sansone, *Blackness without Ethnicity: Constructing Race in Brazil* (New York: Palgrave Macmillan, 2003); Robin Sheriff, *Dreaming Equality: Color, Race, and Racism in Urban Brazil* (New Brunswick, NJ: Rutgers University Press, 2001).

23 The ways in which dance can theorize have been discussed often in Susan Foster's scholarship, beginning with her groundbreaking book, *Reading Dancing*. Her most explicit article on the topic, "Dance Theory?" was published in 2005 in the collection *Teaching Dance Studies*.

24 Linda Tomko, "Teaching Dance History: A Querying Stance as Millennial Lens," in *Teaching Dance Studies*, ed. Judith Chazin-Bennahum (New York: Routledge, 2005), 93–113.

25 Kari Veblen, Carol Beynon, and Selma Odom, "Drawing on Diversity in the Arts Education Classroom: Educating Our New Teachers," *International Journal of Education and the Arts* 6, no. 14 (2005): 1–17.

26 David Gere, ed., *Looking Out: Perspectives on Dance and Criticism in a Multicultural World* (New York: Schirmer, 1995).

TWELVE

A DANCE FLASH MOB, CANADIAN MULTICULTURALISM, AND KINAESTHETIC GROUPNESS

Janelle Joseph

IN LATE JUNE 2012, I SENT AN EMAIL TO A PROFESSIONAL DANCE company to inquire about Caribbean dance classes. In response, I received an invitation to be part of a Canada Day flash mob. The email had a link to an online newsletter, which read,

> We want you, and your friends to be part of the biggest Canada Day Flash mob. Yes that is all the details you're going to get right now, because it's top secret. The Flash Mob is on Saturday June 30th, 2012. The location will be given to confirmed participants. If you're interested in participating in this AMAZING and FUN flash mob please contact us.[1]

With great excitement—and trepidation—I contacted the organizers and received an email with links to unlisted YouTube videos and instructions about the time and place of the one and only rehearsal. I practised on my own and nervously attended rehearsal two weeks later with thirty other amateur dancers of all ages, sizes, sexes, and ethnicities. At the rehearsal we were taught how to execute the moves and were given a brief cultural and historical explanation of the dances we were performing. It was not until the end of the rehearsal that we learned the whereabouts of the flash mob location: Harbourfront Centre's Redpath Stage, one of Toronto's premier outdoor arts venues that typically hosts a full weekend of Canada Day entertainment.

Upon arrival at the venue, I surveyed the area around the stage. The circular platform, surrounded by grass, was adjacent to vendors of crafts, fashion, jewellery, and art from around the world. The crowd was a mixture of ethnically and racially diverse couples and families, young and old. Most were sitting in comfortable, brightly coloured Adirondack chairs, on picnic tables, or on the grass. I counted nearly four dozen people wearing red and white: the prescribed flash mob costume colours. I recognized many of them from the single rehearsal we'd had two nights earlier. I soon learned that a few of the rest I didn't recognize were regular citizens celebrating Canada Day with their sartorial style.

We had been instructed to blend into the crowd—to sit, stand, and pretend as though we were waiting for the next set of performers to come to the stage. When we heard the musical cue, we were to rush to the area in front of the stage and start dancing. Our Bollywood, soca, dancehall reggae, jazz, and hip-hop dance routine followed suit. We screwed the light bulb, tapped our wrists, wined, butterflied, Willie bounced, gave them a run, and pumped it up to a fast-paced five minutes of contemporary tunes. Onlookers moved closer for a better view, their expressions shifting from confusion to delight. Once we'd struck our final pose, we joined the audience in clapping and cheering before hugging each other and dispersing as quickly as we began.

The politics of belonging in a culturally diverse Canada hinge on the complexities of nation, race, ethnicity, culture, and their ever-shifting intersections. An analysis of these complexities certainly warrants scholarly attention. This chapter examines how flash mob dances may serve to engender multicultural solidarity by potentially giving participants and observers a kinaesthetic sense of groupness through the physical and artistic movements of the body and the proximity between dancers and audience. Brief mob dances might seem to offer nothing more to participants and spectators than cultural appropriation of dance moves or costuming, or superficial entertainment. I contend, however, that the flash mob dance described above encouraged participants and audience members to reflect upon the foundational multicultural principle of cross-cultural interaction. With its democratized participation (no professional training or ticket purchase necessary), the Bollywood, soca, dancehall reggae, jazz, and hip-hop routine that took place on a day reserved for celebrating belonging in Canada can help us understand how racial and cultural barriers may be transcended. Below, I describe the flash mob phenomenon and the literature on Canadian multiculturalism and dance before discussing the potential for dance flash mobs to generate what I am calling kinaesthetic groupness.

FLASH MOBS

The research on flash mobs is replete with all the hallmarks of a nascent field of study: a focus on examples, definitions, and typologies. After nearly ten years of research on the topic, the question of, "What is a flash mob?" has shifted to, "What are the social and political implications of flash mobs?" However, the shift to a political and social perspective is not without controversy. Behaviours of flash mobbers, who gather temporarily in one location to complete a specific, brief act, have been defined as "absurd,"[2] and "unusual or notable."[3] Some scholars and mobbers argue that flash mobs are intrinsically apolitical, with "no other message than its sheer and unexpected physicality."[4] This critique, as Sangita Shresthova notes, "underestimate[s] the important ways in which [flash mobs] contribute to popular culture and expression… Flash mob organizers' disavowal of political action, in fact, helped create the participatory and open-ended conditions in which performance could connect to political action."[5] Organizing joyful chaos and unexpected physicality through the flash mob can be read as inherently political because gathering en masse in public space, however temporarily, disturbs the social order. In a capitalist society, space (and especially urban space) is never neutral but always a site for the assertion and contestation of power.[6] Temporarily unsettling the predictable and seamless choreography of public space with "spatial figures of resistance that require circumnavigation, pausing, spectating"[7] allows non-elites to create a counter-hegemonic space for critical thought and activism.

Dance flash mobs in particular are amenable to political analysis because they are closely aligned with older socially disruptive performance genres (e.g., street theatre, prankstering, and protest movements) that creatively mix art and politics in public urban spaces. The use of public space is crucial here: flash mobs move performance art "out of the insular and exclusionary world of art galleries and theaters to the open space of the city and [involve] large groups of strangers as opposed to a few artists in the role of professional provocateurs."[8] Flash mobs are what Michel de Certeau calls a "tactic,"[9] an imaginative way for non-elites to insert themselves into spaces they do not control and reconfigure the use of public space, which "forces attention on the performance, thus constituting a heterogeneous public into a community with a shared focus—the audience—even if only for the space of a song."[10]

While dance flash mobbers' performances may or may not contain intentional or inferred political messages, the very fact that such performances occur in public space opens up possibilities to transform dancers and audience members' values, beliefs, and practices; they are a way of engaging in a politics of visibility and staking larger claims for recognition and group belonging.[11] If public dance disturbs the social order, then organizing an "ethnic dance" with a multiethnic group of non-professional dancers disturbs the Canada Day multicultural dance order.

CANADIAN MULTICULTURALISM AND DANCE

The nation is far from a natural phenomenon. Relatively young nations, such as Canada, may be especially prone to utilizing a range of popular culture discourses to shore up feelings of belonging. Popular culture is one way of communicating and representing national belonging in part because it is "where the production and reception of knowledge and aesthetics come together for the majority" of people in a geopolitically bounded territory.[12] In Canada, one of the popular concepts used to assert a national societal order is multiculturalism, which is based on the principles of sharing cultures. The Canadian Multiculturalism Act promotes both the "freedom of all members of Canadian society to preserve, enhance and share their cultural heritage"[13] and the "understanding and creativity that arise from the interaction between individuals and communities of different origins."[14] This top-down policy that relies on essentialized notions of origins and cultural heritage reflects an interesting paradox: ethnic minorities draw from *foreign, ethnic* cultures to define their local, national identities. Through expressions of their ancestral heritage, all Canadians should gain a sense of belonging in, or "full and equitable participation ... in the continuing evolution and shaping of all aspects of Canadian society."[15]

In a typical multicultural "mosaic" display, people of specific ethnic groups exhibit their ancestral heritage through dance. Some scholars have elucidated how dance is tied to ethnic beliefs, values, and visions of the world and allows for the survival of a group's cultural elements.[16] These sorts of ethnic dance performances can, moreover, unsettle a nation's "race hierarchies and open up possibilities for young people who are minoritised and excluded through these race hierarchies to be recognised as legitimate."[17] Ethnic dance performance is an embodied preservation of ethnic culture and can help marginalized populations find a place within a nation; dance is a means of expressing belonging in Canada. Typical multicultural displays offer interactions between individuals and communities of different origins across the distinct performer/audience divide.

Other more critical approaches have analyzed how multicultural dance performances are sites of abjection that promote a sense of outsiderness: the very opposite of inclusion and belonging. Scholars claim that multicultural dance performances reify and exoticize culture by showcasing the differences between majority and minority cultures, thereby casting ethnic groups as fixed and unchanging and setting them apart from the dominant culture. Audience receptions of these seemingly exoticized displays of dance may also be seen as merely tolerating difference with no real change occurring in the structural factors that disadvantage minority groups. From this perspective, multicultural shows and dance performances do little to dismantle what Taucar refers to as "barriers to full participation and equality by not challenging the public's complicity in their creation or their passivity regarding issues like racism."[18] Rather than promote inclusion and diversity, they are seen as promoting an outsider status. They may operate to frame ethnic minorities as authentic Others for the pleasurable consumption of dominant groups, thereby obscuring similarities to both majority and minority ethnic groups/heritages.[19] Like Taucar, Janice Gross Stein suggests that such performances are a form of "multiculturalism-lite, which raises no hard questions at all."[20] Stein also contrasts dance with "important" multicultural issues that "matter," such as human rights and religious freedoms.

However, just as the debates over secular dress codes in Québec are about more than sartorial style,[21] I contend that expressions of the body through an ethnic dance "matter" and are about more than the trite consumption, exoticization, and performance of culture. Multicultural performances generally, and multicultural dance performances specifically, are about kinaesthetics, or the embodying of cross-cultural knowledge; this is particularly important to uphold the Canadian multicultural principle of interaction between individuals and communities of different origins. Alternative, bottom-up analyses of multiculturalism examine acts of private or "intimate multiculturalism"[22] and demonstrate how ideas of nation and community are sometimes animated through processes whereby multiethnic groups create their own sense of solidarity. In the flash mob setting, where the performers are strangers—maybe from different ethnic, cultural, and racial backgrounds—and where a performance in a public place is forced onto an unsuspecting audience, the capacity of the dance to unify is particularly powerful.

In his text *Ethnicity Without Groups*, Rogers Brubaker explains belonging as more than being part of a group. Rather, he suggests a process of groupness that is "variable and contingent rather than fixed and given ... [with] phases of extraordinary cohesion and moments of intensely felt collective solidarity... and capacity for concerted action."[23] To create a bounded collectivity, a national solidarity, for example, groupness is described as "an *event*, as something that 'happens.'"[24] The rhythmic and spatial synchrony created through group dance has been explored, through disciplines as disparate as neuroscience, psychology, movement therapy, dance history, and philosophy, as a means of creating empathy, social bonding, and group solidarity.[25] Here, I refer to this notion as kinaesthetic groupness and argue that the collective solidarity created through moving the body to music (or watching it do so) can be linked to national identity through the process of group-making—even if only temporary—in which participants engage.

An examination of a flash mob dance that incorporates movement from soca, dancehall reggae, hip-hop, jazz, and Bollywood within the Canadian context reveals how dance might be instrumental in generating an inalienable human right: the right to belong. Participation in these sorts of multicultural dances opens up the possibilities of challenging the popular meaning of multiculturalism for performers and audience members alike. The flash mob's democratized recruitment combined with the collective movement ritual and muscular bonding of dance, as well as the fusion of varied styles of ethnic dance, allows performers to see themselves as an intercultural, unified group. The flash mob's aggressive insertion into public space allows the kinaesthetic groupness to transcend the performer/audience divide, pulling the audience into a liminal scene that is analogous to the boundary loss experienced by dancers. This chapter adds to the nascent research on dance, pluralism, and flash mobs by suggesting that bodily movement is not merely about joyful, organized chaos, celebration, or superficial issues, but has serious consequences for a sense of group—that is, national belonging or kinaesthetic groupness.

A comprehensive framework for analyzing groupness, according to Kristina Cantin, "must not only attend to cognition and practice, but also to emotion."[26] The feelings of elation, exchanges of grins, and sharing of laughter precipitated the trading of email addresses in some cases and suggest that the dancers experienced a sense of themselves as a group connected both through their muscular bonding and their intervention in public space. The ability to perform the sequences at the same time, moving to the same beat and punctuating their actions in the same way allowed them to adopt the group habitus, feel comfortable with each other, and know themselves as part of a whole. The red and white costumes and Canadian flags made the link to the nation explicit. Body techniques are not natural acts, but complex, socially constructed, and culturally loaded skills.[27] Once a person makes a decision to enter a cultural contact zone and invest in learning a culturally specific physicality, the intimacy that results "has both discursive and material effect, and often has the body as its signifier."[28]

This chapter draws on and extends Wise and Velayutham's notion of everyday multiculturalism,[29] which points to the need to research informal, vernacular, intercultural negotiations that happen in informal places of leisure and that shape and reshape social relations and identities. Official multiculturalism offers only limited forms of public recognition through participation in a "mosaic" of cultures through identifiable, essential, national, or ethnic origins. I put this notion of everyday multiculturalism into conversation with kinaesthetic literature[30] that suggests that physical, embodied, intercultural encounters are foundational group-making processes that allow participants to develop a physical habitus, which can extend to ways of seeing and interpreting the social world in "neo-traditional communities."[31] The group may not be named with a single national moniker (e.g., Jamaican or Canadian); rather, it is a temporary group of like-minded, multicultural dance enthusiasts. The public setting is important to the politics of recognition and visibility that performers enact. By performing dance in public they stake a claim on the space and signal the ability to resist the social order using "popular procedures ... [to] manipulate the mechanisms of discipline and conform to them only in order to evade them."[32] A Canada Day flash mob allows people to "reinvent themselves, question their belonging to one national imagined community and embody other forms of being."[33]

THE CANADA DAY FLASH MOB

The sweaty hugs and wide grins I shared with the other flash mob participants after our performance signalled that we were overjoyed that we had translated our online and in-person cross-cultural kinaesthetic education to a successful performance. We had worked together towards a common goal and briefly shared a sense of sociability. Sociability, or the gathering of strangers for pure, purposeless, joyful interaction, free of material exchange, and without social hierarchies, is a feature specific to short-lived groupings.[34] All participants are welcome, regardless of experience, talent, or ethnicity, in most short-lived flash mobs—a situation that promotes the experience of sociability. This camaraderie is further promoted through a group choreography, whereby bodily movements are arranged in space and performed in unison.[35] Kinaesthetic bonding through dance permits the formation of a group identity based on shared embodied understandings of ethnicity and culture.

If we examine the soca dance that flash mobbers performed, we must consider the history of soca in Toronto articulated by Camille Hernandez-Ramdwar.[36] Due to its link with carnival, Hernandez-Ramdwar states, soca

> acts as a pressure valve by inducing a catharsis that actually allows people to survive oppression and stress. Soca, a dance originating in Trinidad and Tobago that blends soul and calypso, can be a healing force, especially for people who face daily racism, hardship and a sense of exclusion and alienation from the Canadian mainstream.[37]

When this dance is performed by a multiethnic group in a flash mob setting, all dancers learn to feel with their bodies what it means to leggo (let go) as they engage in "face-to-face stranger relations in urban space"[38] and transcend their differences, if only temporarily.

Randy Martin's work on a mainly white group of hip-hop dancers is also instructive here.[39] In contrast to scholars who emphasize white participation in hip-hop as nothing more than appropriation or imitation of black art(ists),[40] Martin suggests that a sense of connectedness between white and non-white Others is made available during those moments in which the body breaks out of its usual space. Dancers connect with the racialized lyrical and melodic music and with each other, and are then less likely, according to Martin, to look on the news, rampant with racism that it is, and see an Other. In contrast, cultural appropriation of dance includes a superficial uptake of movements that includes stereotyping, essentializing, or otherwise fixing difference into a static otherness, lingered over because it is strange or exotic. Therefore, if choreographers make a point of incorporating dance history, cultural values, and national beliefs into their teachings, participants in racialized dances such as soca, Bollywood, and dancehall reggae may discover the deeper artistic and cultural origins of the art forms, and the contributions of both white and non-white groups in the global dissemination of ethnic dances. Being able to see themselves in the dance, and not maintaining boundaries that keep the Other as foreign, moves participation in multicultural dance out of the realm of cultural appropriation and into the domain of cultural transformation. This type of participation can create a sense of solidarity beyond the specific dance space, which can ultimately transform communities.

While a sustained analysis is necessary to determine if the brief encounter of the flash mob merely offered a chance to superficially appropriate cultures, or has lasting effects, the scholarly literature about dance as a transformative moment and my experience with the Canada Day performance speak to the immediate power of kinaesthetic groupness for cross-cultural interactions and multicultural sociability—integral aspects of Canadianness.

Multiculturalism is described as "shallow" when it "strengthens each culture within its own boundaries."[41] This is typically the case when dance companies or ethnic associations perform on Canada Day, reinforcing the dominant Canadian multiculturalism rhetoric of bounded and fixed cultures on corporeal display in service of a mosaic ideology where ethnic "essential difference" is staged and heritage preserved.[42] In Chapter 11 of this book, Robinson and Domenici suggest that modern university dance programs should move beyond simple inclusion and work towards greater cross-cultural integration to deepen pluralism. Along these lines, the flash mob organizers advertised virtually through their websites, Facebook, and dance company/community bulletin boards in an attempt to dismantle notions of essential difference among dancers. Organizing over the internet and inviting open participation allowed for the inclusion of a wide variety of participants in terms of cultural background, ethnicity, age, and dance experience and helped to promote a "deep multiculturalism [that] builds bridges across cultures."[43] While the organizers, two of Toronto's pre-eminent black Caribbean dancer/choreographers, both experts in the varied styles of dance they taught, could have easily amassed a cadre of elite black or Indo-Caribbean dancers to perform and chosen one or two Caribbean styles of music and dance, they were explicit that no participant was turned away, as their objective was to "get as big a group together as possible... to show all the differences Toronto has to offer."[44] They put Asian and African diasporic dance traditions in dialogue, refusing to separate genres, as Robinson and Domenici suggest. This dialogue, in combination with including dancers of all ethnicities, helped to create a cross-culturally integrated performance.

We connected to each other through the synchronized movements of our bodies, outpouring of our sweat, and racing of our heartbeats. This sociability has the potential to generate a sense of belonging or groupness that not only transcends the boundedness and fixity of ethnic dance mentioned above but also holds out the promise of transcending the performer/audience binaries inherent in most staged dance performances. The encounter between audience and artist in a flash mob generates, according to Megan Steinman,[45] an empathy that assures audiences—due to proximity of and seeing performers from a range of ethnicities, races, ages, genders, and abilities dance—that they too could possibly be part of the action and part of the community. Whether we are watching or participating in a dance performance, we become aware of our own capacity for movement and are thus connected to the dancers and each other.[46] If flash mobbing is, following Gore,[47] like soft terrorism because its guerrilla tactics force the audience to retain the message due to its difference from the habitual, then it follows that in a flash mob dance that utilizes multiethnic dance styles and multiethnic performers, audiences are more likely to recognize that the essentialist links between dances and ethnic groups are fictions. When dancers use public spaces to move to music with African and Indian roots, wine their waists to soca and dancehall reggae music, or wave Trinidadian and Canadian flags on the Canadian national holiday, they present a unique opportunity to imagine and reify the idea of a multicultural Canada.

It is possible, then, to understand the flash mob as "a pleasurable implication of the body within the city, in which categories of citizen, stranger and outsider may become blurred through shared performance that interrupts conventional spaces."[48] While it may be argued that participation by some folks was based on a superficial colonial desire or was an example of cultural appropriation, I concur with Jobbitt's findings, Chapter 17 in this book, that glaring limitations of deeply essentialist versions of multiculturalism, reducing people and cultures to national costumes and other traditional stereotypes, can be superseded through participation in dance forms where participants embody Canadian Prime Minister Trudeau's ethnic multiculturalism by overcoming their own perceived "monoculturalism" and being counted among the Others. Dance performance at once reproduces the invented traditions and (sometimes problematic) narratives of diasporas at the same time as it contributes to community-building processes. I danced alongside South- and East-Asian men and women, and people with European and African backgrounds who did more than perform the prescribed Bollywood, soca, dancehall reggae, jazz, and hip-hop routine. The dancers (a group of strangers) connected with an audience (a larger group of strangers) in service of celebrating the nation. They articulated their groupness, belonging to a multicultural Canada that was "both uniquely theirs and simultaneously in conversation with a wide array of cultural expressivity."[49] Through the location and date of the dance flash mob I describe here, performers claimed public space, demanded visibility, and questioned how Canadian multicultural groupness, togetherness, or sociability may be articulated by and through corporeal movement.

CONCLUSION

Rather than wait for a "Multicultural Day" or navigate the bureaucracy associated with sanctioned professional dance performances, choreographers may turn to the dance flash mob genre as a guerrilla tactic in the fight for claims to belonging. Although they may appear spontaneous, irrational, or apolitical at times, flash mobs—particularly those of the performance variety—require meticulous planning, rehearsal, and political choices such as costumes, dates, and locations. Through its ephemeral and jarring presence, the flash mob allows for reconsidering how subjects embody the city and how dominant multicultural discourses are performed and resisted. It is my assertion that a Canada Day Caribbean dance flash mob is interesting precisely because it provides insight into the intersections between pluralism, nationalism, and belonging. This flash mob cannot be seen simply as an "ethnic cultural form" carried out by a specific diaspora. Rather, it operates as a temporary appropriation of public space that has the potential to create multicultural groupness in at least three ways. First, by joining people of many backgrounds together for intense conviviality, or "intimate multiculturalism,"[50] cultural barriers may be transcended. Second, by inviting a multiethnic group to perform dances usually considered to belong to one ethnic or racial group, stereotypes are debunked and an embodied understanding of culture, or "sensuous multiculturalism,"[51] is generated. Third, when an unsuspecting audience is forced to watch a group of amateur dancers who, moments before, had been part of the crowd just like them, they have the opportunity to begin to shift their understanding of self and other within a multicultural community.

Multicultural dance shows are critiqued for reinforcing Othering and maintaining apolitical attitudes among audience members.[52] Despite their potential for political interventions, Cayley Sorochan argues, flash mobs are similarly flawed: due to their fleeting nature, "flash mobs often reinforce dominant ideologies rather than question them. Hierarchies are not overturned, and the everyday flows of the city are not suspended in such an extreme degree."[53] Clearly, a five-minute dance flash mob in Toronto cannot carry the weight of reimagining community for all of Canada, but reflection on my own experiences allows me to hint at longer-lasting effects and the potential for more than the simple tolerance of difference or consumption of essentialized Otherness by the audience.

I speculate about other unanticipated consequences of the flash mob. After participating in or being forced to see the Canada Day flash mob, might dancers or audience members be more open to enrolling in a dance class? Would they be more ready to purchase tickets for Ballet Creole or the Collective of Black Artists, to name just two companies that bring African diaspora dance to formal stages? I believe this flash mob and others like it can serve as an instance of public pedagogy; popular culture can be an expression of activism, one that might move us towards social justice through the bridges that it permits to form between audience and dancer. The cultural processes put into motion by a dance flash mob may never fully come to rest.

Through choreographing, performing, and/or witnessing dance, new ways to imagine belonging in Canada are enacted. Multiculturalism is realized when minority groups demand more and more visibility and recognition: "Multiculturalism is the visible manifestation of outsiders' codes of conduct becoming diffuse vertically and laterally, penetrating not only social institutions but also the Canadian personality structure."[54] In learning and performing a flash mob dance, I developed a kinaesthetic groupness. I expressed an embodied belonging to many cultures and used my dancing body to illuminate the complexities of the discourse of multiculturalism in Canada. I also suggest that the choreographers, and subsequently the dancers and audience, all participated, at the level of public discourse, in a re-education of nationalism and belonging. They too, I surmise, experienced and learned about kinaesthetic groupness within the context of Canadian multiculturalism.

NOTES

1 Kay-Ann Ward, "Participants Needed for Upcoming Flash Mob," accessed June 6, 2012, http://www.kayannward.com/uncategorized/participants-needed-for-upcoming-flash-mob/. The original spelling, punctuation, and grammar of this email has been preserved; the URL has since been removed.

2 Cayley Sorochan, "Flash Mobs and Urban Gaming: Networked Performances in Urban Space," (master's thesis, McGill University, July 2009), 1.

3 Anne Duran, "Flash Mobs: Social Influence in the 21st Century," *Social Influence* 1, no. 4 (2006): 301.

4 Thea Brejzek, "From Social Network to Urban Intervention: On the Scenographies of Flash Mobs and Urban Swarms," *International Journal of Performance Arts and Digital Media* 6, no. 1 (2010): 118.

5 Sangita Shresthova, "Bollywood Dance as Political Participation? On Flash Mobs, New Media, and Political Potential," *Convergence: The International Journal of Research into New Media Technologies* 19, no. 3 (August 2013): 311–17

6 Michel de Certeau, *The Practice of Everyday Life* (Berkeley, CA: University of California Press, 1984).

7 Brejzek, "From Social Network to Urban Intervention," 120.

8 Virág Molnár, "Reframing Public Space through Digital Mobilization: Flash Mobs and the Futility (?) of Contemporary Urban Youth Culture," *Space and Culture* 17, no. 1 (2014): 50.

9 de Certeau, *The Practice of Everyday Life*, 20.

10 Georgiana Gore, "Flash Mob Dance and the Territorialisation of Urban Movement," *Anthropological Notebooks* 16, no. 3 (2010): 128–29.

11 George Yúdice, *The Expediency of Culture: Uses of Culture in the Global Era* (Durham, NC: Duke University Press, 2003).

12 Randy Martin, *Critical Moves: Dance Studies in Theory and Politics* (Durham, NC: Duke University Press, 1999), 124.

13 *Canadian Multiculturalism Act, Revised Statutes of Canada* 1985, c. 24, 3a, accessed August 7, 2014, http://laws-lois.justice.gc.ca/PDF/C-18.7.pdf.

14 Ibid., 3g.

15 Ibid., 3c.

16 Andrew M. Robinson, *Multiculturalism and the Foundations of Meaningful Life: Reconciling Autonomy, Identity and Community* (Vancouver: UBC Press, 2007); Sangita Shresthova, *Is It All about Hips? Around the World with Bollywood Dance* (New Delhi: Sage, 2011).

17 Deborah Youdell, "Fabricating 'Pacific Islander': Pedagogies of Expropriation, Return and Resistance and Other Lessons from a 'Multicultural Day'," *Race Ethnicity and Education* 15, no. 2 (2012): 141.

18 Jacqueline Taucar, "(Per)Forming Ourselves and Others in Toronto's Multicultural Caravan Festival," *Canadian Theatre Review* 140 (Fall 2009): 54.

19 Neil Bissoondath, *Selling Illusions: The Cult of Multiculturalism in Canada* (Toronto: Penguin, 1994); Taucar, "(Per)Forming Ourselves"; Janice Gross Stein, "Searching for Equality," in *Uneasy Partners: Multiculturalism and Rights in Canada*, eds. Janice G. Stein et al. (Waterloo, ON: WLU Press, 2007); Sunera Thobani, *Exalted Subjects* (Toronto: University of Toronto Press, 2007).

20 Stein, "Searching for Equality," 17.

21 In Québec, since the early 1990s, debates have raged over how to integrate immigrants: whether to encourage assimilation to a common Francophone culture given that Québec's minority status in Canada is under siege, or to encourage interculturalism and maintenance of ancestral cultures. These debates have manifested in calls by some groups to ban wearing of religious items such as hijabs (Muslim headscarves) and kirpans (Sikh swords) in public.

22 Cristina Wulfhorst, Cristina Rocha, and George Morgan, "Intimate Multiculturalism: Transnationalism and Belonging amongst Capoeiristas in Australia," *Journal of Ethnic and Migration Studies* 40, no. 11 (2014), accessed August 9, 2014, doi: 10.1080/1369183X.2014.894875.

23 Rogers Brubaker, *Ethnicity without Groups* (Cambridge, MA: Harvard University Press, 2004), 12.

24 Ibid.

25 Andrea Behrends, Sybille Müller, and Isabel Dziobek, "Moving In and Out of Synchrony: A Concept for a New Intervention Fostering Empathy through Interactional Movement and Dance," *The Arts in Psychotherapy* 39, no. 2 (2012).

26 Kristina M. Cantin, "Process and Practice: Groupness, Ethnicity, and Habitus in Carpathian Rus'," *Nationalities Papers: The Journal of Nationalism and Ethnicity* 42, no. 5 (2014): 849.

27 Janelle Joseph, "Going to Brazil: Transnational and Corporeal Movements of a Canadian-Brazilian Martial Arts Community," *Global Networks* 8, no. 2 (2008).
28 Wulfhorst et al., "Intimate Multiculturalism," 6.
29 Amanda Wise and Selvaraj Velayutham, "Introduction: The Study of Everyday Multiculturalism," in *Everyday Multiculturalism*, eds. Amanda Wise and Selvaraj Velayutham (Basingstoke, Hampshire: Palgrave Macmillan, 2009).
30 For example, Michael Atkinson, "Enduring Bodies in Triathlon," in *Tribal Play: Subcultural Journeys through Sport*, eds. Michael Atkinson and Kevin Young (Bingley, UK: Emerald Group Publishing, 2008); Wulfhorst et al., "Intimate Multiculturalism."
31 Hal Niedzvecki, *Hello, I'm Special: How Individuality became the New Conformity* (Toronto: Penguin Books, 2004).
32 de Certeau, *The Practice of Everyday Life*, xiv.
33 Wulfhorst et al., "Intimate Multiculturalism," 2.
34 Georg Simmel, "The Sociology of Sociability," trans. Everett C. Hughes, *American Journal of Sociology* 55, no. 3 (1949).
35 Paul Spencer, "Introduction: Interpretations of the Dance in Anthropology," in *Society and the Dance: The Social Anthropology of Process and Performance*, ed. Paul Spencer (New York: Cambridge University Press, 1985).
36 Camille Hernandez-Ramdwar, "Feteing as Cultural Resistance? The Soca Posse in the Caribbean Diaspora," *Topia* 20 (Fall 2008).
37 Ibid., 73.
38 Sorochan, "Flash Mobs and Urban Gaming," 56.
39 Martin, *Critical Moves.*
40 For example, Russell A. Potter, *Spectacular Vernaculars: Hip-Hop and the Politics of Postmodernism* (Albany, NY: SUNY Press, 1995).
41 Stein, "Searching for Equality," 19.
42 Bissoondath, *Selling Illusions.*
43 Stein, "Searching for Equality," 19.
44 Co-organizer, personal communication, June 30, 2012.
45 Megan M. Steinman, "The Kinesthetic Citizen: Dance and Critical Art Practices" (master's thesis, University of Southern California, May 2011).
46 Ibid., 2.
47 Gore, "Flash Mob Dance."
48 John Saunders, "Flash Mobs," in *Acts of Citizenship*, eds. Engin F. Isin and Greg M. Neilsen (London: Zed Books, 2008), 295–96.
49 Rinaldo Walcott, "Caribbean Pop Culture in Canada; Or, the Impossibility of Belonging to the Nation," *Small Axe* 5, no. 1 (2001): 125.
50 Wulfhorst et al., "Intimate Multiculturalism."
51 Amanda Wise, "Hope and Belonging in a Multicultural Suburb," *Journal of Intercultural Studies* 26, no. 1–2 (2005).
52 Taucar, "(Per)Forming Ourselves"; Youdell, "Fabricating 'Pacific Islander.'"

53 Sorochan, "Flash Mobs and Urban Gaming," 124.

54 David M. Matsinhe, "Nightlife, Civilizing Process, and Multiculturalism in Canada," *Space and Culture* 12, no. 1 (2009): 133.

THIRTEEN

CONTEMPORARY INDIGENOUS DANCE IN CANADA

Santee Smith

in conversation with Samantha Mehra and Carolyne Clare

"The fact that I'm creating work… is a political act."
—Santee Smith, Kaha:wi Dance Theatre

SANTEE SMITH IS THE FOUNDING ARTISTIC DIRECTOR AND PRINcipal choreographer of Kaha:wi Dance Theatre based in Six Nations Reserve and Toronto. Founded in 2005, the company presents Smith's distinct contemporary performance, a confluent expression of settler and Indigenous dance forms. Her work has been presented internationally, and Smith has been awarded numerous prestigious prizes, including a Dora Mavor Moore Award for Outstanding Choreography in 2013. In addition to creating original works, Kaha:wi Dance Theatre delivers educational programs for aspiring dance professionals and elementary and high school students. These programs seek to enlighten participants about Indigenous performance, cultures, and worldviews. Smith's work as choreographer, performer, researcher, and educator has increased awareness of Indigenous politics as well as Indigenous performance practices in Canada.

The following transcript summarizes a series of interviews with Smith that took place in Toronto in 2013 with Samantha Mehra and Carolyne Clare. The interviewers are both emerging dance professionals: Mehra is a writer, editor, historian, and emerging scholar, while Clare works as a dance archivist. During these conversations, Smith describes her path to becoming a leading contemporary artist in Canada and discusses how her art has been inspired by her Kahnyen'kehàka (Mohawk) heritage. In addition, having received intensive dance training at Canada's National Ballet School and being immersed in Six Nations dance traditions, Smith explains how both ballet and Indigenous dance express themselves through her body and the impact both have on the content and aesthetics of her choreographic work and educational outreach. Smith also discusses how several dance forms have given momentum to the decolonization of bodies, communities, and environments.

In our conversations, Smith also calls attention to her artistry and self-aware engagement with the political implications of her dance-making. Smith often uses her art to combat and transform negative public perceptions of Indigeneity. The content of two of her choreographies, *The Threshing Floor* (2006) and *The Honouring* (2013), are cases in point. For example, *The Honouring,* commissioned by the city of Toronto, is a site-specific work that premiered at Toronto's Fort York heritage site. The work focuses on the War of 1812, specifically commenting on the participation of thousands of Haudenosaunee soldiers who supported British troops. Dance critic Paula Citron suggests that this work elicits a sense of melancholy in the audience and takes the public on "a heartfelt journey through war, death and grief, but always with a dignified ceremony."[1]

While *The Honouring* has explicit political content and communicates the complexities of Indigenous history in Canada, in *The Threshing Floor,* Smith intentionally chooses not to represent a historically specific or political story. Instead, *The Threshing Floor* uses contemporary dance to tell a tragic love and loss story of a couple. The emotionally layered work, co-choreographed and performed with Michael Greyeyes, demonstrates Smith's ability to dance with both technical mastery and emotional impact (Greyeyes is also a former student of Canada's National Ballet School, has danced professionally with the National Ballet of Canada, and works as an actor, choreographer, and director). Smith explains how the presence of their two bodies onstage, engaging in a representation of a contemporary relationship without overtly referencing political issues, histories, or cultural signifiers related to Indigeneity, is in itself political.

In introducing our interview, it is important to reaffirm scholarly critiques of the role of culture in Canadian politics. In short, positioning Indigenous nations as cultural rather than political communities obscures the distinct status of Indigenous nations in Canada: political communities that enacted nation-to-nation treaties with settler colonialists prior to being dispossessed of their land. Scholars have analyzed how settler governments have used the concept of cultural diversity to belittle Indigenous claims to cultural and political sovereignty, thereby perpetuating Canadian colonialism. At the same time, as Smith does in the following interview, Indigenous artists, scholars, and activists have also shown how culture can be used to resist colonialism and support Indigenous resurgence through the twenty-first century. We invite readers to keep various understandings of culture in mind while reading our interview.[2]

Carolyne Clare: What inspired you to dance?

Santee Smith: I don't remember having dance come into my life. My family says that I danced as soon as I could walk. When I heard music, I would get lost in a world of dance. I started exploring physicality and the relationship between music and movement at a very young age. At age three, I got into a car accident and broke my femur. I was in traction for a month and then a body cast for a month. Shortly after that, I broke my ankle in a bike accident and a collarbone. As a result of those injuries, my body was weakened, and my doctors suggested that I take up a physical activity in order to redevelop my strength and alignment. Knowing that I loved moving, my parents put me into ballet.

CC: What brought you to Canada's National Ballet School?

SS: At age ten, I asked to audition for Canada's National Ballet School. My parents said no. I was an only child, and we were a tight-knit family. They did not want to send me away to boarding school. They consoled me by suggesting that I audition the following year; they assumed I might forget about the audition. When the next year rolled around, I asked them again. They decided that I could go to the audition. Since the process is very competitive, who knew if I would get in? I passed the audition in Hamilton and, after the summer school, I was accepted into the full-time program in 1982 for grade six.

CC: Did you graduate from Canada's National Ballet School?

SS: I completed grade eleven at the school, but I decided that I did not want to return for grade twelve. I wanted to move back to Six Nations to be home. I was feeling disconnected from my family, our traditions, and my own cultural identity. So I stepped away from the ballet world in a very abrupt way. It felt like a huge change in my identity; I did not think I would become a professional dancer anymore.

Samantha Mehra: Did your training at Canada's National Ballet School play a part in your exploration of your identity?

SS: No, while I was training at the ballet school, I did not consciously think a lot about my Indigenous identity. I was so focused on ballet. My artist parents worked hard to keep me connected to our worldview by keeping our stories relevant, [as] a way to keep me strong. Nor did I do much exploration of Indigenous dance, although it might have been nice to do so. National Ballet students were offered a dance course that introduced us to various dances from around the world, mostly Euro-based. I remember a Bharatanatyam artist coming in for a demonstration. I don't recall having learned any Indigenous dance, although it is possible that we did.

CC: Did you continue dancing in some capacity after leaving Canada's National Ballet School?

SS: While finishing high school, I consciously put myself out into my community and continued learning about my own culture. I went to Longhouse, participated in ceremonies, and took part in the traditions that I missed out on by being away from home.[3] I learned the dances through observation, and I would also ask my mom how to do different steps. We would practise together in our kitchen. Being home gave me the chance to reconnect with my family, community, and culture—connections that my ballet lessons had interrupted.

CC: Did you feel welcomed back into your community?

SS: Yes, because my family is very active in the community. My family on my mother's side has been going to Longhouse for years and years. My great-grandmother was a Kahnyen'kehàka clan mother, and my aunt is now our clan mother. Longhouse welcomed me, in that my family goes, but people also noticed that I was a new face. Even today, I'm very busy with my dance company, and so I don't get to participate in ceremonies consistently.

CC: Why did you start choreographing?

SS: I attended McMaster University to pursue a degree in kinesiology. After stepping away from ballet, there was a huge void in my life, and I knew that I should keep trying to find a career that would be fulfilling. I thought that becoming a physiotherapist or chiropractor would fulfill my interest in the mechanics of the body. At the same time, I studied psychology, which I preferred to my kinesiology courses. I thought I would become a clinical psychologist.

However, while I was at university, a friend of mine, Gary Farmer, asked me to choreograph for a National Film Board documentary called *The Gift*. Being from Six Nations he knew about my background as a dancer. He asked me to create two short dance choreographies based on Onkwehon:we [Iroquois] stories, such as the teachings of Corn, Beans, Squash, and Sky Woman from our creation story.[4]

As soon as I went back to the studio, I was listening to music and moving, and I fell right back into dancing. The process sparked the seed that has kept me in dance but as a choreographer. I recognized my desire to explore movement that was sourced from a more personal place. Choreographing allowed me to develop a personal artistic expression incorporating Indigenous understanding and narratives.

CC: Can you tell me more about the creation of your choreography named *Kaha:wi*?

SS: In 1998 I was developing my first major choreographic work, *Kaha:wi*. It was inspired by three generations of women, a family creation story; it explored the passing of my grandmother and the birth of my daughter. I wanted to weave in cultural concepts related to birth, death, and ceremonial life. I therefore talked to people in my community and honed some of the knowledge that I had already been investigating. Documenting my own culture from an Indigenous perspective was also important to me. Finally, I thought, well, I'm doing intensive research. So, in 2002, I decided to enrol in the MA Dance program at York University with a focus on dance ethnography. The MA was rolled into a process of research and creation for the production of *Kaha:wi*; it was an autoethnographic process.

CC: Did you learn how to choreograph contemporary dance?

SS: Before starting my research on *Kaha:wi*, I was not formally introduced to Western-based contemporary dance or choreographing. I took a few contemporary dance classes but didn't study a specific modern technique like

Horton, Graham, or Limón.[5] However, I've been lucky to have excellent mentors along the way and opportunities to learn Indigenous dance styles from around the globe.

CC: In what context did you meet your mentors?

SS: I met some of my greatest mentors through the Banff Centre for the Arts' Aboriginal Dance Program. I participated in the program from 1996 to 2001, first as a dancer and then as an assistant choreographer. It was an excellent program that brought in outstanding Indigenous dance instructors from around the world. At that time, Alejandro Ronceria was the director of dance, and he was exploring contemporary Indigenous dance work. Ronceria is a Colombian-born artist and was the first director of the Banff Centre's Aboriginal Dance Program; the program director was Marrie Mumford. Ronceria remains a key collaborator and continues to support my work. He teaches at Kaha:wi Dance Theatre's four-week-long summer dance intensive and facilitates at our Creation Labs. In general, the early years at the Aboriginal Dance Project offered a place for me to connect with a community of Indigenous artists who were interested in contemporary dance and performance infused and inspired by traditional dances and methodologies.

CC: Did the Banff Centre program focus on Indigenous dance across diverse nations?

SS: Yes, the dance styles we studied were from different nations—from Greenlandic dance, Aztec dance, Inuit styles, Powwow styles, and various other dance forms emerging from across the Americas and internationally. I should mention that the dance program also focused on movement-based theatre as well, exploring how we create dance, song, text; Indigenous artists don't silo disciplines. From a holistic Indigenous view, a performer can be a singer, dancer, drummer, and storyteller. It's all interconnected.

CC: What does it mean to explore Indigeneity across diverse nations?

SS: There is great diversity amongst the nations. We tried to avoid treating Indigeneity as a homogenous pan-Indian concept, and we recognized the distinctions amongst nations. However, it was also important and empowering to acknowledge overarching similarities across the nations.

CC: What kinds of similarities exist?

SS: The dances tend to all be based around a cosmology; they have spiritual significance. Although the ceremonies have different purposes across nations, the dances tend to be a major part of ceremonial life. Dance is also a central form of celebrating your humanity and is a way of making a real connection to the earth and to the animals and natural cycling. The drumbeat links us to the pulse of the earth.

CC: How did you integrate your training in different dance styles within your body?

SS: While developing my choreography, I pursued my research in order to use movements from a traditional source. But then, I also have this ballet body with extended lines and uprightness. Ballet is still in my body. I had to learn to bring my feet into parallel and work with the ground. Now, I have a sense of weightedness and being grounded in the lower half of my body, which is my driving engine. My upper body is more connected to the sky; it is fluid and treelike. I've developed my Indigenous base in the legs and pulse through the core, and I also use my extensions and fluidity on the top half of my body.

CC: What kind of training do the dancers from your company have?

SS: Some of the dancers that I work with come from modern dance training, primarily in Graham technique. Occasionally, I will choreograph a sequence and my dancers exclaim, "That is so Graham!" From my perspective, the sequence just reflects the way I like to move. I never studied Graham! I work with dancers who are traditional dancers—hoop and Powwow styles—as well as actors.

CC: Do the participants in your four-week-long summer intensive program[6] also mostly have Graham training?

SS: No, those students come with varied dance backgrounds. They must have some rigorous dance training, but it can be in Indigenous, ballet, modern, or other styles. During the summer intensive, the students must take classes in various styles, and so most of the students have to face the gaps in their training. There tends to be a steep learning curve for all of the participants, which is quite exciting.

CC: I had the opportunity to chat with some of the participants in your summer intensive. A few mentioned the challenges they faced in accessing dance training. Can you comment on those challenges?

SS: It's a vast generalization; however, I could say that Indigenous dancers usually begin intensive dance training later in their lives than most professional dancers. Young Indigenous people might not have the opportunity to access intensive training because they come from isolated communities or lack the necessary financial support and resources. In addition, the idea of dancing as a profession, as conceived by modern or ballet dancers, may not be part of their community's worldview.

CC: What hopes do you have for the students who participate in your summer intensive?

SS: My aim is to offer them some of the training they need to become capable and versatile professional artists. I want them to be able to have careers in dance and to get jobs. As the program grows each year, the focus is also on offering artists new ways of creating, working with their bodies, [and] understanding Indigenous processes to develop their voice and bodies in ways that do not necessarily follow the mainstream Euro-Western training and praxis.

CC: What kind of challenges do you face now?

SS: Even though Kaha:wi [Dance Theatre] is approaching its tenth anniversary, I still find it challenging to find continuous financial support for my work and to support time to invest in the creation process while at the same time researching, writing, and dialoguing about the way in which I am creating. Time to explore Indigenous methodology is limited. Nonetheless, the artistic side is full of little treasures. With the little time we can support the actual art-making, I love being in the studio, working with collaborators, students, [and] mentors, and performing.

SM: When you apply for funding, do you have to explain your choreography in relation to ballet or modern dance?

SS: No, I try to describe the essence of the work. For example, I might describe my dancers' "use of breath" or their "connection to the earth." However, I might also draw upon ballet expressions such as "extensions" or "lines" to describe my dancers' movements. Overall, I don't feel the need to relate my work to ballet but rather what I am investigating in the vision of a work and Indigenous process.

SM: Do you feel a pressure to categorize your choreography in order to attract new audiences to your shows?

SS: Although I consider my choreography to be contemporary Indigenous, I sometimes have to reconsider how I explain that to other people. I question whether to market our work as traditional, modern, avant-garde, postmodern, or other categories. In part, it is necessary to choose the right words to describe our work because presenters are not always comfortable collaborating with First Nations artists or communities. They are not sure who to talk to and how to talk to them. I've tried to help communities overcome those patterns by connecting with First Nations communities whenever we go on tour.

SM: What are your goals for your company's tours?

SS: Outreach is very important to me. When we go on tour, in addition to performing, we also offer workshops for various community groups. For example, my company just finished a tour of Northern Ontario, which doesn't get a lot of exposure to live performance. The school groups we worked with were excited that we were in their community. [7]

We taught some traditional stories and introduced children to creative movement and improvisation. I hope to promote healthy lifestyles and physical activity. I hope that kids will learn to express themselves, and I encourage them to discover what they enjoy doing and to find a way to do it. When I work with First Nations children, I also hope that they will feel empowered by telling our stories through song and dance.

CC: How does your work help empower people? Is your work political?

SS: Generally, my work does not make explicit political statements; however, it is political because it provides students, artists, and the public with a more positive impression of my culture. The media generally prints negative headlines about Indigenous people. My work highlights the positive and provides a way of celebrating Indigenous culture where there has been a lack of celebration. Especially in the early stages of my career, it was empowering to me to find beauty, power, and strength in my culture and stories. Today, it continues to be important to me to give voice to my culture, which is intact, living, and holds past, present, and future in one. My recent works do take on the topics of residential school experience, murdered and missing Indigenous women, and decolonial processes and themes with the intent to educate and empower.

SM: Do any of your dances have an explicit political message? Do they explore decolonization or colonization?

SS: To begin, the fact that I'm creating work as a First Nations person living in Canada (Turtle Island) is a political act. Also, as I mentioned, early in my career, I decided not to create work that perpetuates negativity nor only represents struggle. I wanted to uplift, show strength, and move towards the beauty and power of my culture. My positive perspective might have to do with the fact that I was close to my family, [and that I] grew up and [currently] live on Six Nations. As part of reclaiming my traditions, working within Canada's public education system is very important to me. I want to fill gaps of consciousness within the education system and public understandings of the truths about Canadian history. More recently, my work explores the fractures from colonial impacts and the ways in each we can heal.

CC: Do you feel like you must continue to overcome stereotypes?

SS: Yes, there is still a tendency for people to stereotype the First Nations. The media's representations also tend to be one-dimensional. I'm combatting stereotypes about what Indigenous people look like and how they speak and move. For example, I recently staged a duet called *The Threshing Floor,* which I co-choreographed with Michael Greyeyes, a Cree artist who also trained at Canada's National Ballet School. For this dance, we decided to simply depict a couple's relationship. We did not draw upon Indigenous singing, nor drumming, and didn't want to be viewed as historicized nor culturally and nationally specific bodies. Why? Because for the most part, media and dominant culture does not depict First Nations people as human, as capable of having emotions and loving relationships.

CC: How did the audience react?

SS: We had a very positive reception, especially from First Nations audiences. One audience member from the Six Nations expressed that she saw herself in the work and related to the couple on stage because it was her experience. By contrast to other dance performances she had seen, she felt especially connected with this choreography. It was interesting to note that several non-Indigenous audience members experienced surprise and confusion to the work because the show did not align with their expectations or preconceptions of Indigenous dance. Some people expected to see Powwow dancing, but there were no feathers!

CC: Can you comment on who comes to see your shows?

SS: My choreography called *TransMigration* explored the work of Norval Morrisseau, the Ojibwa visual artist. We performed the piece at the Fleck Theatre in Toronto in 2012. The choreography described Morrisseau's life, including his experience with residential school, alcoholism, and homelessness. It was a theatrical piece that was also visually engaging, since it drew upon Morrisseau's aesthetics. We received a lot of media attention. Our shows tend to attract minimal interest from the Toronto dance community. One of my Toronto dance colleagues came to see the show and commented that she didn't recognize many people in the audience from the community. Audiences who attended were generally interested in Morrisseau's life and Indigenous stories. It was a very unique audience.

CC: Is your public often surprised by the content of your choreography?

SS: Yes, many Canadians tend to lack knowledge of Indigenous histories. Recently, the company premiered *The Honouring,* which discusses Onkwehon: we families' contribution to the War of 1812. Haudenosaunee ancestors chose to take part in the war and protect our sovereignty, culture, and land. This decision took place at a time of profound cultural change, but my ancestors considered how their decisions would impact seven future generations. I tried to represent this story as best I could within my choreography. I would say that is overtly political.

SM: Have you read critical reviews of your choreography that interpret your work in an overly political way?

SS: My reviews have been even-handed. At times, critics or scholars don't understand Indigenous dance and suggest that my work does not step outside of traditional dance. However, if they knew what traditional dance really looks like, they would understand that my choreography utilizes traditional aesthetic as a leaping-off point. At the same time, some critics suggest that the work is simply modern dance, which I would also disagree. Indigenous aesthetics usually appear in my choreography. Overall, I would like to be presented as an artist, first and foremost. I am not necessarily always working with themes that relate to First Nations, although it is my driving inspiration. What I do, really, is about reframing and restorying our narratives, accessing Indigenous creativity, and perpetuating the role of artist as storyteller and transformer.

CC: What are you working on now?

SS: I have decided to challenge myself by developing a solo work, which I have called *NeoIndigenA*. I presented *NeoIndigenA* in May of 2014 as part of the Harbourfront Centre's NextSteps dance series in Toronto. I had spent the past few years focused on building the foundation of my company, developing the ensemble and its movement vocabulary. I wanted to try to embody the information we have been exploring and bring it into my own body.

Although I have performed solos, and I continue to perform in my work, it was a frightening undertaking and was a big challenge. I looked forward to it, and I worked with mentors. Alejandro Ronceria, who I met at the Banff Centre, was one of my key mentors. I also worked with Charles Koroneho, who is a solo artist, teacher, dramaturge, and director. Margie Gillis was also a mentor; she has a large repertoire of solo work.

CC: What did *NeoIndigenA* investigate?

SS: I was interested in identifying the continuous aspects of my Indigenous culture from ancient, contemporary, and future. I wished to represent that which has remained the same, minus the blip of colonization. Decolonization is, in part, bringing the essences of my culture into the future.

CC: What does decolonization mean to you?

SS: To move away from colonizers' behaviours, beliefs, values, and structures. I look to integrate my culture's worldview, ways of living, and teachings into contemporary life. We don't really realize how much colonizers have impinged on our thoughts and bodies. My dancing aims to put those traditional essences back into motion.

CC: We look forward to your future performances!

SS: Thank you.

NOTES

1 Paula Citron, "Native-Inspired Performances at Fort York Mostly Hit the Mark with Melancholy Subject Matter," *Globe and Mail*, June 25, 2013, accessed July 2013, http://www.theglobeandmail.com/arts/summer-entertainment/native-inspired-performances-at-fort-york-mostly-hit-the-mark-with-melancholy-subject-matter/article12815061/.

2 To read further on the role of culture in perpetuating and resisting Canadian colonialism, we encourage readers to engage with work by Michael Asch, Glen Coulthard, and Leanne Simpson.

3 Longhouse can refer to the building in which the Haudenosaunee hosts its ceremonies. The term has also been used to represent various political, cultural, and national meanings. Kaha:wi Dance Theatre explains, "embedded within all [Iroquoian] ceremonies are elements of storytelling, song and dance. It is believed that song and dance were gifts given to the people to honour Life. They follow a calendar of ceremonial festivals that are celebrated in the Longhouse." See Kaha:wi Dance Theatre, "A Story before Time: Study Guide" (Toronto: Kaha:wi Dance Theatre), accessed July 2013, http://kahawidance.org/wordpress/wp-content/uploads/2011/04/kdt-asbt-study-guide.pdf.

4 Sky Woman is a central character in the Iroquois creation story. Sky Woman falls through the roots of the Celestial Tree to the Water World below, which allows Life to take shape on Turtle's back. Sky Woman sings and dances her world into existence. The Iroquois nation refers to Corn, Bean, and Squash as the Three Sisters. The Three Sisters are the main food spirits and are the sustainers of life. There are specific ceremonial and social dances that honour the plants.

5 Each of these techniques has a distinctive aesthetic and movement vocabulary defined by the interests and movement qualities of their founders. For instance, the Graham technique (founded by Martha Graham) is characterized as grounded and angular and makes extant use of the floor; its emphasis on the spiralling, contracting, and releasing of the core is central to the dramatic plots to which Graham set movement. The Limón technique (founded by José Limón) is characterized by a more lyrical, breath-like quality, the energy of movements through space often made possible by falling and rebounding yet still emanating from the body's core. The Horton technique (founded by Lester Horton) explores the structural underpinnings of the body, particularly the way the hips hinge the body in multiple directions, and the lengthening of the spine via a flattened back; the technique explores the lower body's relationship to the ground via deep lunges and squats.

6 The summer intensive is a month-long training program that aims to expose participants to Smith's hybrid dance style. Students participate in approximately thirty hours of dance classes each week. In 2014, the program included classes in improvisation, choreography, contemporary dance, and contemporary Indigenous dance.

7 For more information about Santee Smith's work with young audiences, see Heather Fitzsimmons Frey's chapter entitled "'There Is the Me That Loves to Dance': Dancing Cultural Identities in Theatre for Young Audiences" published in this collection.

FOURTEEN

"THERE IS THE ME THAT LOVES TO DANCE"

DANCING CULTURAL IDENTITIES IN THEATRE FOR YOUNG AUDIENCES

Heather Fitzsimmons Frey

Just before the climax of Theatre Direct's production of *Beneath the Banyan Tree* (2005), there is a blackout.[1] Then the lights come back up, and the main character, newly arrived immigrant Anjali, begins her "All about Me" presentation for her elementary school class in Canada. Facing the audience as if we were her classmates, she tells us she was born in Bangalore and that moving to a new country has been difficult for her, especially when kids at school make fun of her for the way she talks and dresses and the food she eats. As she speaks, she begins to introduce Bharatanatyam-style gestural language, such as a sign to represent her grandmother, placed near her heart, or using her hands and arms to make the undulating motion of waves to indicate travelling a long distance. Then she announces, "There is more to me than the food I eat or the clothes I wear.

There is the me that loves to dance. I'm going to tell you the rest of my story the best way I know how." She takes off her shoes and reties her scarf. As the music starts, she begins to dance.

Choreographer Lata Pada has created a Bharatanatyam-based movement vocabulary for the character of Anjali that is simple, though not simplistic. It uses broad, straight-armed movements, intricate hand gestures, flexed feet, strong accented rhythm work, and angular, asymmetrical poses. The actor performs the character's nervousness by initially avoiding eye contact with the audience. Gradually, after her danced story brings her across the ocean, she conveys, through dance, that she is surrounded by family. She smiles, looking directly at the audience for the rest of her performance before closing with a respectful bow. As the action of the play continues, her new friend, Mason, tells her how much he loved her presentation. Anjali is uncertain. "I don't feel like everyone *got* it…they didn't understand what I was doing," she moans. "We didn't have to," insists Mason.

This scene is indicative of the potential of dance in a theatrical genre known as Theatre for Young Audiences (TYA) and demonstrates how the combination of story, text, and dance can address complex issues related to cultural diversity, multiple identities, immigration, and ways of communicating. In this chapter, which references interviews with Canadian directors and choreographers[2] from across Canada to augment my discussion of *Beneath the Banyan Tree,* I examine ways dance in TYA productions can be, and often is, more than ornamental, spectacular, and colourful entertainment; it can be used to foreground marginalized cultural performance styles to provoke young spectators to think more deeply about how what we *do* is as important as what we *say*. As a result, dance in TYA productions can inspire children to ask challenging questions about cultural and racially constructed differences—about who they are, who they would like to be, and what it means to be Canadian.

THE SCENE: TYA, DANCE, AND PUBLIC EDUCATION

Early Canadian TYA experiments with multicultural performances began, like multicultural education, "with emphasis on culture as exotic and as an artifact."[3] For example, Salamander Theatre's production of *A World of Stories* (1991) toured for twenty years and offered seven stories from Africa, Asia, and

Europe, told in a variety of performance genres, including dance. In 2011, I asked permission to attend an Ottawa school performance of *A World of Stories* as an observer. Children seemed to delight in the production, but the piece reinforced what Canadian literary scholar Laura Moss describes as one of the most long-standing criticisms of official multiculturalism: "superficial, overly celebratory, and impractically ideological... *just* 'song and dance.'"[4] As multicultural education scholar Ratna Ghosh puts it, "the song-and-dance routine completely de-politicised culture and avoided issues of discrimination and race relations."[5] Indeed, popular as it was with many children and teachers, *A World of Stories* did not encourage critical thinking about the multiple identities of Canadians.[6]

Since the premiere of *A World of Stories*, TYA's approaches to cultural diversity have changed. Whether or not they have a commitment to multiculturalism or to featuring cultural diversity in their company mandates, in order to make their performances more marketable, TYA companies adopt casting practices that reflect cultural and racial diversity in alignment with provincial education curricula, which began to integrate Canada's multiculturalism policy in 1971.[7] Many contemporary TYA theatre companies also offer production study guides that include links to dance learning objectives and curriculum connections, including references to issues such as race, inclusivity, diversity, difference, and empathy.[8]

Another potential reason for this shift is that, although mainstream theatre audiences in Canada tend to be well-educated, middle- to upper-class, with roots in North America or Europe,[9] TYA audiences reflect Canadian demographics more accurately. In general, child spectators are diverse in terms of socio-economic class, geographic location, and racial, ethnic, and linguistic backgrounds. These differences can be explained by the fact that many TYA companies make an effort to reach schools serving students of all socio-/economic classes and often tour to rural areas, reserves, and suburban and urban schools.[10] As a result, today, none of the TYA artistic directors or choreographers I interviewed assume that their audiences fit a single demographic profile, and they choose, create, and cast their work accordingly. As Theatre Direct's then-artistic director Lynda Hill put it, "Our audience inspires us to create theatre that draws on all the different cultural influences that make up Canadian society. I can't imagine presenting an entirely white/European view to culturally diverse audiences. It would be irresponsible."[11]

DANCE, TYA, AND PERFORMING CULTURAL IDENTITIES

When I spoke with choreographers and artistic directors about the significance of dance in their TYA performances, many chose to highlight that using dance in a production can demonstrate how Canadian identities—cultural and otherwise—are often multiple and performed, not just on stage, but also in daily life. Couched in the context of a particular narrative, rather than an abstract form, dance in TYA can convey a variety of identities, complicate and trouble cultural difference, and help spectators to understand their own cultural identities.

Theatre Direct's *Beneath the Banyan Tree* is a good example of a TYA performance that both constructs and conveys cultural identity. The ideas present in Lata Pada's choreography intentionally interact with the narrative and include Bharatanatyam, Bollywood, and hip-hop. Together, the story and the dance refuse to offer simplistic portrayals of cultural identity performances. Dance allows Anjali to communicate differently than the non-Indian characters. While parts of her dancing remain inscrutable to some of her classmates, Anjali finds that, by dancing, she is able to understand her own identity better. By embracing dance, she articulates and accepts her roots as a part of who she is.

Dance also allows Anjali to explore new cultural experiences. After her class presentation, Anjali embraces Mason's gesture of friendship by dancing to spoons he plays for her (the traditional Québec folk music rhythm instrument) instead of a tabla. The movements are reminiscent of her performance in class, but more casual and playful—she twirls and spins as she stomps and gestures in the relaxed, nearly informal ways of schoolyard play.

The way dance means to the "onstage" audience of Anjali's classmates is no more fixed or definitive than it might be for the spectators attending *Beneath the Banyan Tree*. As Lata Pada argues,

> TYA must be a response to the realities of young Canadians growing up in a pluralistic society.... Theatre must go beyond the "dominant" culture and find ways to weave our rich and diverse cultures into work that is engaging, entertaining, and most importantly speaks to who they are and who they can be.[12]

Pada uses specific classical dance forms, not as sedimented cultural artifacts, but in order to use particular, and possibly unfamiliar, ways of moving to share cultural specificity at the same time as performers demonstrate the possibility of fluid, multiple identities. At the end of *Beneath the Banyan Tree*, Anjali loves the part of her identity that she sees as Indian. By sharing her dance with other children, she sees them experimenting with their own versions of her performance on the playground. Her school classroom culture shifts, and the audience can see how her own cultural identity can be simultaneously multiple. *How* culturally specific forms of dance are approached in productions aimed at young people has the potential to help children to engage with living, breathing, and constantly changing cultures.[13]

Enabling children to see and hear people and voices from marginalized Canadian cultures is central to why many artists working in TYA believe cultural diversity on stage is valuable. For Tekaronhiáhkhwa Santee Smith of the Toronto-based Kaha:wi Dance Theatre, and of Kahnyen'kehàka Nation, Turtle Clan, Six Nations of the Grand River, Haldimand Treaty Territory, (Ontario), even more significant than simply making difference visible, however, is the opportunity to use performance as a tool to promote positive images of marginalized cultural groups, like her own Indigenous community.[14]

Smith argues that even though Indigenous work is accessible to mainstream Canadian audiences, it is still systemically marginalized; it "lacks public attention and honour" and is "too easily made invisible."[15] She believes the negative news that perpetuates stereotypical notions regarding Indigenous cultures and peoples is more popular than positive news, so favourable visibility made possible through staging Indigenous stories and Indigenous identities is extremely important. Smith emphasizes that her performances reveal complex aspects of her Indigenous culture, how she works, and why dance is central to the way she creates:

> Dance isn't just about the body: it's body, mind, spirit—that's how we work [at Kaha:wi]—watching and participating in dance, we're trying to make those connections. For me, every ceremony, every cultural event has music and dance. It's important for Iroquois people living today to share that. Music and dance impacts body, mind, spirit, and for us, with our ceremonies, that is how we celebrate life, and that is why I continue to do the work I do. I feel my work is a continuation of that concept.[16]

Her positive performance of Indigenous culture, both through her creation methods and what is visible on stage, demonstrate the power of presenting marginalized cultural performances on the TYA stage. For instance, when Smith began workshopping her interpretation of *A Story Before Time*, a Six Nations creation story her parents told her, she experimented with what she called a "purely dance" performance—but her audiences on her reserve were frustrated and missed plot points, even though some audience members knew the story as well as she did. Since she planned to share the show with non-reserve schools, and because she was not sure if *A Story Before Time* might be those audiences' first contact with Indigenous culture, ensuring young people understood the stories was essential. After numerous revisions, she augmented the athletic choreography (which includes physical references to Powwow round dances, fancy dances, stomp dances, animal-inspired movements, contemporary dance, and breakdance) with narration and spoken parts for the characters.[17]

Like Smith, Pada feels that sharing stories with young people through dance is a way to increase the circulation of positively framed cultural identities. She says, "The body is an incredible instrument of expression. It conveys so many things. For me, it's a sense of finding yourself in the dance, and it's also important in discovering who you are, as a Canadian, not creating a sort of 'one-size-fits-all' attitude or identity."[18] Her community of Mississauga is home to large numbers of immigrant youth. She notes, "It is a new world to them—new languages, new cultural norms, difficulties of integration and assimilation. So a work like *Beneath the Banyan Tree* is one way of telling their stories with a hope that this opens new windows into intercultural understanding."[19]

Of course, *Beneath the Banyan Tree* does not retell all immigrant children's stories, but it acknowledges some of the challenges and tensions that shape immigrant lives in Canada, while portraying difference in a positive way. Pada suggests, "We need to celebrate our diversity, origins. We all come with stories when we came to Canada, even if you were born here, somebody in your family has stories about who you are and where you come from.... Dance is about those stories we tell each other as Canadians."[20] Pada's remarks allude to the value of dance in exploring and presenting positive cultural identities while addressing the transitional, liminal state of childhood and adolescence, and especially immigrant adolescence, where young people are making choices about who they want to be and how they want to see themselves.

EDUCATION AND PERFORMANCE: INTERPRETING, EMBODYING, AND CRITICALLY DISCUSSING

Interpreting meanings produced through dance and TYA involves the partnership inherent in the conditions of TYA creation described at the beginning of this chapter: the connection between education and performance. After a performance, post-show discussions, workshops with artists, and engagement with study guides are opportunities to go beyond easy questions like, "Did you like it?" Instead, the goals of these performance supplements are to help young people analyze what and how dance can mean, how bodies represent culture on stage, and how identities can shift and change. A well-run facilitated discussion ideally can help spectators to navigate unfamiliar ethnoculturally rooted dance performances, and expert-led workshops can give them an opportunity to attempt to embody diverse forms of cultural expression—trying on movements, experiencing ways they feel unnatural, exciting, or familiar.

In dance workshops, choreographers regularly share aspects of the choreography from the production the young people just saw and relate it to ethnocultural heritage. Pada observes that when her performances include workshops, even children in Canada from South Asian backgrounds are not necessarily familiar with Bharatanatyam. Yet, regardless of ethnic background, she feels that the young participants do not appear troubled by unfamiliarity, or what she calls "foreign-ness." She finds that students take to Bharatanatyam "as easily as they would a hip-hop class," and believes they conclude, "'I can relate to that. That speaks to who I am.'" In Pada's experience presenting Bharatanatyam dance vocabularies in workshops, exposure to difference intrigues rather than intimidates or alienates young audiences; unlike Anjali, who worries to Mason that her "All about Me" presentation was lost on her classmates, Pada says, "I feel they *get* it." She explains, "They are very open ... they are very intuitive and perceptive."[21]

Smith's experience is different: when she conducts workshops with school children, the response to dance is "pretty individual ... out in the lobby after shows [some] are really very animated, moving physically, and you do see some of them doing some moves, like the hunter in *Medicine Bear*." But she notices that in her workshops there are other children who seem to be "resistant to move.... They are more restricted in their reception of it.... It's a bit sad for me, as a mover, to see kids who are so young and are detaching from their bodies or wanting to hide."[22] She wonders if there may be a certain age when that starts to happen, but she suggests that "it may also be their lives"—that they are in their heads or computer games and lack that important mind-body-spirit connection. Whether students choose to engage or not, workshops following ethnoculturally specific performances invite young people to experiment with embodying cultural difference in an environment that encourages respectful engagement with a specific culture, rather than something that might be construed as "dress-up" or "spectacle," or even "*just* song and dance."

Workshops invite young audiences to try out culturally specific dances, while post-show discussions can provide a forum for young people to think through meanings in the often-complex aesthetic experience they have just had. A skilfully lead discussion is ideally a force against reductive interpretations and stereotyping, and can open young minds to what it means to perform cultural identities, and how dance can mean on stage. Being a good facilitator necessitates an understanding that not all audiences have the same knowledge base—and here are three examples to show why that could be important.

Playwright Marty Chan noticed a significant difference between Edmonton audiences for *The Forbidden Phoenix* (2008), a Peking opera–rock musical hybrid, when there were a large number of Chinese Canadians in the audience compared to when there were few. The Monkey King character wore traditional makeup and performed expected acrobatic and humorous dance/fighting choreography. Chan recalls, "They [the Chinese Canadian children] didn't need to wait to get to know the Monkey King before they could laugh at him. As soon as he walked on stage, they knew he was funny, so they laughed."[23] Chan observed that children who did not initially recognize the Monkey King had to get to know the character before they found him entertaining. Regardless of familiarity with jingju (Peking opera), it is possible that thoughtful discussion can help young people think more deeply about the issues presented through the performance.

In the *Forbidden Phoenix* study guide,[24] Chan describes how his play addresses racism through an allegorical retelling of the story of Chinese "bachelor men" who came to Canada to build the railway. Chan explains why he chose to make the play neither pure Peking opera nor pure rock musical, in terms of musical score, performance style, and even narrative. The dancing and athletic acrobatic performances had become hybrid—neither one, nor the other—by virtue of being in Canada, and that hybridity, especially as it relates to racism and constructions of race, is worth discussing.

In contrast, director Nina Lee Aquino planned to use dance and movement to defamiliarize culture and intentionally alienate audiences in her TYA piece at Young People's Theatre, *Sultans of the Street* (2014). She hoped that through a whirl of colour, unfamiliar instrumentation, and Bollywood-style dancing, audiences would feel transplanted into a world far from Toronto. In particular, scenes in which the beggar children dressed as gods and danced to draw attention to themselves were intended to be uncomfortable for spectators. She anticipated the responses of some audiences of children from mainstream Canadian cultures and asserted that when Canadian schoolchildren enter the world of the play, "it's the audience that is going to feel Other."[25] During post-show discussions, she hoped young people would talk about whether or not they had learned something new, and whether they thought differently about distant children who had to beg to stay alive—stories that might well be shared by some Canadian families but were usually hidden in the intercultural fabric of Canadian life. In these post-show conversations, Aquino resisted pulling "universal heartstrings, suggesting, hey, we're the same, and it's all okay. No. Why can't [a performance] be good if you *don't* relate to it?"[26]

Finally, post-show discussions can also help to complicate young people's assumptions about what they think they know about the multiethnic nature of North American culture. Dancer Seika Boye's early training included jazz, tap, and ballet, and her pre-professional and professional training was in modern and contemporary dance. Yet, because her father was Ghanaian (her mother is a Scottish New Zealander), Boye's body can be read as "black" on stage. During the run of one dance-theatre production for young audiences, she performed a wide range of dance forms and wondered if, in the eyes of the audience, she was performing the "unexpected" when she danced contemporary or ballet, in which she was trained, and the "natural" (because of the colour of her skin) when performing hip-hop dancing, even though she was neither trained in it nor was she entrenched in that culture.[27] The partnership between education and TYA is often criticized because it can stifle aesthetic creativity in favour of curriculum links,[28] but clearly a thoughtful post-show discussion can help young people to think about dancing bodies, assumptions about what is "natural" for people, and how people's cultural performances can be multiple and ever-changing in the Canadian context, while still being *theirs*.

CHALLENGES AND OPPORTUNITIES

I have already alluded to some of the issues that concern choreographers, directors, and dancers related to the performance of ethnoculturally specific dance forms in TYA, but I now wish to pursue a few of the main challenges and opportunities that are of current interest. First, TYA choreographers need to consider the extent to which it is truly possible to communicate abstract ideas about cultural identity. Artists like Santee Smith augment their TYA shows with text, while many TYA directors frame productions with workshops and post-show discussions to encourage complex thinking about performances. Young People's Theatre's Artistic Director, Allen MacInnis, does not believe most young audiences are ready for completely abstract dance performances,[29] and, for that same reason, other artists with whom I spoke, such as Nikki Loach from Quest Theatre, Calgary, and independent choreographer Nicola Pantin, like to ground their movement work for young people in narrative. As children learn how to read various forms of dance and moving bodies on stage, workshops supporting their "dance literacy" in which they can try to embody what they have seen, and facilitated discussions where they are guided to consider meanings in the aesthetic experience, can go a long way in addressing the ability of dance in TYA to communicate.

TYA artists also need to be ever vigilant that the dance performances incorporated into theatrical productions do not reinforce superficial and stereotypic representations of marginalized cultures. Performances like *Beneath the Banyan Tree*, *A Story Before Time*, and *The Forbidden Phoenix* all promote complex thinking about cultural identity performances: the first because, as a newly arrived immigrant, Anjali is trying to determine how to perform her own identity; the second because it presents a positive, non-static, contemporary visioning of the creator's Indigenous culture; and the third because it intentionally employs hybridity to foster discussions about racism and immigration. But, of course, there are other performances that are less successful. Theatre scholars Ric Knowles and Ingrid Mündel suggest reducing focus on how performance

OPPOSITE: *Figure 14.1.* The Monkey King fights to keep his baskets of rice. *The Forbidden Phoenix* book and lyrics by Marty Chan and lyrics and music by Robert Walsh, Citadel Theatre, 2008. Direction by Ron Jenkins. Performed by Jonathan Purvis, John Ullyatt, and Allen Keng. Photograph by Meryl Smith Lawton, EPIC Photography.

reflects racial, cultural, and linguistic differences in Canada and instead recommend considering what meanings are *produced* through intercultural performance, whether "new, negotiated, and hybrid diasporic subjectivities, racist stereotypes, or exotic fantasies."[30] These issues are no less relevant for TYA than they are for theatre for general audiences—in fact, the stakes may be higher when the intended spectators are school children being taught something.

The final issue I would like to address is whether artists present a disservice to children when dance forms are a part of a theatrical performance rather than presented separately. One factor influencing the meaning produced through dance-infused TYA productions is that TYA audiences are often exposed to the *idea* of a particular dance form rather than a full expression of it. While some companies—including Red Sky Performance, Judith Marcuse Productions, and Kaha:wi Dance—cast trained dancers, many directors focus on acting skills and cast good movers who are not trained in the specific dance form they are expected to represent. Casting decisions mean dance forms may be distilled or hybridized—but also diluted. As Pada explains, her use of the Bharatanatyam cultural aesthetic in *Beneath the Banyan Tree* is merely "a little window onto the form... a window into another culture."[31] Pada's choreography in *Beneath the Banyan Tree* is central to the narrative, but she observes that the actors who played Anjali were rarely familiar with Indian dance forms, so her choreography had to incorporate existing actor skills, simple Bollywood gestures, and more familiar hip-hop references. *The Forbidden Phoenix* cast faced similar challenges. Chan's play blends jingju (Peking opera) and American musical theatre, but while some of the cast had previously trained in musical theatre, none had trained in Peking opera. Expert coach William Lau recalls, "It is hard to condense a thousand-year-old art form into a short orientation, so I was only looking for the essence."[32] The fight choreographer combined Lau's brief training for the actors with ideas to develop movement and dance that was exciting, athletic, and certainly hybrid. In both *Banyan* and *Phoenix*, the choreographers hoped

OPPOSITE TOP: *Figure 14.2.* Dream dance. *Beneath the Banyan Tree* by Emil Sher, Theatre Direct, 2015. Choreography by Lata Pada, direction by Lynda Hill. Performers (left to right): Rachelle Ganesh, Qasim Khan, Natalia Gracious, Kyle Orzech. Photograph by Naz Afsahi.
OPPOSITE BOTTOM: *Figure 14.3.* The Phoenix chases winter away. *The Forbidden Phoenix* book and lyrics by Marty Chan and lyrics and music by Robert Walsh, Citadel Theatre, 2008. Direction by Ron Jenkins. Lori Nancy Kalamanski as the Phoenix. Photograph by Meryl Smith Lawton, EPIC Photography.

actors would, as Lau puts it, "achieve the right look," but the actors' specific skills created something hybrid by necessity. Young audiences were introduced to the idea of Bharatanatyam or Peking opera, but not the actual art forms.

Whether or not the distilling approach presents a cultural shorthand that risks reinforcing stereotypes rather than challenging them, or offers accessible exposure that potentially introduces a craving for something deeper and more profound, has a great deal to do with how the dance is constructed and who makes the creative choices. A master dancer/choreographer like Lata Pada can choose how to work with Bharatanatyam, just as the highly trained and knowledgeable William Lau can choose how to present the essence of jingju, in ways that a choreographer who is inspired by those forms but not trained in them cannot. The training means that it is possible to make artistically relevant and powerful choices *grounded in knowledge of the form* on what to present and how, and that knowledge, understanding, and respect for the dance means creating work that avoids exoticization. Knowledgeable choreographers can also make use of dance form "sampling" in ways that strengthens the performance in relation to a dancer's skills. I suspect that the choreography in *A World of Stories* was not developed by masters of the dance forms they purported to present, and that contributed to the impression that the work was superficial. But if the choreographic core comes from a place of knowledge, the performance should be, as Pada put it, "intriguing" and may encourage a young audience member's interest in further exploration.

Furthermore, hybrid dance may provide an answer to a prime criticism of multicultural performance. Carefully constructed hybrid performances discourage young audiences from uncritically thinking with stereotypes and fixing or historicizing living cultures. Bringing the Monkey King character to Canada in *The Forbidden Phoenix* changed him: he wasn't a purely Peking opera character anymore, but his physical performance was still recognizable, funny, and interesting to watch. In Red Sky Performance's production of Drew Hayden Taylor's retelling of the Haida tale *Raven Stole the Sun*, Sandra Laronde uses dance to challenge the notion of an exclusively historical Indigenous identity. Raven, the trickster, performs "The Raven Hop"—a dance Laronde created connecting the men's prairie dance "the crow hop" with contemporary hip-hop.[33] Laronde's traditional/contemporary hybrid choreography locates the story in the audience's current world; ensures that the performance of Raven's identity (and by association, that of Indigenous culture) is neither fixed nor historicized; and decentres Indigenous identity stereotypes by humorously and playfully incorporating a pastiche of contemporary popular dance with traditional dance forms.

Avoiding historicizing or "fixing" the danced identity combats stereotypes, especially false notions that Indigenous culture is not contemporary, living, and changing. Red Sky's complex ways of working with traditional dance skills may even offer what Jill Carter calls "a survivance-intervention"—an act that asserts Indigenous presence, refuses to accept myths of Indigenous peoples as vanished or vanishing, and thus, means Indigenous peoples can imagine a future for themselves and their nations.[34] Yet avoiding fixing dances and peoples in a contained moment of the past is not the same as encouraging awareness about histories and historical contexts; Janelle Joseph (in her chapter in this volume) encourages choreographers to "incorporate dance history... into their teachings," particularly if they are working with "racialized dances such as soca, Bollywood, and dancehall reggae," because participants may discover the multiple origins of dances, and can create "solidarity beyond the specific dance space, which can ultimately transform communities." Providing young audiences and teachers with information about some traditional dances may further complicate audience understandings of Raven, and it may provide additional ways to "transform communities." Laronde asserts that for her, "the traditional is contemporary."[35] Notably, in three of the Red Sky Performance study guides for *Raven Stole the Sun*, teachers are given the lyrics to the Raven Hop. Grade 3 and 4 students are encouraged to reinterpret the dance in their own way, placing the emphasis on the idea of Raven as present, here, and now.[36] While it is true that TYA rarely offers audiences highly skilled performers in a particular traditional dance form and runs the risk of misrepresenting cultural traditions, creative responses from directors and expert choreographers react to performer limitations and have the potential to expose profound ideas related to cultural identity performances and presence.

VALUING DANCE IN CANADIAN TYA

In *Beneath the Banyan Tree*, Anjali has a special relationship with a banyan tree that tells her animal fables from the *Panchatantra*. When Anjali, confessing to feeling lost, despairs, "I'm not in India anymore," her banyan tree, Maitri, answers, "But India is in *you*." The music starts, and Anjali discovers she is doing a simple Bharatanatyam routine in unison with characters she knows well: Elephant, Monkey, and Peacock. Moments later, the animals drift offstage and Anjali is left dancing with Maitri, slowly spinning, an unrefined gesture of a child's pleasure. The beautiful dreamlike moment could be defined as "spectacle" and "*just* song and dance," but within the context of Pada's choreography, it is part of a complex exploration of what it means to perform cultural identity.

Creating and performing is always risky, and TYA carries with it the burden and responsibility of educating young people. Because it is non-verbal and often well suited to emotional expression, using dance to promote, challenge, and question cultural identities and assumptions opens up discussions and possibilities rather than insisting on static meanings and closure. At the same time, ethnocultural dance can be used to stage positive alternatives to common assumptions about cultural identities, to provoke discussions about multiple identities, and to present cultural difference as a significant reality. Furthermore, conscientiously performing hybridity does not have to be a disservice to children or necessarily a misrepresentation of dance forms—it can point towards powerful ideas about difference, presence, and change. Because of the relationship between TYA and the education system, artists and children can expect to encounter challenging discussions about these complex issues and to experiment with embodying dance forms through workshops, giving young people a chance to share their own experiences with the arts and their own histories, as well as their cultural identities. If directors and choreographers thoughtfully work with design, music, dance, and story, they can be challenging and provocative, raising issues related to cultural diversity, multiple identities, immigration, and dance as a way of communicating. As Lynda Hill puts it, "working in an interdisciplinary way with expert artists means ... we [TYA] can be the most innovative and experimental work out there!"[37] Experiencing ethnocultural dance through TYA has the potential to challenge young people to consider the multiple identities of Canadians, their own identities, how they perform who they are, and who they want to become.

NOTES

1 *Beneath the Banyan Tree* was a commission by Sampradaya Dance Creations that premiered in association with Theatre Direct Canada in 2005 and had subsequent

productions in 2006, 2009, 2010, and 2015. These notes are based on Theatre Direct's video of the performance at the 2005 Milk International Children's Festival, Toronto Harbourfront Centre.

2 Between 2008 and 2014, the author interviewed over twenty directors and choreographers working in seven different provinces who work or have worked in TYA. One of the limitations of this study is that TYA can refer to work for babies, elementary school children, or young people finishing high school. Sometimes the work is considered to be for "families," which usually means that all ages are appropriate (*The Forbidden Phoenix* was promoted that way at Edmonton's Citadel Theatre). In conversation, artists did not always differentiate between the ages of the audiences for whom they performed and/or conducted workshops.

3 Ratna Ghosh, "Public Education and Multicultural Policy in Canada: The Special Case of Quebec," *International Review of Education* 50, no. 5–6 (2004): 554.

4 Laura Moss, "Song and Dance No More: Tracking Canadian Multiculturalism over Forty Years," *Zeitschrift für Kanada-Studien* 31, no. 2 (2011): 54.

5 Ghosh, "Public Education," 554.

6 Steven Jobbitt (whose chapter is in this volume) also gestures to this period of Canadian history in which multiculturalism was limited to a "deeply essentialist" portrayal that was "'kitschy,'" but also, for its time, "somewhat radical," and fuelled for Jobbitt (and possibly other Canadians) "multicultural desire." He argues that the early ways cultural diversity was taught might have fostered what he views as "openness to multiculturalism," although he recognizes that might also be seen as "a form of colonial desire or cultural appropriation." *A World of Stories* is also part of an attempt to challenge Anglo monoculturalism, and the idea that young people could have aesthetic experiences that might go beyond what was already familiar contributes to why it was so successful.

7 Some current provincial curricula for dance, language arts, arts education, and social studies use the word "multicultural" or "intercultural"; others reference "other cultures," diverse cultures, or ethnocultural groups. Provincial curricular changes happened at different rates and focused on different subjects; not all employ language related to multiculturalism and/or diversity. See Kogila Moodley and Heribert Adam, "Shifting Boundaries and Flexible Identities within a Multicultural Canada," *Intercultural Education* 23, no. 5 (2012): 430.

8 For example, Theatre Direct's *Beneath the Banyan Tree* study guide has a section of "curriculum based activities," including ones related to "the immigrant experience: cultural differences, generation differences, fitting in with the new while not letting go of the old" and "anti-bullying and anti-racism." The companion study guide highlights curriculum connections like Canadian and World Studies, Equity and Inclusive Education, and Character Education Connections like "empathy."

9 Hill Strategies Research, "Factors in Canadians' Cultural Activities: Demographics and Cultural Crossovers Involved in Book Reading, Performing Arts Attendance, Art Gallery Attendance and Movie-Going," *Statistical Insights on the Arts* 6, no. 3

(February 2008); Hill Strategies Research, "Factors in Canadians' Arts Attendance in 2010: An Analysis of Attendance at Art Galleries, Theatres, Classical Music Performances, Popular Music Performances, and Cultural Festivals," *Statistical Insights on the Arts* 11, no. 1 (September 2012).

10 This assertion is based on anecdotal evidence provided by several TYA companies the author interviewed who tour extensively and have reported performing for diverse audience demographics. For instance, Kaha:wi Dance Theatre has toured their two TYA shows across Canada in schools and theatres in small and large communities; they have limited artistic activity on reserves to workshop performances (Kaha:wi Dance, personal communication with author, September 30, 2014). Quest Theatre Calgary has toured to over 350 communities in Alberta and Saskatchewan, including northern towns like Fort McMurray and southern Alberta Blackfoot reserves (personal communication with author, September 24, 2014). In 2010–2011, Green Thumb Theatre toured to sixty-three communities as far north as Charlie Lake, British Columbia. In 2011–2012, Green Thumb Theatre toured to thirty-seven communities in British Columbia, twenty-two communities in two other Canadian provinces, and also visited the United States. The report states that the furthest north they travelled was Prince George, BC, the smallest community was Cache Creek, BC (population 1,037), and the largest community was Toronto, Ontario (population 2.5 million) (Green Thumb Theatre, "Green Thumb Theatre Annual Report" [2010–2011]: 2, 3; and "Green Thumb Theatre Annual Report" [2011–2012]: 2, 3).

11 Lynda Hill, personal correspondence with author, March 5, 2011.

12 Lata Pada, interview by author, June 7, 2013.

13 See Dominique Rivière's important work on "living culture" in Dominique Rivière, "Identities and Intersectionalities: Performance, Power and the Possibilities for Multicultural Education." *Research in Drama Education* 10, no. 3 (2005): 342.

14 Verna St. Denis, a professor in the College of Education at the University of Saskatchewan, provocatively argues why it might not make sense to discuss Indigenous cultural expressions within a multiculturalism context, suggesting that multicultural discourses may not only exacerbate racism against racialized people, but also trivialize Indigenous concerns about sovereignty, colonialism, and oppression and increase resentment in what she calls "Aboriginal knowledges and history" and "Aboriginal content and perspectives." Verna St. Denis, "Silencing Aboriginal Curricular Content and Perspectives through Multiculturalism: 'There Are Other Children Here,'" *Review of Education and Cultural Studies* 33 (2011): 315. St. Denis's argument is relevant beyond the context of multiculturalism: it is important to consider how we address Indigenous dance, knowledge, and practice within and alongside other contexts and discourses, including (but not limited to) cultural diversity, transculturalism, transnationalisms, and migrations. While it is beyond the scope of this paper to consider issues concerning TYA, colonialism, and settler futurity, or the significant differences between dancing Indigenous identities and the

TYA stage and dancing other marginalized identities, the author wanted to include Indigenous dance practices in this chapter because she believes that in the context of Canadian TYA and dance, some issues concerning dancing marginalized identities (Indigenous and non-Indigenous) share similarities worth considering together.

15 Santee Smith, personal correspondence with author, September 26, 2014. For further details about Santee Smith's artistic practice, see the interview in this volume, conducted by Carolyne Clare and Samantha Mehra. In particular, Smith's marketing and outreach, her discussions around "What does it mean to explore Indigeneity across diverse nations?" and her response to the question "Is your work political?" speak to the issues explored in this chapter.

16 Santee Smith, interview by author, June 14, 2013.

17 For further insight, see Smith's comments in Carolyne Clare and Samantha Mehra's interview in this volume regarding "reframing and restorying our narratives."

18 Lata Pada, interview by author, June 7, 2013.

19 Ibid.

20 Ibid.

21 Ibid.

22 Santee Smith, interview by author, June 14, 2013.

23 Marty Chan, interview by author, December 10, 2008.

24 Marty Chan, "Playwright's Note," in *"Forbidden Phoenix" Study Guide,* by Karen Gilodo and Christina Sangalli, Lorraine Kimsa, *Theatre for Young People,* 2008, 7.

25 Nina Lee Aquino, interview by author, December 13, 2013.

26 Ibid.

27 Seika Boye, interview by author, January 17, 2011.

28 The influence of schools on TYA is well documented. See Lois Adamson, "Why Bring Students to the Theatre? An Exploration of the Value of Professional Theatre for Children" (MA diss., University of Toronto, 2011); and Roger L. Bedard, "The Cultural Construction of Theatre for Children and Young Audiences: A Captive Eddy of Recursive Harmonies," *Youth Theatre Journal* 23, no. 1 (2009): 22–29.

29 Allen MacInnis, interview by author, March 4, 2011.

30 Ric Knowles and Ingrid Mündel, "Introduction," in *"Ethnic," Multicultural, and Intercultural Theatre,* eds. Ric Knowles and Ingrid Mündel (Toronto: Playwrights Canada Press, 2009), iii.

31 Lata Pada, interview by author, June 7, 2013.

32 William Lau, interview by author, January 23, 2009.

33 Sandra Laronde, interview by author, March 28, 2012.

34 Jill Carter, "Discarding Sympathy, Disrupting Catharsis: The Mortification of Indigenous Flesh as Survivance-Intervention," *Theatre Journal* 67 (2015): 420, 23n.

35 Sandra Laronde, interview by author, March 28, 2012.

36 Ibid.

37 Lynda Hill, interview by author, April 6, 2011.

V

BUILDING COALITIONS / BELONGING TO COMMUNITIES

FIFTEEN

THE PRESENCE AND FUTURE OF DANISH FOLK DANCING IN CANADA

Suzanne Jaeger

There is a spry but small assembly of Danish folk dancers who meet Friday nights in the basement of the Danish Lutheran Church on Finch Avenue in Toronto, Ontario. Although the membership is not exclusively Danish, the group meets in order to practise and perform various kinds of traditional Danish folk dances. The group has existed for over thirty years, but their numbers are diminishing, as many of the dancers who started the group no longer attend and have not been replaced by new, younger participants. It appears that Danish folk dancing no longer appeals to contemporary Canadians, neither new Danish Canadians nor first- and second-generation children of Danish immigrants. Daniel Walkowitz, commenting on similarly waning aficionados of English country dancing, suggests the problem is the exclusive nature of the practice.[1] Like English country dancing, Danish folk dancing is predominantly a white person's practice, as well as heteronormative and nationalistic. The survival of Danish folk dance may depend, as Walkowitz suggests for English country dancing, on its

Figure 15.1. The Toronto Danish Folk Dancers at Sunset Villa, Puslinch, Ontario, celebrating Danish Constitution Day, June 1, 2014. Photograph courtesy of the Toronto Danish Folk Dancers.

capacity to become more inclusive. But what would this mean? Would it still be Danish folk dancing?

In the following chapter, I discuss the continued existence of Danish folk dancing in Canada. My starting point is the suggestion that Danish folk dance no longer attracts new dancers because it is an antiquated practice within a now more diverse Canadian culture. By looking more closely at the practices of the Toronto Danish folk dance group, I seek to understand better its potential for transformation and continued existence. The theoretical interest is to observe in the practice the negotiation between the desire to reproduce the past in the present, which is the conservative action of aiming to recreate the familiarity of a tradition, and the idea of multiculturalism as "a collective one-worldness" without historical, cultural, and localizable specification. This latter notion is celebrated in the phenomenon of flash dance mobs and in practices such as Zumba fitness classes, which I consider towards the end of my discussion.[2] Although not the main focus, the concept of nationalism, to some extent, underlies these discussions. A question arises about how nationalism is understood: are there different versions of nationalism, such that national folk dance traditions as "imperfect multicultural practices" could also be understood as communities of people who have chosen to participate in culturally meaningful practices that celebrate differences while remaining open to transformation within peaceful boundaries that are respectfully and collaboratively established?[3]

The research conducted is based on an autoethnographic methodology, and more particularly, a "layered" approach.[4] Autoethnography combines autobiographic strategies with the aims of ethnography, thus seeking to understand cultural experience by describing and systematically analyzing personal experience. Layered approaches go beyond the personal, however, by including storytelling, reflection, and introspection together with more objective research methods such as data collecting, interviews, and the review of relevant literature. The aim is to evoke questions and comparisons while also holding to the idea that "the measure of truth" in ethnographic research is a complex, experience-based, "emergent process."[5]

I chose autoethnography for several reasons, first, because as a member of the Toronto Danish folk dance group, I am a participant observer. My goal is to think critically about folk dance, national identity, heteronormativity, and whiteness without alienating my fellow participants or dismissing either my own or their reasons for engaging in the practice. This is, in part, an ethical concern for the relationships that have been the basis for the research process and that I hope to keep as a continuing member of the group. The concern is connected with a valuing of empathy as a relatedness through which the complex meanings that the practice has for its participants can be understood. To put it a bit differently, autoethnography aims to be self-consciously value-centred, rather than to pose as value-free, emotionally distant, or scientifically objective.[6] In the following analysis, the notions of rational argumentation and coherence are affirmed, as is the value of lucid, compelling descriptions. However, the objective is not only to provide historical and cultural information about Danish folk dancing, but also to explore the meanings it has for its participants from an insider's perspective, and from these meanings, to discern new possibilities that might secure its continuation as a practice.

The discussion begins with background information about my interest in Danish folk dancing and then moves to the history and significance of Danish folk dancing both in Denmark and in Toronto. I then consider some of the reasons for the currently diminishing numbers of participants and explore possible changes that might lead to the preservation of Danish folk dance, albeit in a different form than as a predominantly white, heteronormative practice. The conclusion draws together suggestions for the preservation of Danish folk dancing in such a way that it can retain its aesthetic richness and meaningfulness as a distinct practice.

My interest in Danish folk dancing began as a way to connect with my heritage after my father, who was a Danish immigrant, passed away. It became a means of reconnecting to a distant Danish family, to Danishness, and to the sound of the Danish accent, which brings back reassuring childhood memories. Both my parents loved recreational social dancing, and with most of the dancers in my Danish folk dance group being fifty-plus, like me, participating in their Friday night dances became both meaningful social time and an enjoyable form of exercise. It offers as close to bacchanalian revelry as the typically reserved Danes get.[7] By contrast, on Friday nights in the basement of the Finch Street Danish Lutheran Church in Toronto, after about an hour and a half of gallops, chassés, hopsas, buzz steps, and polkas, the dancers move into the church kitchen for a traditionally Danish hyggelig (friendly/cozy) coffee break with Danish baked goods; here, I can talk about *Æblekage*, Jutland, smørrebrød, snaps, and Danish humour, and these people know what I am referring to. Participation in this Friday night ritual of Danish folk dancing is not so much about national pride if "pride" is understood to be an aggressive form of patriotic separation from others. The Danish folk dance nights are more about familiar cultural references and participation in an imagined shared heritage of food, language, and geopolitically defined communities.

Among the dances performed by the Toronto Danish folk dancers are those believed to have been danced by Danish farmers and poor people roughly between the mid-eighteenth and nineteenth centuries. During this time, and until fairly recently, Denmark was primarily an agrarian, culturally homogenous "white" society.[8] While the nobles—including members of the royal family and political and other wealthy associates—danced the minuet from France, the rural folk dances were various kinds of coupled formations that adapted the minuet, the waltz, and the polka into a distinctively rural Danish repertoire. Also at this time in Denmark, there was political and academic interest in nationalism, similar to what was happening in other European countries, and which motivated research on folktales, poetry, songs, and dance with the idea that the practices of the peasant folk preserved an identity tracing back generations.[9] Such ideas inspired the documentation of the peasant folk dances and costumes from the middle of the nineteenth century and ensured fairly bountiful records of Danish folk dancing in coloured sketches and descriptive writings.[10] Given that the basic steps of Danish folk dancing were common to dances from other European countries, the distinctiveness of Danish dancing tends to be attributed to subtle differences in music, costumes, and couple formations, rather than on the steps themselves.

The leaders of the Toronto group work from archival material gathered from various sources, including notes taken at workshops and folk dance courses in Denmark, articles written in Danish available on the internet, and from the magazine published by the National Association of Danish Folk Dancers (Landsforeningen Danske Folkedansere).[11] Although the Toronto group focuses primarily on Danish folk dances, anyone interested is welcome to participate. Non-Danish-speaking Canadians are at a disadvantage only when it comes to the written sources for learning the dances because, other than the early-twentieth-century American educator Elizabeth Burchenal's translations of Danish dances, the available information is mostly in Danish.[12]

When learning the dances on Friday nights, arguments sometimes break out in the group about the steps and how they are to be executed, their order, and the kinds of holds the couples should be using. Various documents are consulted to sort out the discrepancies, but most often the more experienced dancers listen to the music to resolve their differences. Their knowledge of the choreography—that is, their memory of what they learned in courses taken in Denmark and at international festivals—is tied closely to the music. Each new phrase signals a new step, and the experienced dancers listen for repeated phrases that signal the repetition of a particular step in a chorus and verse structure. The number of times a particular step is repeated depends on the musicians. Even with the recorded music, a dynamic relationship exists between the dancers and the musicians. Different recordings of music for the same dance dictate how it is to be done; that is to say, the dancers are trained to respond to cues in the music, which makes the dance a little different depending on the recording used and how a particular group of musicians play the chorus and verses. There are also regional inflections for specific dances and contemporary adaptations created by virtue of forgotten choreography and the challenges of translating verbally described steps and movement patterns from written sources into physically performed movements. Now that the Toronto dancers are getting older, the dances are sometimes cut shorter and the steps made easier on the knees and feet. Some of the more contemporary dances performed by the group are also fusions of other Scandinavian dances. Transformation of the Danish dances is, thus, an integral part of the contemporary practice, and while comparisons between Danish, Finnish, and Swedish dances are common, flexibility and fusion are integral to the performances, including with the costumes.

When I first started with the group and had not yet seen the costumes worn for performances, I mistakenly anticipated that they would be generic and somewhat shabby caricatures of folk costumes according to ideas I retained from the "national dances" I learned as a child for Cecchetti ballet exams in the late 1960s and early 1970s. I soon discovered, however, the folk dancers' considerable pride in their clothes, and in the distinctiveness attributed to Danish costumes in comparison with those from other Scandinavian countries, such as Sweden and Finland. Yet, despite the nationalistically prescribed differences, the costumes of the Danish folk dance group contained a surprising heterogeneity.

Some of the dresses worn by the Toronto Danish folk dancers are made from patterns copied from those created by the Danish Society for the Promotion of Folk Dancing (Foreningen til Folkedansens Fremme).[13] However, not everyone belonging to the Toronto group has a Danish costume. Among the national dresses worn are those from Estonia, Sweden, and Finland. The costumes are alike by being primarily red and white, the colours of the Danish flag. They are also similar in that for women there are long skirts plumped full with petticoats underneath, white aprons, puffy-sleeved blouses, and bonnets or scarves for the head. The men wear red caps or top hats and calf-length pants or "knee breeches" and either long or waist-length coats or vests with white shirts underneath. The women also wear shawls or capes with lace frills, and there is often embroidery or lacework on the blouses, aprons, and skirts. Bobbin lacing was a common practice for rural women. My great-grandmother and great aunts, who lived in a rural village in Denmark where my father also grew up, continued to do bobbin lacing and knitting up to the late 1960s, before they passed away. Their handcraft practices were a link to the agrarian culture of the past, but that link has long since died out. Danish folk dancing is now the celebration of a rural past that no longer exists, and it is far enough away to no longer be as meaningful to younger generations. It is not surprising that dressing up in this way to perform dances from Denmark's rural past holds less interest for the second and third-generation children of urban Danish immigrants.

Certainly, diminishing interest among second and third-generation children explains, in part, why there are now fewer participants in the Friday night dances at the Danish Lutheran Church. The decrease in numbers is also a result of changing immigration patterns. In the mid-twentieth century, large numbers of Danes, including my father, immigrated to North America.[14] This influx of new Danish Canadians coincides with the Toronto Danish folk dancers' heyday in the 1980s and 1990s, during which there were over thirty-five members and the possibility of live music played by Danish musicians.[15] The group performed regularly at Nordlek, a Scandinavian folk dance festival held every three years in different Scandinavian cities as well as at various regional multicultural festivals in Canada and the United States, and at Sunset Villa, a Danish retirement community created in the 1960s in Southwestern Ontario. Since the 1990s, however, there are not only fewer Danes leaving Denmark, but fewer immigrants to Canada from other Scandinavian countries, as well. Decreasing numbers have led to the creation of more broadly construed folk dance groups, such as the Skandia Folk Dance Society in Seattle and the Scandinavian Dancers of Vancouver, British Columbia, both of which are amalgamations of formerly separate Danish, Finnish, Swedish, and Norwegian dance groups.[16] In 2012, at the time of the thirty-first Danish Canadian Conference in Toronto, there were only thirteen members in the Toronto Danish folk dance group, and they were now relying on recorded music. Moreover, because of their small size, they too sometimes invited a Toronto-based Finnish folk dance group to perform along with them.

Notwithstanding these North American amalgamations, Danish folk dancing is still a recreational practice in Denmark, as well as a thriving part of an international Scandinavian folk dance scene supported by summer dance camps and festivals throughout the Scandinavian countries and the United States.[17] The National Association of Danish Folk Dancers, together with the long-standing Society for the Promotion of Folk Dance, continue to promote the practice of Danish folk dancing in Denmark and for diaspora communities, such as the Toronto Friday night group. Despite their decreasing numbers, the Toronto group continues to perform regularly at church festivals and at Sunset Villa for special events such as Grundlovsdag, the Danish Constitution

Day. Those who keep the Toronto group going describe themselves as "large in spirit and enthusiasm," and those who are Danish in background hope to keep this part of their "Danish Heritage going for many years."[18] Unlike other North American Scandinavian folk dance groups, the Toronto Danish folk dancers are aiming to retain something of their distinctive national identity.

I turn now to consider alternative possibilities for the future of Canadian Danish folk dance by returning to ideas proposed by Walkowitz in his analysis of the future of English country dancing. Walkowitz draws attention to the prevailing Anglo-Saxon character and heteronormativity of English country dance, which both defines and limits its survival in the demographically diverse urban communities of today. He suggests that the needed increase in a participant base depends partly on whether English country dance engages with "the inclusive-exclusive contradictions of modern liberalism."[19]

What would it mean for Danish folk dance to become more inclusive? The Toronto Danish folk dance group welcomes dancers from all ethnic backgrounds. Similar to Steven Jobbitt's enthusiastic participation in Ukrainian dance as a non-Ukrainian, there are regular non-Danish participants who eagerly learn and perform the Danish folk dances.[20] However, despite the pleasure of participating in real and imagined cultural practices, the question to be considered is whether ethnic and nationalistic identification are no longer appropriate in the context of contemporary pluralism. Perhaps Danish folk dancing should embrace "the pluralism and multi-generic" aesthetics of the late twentieth and early twenty-first centuries and lose its identification as "Danish."[21]

The Toronto group sometimes has more non-Danes than Danes attending on any given evening. Laments about the group's weakened Danishness have been expressed by long-standing, Danish members of the group.[22] Such feelings are understandable when one considers that the enjoyment of Danish folk dancing for some participants goes beyond the dancing to a more complex experience of cultural belonging, cultural heritage (including shared language, foods, geographically based history, and temperament), as well as the positive contributions to emotional recuperation from losses and life changes made possible through participation in nostalgic experiences and practices.[23] Moreover, while non-Scandinavians tend to group people from the Scandinavian countries together, often confusing the Danes with the Dutch, by contrast, the Norwegians, Finns, Danes, and Swedes distinguish themselves from one another through language, customs, temperament, geography, and history. In subtle ways, these kinds of distinctions are celebrated by the Danes participating in the practice of Danish folk dancing.

In writing this chapter and contemplating it being read by my fellow Danish folk dancers, I wondered whether bringing to bear academic criticisms of national identity on their seemingly benign Friday night dance practice might be perceived as a surprising, esoteric, and somewhat offensive imposition that makes what it wants of the practice regardless of the meanings that it has for the practitioners. This difference in perspectives doesn't necessarily lead to the conclusion that academic interests are irrelevant to the practice, but it does highlight the differences in forms of consciousness, and if the academic perspective is to avoid its hegemony over the practitioners' as naive or unreflective, then a negotiation is required between the two perspectives—a negotiation in the form of a conversation. This chapter aims not so much at making definitive claims about what the future of Danish folk dancing ought to look like; instead, my objective is to begin the conversation about what might make its future more certain.[24]

One possibility is that Danish folk dancing might have a better chance of surviving if it makes some specific changes to its practice. There are ways, for example, in which it could be made more gender inclusive.[25] Moreover, Denmark is no longer a homogeneously white society, having received in the last twenty to thirty years large numbers of immigrants from Asia, Africa, the Middle East, and Eastern Europe. Folk dancing might be a way for the Danes, old and new, to come together in a celebration of contemporary Danishness by creating new contexts in which folk dancing serves as a form of exercise, as well as a celebration of national identity that acknowledges the losses of a past (which had value and meaning for its inheritors) while also creating the future with all its complexity and diversity in cultural composition. This approach would mean rethinking the practice of Danish folk dancing so that it is more inclusive and flexible to further adaptations in relation to new, culturally blended participants.

A good example of this kind of approach is found in contemporary innovations of the French-Canadian gigue. Québec choreographers such as Lük Fleury, Marie-Soleil Pilette, Nancy Gloutnez, and Luca Palladino have preserved the traditional gigue while incorporating new elements that reflect a more accurate representation of today's culturally diverse Québécois society. The Toronto Danish folk dancers could similarly consider adapting their practices, in small but significant ways, to be more open and affirming of contemporary Danish and Canadian pluralism. The goal is to become more inclusive, blended, and open to integrating movements from other folk dance traditions while also affirming significance for those participants for whom the "traditional" Danish practice is meaningful in multifaceted ways.

I would like to consider briefly a contrasting model for folk dancing that has emerged in Zumba fitness classes. Zumba Fitness was created in the 1990s in Columbia by Alberto "Beto" Perez. He later moved to Miami, Florida, and by teaming up in 2003 with business partners Alberto Perlman and Alberto Aghion, created what soon became an internationally practised dance fitness program selling licensing rights, music, DVDs with choreographed dance routines, and fitness wear. On their website, Zumba Fitness is described as

> a global lifestyle brand that fuses fitness, entertainment and culture into an exhilarating dance-fitness sensation! Zumba® exercise classes are "fitness-parties" that blend upbeat world rhythms with easy-to-follow choreography, for a total-body workout that feels like a celebration.[26]

Although at first primarily rooted in Latin American music and dance, Zumba dance routines now include flamenco, cha-cha, reggaeton, hip-hop, Indian dance, various kinds of African dance, Middle Eastern belly dancing, and tango, among others.[27] In a single routine, it is possible to move across many different ethnic dance styles, mixing, for example, Bharatanatyam steps and arm movements with Latin American music, followed by Middle Eastern belly dancing blended with hip-hop choreography. The music is contagiously exuberant, setting the ambience of the class as a dance party where it doesn't matter whether the steps are done correctly. Instead, what is promoted is doing the steps "in your own way," according to a participant's own rhythm, physical ability, and enjoyment of the music.

Zumba classes are popular, and the different kinds cater to various age groups and different physical abilities and exercise interests, from Zumba Gold for "active older adults" to Zumbini for infants aged zero to three years. Zumba classes are available at almost any fitness club offering group classes, but also at community recreation centres, YM and YWCAs, and retirement homes. The strength of the Zumba model is its inclusiveness; the classes at my university gym are attended by students for free, and by staff and faculty members for a very modest program fee. There are women wearing the hijab, students from China, India, and Brazil, Caucasian women, and quite possibly other women of Scandinavian descent, like me. Some Zumba routines include steps very similar to what we do on Friday nights and common to many folk dance traditions, including versions of the grapevine, triple steps (or ballet balancé), and the jazz step-ball-step. Given its capacity for integrating new moves, it would not be surprising for Zumba Fitness to incorporate eventually more steps common to European folk dance practices, especially as licensed instructors proliferate globally.

Of course, for some, the downside of the Zumba model is the imprecise quality of the movements and the loss of explicitly identified cultural origins for the music and dance moves. Zumba Fitness draws attention to how identifying the national or ethic origins of movements and style is a choice depending on the interests of a group of individuals. As Janelle Joseph points out in her chapter on flash dance mobs, it can be pedagogically and politically advantageous not to do so.[28] Zumba Fitness clearly offers a model for enjoyable, accessible folk dancing that successfully negotiates the inclusive-exclusive tensions within modern liberalism. What Zumba offers is a model of radical aesthetic flexibility, possibly at the opposite end of the spectrum from the more culturally and historically conservative aesthetic assumed by the Toronto Danish folk dancers. Conservative aesthetics may, nevertheless, be an enjoyable, understandably meaningful, and politically benign choice for particular communities within a larger democratically organized state. Rather than effacing cultural distinctions altogether, aesthetically conservative national folk dances can be seen as an acknowledgement of, and interest in, differences.

However, the questions raised at the beginning of this discussion remain: Will Danish folk dancing continue to exist in the future? Will the Finch Avenue Toronto group survive the current downturn in its membership and retain its distinctive Danishness? In conclusion, all that can be said is that there are still some people interested in attending the Friday night dances in the basement of the Danish Lutheran Church and for whom the current practice is meaningful. An international folk dance scene exists for those participants with the leisure time and disposable income to take dance classes, music lessons, and attend international celebratory festivals. For the time being, folk dancing exists in different contexts, from ultra-inclusive Zumba classes to more ethnically, heteronormative exclusive groups like the Toronto Danish Folk Dancers. There are different contexts for different tastes and interests. There is also, however, the possibility of reform for the more traditional practices by introducing, for example, more aesthetic flexibility and gender-neutral terminology for the steps and couple formations. Implementing these kinds of changes would, I suggest, increase the chances of survival in the Canadian and global contexts, and perhaps also provide a political tool in the international context for the celebration of blended cultures.

NOTES

1 "It remains to be seen, as the [English] dance community seeks to expand its base, if and how it will engage the inclusive-exclusive contradictions of modern liberalism and, in doing so, determine its future." Daniel J. Walkowitz, *City Folk: English Country Dance and the Politics of the Folk in Modern America* (New York: New York University Press, 2010), 11.

2 In her chapter, "A Dance Flash Mob, Canadian Multiculturalism, and Kinaesthetic Groupness," Janelle Joseph considers the political meanings of participating in a flash dance mob in which neither the dancers' varying ethnicities nor the cultural affiliations of the different movements are ever identified. The flash mob is a fusion of different styles that "allows performers to see themselves as an intercultural, unified group."

3 In his chapter, "Dance and the Fulfillment of Multicultural Desire: The Reflections of an Accidental Ukrainian," Steven Jobbitt discusses Ukrainian dance as a national folk dance with politically complex affiliations.

4 My understanding of a layered autoethnographic approach has been drawn primarily from Carolyn Ellis, Tony E. Adams, and Arthur P. Bochner, "Autoethnography: An Overview," *Forum Qualitative Sozialforschung/Forum: Qualitative Social Research* 12, no. 1 (2011): 1–13, accessed June 28, 2014, http://www.qualitative-research.net/index.php/fqs/rt/printerFriendly/1589/3095.

5 Ibid.

6 This theoretical/methodological standpoint has emerged from the postmodern epistemological "crises of confidence" of the late twentieth century and from the works of philosophers such as Derrida, Foucault, and Rorty, among others, who drew attention to the multiple perspectives from which knowledge might be generated and also inflected by structures of power and hegemony. See Ellis et al., "Autoethnography: An Overview."

7 See, for example, the 1987 film *Babette's Feast,* which presents an extreme version of Danish Nordic reserved stoicism.

8 I am indebted to Laine Ruus from the Toronto Danish Folk Dance group for drawing her attention to the quadrille folk dances performed in the Virgin Islands. The origins of these dances are attributed to the 18th century folk dances brought

by French and Danish colonists. Denmark colonized four of the Virgin Islands including St. Thomas, St. John, Water Island, and St. Croix beginning in 1672. At that time, the islands were known as the Danish West Indies. Denmark eventually sold the islands to the U.S. in 1917 at the start of World War I. For an example of the quadrille dancing still performed on the Virgin Islands, see the YouTube video of the We Deh Yeh Cultural Dancers of St. Croix: https://www.youtube.com/watch?v=U7EbQXQoSYs.

9 Although nineteenth-century romantic conceptions of national identity and authentic cultural origins culminated in Germany in horrifying claims of racial superiority and inalienable rights to a heartland or homeland, the political atrocities of the German Empire and later German National Socialism are not the universal or inevitable result of culturally distinctive practices. "Nationalism" as a theoretical concept is complex, with both potentially and historically widely varying political effects.

10 Research and archives were compiled in the nineteenth century by Svend Grundtvig, Henning Frederik Feilberg, and Evald Tang Kristensen. A number of nineteenth-century artists were also famous for their documentation in lithographs and watercolours. For example, the artist Frederik Christian Lund travelled across Denmark sketching people in local costumes. His collection of thirty-one coloured lithographs was published in 1864 in *Danske Nationaldragter* (Danish National Costumes). See Sigurd Müller, Luplau Janssen, and F. C. Lund, *Danske Nationaldragter* (Kolding: P. Blicher, 1916).

11 The National Association of Danish Folk Dancers (Landsforeningen Danske Folkedansere) was founded in Aarhus, Denmark, in 1929 and, in cooperation with the Folk Dancers Fiddler Circuit (Danske Folkedanseres Spillemandskreds), aims to raise awareness of the folk dances, costumes, and folk music of Denmark. This information was provided by Poul Rassmussen, a member of the Toronto Danish folk dance group, who translated an article from Danish describing the history and mandate of the National Association of Danish Folk Dancers, which is distinct from the Society for the Promotion of Folk Dancing (Foreningen til Folkedansens Fremme).

12 Elizabeth Burchenal published a number of books providing English translations of various kinds of European national dances, including those of Germany, Finland, and Denmark, as well as collections of dances and singing games from several Scandinavian countries. See Elizabeth Burchenal, *Folk-Dances of Denmark, Collected and Described* (New York: G. Schirmer, 1915).

13 Influenced by a Swedish revival of traditional folk dances and singing games, the Danish Society for the Promotion of Folk Dancing was created in Copenhagen in 1901. In the early part of the twentieth century, the Society initiated research into the folk dances and costumes of Denmark, seeking help from the Danish costume collector, Bernhard Olsen, who had created an exhibit of Nordic national costumes for the Copenhagen Exhibition of Art and Industry in 1879. He had founded the

Dansk Folkemuseum that same year, a national ethnographic museum with wax mannequin displays of folk costumes. See B. Stoklund, "Between Scenography and Science: Early Folk Museums and Their Pioneers," *Ethnologia Europaea* 33, no. 1 (2003): 21–35. The Society drew up patterns using the original clothes from Olsen's collection. The artist Rudolf Peterson, using the Society's numerous resources, created a frieze of national importance that portrayed the national costumes, a copy of which can be seen on the cover of Burchenal's Folk-Dances of Denmark, published in 1915. The cover of Burchenal's book can be viewed on Cornell University's open source database: https://archive.org/details/cu31924019899586.

14 The first known Danish Canadian folk dance group was started in Toronto by John Madsen and his wife, Betty Hansen, in 1932. At this same time, between the 1930s and 1950s, when Canada received a high number of immigrants from the Scandinavian countries, a number of distinctively ethnic clubs, support organizations, and dance groups also formed in the Vancouver area. See "Scandinavian Dancers of Vancouver. The First Twenty Years: 1970–1990," *Scandinavian Dancers of Vancouver, BC*, accessed April 3, 2015, http://www.vcn.bc.ca/scandi/First20YearsHistory.pdf.

15 The current group at the Danish Lutheran Church on Finch Avenue was created in 1986 by Emilie Esbjørn, the pastor of the Danish Lutheran Church. Its heyday lasted throughout the 1990s. At the time of its inception, the pastor's husband, Frode Else Staal Nielsen, played the violin. Maria Skov Jensen was the pianist, and Tony Christensen played the clarinet. Later, as group members left, Verner Mikkelsen, an accordionist, became the sole musician until his death in 2011. See Audrey Urszulan, "The Danish Folk Dancers of Toronto," in *2012 Heritage Book: Vikings in Canada 2012, Proceedings of the 31st Danish Canadian Conference, Toronto, Ontario, May 24–27, 2012*, edited by Svend Berg, 54–57. Federation of Danish Associations in Canada.

16 See "Scandinavian Dancers of Vancouver."

17 See, for example, festivals such as Nordic Fiddles and Feet in New Hampshire; the Scandinavian Dancers of Vancouver, BC; the Eastbourne International Folk Dance Festival; and the National Folk Festival in Australia.

18 Urszulan, "The Danish Folk Dancers of Toronto," 57.

19 Walkowitz, *City Folk, 11.*

20 See Jobbitt's chapter, "Dance and the Fulfillment of Multicultural Desire."

21 I am borrowing the idea of a plural and multigeneric aesthetics from Gillian Mitchell's description of folk music traditions in her book, *The North American Folk Music Revival: Nation and Identity in the United States and Canada, 1945–1980* (Hampshire, UK: Ashgate Press, 2007), 170.

22 From interviews with members of the Toronto Danish folk dance group, April 4, 2014.

23 Numerous studies have recently been published concerning the positive benefits of nostalgia, especially for ageing populations. See, for example, Wing-Yee Cheung et al., "Back to the Future: Nostalgia Increases Optimism," *Personality and Social Psychology Bulletin* 39, no. 11 (November 2013): 1484–96.

24 In recent years, scholars have been encouraged by government funding agencies to understand knowledge creation differently. Knowledge is no longer to be conceived as generated and disseminated only by academics, but as a partnered activity with non-academic partners and communities. The most useful, accurate knowledge is co-created, shared, and interdependently generated between invested participants, including non-academic stakeholders.

25 For example, Dovercourt House in Toronto is a facility offering social dance classes in a variety of styles, including swing, salsa, and tango, among other dance forms. The instructors use gender-inclusive language that replaces "male" and "female" with other terms, such as lead and follow positions, or first and second positions. In *City Folk*, Walkowitz documents a new community of English country dancers begun by Carl Wittman and in which there were no gendered dance roles. See chapters 6 and 7.

26 http://www.zumba.com/en-US/about.

27 It is worth noting that Zumba incorporates dance forms and music primarily from non-European countries, the reasons for which would be worth investigating.

28 See Janelle Joseph, "A Dance Flash Mob."

SIXTEEN

GLIMPSES OF A CULTURAL ENTREPRENEUR[1]

Yasmina Ramzy

in conversation with P. Megan Andrews

Choreographer, dance artist, and teacher of Middle Eastern dance Yasmina Ramzy was born to white Scottish-Irish parents and raised in Toronto, Ontario. She discovered Middle Eastern dance by accident in her early twenties at a restaurant featuring live performers. Soon after, she attended an informal showcase of Middle Eastern dance where friends performed, and she improvised for fun in her street clothes. The musicians there recognized her innate musicality and encouraged her to continue. She says she embraced it as an opportunity to overcome her shyness.

When she began performing in the Middle East in the 1980s, she legally changed her name to Yasmina Ramzy. More than just a stage name, it reflects her sense of herself as an artist. It is also a name that has become known in the Middle Eastern dance community. In her book *Belly Dance, Pilgrimage and Identity*, dance scholar Barbara Sellers-Young offers a profile of Ramzy, her influences, and choreographic works, as well as the development of Ramzy's Arabesque Dance Company and Orchestra. In examining how and why

Ramzy decided to pursue belly dance, Sellers-Young points to the influence of a Tibetan meditation teacher:

> One of the major influences on her upbringing was Tibetan meditation, her guide in it, Lama Jampa Rabjampa Rinpoche, and the Orgyan Osal Cho Dzong Temple he founded in the middle of the forest of eastern Ontario. In her late teens she spent several years living with the monks and nuns of the monastery and she still spends part of each day in meditation and visits the temple on a regular basis. It was Lama Jampa Rabjampa Rinpoche who advised her in 1980 to learn to belly dance and never stop as it would play an important role in reviving women's spirituality.[2]

Ramzy has crafted a dynamic path in Middle Eastern dance in Canada, launching many initiatives and advocating for the art form. She is frank about the challenges in practicing and presenting an art form that is fraught with issues relating to Orientalism, femininity, sexuality, entertainment, commerce, and globalized media. For instance, Ramzy embodies inherent cultural tensions as a white woman practising Middle Eastern dance. Elsewhere Ramzy has acknowledged that the phrase "belly dance" is problematic.[3]

Despite the difficulties and politics of the art form, and her place in it, Ramzy has worked to educate herself and others and to shift negative attitudes about belly dance. As part of this effort, she wrote a column for the online magazine *The Gilded Serpent* from 2008 through 2012 and has contributed articles to other publications, including *The Dance Current* in 2009, when I was publisher and editor.[4]

Ramzy's perspectives are shaped by the complexities and plurality of issues and identities activated by her dancing and through her projects: artist and entrepreneur, Eastern and Western, professional and amateur, teacher and choreographer, performer and advocate, culture and commerce, dream and practicality. She says she has never loved performing, yet she glows with charisma and confidence on stage. She resists being called a businesswoman, but she has created and successfully managed multiple organizations, events, and initiatives over her forty-year career thus far. She describes how, in the early 1980s, she travelled to the Middle East and became an accomplished and celebrated performer; she was invited into audience members' living rooms to learn new material, and even became somewhat famous for a time in

Syria. She is recognized by many in the Arabic community in Canada for her knowledge and respectful articulations of Middle Eastern dance and music. An "advocate," she says, is how they would describe her. And yet, she has struggled to convince arts councils to fund her ten artistic productions with Arabesque Dance Company and Orchestra.

In 1987, Ramzy started Arabesque Academy, one of the first major schools for Middle Eastern dance in Toronto. At its height in the 1990s and early 2000s, the school had upwards of three hundred students per week pass through its doors. Through the Academy, Ramzy has helped train multiple generations of dancers, effectively raising the profile of the art form in Canada—as well as fostering her own competition, as her students have moved on to form their own schools and perform for audiences already primed, to some degree, by Ramzy's activities. She has taught across Canada and internationally in the United States, Mexico, Europe, the United Kingdom, China, and the Middle East. Her multiple troupes, primarily of students, also perform regularly, including the Folklore Troupe and Earthshakers, the latter of which is a group of full-figured women performers. In addition, she has mounted four international conferences and three festivals (the most recent one in 2018) to advance the creative practice and the discourse around the art form, leading discussions on issues in the field (including cultural appropriation, the question of over-sexualization, pedagogical responsibilities, and social activism), and stimulating engagement in creative process and collaboration.

Ramzy also runs a commercial agency called Arabesque Entertainment, which hires out dancers and musicians from her school and company for corporate events, weddings, and cultural celebrations, and, through her Planet Egypt Tours initiative, she takes groups of dancers and drummers on cultural trips to Egypt. She has embraced the digital public sphere, teaching classes online. She even engages dancers who live at geographic distance from Toronto to perform in her company; these dancers learn the material through online video and coaching sessions and arrive at dress rehearsal, able to fully integrate with the rest of the performers. Ramzy calls this digital extension the Arabesque Dream Company.

In 2011, Ramzy received a grant from the Canada Council for the Arts to travel to Egypt to interview an ageing generation of pioneers in the art form, some of her former teachers among them. The project was interrupted by the political turmoil in Egypt at the time; however, she managed to complete the work in 2014–2015, including a six-part interview with Farida Fahmy, principal dancer with the internationally celebrated Reda Dance Troupe of Egypt, and a set of blog posts about her conversations with renowned choreographer Mahmoud Reda.

In *Belly Dance, Pilgrimage, and Identity*, Sellers-Young examines the position of belly dance on the concert stage and the impacts of globalization and commercialization on the proliferation of the form, specifically mentioning Ramzy's contributions:

> The history of belly dance from the nineteenth century to the twenty-first century is an example of the impact of the desiring imagination on the (re) definition of a cultural form. In the process, the dancing Arab body, male and female, has been reified within the concept of Orientalism and propagated by the forces of commercialization. Mahmoud Reda and Yasmina Ramzy, in their communities of origin, Cairo, Egypt and Toronto, Canada, have presented a counter-discourse that has had an impact on the global dance form's reception.[5]

The basis for this comparison lies in Sellers-Young's assessment of the commitment of each of these artists to the aesthetic rendering of Middle Eastern choreography and performance, to a genuine investment in creative process, and to advancing an understanding of the rigour and complexity of the art form.

Sellers-Young cites multiple reviews of Arabesque Dance Company performances, concluding that:

> The critical reception of the Arabesque Dance Company and Orchestra has been positive from its inception…The visual revelation of the dance's vocabulary is in emotional synch with the onstage musicians and the audience's experience is that the dancers are the realization of the music. Yasmina Ramzy's ability to choreograph this visual and aural integration is the result of her discovery of *tarab*, the relationship between dancer, musician and audience she experienced during her years of performing in the Middle East.[6]

As she turns sixty, Ramzy dreams of passing on her organizations' business responsibilities and focusing on her artistic work. She recently rebranded to identify her artistic and mentorship activities under the moniker Yasmina Ramzy Arts and, for now, will continue the more commercial activities through Arabesque Academy and Arabesque Entertainment. She says she hopes to sell this suite of activities—to the right person—in the future.

Many artists, like Ramzy, strongly feel the competing priorities of pursuing one's creative vision without compromise while ensuring its viability in a market-driven economy; however, the art–business relationship is not an inherent antinomy. Artistic and cultural activity generally requires an economic structure of some kind, and it's no different for dance companies, dance schools, performance productions, festivals, and events. In fact, Ramzy's work finds many complementary possibilities among these to generate the necessary resources for her work. However, working in a non-Western cultural form in Canada means that public funding sources through arts councils have been slower to develop and, for Ramzy, still difficult to access. Indeed, even though the Applebaum-Hébert Report, which was published in 1982, recommended that the Canada Council for the Arts change its practice of only funding ballet and modern dance, it was just in 1988–1989 that the Council began a consultation process on cultural diversity and in 1989–1990 that it established the Racial Equity Committee. In 1992–1993, the Council finally expanded the scope and criteria for its dance programs to include all professionally practised forms of dance.[7]

This history of access to federal funding aside, Ramzy has continued to find ways to realize and finance her projects, driven always by her underlying commitment to her art form. It is this underlying commitment that arguably stirs her frustration with some in the field who choose to prioritize economic potential over—or at the expense of—artistic and cultural integrity.

In recent years, the term "cultural entrepreneurship" has become a catchphrase, and now around the world, post-secondary courses and programs in cultural entrepreneurship are being established, along with a field of research and a growing literature. While Ramzy accepts the phrase as a frame for understanding her work, it does not categorize her. To understand Ramzy's work is to understand that her activities and enterprises traverse the spectrum from the primarily artistic to the more commercial. Her resistance to formal not-for-profit structures aligns with her entrepreneurial impulse to seize opportunities where they arise, to activate ideas in immediate and instinctive ways, and to adapt and flex in response to changes in the field, the market, and the cultural dynamics. The way she speaks about her business sense belies the evident success of her efforts, which are ultimately driven by her creative instincts, passion, and drive to advocate for the art form.

Our interview ranged broadly; however, these focused excerpts in the edited transcript that follows are primarily limited to Ramzy's experiences in relation to the economic and business aspects of her career.

Megan Andrews: If you could, in your own words, introduce yourself and your work.

Yasmina Ramzy: Okay. So, my name is Yasmina Ramzy. I began practising Middle Eastern dance in 1980, so it's been thirty-nine years. It's been my whole career/life, and it's all I've really done. I happened on to it by accident, and I'm still here doing stuff; it never seems to end. And I've done a lot.

In the beginning I was performing in the Middle East, primarily in Syria and Jordan, and also in Lebanon and Egypt, on and off, for about fifteen years. Then I opened a school here in Toronto—I've opened a school here twice. I closed it to go back to the Middle East and then opened it again. Both times I really opened it so I would have a home—a place to be planted—get a "life" kind of thing, because I was living in hotels all the time—but I'm not a businesswoman. I'm terrible at it, I hate it, I struggle with it, and now that I'm about to turn sixty I'm reflecting on all that. And I've decided that I just want to try and let go of a lot of that; there's always been a struggle of what I want to do artistically and what I need to do—well, what I should be doing—to be a business person.

The rest of the world wants me to be a business person—but I really, really don't. I've always tried to find a way out; and both [the art and the business] suffer because of it. So I always do just enough business to maybe sort of almost pay the rent, and then I'm off doing my artistic things, and I can never really fulfill that because I'm pulled back and anchored to this horrible business stuff. So I've decided in my last years that I don't care—at whatever cost—and I just want to do my artistic projects. I've been working my way towards that in the last two years, and I hope that happens sooner than later, but we'll see [*crosses fingers and laughs*].

MA: You have all these initiatives, but what I want to get at is what is the financial infrastructure, to the degree that you can share that, I'm just wondering—do some things resource others?

YR: I would say, in general, each activity pays for itself. But the school generates artists and audience members for the company shows. Since the early 1990s, I have received about eight grants from Ontario Arts Council (OAC) for "Culture Specific" professional dance training, which funds bringing specialized teachers to the school or company for professional training; maybe three grants from OAC for dance production out of ten productions, two for seven of the dance festival/conferences and about two small grants for music composition; about two grants from Toronto Arts Council for festival/conferences and five for productions; and one grant from Canada Council for the Arts for production and one for research. I think we got one grant from the Laidlaw Foundation a long time ago for a production. These are estimates. When there was not enough funding for a production, I depleted my own resources from family, and so on. When the festival/conferences did get funded, then I could pay myself, which then got absorbed by productions.

MA: So, in terms of that whole big picture, you're obviously paid, somehow, by the work.

YR: No, I'm in debt, always [*laughs*]. And I borrow from my family, and I borrow from my friends [*laughing*]. I borrow from everybody. And that's why I've got to—I'm really trying to—streamline things so that it's very, very simple, and I'm not always using one festival to pay for another thing to pay for another. I want to really simplify it and not be borrowing money anymore.

MA: The school, the Academy, presumably has a more formalized [structure]—I mean, people pay for their classes. So that feeds the structure with you as the director and any teachers you hire, and . . .

YR: Yes [*nodding emphatically*]. So, when the school was really going gangbusters—because we were the only school—then the teachers got paid. I got paid. The money we earned from it paid for the costumes and production needs for the next project. The school financed a lot. I've always used the money that was earned, be it the agency—the commercial gigs—or the school, or my inheritances, anything like that, for productions.

MA: Do you pay your Arabesque Dance Company dancers to perform—like a professional dance performance? How does that work?

YR: They all get paid—mostly from the commercial stuff. So, for instance, if we do something on an outdoor stage and I get an honorarium for $1,000, I may give them all the money for parking and whatever, you know. But they get good money when they do commercial gigs. When we do a corporate event, or a wedding, even [with] a group of twelve dancers, they still all get paid really well.

MA: Are any of these entities incorporated as not-for-profit? Or for-profit?

YR: Well, in 1988, I incorporated. Yasmina Ramzy Dance Association was incorporated, non-profit. I didn't understand. I was told that I couldn't get grants unless I did that. As the years went on, then more and more you didn't need to be incorporated non-profit. For Canada Council you did, but for the other two [Ontario Arts Council and Toronto Arts Council] you didn't. It was very problematic—the corporate structure. First of all, if people are actually going to donate money to you, then it's a worthwhile venture. But no one's ever going to donate money to a Middle Eastern dance company—this doesn't happen [*laughs*]. So, what was the point [of incorporation]? You know I have to do all this extra bookkeeping, and I was told, "You're going to save on GST," but then I found out it's the same, and so eventually I just gave it up.

MA: So that organization doesn't exist anymore?

YR: No, it doesn't exist as non-profit. And I can apply as—what do you call it?—collaboration, or something—for Toronto Arts Council and Ontario Arts Council. The Canada Council, I can't, but I think I got one Canada Council grant in all the years for Arabesque. So it really wasn't worth it. And as for having a board of directors, I tried that once, and that was a disaster. They all wanted me to do—I don't know what it was. And it was all to do with money. They said, "Oh, you can't do this, and you can't do that, and I'm saying to myself, "If I thought like you guys, I wouldn't be here today. There wouldn't be an Arabesque!" And so I said, "Okay, fine. You guys, you run the Arabesque. No problem. I'm going down the street and starting something else" [*laughs*]. So when it came to that, they all said, "Okay, okay." And then I ended up just putting my best friends on the board because it just wasn't working otherwise. And I heard that many other dance companies had the same problem, and so I just thought, *What's the point?* Now we're more non-profit—in the sense that there's less money now—than we've ever been [*laughs*]. But just not officially non-profit.

MA: So are all of these activities just under you, as a sole proprietor?

YR: Yep, pretty much. Honestly, I'm just so not good at business. It's a miracle I exist. I just get these ideas, and I do them. And apparently sometimes they work, and they bring in some money, but then it's gone. So, I don't know [*shrugs and laughs*].

MA: Do you have someone as a manager, a business manager or a mentor or…

YR: [*Shakes head "no" at length*].

MA: You've always just done it yourself?

YR: Yeah. I mean, so many people have come along and said, you know, oh, they love what I do, they want to help me—so many times [*shrugs*]. You know, they help a little bit. But at the end of the day, it all lands in my lap, especially when it's not going well. And they all have jobs and lives—things like that. I mean, I've had paid staff, and I still do—[and] I've done a lot of bartering. I just had a new website created by bartering. The website designer is going to take my Pro Course [an intensive training course for dance artists, teachers, directors, and advanced students] probably, and so she made me a website. So a lot of the work is done through bartering. I have receptionists who work part-time as barter and take classes.

MA: So you've used the word "agency" a couple of times. Is that a good way to understand [your overall activity] as a whole?

YR: No, no—agency. I'm sorry—"agency" is the entertainment, meaning people who hire commercial dancers or musicians for weddings and corporate gigs. That's what I mean by "the agency." I hate running that, as well.

MA: So people pay you for those things, and then you pay out people who perform, but you take some sort of…

YR: Commission. Yeah.

MA: Commission. So that's one financial structure that's in place.

YR: Yeah, if I ran just [the agency] alone, and if I had my heart into wanting to do it, I could have made money. But I hate doing it. I had somebody else running it for years because I hate dealing with "bridezillas." Mostly I hate people phoning me up, and they want to know, "Is the dancer young? Does she have a good body? Is she this or that?" These are my girls, my students. When I hear people talk about them in an objective way like that, it makes me very upset. They're concerned about race; they don't want this race or that race. And it makes me very angry. So I get angry at my clients [*laughs*]. And then they go somewhere else. I can't be a good businesswoman for the agency. I'm terrible. And also, I don't care. I don't care about those agency shows. I don't want to do them.

MA: But then all of these students are getting work as a result, and from the outside, it looks very successful.

YR: Yeah. But at the end of the day, I never wanted an agency. I never even wanted a school. I didn't want any of these things. It all happened because I put on some show somewhere—because I've been doing that since I was like seven years old. I like organizing girls, and I like creating choreography and putting on a show, and that's where it ends. That's what I like to do. I do that, and then I get this response afterwards. People want to hire dancers, people want to take classes, people want to be like this, or like me, or whatever. And so they're willing to pay, and I think, *Well, maybe I better get a studio,* and then one thing leads to another. But at the heart of it are just these ideas—like the conference, like the choreography. And then it gets a response. But I never ever intended any of them to be a business.

MA: So, here's a definition of entrepreneurship: "The term entrepreneurship, generally speaking, describes the discovery of new means-ends relationships, and includes the exploitation of an opportunity as well as the creation of a new organization to implement a novel idea ... An entrepreneur establishes an organization to realize that opportunity and is at the same time responsible for the continued existence of this organization."[8] Does that resonate with you?

YR: I guess so. But I think I'm a starter, not a continuer—meaning the continued responsibility. I never wanted it.

MA: But you do it. So, in a way, I think this describes you, even though you rail at it, you fight back against it.

YR: [*Nods vigorously*].

MA: You say, "I'm not a businesswoman! I don't do this! And yet, you have created many different organizations and initiatives in your career, so far, and you're about to move in a new direction with new organizational structures, however unstructured they might be. You're the one who gets the idea and says "we need to do something about this," or "here's an opportunity, so I'm going to meet this opportunity with this idea."

A cultural entrepreneur—this is another quote—"is an entrepreneur who creates a business that is grounded in the arts, creatively inclined or relevant to the cultural heritage of a specific community. The goal of their business is to address social problems by shifting belief systems and attitudes. In other words, a business visionary who wants to transform the world."[9]

YR: Well, that, I would say, is more me than the other one.

MA: That describes you more, because it brings in the cultural mission piece that's at the heart of your work. But then it creates all this invisible labour—cultural labour that isn't necessarily remunerated or, you know, you're always looking for the money. Somehow you must be always looking for the money.

YR: Oh my god. I'm always stressed out about money. I wake up in the middle of the night, I have nightmares—only about money. And that's why right now, I'm trying to keep things simple so I can actually know where the money is, what's actually happening, so that I can have some kind of control, so that when I turn sixty-five...When I was thirty-three, my mom was worried about my future, and I said, "I'm probably going to be a bag lady." But I can't not be a dancer—this is what I love, right? But it may turn out that I am a bag lady [*laughs*]. It's worse right now because the economy is bad, and the genre that I'm in has become so appropriated by people who are taking it in another direction in which I can't go, you know.

[*Author's note: Here, Ramzy is referencing comments made elsewhere in our interview regarding her resistance to belly dance competition culture and the mediatized spectacle that dominates popular consciousness with its tendency toward overt sexualization and tricks and gimmicks over artistic nuance, expressivity, and the fundamental musicality of the form.*]

YR: So anyway, I don't know, we'll see what's going to happen [*shrugs*]. I do know one thing: every time I've gone kind of against the grain and followed my heart, it's always been successful. So I figure I just have to be brave and do that again. That's what the Yasmina Ramzy Arts thing is. Whenever I follow my heart really strongly, it always ends up being very successful. Belly Dance Blossom Festival[10]—well I told you, seven people did it the first year, and then boom, you know—

MA: And then 115 people came the next year.

YR: Not [just] "*came.*" More than that many came. One hundred-fifteen people wanted to be part of the creative process alone.

MA: Right, so that's even a whole different thing. So, your sources of funding are sometimes the arts councils. And then other sources of revenue would be the initiatives themselves, the agency, like the commission fees that come in, the school, like the teaching fees, and things like that. What about sponsorships? Donors?

YR: Only when we did Kickstarter. We did Kickstarter once, and it was hugely successful. But you know what? It was hugely successful because one or two very rich people just went and plopped a couple of grand on it. And it can't be done again. It was a one-time thing. We'd only ever ask for money from the public once. And we've been known, and we've been doing stuff for so many years, so I think people were really on board. But I don't think I could do that again.

MA: When was the Kickstarter campaign?

YR: We did it for the last production, for *Sawah* (2014). We asked for twelve thousand dollars, and we got fifteen thousand. And part of that was because my father was still alive and somewhat healthy, and my parents also went to all of their friends. But it was also the belly dance community—people who had watched us for many years and thought, *Wow, you know, I want to help them.* But I don't think we could do that as an ongoing thing. I think it was a one-time phenomenon. And interestingly enough, it was great—we needed the money, and that was great. But what was more ... beautiful about the whole thing was the artists involved. The dancers and musicians who'd been with me for many years felt so validated that people believed in them enough to donate fifteen thousand dollars. They were so excited [*smiles*]. It really boosted their sense of "wow, we're doing something good."

MA: And your instinct is it wouldn't work again. Why?

YR: Well, maybe. But I don't know. I don't like asking for money, anyway [*laughs*]. So I don't want to do it again ... I don't know that we could go back and ask—a lot of the people have died since then. They were friends of my parents who died. If I don't get grants from Toronto Arts Council and Ontario Arts Council for my new project, I do intend to at least go to a few wealthy Arabs who believe in what I do and try to raise money that way, or some kind of corporate sponsorship. But it's problematic. I remember on an Arab TV show, a producer-type once said, "Oh, Arabesque is so amazing, we love Arabesque; too bad it's belly dance!" And one of my musicians was there—he's Arabic—and he says, "What in that show did you see that in any way resembled what you think belly dance is?" The producer-type said, "Oh, no, nothing; it's not what I think belly dance is." So, there's always this perception problem.

A difference between our company and any other dance company, be it flamenco, Indian dance, or modern dance, is that—especially when it comes to ballet—you have patrons. We don't have that in our art form. When it comes to flamenco or Indian dance, you have a cultural community who will support their art form as a cultural thing for their own children. In Middle Eastern dance, it's never been the case. If you have a multicultural event, be it a parade or anything, up until recently, the Arabs are not there. And I always get called by these cultural event organizers who say, "We can't get the Arabs out; who's going to represent the Arabs? Would you please represent the Arabs?" So I end up doing it.

If Arabs are going to invest in any kind of art, then it's going be the art that *they* think will help them have a better PR with the rest of the world. They're being badly represented. They're very afraid of their image. They will do anything to fix that image. So, if it's a bunch of musicians with suits and ties with a violin, which looks Western, that's what they'd much rather put out than girls with their belly button showing.

So no one in the Arab community would ever donate money to us[11]—even though when they get to the theatre and they see what we do, and see the response that the Western community has, they say, "Oh, that's great!" But there're no Arabs who could donate money to a dance performance that has anything that remotely looks like belly dancing because, for the most part, Arabs will have belly dancing at their weddings. It's part of the culture, but they don't want the outside world to think that's part of their culture, because they think the outside world will think they're uncouth or over-sexual or something like that.

They don't want to be perceived as that. So they don't really want me out there doing what I do, in a sense. When they see what I do, they love it. But there's this war there. So, we don't have support from the actual cultural community the way Indian dance does, or any other "cultural" dance. And then we don't have support from mainstream dance, because anything with a rhinestone in a belly button is not art, and basically there's no one who supports us—except us—who really want to do what we do so people will change their minds. You know what I mean?

MA: So speaking of changing people's minds, I wanted to ask you about doing a pitch on the CBC TV show *Dragon's Den*?[12]

YR: [*Smiles*]. Yeah, I was going to bring that up a minute ago. *Dragon's Den* was fascinating.

MA: How did that opportunity come about?

YR: They found us, and they bugged us. And unfortunately, it was a last-minute thing. They were finishing recording their season, and they had a whole bunch of tech guys coming in, and they said they have "nothing colourful." Can you please come in and pitch something? And we were doing a show at Casino-something in Niagara Falls, which was a big three-day ordeal, and I was tired, tired, tired. So I had to come up with something at like four o'clock in the morning. We were coming back from Niagara Falls and had to go into the studio on *Dragon's Den* on Sunday morning. So I didn't know what to do, and I don't know anything about business, and afterwards everybody said, "Well, you should've come talk to me." But I didn't have time, and it was four o'clock in the morning, so I said, okay, I'll just ask for my dream. My dream is this: I would like $800,000 to take Arabesque Dance Company on tour to four major American cities, and to launch the company internationally. What was fascinating was that what you see on TV is not what happened; they always edit to make good TV, right? But what actually happened is first of all Kevin [O'Leary, one of the investor panellists on the show]—and that *is* on TV—you see him, he doesn't attack us. He attacks everybody. He did not attack or make one derogatory comment to me or to the group—except [for] one thing; he said, "Why don't you dump the musicians?" That's the only thing [*laughs*]. But even off-camera, he was very nice. Well, not very nice [*shakes head as if that's the wrong phrase*]. But I expected him to attack me. Arlene [Dickinson, another investor panellist on the show], said, "You know something? People like you, who have a vision and can inspire people… It's magic. If you find the right business person to partner with, you can make magic." But I just never found that partnership. Maybe I will—I don't know.

MA: That's so interesting, because they were all "out"—unwilling to invest—at the end. I watched the episode.

YR: Yeah. There was no way that we were going to be "in" [invested in]. I knew that, but more people from across Canada know who we are from that show than anything else.

MA: From the outside, it looks like you have structures and strategic plans and business objectives and stuff like that. But, talking to you, you're going on instinct.

YR: Oh yeah!

MA: And inspiration. In many ways.

YR: I try to make it look like it's all very intentional and everything [*sighs audibly*]. I do this partially to appease my parents [*laughs*]. Second, to appease the outside world. Otherwise I'm just a flake, right? And I do it for people to have confidence. And this was the problem with having the board of directors, because they wanted that approach. But if I went by doing things rationally, Arabesque wouldn't exist. None of this would have happened. When I opened the first school in 1987, I went to a small business course for three months, or something like that. Everybody had to present their projects. Every single person—the teacher and everybody in the class—said, "Don't do it, Yasmina; it'll never work." My parents, everybody. Every single thing I've ever... done, including Belly Dance Blossom Festival—"Don't do it; it'll never work." A conference on Middle Eastern dance? "Don't do it; it'll never work." Arabesque Dance Company in Fleck Dance Theatre,[13] a bunch of belly dancers? "It'll never work" [*shrugs and shakes her head*]. I've done it all.

With the Belly Dance Blossom Festival,... I just intended to drop a pebble in the water and let it ripple. Plant a seed. And again, a lot of people copied the idea.... I do these things because I feel this need to fix something, but I don't want to run the business. I don't want to be the director of the event, and I don't want to do all the administration. It takes me away from all my other artistic work. I'm so burnt out from all of it. So I refuse to do another festival, another conference—I refuse, I refuse. But every now and again, I get rattled up by something and I think, *I have to teach someone!* And so then I come up with these ideas [*laughs*].

MA: And this resonates with what you're sharing with me today in terms of how you feel about the work that you've tried to do or been inspired to do around this practice, this art form—[that it's about education and advocacy]—and how you feel it's really being shifted by commercialization and competition culture.

YR: Yeah, and I kind of feel like I opened the door. Especially in Toronto—I opened the door for belly dancers to be accepted, and all they did was hijack it and use it in ways that defeats itself, you know.

[*Author's note: Here she is referencing the perceived capitulation to spectacle and financial gain at the expense of the artistic nuance, cultural integrity, and musicality of the form discussed elsewhere in our conversation.*]

MA: Some of them, not all of them.

YR: Oh yeah, oh yeah. But even [with] Belly Dance Blossom Festival, we'll have a great discussion about this or that or where we should go and everything like that, and on the last day I think, *Oh wow, they've all become inspired; they're gonna change their ways and everything,* and they all go back and put on a competition [*shakes her head, laughs*]. A lot of hot air! So that's also why I stopped doing it, because at the end of the day, I know there's a ripple effect. But at the end of the day, not a lot changes as fast and dramatically as I would like.

MA: So, you've had experience as a businesswoman—even though you rail against that and fight back against that. By the outside measure, you've been successful. I mean, whether your financial statements suggest that you've been successful or not, you've been successful in initiating and seeing through many, many, many initiatives.

YR: Yeah.

MA: You've been somehow able to make the business work. And keep going. You keep doing new things, so there's that. You're—at the centre of your heart and soul—you're an artist; that's clear. You're a teacher. You're a mentor. And I would call you an advocate also.

YR: Yep, yeah [*nods*]. And I think in the Middle Eastern—the foreigner Middle Eastern dance community, especially in North America—that's how they would describe me: as an advocate. I'm always called upon any time there's a discussion: "Yasmina, what do you think?" [*Laughs.*]

MA: So what you're saying is [that] the Middle Eastern dance community calls upon you.

YR: Yeah, yeah, I mean not everybody. The new generation doesn't know me from a hole in the ground, but those who do say, "Well, you know, if you're talking about this, you should ask Yasmina." Or you know, very often they'll tag me in a conversation because they want to know what my voice would be in this situation.

MA: Because you're seen as someone who has an expertise and a depth of knowledge and a range of experience?

YR: And an advocate. That I've tried to push attitudes and ideas.

MA: About this art form.

YR: About the approach to this art form, attitudes toward this art form, how we should proceed, you know, things like that.

NOTES

1 Several complex and critical topics are touched on in this interview that invite deeper engagement but are not developed in this edited excerpt of our much longer interview. We acknowledge the tensions in some of this material, the context for which extends beyond our focus in this contribution on the economic and business aspects of Ramzy's experience.

2 Barbara Sellers-Young, *Belly Dance, Pilgrimage and Identity* (Palgrave Macmillan, 2016), 134–35.

3 Megan Andrews, "Yasmina Ramzy," *The Dance Current*, February 23, 2009, accessed August 25, 2019, www.thedancecurrent.com/column/yasmina-ramzy.

4 Yasmina Ramzy, "Feminism and Bellydance," *The Dance Current*, March 1, 2011, accessed September 25, 2019. www.thedancecurrent.com/feature/feminism-and-bellydance.

5 Sellers-Young, *Belly Dance*, 145.

6 Ibid., 141, 142.

7 Shannon Litzenberger, "Dance and Cultural Policy in Canada: Celebrating the Canada Council's 50th Anniversary," *The Dance Current* 9, no. 8 (March 2007): 22.

8 Andrea Hausmann and Heinze Anne, "Entrepreneurship in the Cultural and Creative Industries: Insights from an Emergent Field," *Artivate: A Journal of Entrepreneurship in the Arts* 5, no. 2 (2016): 7.

9 Kathryn Buford, "What is cultural entrepreneurship?" Quora, May 1, 2017, accessed March 1, 2019, www.quora.com/What-is-cultural-entrepreneurship.

10 Through Belly Dance Blossom Festival (2016, 2017, 2018), Ramzy initiated and hosted a gathering of international belly dance artists, scholars, and educators for a three-day in-depth engagement to advance the practice of and discourse around the art form through workshops, performances, creative process sessions, issue-based discussions, and presentations. Ramzy started the festival as a continuation of the International Belly Dance Conference of Canada, which she initiated and hosted four times, the last of which happened in 2012.

11 She does acknowledge several individuals from the Arab community who have financially supported her company.

12 *Dragon's Den* is a reality TV show that originated in Japan. Entrepreneurs pitch their business concepts to a panel of venture capitalists who decide whether or not to invest. They each cast their "vote" by saying they're either "in" to invest, or "out."

13 Fleck Dance Theatre is a mid-sized dance performance venue in downtown Toronto with capacity of 446 seats.

SEVENTEEN

DANCE AND THE FULFILLMENT OF MULTICULTURAL DESIRE

THE REFLECTIONS OF AN ACCIDENTAL UKRAINIAN

Steven Jobbitt

To suggest that I was "discovered" would probably be apocryphal, though there is certainly an element of truth to this statement. It all happened back in August 1995. I was at a party, dancing to Boney M.'s "Rasputin" and doing my best to kick and spin like a Cossack. Among the partygoers that night was Beth Yarzab, a dancer with the Chaban Ukrainian Dance Group in Thunder Bay, Ontario. She liked my moves and told me her troupe was looking for male dancers. I can't recall the finer details of the conversation, and I am sure that, being a twenty-five-year-old non-Ukrainian with no previous dance training, I was more tentative than I now remember. But when she asked if I would consider joining Chaban when the season started up in September, I must have said yes fairly quickly, because only a few weeks later I walked into the Ukrainian Home on Robertson Street with a brand new pair of black leather jazz Oxfords in my hands, ready to begin my first-ever dance class.

I remember being incredibly nervous for that first rehearsal. I also remember that this anxiety was tempered by a genuine excitement for the project I was embarking upon. As a boy, I had always watched my younger sister Michelle dance, and I recall quite vividly not only the fascination I had for the different forms of dance that she perfected over the years, but also the curious longing I felt when I attended her many recitals and performances. I was drawn to the spectacle of these events and beyond this to the physicality of dance and especially to the corporeal expression of a wide range of concepts, narratives, and emotions. Though I often yearned to be on stage with her, dancing was not something boys generally did in Thunder Bay, and so I never really gave it a second thought—at least not until I was invited to join Chaban. The possibility of becoming a Ukrainian dancer, therefore, provided me with an opportunity to fulfill a desire I had long held, but which I had never considered acting upon. The thought that I might finally be able to actualize this boyhood fantasy left me elated, almost giddy. It is a feeling that has stayed with me to this day, and that I get to relive every time I enter the studio to rehearse or teach.

My desire to dance intersected with a second and equally powerful yearning that I had long harboured, one that compelled me to explore, learn about, and ultimately immerse myself in as many different cultural communities as possible. From a very young age I had been drawn to a wide range of cultural forms and ethnic practices that stood outside the narrow confines of my own British heritage and Anglo-Canadian upbringing. Drawn to the history as well as to the languages and unique worldviews and traditions of so-called "others," I became committed to the idea of diversity and multiculturalism long before I had an awareness, let alone a full understanding, of what this meant, either conceptually or in practice. Though I recognize the danger of framing my attraction to the ethnic "other" in terms that might seem on one level to be a form of colonial desire or cultural appropriation, my openness to multiculturalism, one that was cultivated in me as a child and that I continue to nurture to this day, is, I think, key to understanding why I was so quick to accept the invitation to join Chaban.[1] Indeed, though I had never once contemplated joining a Ukrainian dance group before the summer of 1995, and though I came to be part of the Ukrainian community in Thunder Bay quite by accident, I can honestly say that I was already open to this possibility, and that the chance to become part of an organization that constituted an integral thread in our city's multicultural fabric satisfied a deep desire—and even a

Figure 17.1. Steven Jobbitt outside the Ukrainian Home on Robertson Street in Thunder Bay, Ontario. Photograph by Lisa Klymenko.

need—to participate in multiculturalism in a very literal and ultimately meaningful and self-transformative way.

What follows are some personal reflections on multiculturalism and dance based on my experiences with Ukrainian dancing in general and my association with the Chaban Ukrainian Dance Group in particular. I approach these reflections not only as a dancer, but also as a choreographer, dance teacher, and current Assistant Artistic Director of Chaban. In writing this, I also draw upon my knowledge as a scholar trained in Eastern European history and on my research into the history of nationalism and modern identity formation. My entry into Ukrainian dancing may have been spontaneous, but it was never, I hope, a naive undertaking on my part. Through my involvement in Ukrainian dance, I have certainly had ample opportunity to reflect on the many shortcomings, blind spots, and contradictions associated with multiculturalism both as a political project and as a community practice. But I have also come to appreciate the many benefits of multiculturalism, at least as these apply to the question of dance. Though Ukrainian dance as it is practised in Canada no doubt reproduces conservative and even exclusive notions of ethnicity and gender, my very participation in this cultural art form as a non-Ukrainian speaks to the potential for inclusivity that groups like Chaban have exhibited over the years, and especially since the introduction of official multiculturalism at the beginning of the 1970s.[2] Multiculturalism may in the end be fraught with inconsistencies and imperfections, but it is a complex phenomenon, one that, at least on the level of individual experience, warrants serious—if obviously critical—attention.

THE CULTIVATION AND FULFILLMENT OF MULTICULTURAL DESIRE

Though I was born in 1969, I was a child of the seventies and very much a product of the multicultural project unveiled under the leadership of Pierre Elliott Trudeau in 1971. I wasn't, of course, aware of the broader political discussions surrounding multiculturalism at the time, but I certainly felt and obviously internalized the general zeal embodied by this ambitious undertaking, in particular as it was introduced into Canada's public schools. Whether their enthusiasm was genuine or manufactured, our teachers integrated Trudeau's particular brand of "ethnic" multiculturalism into the curriculum with some excitement—or at least this is how it seemed to me. Alongside projects on fire safety, metric conversion, and the importance of wearing seat belts, my schoolmates and I were encouraged to explore and share our personal histories and heritage as Canadians. What countries did our ancestors come from? What languages did our parents and grandparents speak? What particular, even unusual, traditions did we practise in the home and with our extended families? What kinds of food did we eat that might be considered different from the Anglo-Canadian or French-Canadian norm?

There were, of course, glaring limitations to the kinds of narratives and practices we were encouraged to examine, share, and reproduce (at least here in

Thunder Bay). Though there was some effort to incorporate the histories and traditions of Canada's Indigenous peoples in a respectful if ultimately superficial and woefully inadequate way, the bulk of what we were exposed to was European, Christian, and white—very white. Africa and Asia were virtually absent from what we learned, and, from what I remember, the Middle East wasn't discussed at all. Moreover, given the limited and in some ways "kitschy" ethnographic scope of the multiculturalism of that era, what we studied was deeply essentialist, with entire cultures and histories reduced rather simplistically to national costumes and other traditional stereotypes. Yet the whole project was, I suppose, somewhat radical for its time and certainly opened up new perspectives and horizons, at least for me. The very idea of multiculturalism, coupled with Trudeau's vision for a "just society" in which people were proud of their cultural heritage and would be confident and willing to share their "ideas, attitudes, and assumptions,"[3] created (or at the very least reinforced) a profound curiosity in me to seek experiences that were foreign to my own upbringing and heritage. In retrospect, what Trudeau's dream for Canada fuelled in me was something that might usefully be called "multicultural desire."

This multicultural desire was enhanced from the outset by the fact that, as a descendant of immigrant families from the British Isles, I had, in essence, a very "uninteresting" heritage to share with my classmates. Whereas virtually everyone else seemed to have a rich past, mine was somehow impoverished and lacking. In the absence of something more exciting or exceptional, I thus found myself clinging almost desperately to the fact that my grandmother's family on my father's side came from Scotland, and that, at the very least, they had some interesting food to speak of (haggis was curious enough to qualify as an exotic dish in my mind, even though I had never eaten it). I also convinced myself that the Scots had a peculiar national costume (the kilt seemed unique to me), and that they were in possession of a dialect and accent that, if not exactly foreign, was at least somewhat "cool." In the end, this was not enough for me, however, and I couldn't escape the fact that, as a member of the dominant "national" group, I had very little to add to the multicultural Canada that was emerging before my very eyes. I was thus envious of my Finnish friends, whose parents spoke a mysterious language, and of my Polish classmates, who had puzzling Christmas traditions and ate lots of tasty dishes that were unknown in my house. Perhaps ironically, even though Trudeau's multicultural vision aimed to "break down discriminatory attitudes" by eradicating "cultural jealousies,"[4] it was I who was left feeling jealous and even a little incomplete. As much as I was fascinated by my own history and cultural heritage, I somehow wanted to be "more" than I was. I wanted, in short, to be seen as embodying Trudeau's ethnic multiculturalism in a very real way and ultimately to be counted among the Others that we were celebrating as a society.

The desire to overcome my own perceived "monoculturalism" was only heightened at the end of high school when I spent a year in Jyväskylä, Finland, as an exchange student, and then later as I pursued my schooling as an undergraduate at Lakehead University, where I immersed myself in European history and was introduced to world history, and where I studied philosophy and began to dabble seriously in existentialism. Driven by the need to broaden my personal horizons and to resist a narrow, "bad-faith" definition of my "self," I left university for a short period after my second year and spent three years between 1992 and 1995 living and teaching in eastern Hungary. It was during this period, as I worked hard to learn the language and to integrate myself into the society around me, that I had the first real opportunity to satisfy my multicultural desire in a sustained and ultimately noteworthy way. Though I would never suggest that I "became" Hungarian, I nevertheless gained a deep appreciation for the history and culture of a country that I can honestly say I felt at home in. Even though I came to realize that cultural differences are difficult if not impossible to transcend fully, it was encouraging to discover that the borders between Self and Other were fluid and porous, and that they could be crossed and transgressed in profoundly meaningful and deeply satisfying ways.

Returning to Canada in the summer of 1995, I was ready to continue my university studies and, more importantly, was hungry for fresh experiences outside of school that would help open up new pathways to a more culturally complicated and fully-developed sense of self. Ukrainian dance was just the sort of "experience" I was looking for. Beyond challenging me physically and mentally, I hoped that Ukrainian dance would provide a means of engaging meaningfully and respectfully with a local ethnic community whose history in Northwestern Ontario dates back to the end of the nineteenth century.

Despite some of the conceptual misgivings that I would later experience with respect to the nationalist (not to mention heteronormative) aspects inherent in Ukrainian dance, I can say without any hesitation that I was thrilled by the opening that Beth's kind invitation had provided for me. Under the skilful and very ambitious guidance of Artistic Director Cathy Paroschy Harris, Chaban had emerged as a dominant force in Thunder Bay's national dance[5] scene by the mid-1990s and had already laid the foundations for what continues to be a very strong dance company whose senior and junior dancers have toured not just in Canada and the United States, but also in Ukraine and Western Europe.

Impressive as this is, what continues to strike me as important about this group, and about Ukrainian dance in Canada more generally, is not only its fundamental openness to members of non-Ukrainian descent, but also the ways in which artistic directors like Cathy employ dance (and the teaching of dance) as a vehicle for the transmission of cultural knowledge and traditional practices.[6] Though Ukrainian dance, like all national or traditional folk dance, is as much an invented tradition as it is an authentic expression of something uniquely "Ukrainian," many instructors and artistic directors take their cultural mission seriously and make use of dance classes and the choreographic process to teach some of the basics of Ukrainian language, while the regional dances we do provide an opportunity to introduce dancers to the various regions of Ukraine (both past and present) and to their particular landscapes and traditions. Though on some level this sort of knowledge may be dismissed by academics as superficial and even overly simplified, dancers nevertheless become acquainted with the regional composition of Ukraine at a very young age and can become quite adept at distinguishing the unique dance steps, costumes, and music of the major regions of the country.[7] As Heather Fitzsimmons Frey argues in her chapter in this volume, this type of ethnocultural knowledge has the potential to open up more profound discussions on questions of identity and belonging, and may even serve to encourage practitioners and audiences alike to reflect critically on "how they perform who they are, and who they want to become."[8]

In addition to introducing practitioners of Ukrainian dance to the language and the cultural geography of Ukraine, dancing also provides an opportunity for instructors and community members more generally to reflect upon and transmit the history both of Ukraine and of the diasporic experiences of multiple generations of Ukrainians in Canada.[9] As an historian, I have to admit to being impressed and even encouraged by the capacity of groups like Chaban to deal in sensitive and even critical ways with issues like immigration, cultural difference, and, more recently, the Russian annexation of Crimea, and Putin's subsequent incursion into eastern Ukraine.[10] However, this process is by no means unproblematic, nor is it devoid of nationalist simplifications and ethnoracial biases, or of the ideological interpretations left over from the Cold War era.

Of course, as a dance troupe, our main focus is on dancing, and so it might be excusable if we don't delve too deeply into the cultural nuances and political complexities of Ukraine's past and present. However, that being said, it has been difficult for me to overlook some of the more problematic aspects of our group's involvement in the broader Ukrainian community. I was confused, for example, when I discovered in 1996 that our executive committee wouldn't allow our senior ensemble dancers to perform at a venue in Southern Ontario if it turned out that the hall in question was a Ukrainian Labour Temple (they were "Communists," I was told, while we were "Christians"). I was also shocked and a bit uneasy when we were encouraged to take out individual memberships to support a local Ukrainian Prosvita society when they were raising money in the late 1990s to build an extension to their existing hall. On the membership form that I was given, I was required not only to indicate my "race" but also to swear that I was not a member of, nor had any sympathy for, the Communist Party. More recently, while performing at a Ukrainian dance festival in Western Canada, I was confronted with the fact that, though many of the festival-goers were more or less apolitical, there was a handful of people in the audience who were vocal and very visible supporters of Svoboda: a right-wing, ultranationalist party in Ukraine.[11] Perhaps ironically, in my desperate desire to transcend the narrow confines of Anglo-Canadian nationalism, I had inadvertently found myself a member of a group that, consciously or not, helps to reproduce an essentialist form of nationalism that I find both problematic and distasteful.

On some level, I suppose it was a wilful blindness to these glaring contradictions that kept—and keeps!—me dancing. Indeed, the impulse to dance, coupled with the overwhelming need to satisfy my multicultural desire, has helped me to reconcile myself on more than one occasion to the idea of national dance as an imperfect multicultural practice (at least as this is defined in terms of Ukrainian dance's relationship to integral nationalism and to the potential reinforcing of conservative politics and traditions). But I console myself with the fact that there is so much more to Ukrainian dancing than just this. Though as dancers we may be complicit in reproducing the invented traditions and problematic narratives of an existing, diasporic group, we are also simultaneously engaged in a dynamic and somewhat separate community-building process—one that is rooted in the very act of dancing itself. Though by no means fully divorced from the Ukrainian community that supports us and infuses our dance with cultural meaning and aesthetic form, as dancers we are members of a more or less independent and ultimately self-referential community built on the camaraderie and goodwill that comes from the collective pain of hours of rehearsal and from the well-earned jubilation that follows the physical and emotional strains of a public performance.[12]

Essentialist narratives and practices may be one pillar of the broader ethnocultural community we are part of, but, in the end, Ukrainian dancing generates partially self-sustaining subcommunities, and perhaps because of this, it also has the capacity to attract Ukrainian and non-Ukrainian practitioners alike. As a stylized art form, Ukrainian dance is performed as much for non-Ukrainian audiences as it is for the Ukrainian communities that gave birth to these dance groups in the decades prior to the launching of Canada's multicultural experiment in 1971. If the celebration and promotion of multiculturalism has done anything, therefore, it has provided both a broader stage and a richer, more diverse pool of dancers for the performance of Ukrainian traditions, and with this has cultivated the potential for hybrid practices and ultimately for the sustained, if inadvertently open-ended, reproduction of the community itself.

DANCING AND THE (RE)PRODUCTION OF COMMUNITY

In August 2000, I left Chaban and Thunder Bay in order to move to Toronto to pursue a PhD in history. I had only been with Chaban for five seasons by that point, but in many ways it felt like a lifetime. Ukrainian dance, in fact, had become a central part of my life in Thunder Bay, especially after I began teaching children's classes for Chaban in 1996, and after I started assisting with the choreography in my role as the Assistant Artistic Director in 1997. I had even begun taking ballet and jazz classes on the side, just so I could improve my technique and work on enhancing my strength and flexibility. Ukrainian dance was like a gateway drug into the dance world, and I was most definitely hooked. It was so addicting, in fact, that I had even deferred my acceptance to the University of Toronto in 1999 so I could dance for one more year. In the end, however, I had to accept that it was time to move on. As integral as Ukrainian dance was to my life and ever-evolving identity, it was not the basis of a career (despite the fact that I really wished it could have been).

Though I would never cease longing for Ukrainian dance, new opportunities awaited, and before long new experiential horizons opened up to me. As a doctoral candidate at the University of Toronto, for example, I met and married Rafaela, the true love of my life, and we went on to have two beautiful children, Marta and Sunny. Through them I learned the joys of parenthood, and through my wife, an African specialist of Portuguese descent who was born in Mozambique and spent many years in South Africa, I was not only introduced to Africa and African history but also came to learn Portuguese and with this a smattering of Spanish as well. My research and teaching were other avenues that allowed me to explore new dimensions of both Self and Other, and to engage with non-Canadian as well as non-European cultures and histories. The ability to speak and work in other languages, moreover, allowed me to access and perform new identities vocally—to reinvent myself not just through vocabulary and syntax, but also through the modulations of my own voice.

As satisfying as all this was and continues to be, very little outside of my immediate family could satisfy the longing I still harboured for dance, and not just any dance, but Ukrainian dance. It was an art form that I had come to love and appreciate for so many reasons, not least of which was the community into which it provided entry. As much as I missed the kicks and spins and the elation that comes from performing on stage, I missed the people I danced with and the families and friends and long-time community members who supported Chaban. I also missed the hall where we practised and the various venues and events around the city at which we often performed. I missed our yearly concerts at the Community Auditorium and our annual spring performances at the Folklore Festival (an event that has been organized and hosted by the city's Multicultural Association since 1972). Most of all, I missed the opportunity to be part of a spectacle that celebrated Ukrainian tradition (however invented it may have been) and that ultimately promoted multiculturalism more generally. Despite its many shortcomings, the multicultural project was still one I believed in and wanted to be a part of.

In 2013, after nearly thirteen years away from the city and away from dance, I had the good fortune to be able to return to Thunder Bay and to Chaban. Walking into the hall on Robertson Street to register for what would be my sixth season with the group was like coming home. Very little in the hall had changed. A Ukrainian flag still stood on the stage next to the Canadian flag, and the portraits of Ukrainian poets and national heroes still hung next to an image

Figure 17.2. Members of Chaban's Veselka/Ensemble group performing the multi-regional "*pryvit*," or welcome dance at a Malanka (Ukrainian New Year's) celebration in January 2018 at the Port Arthur Polish Hall in Thunder Bay, Ontario. Photograph by Lisa Klymenko.

of Queen Elizabeth and to maps of Ukraine and to plaques and photographs commemorating over half a century of cultural activity in the hall. Costumes and props, some of them dating back to the 1960s and earlier, still cluttered the upstairs storage room, while kids ran around in the chilly basement as their parents signed them up for the coming year.

More importantly, though the faces of the younger dancers had changed, and though new families and individuals had been added to the group, Chaban was still the big family I remembered it to be. If anything, the passage of time only highlighted for me the deep roots and often intimate relationships at the heart of this community, a community that not only remains vital because of a constant influx of new Ukrainian and non-Ukrainian members but also thrives because of its intergenerational richness. Kids that I had once taught in the late 1990s were now grown up, and though many of them no longer danced, some of them did and were now my partners in the senior ensemble group. To close the circle even further, one of my former pupils, Jeramy Luby, was now teaching my youngest child to dance and was thus introducing them to the same basic steps and rhythms that I had once taught him. The thought that one day my child might grow up to teach dancing to his children quite literally thrills me and gives me the profound satisfaction of being embedded within a community that has both a rich past and, from what I can tell, a viable future.

I have just come to the beginning of my thirteenth season with Chaban, and it continues to be deeply satisfying. As an instructor, I am able to exercise my love of teaching, and as a choreographer and Assistant Artistic Director I once again have the opportunity to indulge a creative side of me that I can't always engage as a scholar. As a dancer, moreover, I am not only able to express myself emotionally and physically, but also have the chance to fulfill, in a performative way, the multicultural desire that was cultivated in me as a young boy. As an academic, I am fully aware of the contradictions and problems inherent in Canada's longstanding multicultural project in general and Chaban's cultural performances in particular, but this awareness only enriches my continued involvement with Ukrainian dancing by adding a critical dimension to it, thus making what I do all the more meaningful and significant.

NOTES

1 The troubling issues associated with the adoption and performance of ethnic Otherness have never been far from my mind as a dancer, choreographer, instructor, Assistant Artistic Director, and academic. Though as a Canadian of European descent I can quite easily "pass" as Ukrainian, I still wrestle as a non-Ukrainian with the appropriateness of what Katrin Sieg refers to as "ethnic drag." Such questions become even more complicated when I reflect upon my performance of Ukrainian dances and steps that, over the course of the long twentieth century, have themselves been inspired by—and appropriated from—subnational groups that have been marginalized, persecuted, and otherwise colonized as a result of Ukrainian nation building (I am thinking here in particular of Jewish, Roma, and Ruthenian communities). However, despite my concerns surrounding the appropriation and possible misrepresentation of a complex culture and history that is not my own, I am nevertheless encouraged by the often thought-provoking perspectives that transcultural immersion opens up, and remain as alert as possible to the numerous pedagogical opportunities that are present in what we do as a dance group. For a valuable discussion on the relationship between performance and cultural/cross-racial appropriation, as well as on the potential of ethnic drag to destabilize normative ethnocultural categories that are often considered "ancient and immutable," see Katrin Sieg, *Ethnic Drag: Performing Race, Nation, Sexuality in West Germany* (Ann Arbor: University of Michigan Press, 2002).

2 Like most Ukrainian dance groups in Canada, Chaban is almost exclusively "white." It is not, however, exclusively Ukrainian, nor does it discriminate on the basis of

ethnicity, race, sexual orientation, or gender identity. Dancers of non-European background have belonged to Chaban in the past, as have transgendered individuals. None of this fully reverses the outward markings of ethnicity or heteronormativity that characterize Ukrainian dance as a stylized art form, but it does reflect the inclusive liberalism that is in many ways at the very heart of multicultural practice in Canada. For a more detailed discussion on the question of inclusivity and the future of national dance in the Canadian context, see Suzanne Jaeger's chapter, "The Presence and Future of Danish Folk Dancing in Canada."

3 Pierre Elliot Trudeau, "Multiculturalism," *Canada History*, accessed May 18, 2016, http://www.canadahistory.com/sections/documents/Primeministers/trudeau/docs-onmulticulturalism.htm. Speech on multiculturalism delivered to the House of Commons, October 8, 1971.

4 Ibid.

5 "National dance" is a category of dance that Chaban performs under and is judged in during the annual Lakehead Festival of Music and the Arts. This grouping over the years has included Polish, Portuguese, Italian, Indian, Filipino, Irish, and Scottish Highland dancers.

6 Like Janelle Joseph, the author argues that, by historicizing ethnocultural dance, we have the capacity as choreographers, instructors, and performers to avoid falling into the trap of "shallow multiculturalism." By inviting all members of the broader community into our group either as active practitioners or as an audience, and by further using dance as an opportunity to educate and engage as well as entertain, we open up the possibility for "deep" multiculturalism. See Joseph, "A Dance Flash Mob, Canadian Multiculturalism, and Kinaesthetic Groupness," in this volume.

7 I was asked by the editors of this volume how Chaban describes or categorizes the dancing we do (i.e., do we refer to it as folk dance, national dance, traditional dance, or something else?). Unsure of how to answer this, I posed the question to our Artistic Director, Cathy Paroschy Harris, and this is how she responded: "Our mission is to promote Ukrainian culture and tradition through dance. We do not restrict ourselves to traditional styles, but also do interpretative and character dances that are rooted in tradition. We do dances from the areas of Ukraine that were located within its ethnographic borders in the 1700s, incorporating the regional variations in steps, costumes, and music as this is currently taught in ethnographic dance programs in Ukraine. Many of these regions show influences from neighbouring regions, borderlands, and countries. Within these traditionally styled dances, there are often variations of a theme, be it a wedding welcome "pryvit," or an Easter "haivky," or the classic "hopak," etc. When we do interpretations of Ukrainian dance, we may use modern variations of Ukrainian dance, and/or modern costume creations, and/or modern music (often based on traditional classics). We also do character dances, replicating daily life (often with an agrarian theme)...Whether traditional, interpretative, or character, the dances all tell a story and are intended to entertain the audience/observer, and to promote the appreciation of culture, the

arts, and creativity among the dancers and audience alike." (Email exchange with the author, May 16, 2016.)

8 See Heather Fitzsimmons Frey, "'There Is the Me That Loves to Dance': Dancing Cultural Identities in Theatre for Young Audiences."

9 As Marcia Ostashewski notes in her chapter "Ukrainian Theatrical Dance on the Island: Speaking Back to National and Provincial Images of Multicultural Cape Breton," Ukrainian dance is practised across Canada, and has been since at least the early twentieth century. My own group, Chaban, is now forty years old and is one of two Ukrainian dance companies in Thunder Bay. Situated in Northwestern Ontario, we have significant ties to a number of distinct regional networks of Ukrainian dance in Canada (in particular in the Prairie provinces, as well as in Southern and Northeastern Ontario). From an artistic point of view, our closest and most longstanding ties are with choreographers and instructors in Alberta and Saskatchewan, though we have toured extensively within what Ostashewski refers to as a "transregional circuit" within Canada.

10 Fitzsimmons Frey makes a similar observation in her chapter, noting that ethnocultural dance has the potential to be both challenging and provocative with the stories it tells, in particular as this relates to very complex questions of cultural diversity, identity (and especially multiple identities), and immigration.

11 On the origins of Ukrainian festivals in Western Canada and their relationship to the history of multiculturalism in Canada, see Ostashewski's chapter. Ostashewski also touches on the nature of political and ideological fissures within the broader Ukrainian community in Canada, noting that, despite the existence of sometimes antagonistic factions, dance itself has the potential to transcend existing secular and religious divides (at least within spaces that are focused primarily on performance and the articulation of Ukrainian cultural practices and traditions).

12 Joseph accurately refers to this shared sense of camaraderie and the feeling of community amongst dancers as "kinaesthetic groupness." See Joseph, "A Dance Flash Mob, Canadian Multiculturalism, and Kinaesthetic Groupness."

EIGHTEEN

OLD ROADS, NEW WORLD

EXPLORING COLLABORATION THROUGH KATHAK AND FLAMENCO

Catalina Fellay

In 1996, Joanna De Souza[1] and Esmeralda Enrique began a partnership of collaborative artistic exploration founded on their traditional dance practices, Kathak and Flamenco respectively, which resulted in the discovery of expanded choreographic possibilities. The success of their seminal choreographic work and first joint public presentation entitled *Old Roads/ New World,* performed as part of the 1996 DanceWorks Mainstage series, inspired further artistic exploration between De Souza and Enrique. The processes and products of their work are investigated here through the analysis of primary source materials, including interviews, program notes, newspaper reviews, photographs, and film footage, with support from secondary source materials, including a documentary film featuring De Souza and Enrique.

The impact of *Old Roads/New World* cannot be underestimated; this project expanded to produce ten years of creative collaboration, including *Firedance: Collected Stories,* a Mainstage performance for DanceWorks (1999), which received a Dora Mavor Moore Award for Best Choreography; *Firedance* (video/

film, 2001), directed by Drew Miller; *Firedance* (documentary, 2002), directed and produced by Vishnu Mathur, script written by Rita Mathur; and involvement in the 7th Kala Nidhi International Dance Festival and Conference (March 23–28, 2004), which featured performance excerpts from *Firedance: Collected Stories* in combination with the panel discussion "Process Revealed—Dialogue with Choreographers." In addition, the work produced as a result of the collaboration between De Souza and Enrique facilitated similar experimentation between artists in the Toronto Kathak and Flamenco communities (many of whom met through De Souza and Enrique's projects), such as Flamenco guitarist Jorge Miguel's ensemble, FlamenKathak,[2] and collaborative work between Kathak dancer Bageshree Vaze and Flamenco dancer Ilse Gudiño.[3]

During the mid-1990s, I was a young dancer beginning a Flamenco career in Toronto. As a member of the Esmeralda Enrique Spanish Dance Company, I was fortunate enough to be a part of the creation and performance of *Old Roads/New World* and several works that resulted from the extensive collaborative relationship between Enrique and De Souza. Looking back at this time now as an academic, I reflect on how De Souza and Enrique's productions demonstrate ways in which intercultural collaborations can be partnerships with innovative results. My focus here is primarily on Enrique's experience in reframing Flamenco through collaboration with De Souza. In particular, I look at how elements of tradition and innovation operate simultaneously to produce a cultural blending, made possible in this case because of similarities in the kinetic movements of both dance traditions.

In 1996, as Enrique prepared her first application for an operating grant from the Canada Council for the Arts, she studied the list of past recipients and noticed that she would be competing primarily with modern dance professionals.[4] It also became apparent to her that she would not be able to word her application in a manner that was true to her interpretation of the Flamenco form, as the Council seemed to favour work that employed innovation and risk-taking, judging by the number of modern and contemporary dance companies receiving grants and the kind of work they were producing. For Enrique, a true Flamenco artist pays homage to tradition; this is a matter of respect for the form. She says, "The *tradition* is what we revere and hold dear—what we treasure. This is what we build from; if that gets lost, then we're performing modern dance with a Spanish flavour."[5] She resented the institutional imposition of having to shape Flamenco at the expense of its traditional impetus and read concepts of risk-taking and innovation as compromising the integrity of what qualifies as a Flamenco dance. For her, privileging dance that favoured innovative risk-taking in the context of modern and contemporary dance did not truly promote cultural diversity in Canada.[6]

In the context of this case study, my use of the term "tradition" does not imply that the dance forms described are in any way stagnant museum pieces that have not evolved and are not evolving. I use the term "tradition" to describe the culturally rooted philosophical and aesthetic movement practices present in Flamenco and Kathak dance respectively, as passed down from teacher to student through established dance lineages. I use the concept of "innovation" in dance arts to refer to the exploration of the time-honoured dance lineages of Flamenco and Kathak dance, thus expanding it beyond the conventional use of the term that refers to the rebellion against establishment that motivated many modern and postmodern dance practitioners. How, then, can so-called traditional dance forms such as Kathak, rooted in Indian culture, and Flamenco, rooted in Spanish culture, express innovation within the Canadian dance landscape? I believe *Old Roads/New World* employed an innovative approach for Kathak and Flamenco dance by bringing them together to express aspects of cultural diversity in Toronto at the end of the twentieth and the beginning of the twenty-first centuries.

THE TRAVELLERS ON THIS JOURNEY: JOANNA DE SOUZA AND ESMERALDA ENRIQUE

Both De Souza and Enrique are North American: De Souza was born in Canada and is of Scottish ancestry, and Enrique is a Mexican American who immigrated to Canada in 1981. Neither woman belongs to the ethnicities that originally developed their respective dance traditions, yet both are recognized and celebrated experts in their fields because of their technical skills and artistic talents as teachers, choreographers, and performers. This is not to say that De Souza and Enrique have not experienced criticism in their dance careers. Working in the Flamenco tablaos or cafés of Spain, Enrique experienced harsh criticism of her dancing by management and the deliberate damaging of her costumes by fellow performers.[7] De Souza explains one of the ways in which people question her involvement in an Indian classical dance form because of her Scottish-Canadian heritage: "People ask me all the time, 'Are you Hindu?' and I say 'No.' 'Are you Muslim?', 'No.' 'Are you Christian?' and in all honesty I have to say 'No,' although that is the way I was brought up. I tend to feel the dance is my religion and my way of life ... but rather than religion or religious, I consider it spiritual."[8] Beyond the fact that the two dancers live and work in the multicultural environment of Toronto, and that geographic and cultural proximity facilitated their professional exchange, perhaps it is also their willingness to adopt expertise in dance forms outside of their own ethnic and cultural heritage that facilitated the initial choreographic exploration.

De Souza began her study of Kathak in 1978 under Sri Chitresh Das after being inspired by a performance in 1977 at Fisherman's Wharf, California.[9] Her study became all-consuming, leading to a master's degree in Kathak dance through Prayag Sangeet Samiti in Allahabad, India. In 1988, she and tabla master Ritesh Das co-founded the M-DO/Kathak Toronto and Toronto Tabla Ensemble Centre for World Music and Dance, where cultural understanding through music and dance were pursued for professional and recreational purposes. Before collaborating with Enrique, De Souza had already worked on numerous traditional Kathak as well as cross-cultural choreographic projects with, for example, Indigenous singer Sadie Buck, Indigenous actors Jack Burning and Madeline Bergeron (1992), and the Japanese taiko drum ensemble Suwa Daiko (1991).

Enrique was similarly inspired to dance as a child when she first witnessed a Flamenco performance at ten years of age and was drawn to the range of expression conveyed by the dancer.[10] Hailing from a large and artistic family, Enrique studied and performed with her older sister, Carla, who is also a Flamenco dancer,[11] and in this way describes herself as having grown up "in the Flamenco tradition."[12] She studied Flamenco dancing as a child in the United States and began working professionally by the age of fourteen, touring North America with Luisa Triana's company and later with José Greco's influential company. After high school, she moved to Spain to perfect her art at the prestigious dance studio Amor de Dios.[13] Enrique further expanded her knowledge through the invaluable education gained by performing as a professional at Los Canasteros, one of the most respected tablao Flamenco of Madrid.[14] She toured throughout Europe, the Middle East, Mexico, and the Caribbean.[15] In 1982, Enrique established the Academy of Spanish Dance and the Esmeralda Enrique Spanish Dance Company in Toronto.[16]

EXPLORING A "NEW WORLD" THROUGH COLLABORATION

De Souza and Enrique knew each other through the Toronto dance community years before coming together creatively in 1996. They had attended each other's concerts and were both in touch with Mimi Beck, dance curator of DanceWorks, which has grown significantly since its creation as a collective of independent dance artists in 1977.[17] As Enrique recalls, Beck was one of the sparks that ignited the partnership between herself and De Souza when she agreed that a concert featuring the coming together of Kathak and Flamenco would do well in the DanceWorks Mainstage series.[18] It is notable, but not surprising, that a presenter with a focus on contemporary dance known for "celebrating past and present and embracing future choreographic voices" would encourage the blurring of perceived boundaries between cultural dance forms by creating this first venue.[19] It is precisely this understanding of cultural diversity that facilitated this and future choreographic cross-cultural explorations.

During our interview, De Souza recalls months of meetings and discussions before she and Enrique ever set foot in the studio to choreograph. They discussed their personal histories, the paths each travelled in their careers as dancers and choreographers, and the directions they might take together through collaborative work. Although De Souza and Enrique come from very different personal and professional backgrounds, they were struck by the similarities in the methods of their dance education. Certainly, De Souza and Enrique agree that their time as young dancers involved a great deal of study through immersion; cultural context and artistic reasons for movement choices were passed directly from teacher to student. In both Kathak and Flamenco there is an expectation that the dancer be simultaneously aware of established technical requirements and the possibility of improvisational expression. These expectations go beyond the iconic aesthetic standards of Kathak and Flamenco as genres; practitioners must be open to the very spirit of each form. It is no surprise then that when at last they entered the studio, De Souza would remember the very first movement she and Enrique took together as one of beauty and harmony.[20] Both De Souza and Enrique prepared themselves to dance by standing with shoulders and hips square to the mirror, arms held toward the left of the body, each dancer simultaneously grounding herself through the legs and feet while pulling up vertically through the spine. This small and relatively simple pose, a default starting point for each discipline, anchored the aesthetic compatibility of the forms and these two women as artists.

As their collaborative work moved from the studio to the stage, this exploration revealed the mutual goals of the artists aimed at creating work to which Toronto audiences of Flamenco, Kathak, and dance in general could relate. When discussing their collaborative relationship, for instance, De Souza recalls working within compatible creative processes, which she attributes to a mutual respect between herself and Enrique. As a seasoned collaborating artist in various forms, De Souza explained that, in her experience, success in the collaborative process "has little to do with the art forms and more to do with the chemistry between the artists."[21] Yet, the compatibility between the artists in this case also mirrors the compatibility between the two dance forms. De Souza described the creative process as an investigation of what is shared by the two forms and the possibilities that exist between them.[22]

ESMERALDA ENRIQUE'S NAVIGATION IN WORKING WITH KATHAK

Although Kathak and Flamenco represent distinct dance genres, there are, in fact, many similarities between them, the most obvious of which are a preference for the use of the vertical axis of the body, percussive footwork, rhythmic hand clapping, and play on specific rhythmic cycles. Moreover, the structure of a conventional Kathak performance follows a progression of tempo from sustained to quick, ending with a climax, a dramatic technique often employed in Flamenco dancing as well. Enrique, however, has described the creative process as a blending of the two forms rather than a fusion based on inherent similarities, stressing that essential structural elements in each form mirrored one another comfortably.[23] She emphasizes an important distinction between "blending" and "fusion." From her perspective, fusion calls to mind a liquefying process that takes separate elements and renders them indistinguishable from one another in order to create something new.[24] In contrast, blending represents a coming together of elements where they complement rather than compromise each other. To this end, the collaborative choreographic works she and De Souza have created were intended to present an equal partnership between Flamenco and Kathak, and not the invention of a new fusion form.

Fundamental elements from both dance forms complement one another, I would argue, because this familiarity actually comes from a shared history. Scholars connect part of Flamenco's history to a Kathak lineage brought to Spain by nomadic bards called Kathakars, or storytellers, from North India.[25] The syncretism between Flamenco and Kathak then, for Enrique and De Souza, is like the reunion of distant cousins: similar but different, with a shared familial bond. In this case, common roots were easily highlighted and identified, holding a base from which a new syncretistic dance expression could emerge between them, facilitated by the fact that both dancers also share the cultural commonality of living and working in Toronto.

Aspects of each dance form are also comparable in mood and aesthetic. In Kathak, choreographed sections intended to highlight specific elements of the dance are called a thaat. A thaat can, for example, focus on a beautiful gait, demonstrating grace, and/or perform stylized scenes from daily life. This is comparable to a silencio from the traditional structure of a Flamenco dance where stylized and often sustained movements focus on the graceful portrayal of emotion. Similarly, a Kathak lari is echoed in a Flamenco escobilla: both are footwork compositions consisting of rhythmically complicated variations on themes employing counterpoint and accentuation that is complementary to the rhythmic cycle being used.

The expected complexity of rhythmic interpretation has resulted in both dance forms using identifiable footwork sequences as punctuation to signal an end. In Flamenco this rhythmic "cadence" is known as a llamada, and in Kathak as a tihai. Both forms also use sharp stops with sudden stillness for dramatic effect that not only provides visual accents but also auditory suspense. Often used to end a footwork section, this practice of ending sharply is known as a kurant (or sam) in Kathak and as terminando bien parado in Flamenco.

Also notable is the cyclical conceptualization of rhythmic patterns where in both Kathak and Flamenco the last and first beat of a cycle are the same. In Flamenco there is no word for this practice, but in Kathak it is known as sam. Sam is the beat that a dancer will both begin and end on in a given composition. I posit that this concept goes beyond the use of an upbeat in classical Western music in that it drives the movement and music with a feeling of continuity making the beginning and end always present. De Souza explains that, in Kathak, sam promotes a sense of balance and equality,[26] while I assert that in Flamenco it establishes a tension within the rhythmic pulse that gives the music a feeling of forward momentum.

The similarities between these mirrored aesthetics and structures of Flamenco and Kathak provided fertile ground for creation. De Souza and Enrique each stated that they aimed to work with these similarities while retaining the individual integrity of each form. For Enrique, one of the most interesting and challenging aspects of the collaboration was working with the rhythmic cycles of Kathak.[27] For example, involvement in transposing Flamenco technique onto the emotions and aesthetic implications of the Kathak rhythmic cycles proved interesting. Often a different perspective can inspire a change of approach towards the familiar, and for Enrique this was certainly the case.[28] Subsequent material involved the increased layering of rhythmic cycles unique to Flamenco onto each other, thereby providing sensational new interpretations of the traditional. Notably, original music was created for their dance works because one of the most important aspects of the blending of the two forms involved the play between the traditional rhythmic cycles from each.[29]

Despite these numerous similarities between the forms, which also facilitated a smooth collaborative process with De Souza, Enrique found that she needed to "temper the attack" of Flamenco for these collaborative works in order to avoid drowning out the sound of De Souza's footwork.[30] Her approach towards choreography for these projects required that, to a large extent, she put aside her spontaneous and deeply rooted improvisational knowledge as a Flamenco dancer and choreographer as it tended towards a more individual expression.[31] Did this make Enrique's contribution any less Flamenco in essence? It is evident through the work that resulted from this collaboration that Enrique's contributions retained their Flamenco qualities and that those qualities are distinct from De Souza's Kathak expressions. Enrique simply worked within her medium but challenged herself to access creative impetus through a different framework as she negotiated collaborative outcomes with De Souza.

In many ways, Flamenco dance traditionally emerges from collaboration. There are three essential elements to Flamenco art: the cante (song), toque (guitar), and baile (dance). In a traditional setting, all three elements work together and feed off each other through improvisation. The result is much like a conversation unfolding in a shared, abstract expression of emotion that includes both performers and spectators as active participants. The impetus comes from the songs, which are driven by the rhythmic patterns of the compás[32] and additionally identified through harmonic qualities. The toque draws from those qualities once established and adds expressions that are both unique to the possibilities of the instrument and the talents of the guitarist, while remaining complementary to the palo. The baile draws inspiration from both the cante and the toque, but it also has influence over the creative direction of the shared experience. The dance then is not only the physical representation of Flamenco, but it also contributes to the overall creation and interpretation of the "Flamenco spirit."

In collaborating with De Souza, the process for Enrique became less about the traditional interpretation of cante and compás through abstract movement and more about an exploration of aesthetic elements and structural form. All of this, although interesting and informative, Enrique found somewhat disorienting.[33] She found herself making conscious decisions to subdue the Flamenco. Sometimes that decision to "temper the attack" of Flamenco came out of a mutual artistic decision between both choreographers to express certain elements common to both forms.[34] At other times, it was a practical choice made to promote balance between the forms, as was the case with footwork. For example, acoustically, Enrique's hard-hitting Flamenco shoes could easily overpower De Souza, who was dancing barefoot with bells on. Neither of these dance forms had traditionally developed for performance on a proscenium stage, so the issue of audible footwork did become a problem. In response, for their second stage show, *Firedance: Collected Stories* (1999), both De Souza and Enrique used a microphone as a technical aid. These microphones, which ran discretely down the leg of each dancer, helped amplify the sound of their footwork that was now not only in competition with one another, but also with the numerous tabla drums onstage.

NEW ROADS

One result of De Souza and Enrique's collaborative work was an underscoring of the openness and sophistication of their audiences. Over the years, both had established and educated significant audience bases. At the time *Old Roads/New World* was produced, there were several notable Flamenco and

Kathak dance institutions in operation beyond M-DO/Kathak Toronto and the Esmeralda Enrique Spanish Dance Company and Academy of Spanish Dance in the Greater Toronto area, including the Paula Moreno Spanish Dance Company, ¡Arte Flamenco!, Theatre Flamenco, Company Carmen Romero, and Sampradaya. The collaborative work brought together Kathak and Flamenco dance in ways that were relevant to artistic communities as well as the local Indian and Spanish communities. Since the presentation of their debut work, the Indian community of Toronto in particular has supported subsequent presentations in more intimate settings by requesting Kathak/Flamenco dancing at important social occasions, such as weddings.[35] What might at first have been considered a novelty act through the combination of tradition with innovation in the coming together of Kathak and Flamenco holds enduring relevance within the multicultural reality of Toronto's dance culture; what Enrique and De Souza did effectively was to negotiate their personal identities and the identifying signifiers of their perspective dance forms as they created collaboratively from those two highly stylized cultural expressions.

NOTES

1 Joanna De Souza was performing under the name Joanna Das in 1996.

2 FlamenKathak often features Flamenco dancer Ilse Gudiño, Flamenco dancer Lisa La Mantia, Kathak dancer Tamana Koovarjee, tabla player Ravi Naipalli, and dhol player Gurtej Singh. See Harbourfront Centre, "Hot & Spicy Food F estival: FlamenKathak Performance," accessed September 5, 2018, http://www.harbourfrontcentre.com/whatson/music.cfm?id=5406.

3 Tamara Baluja, "A Festival That Celebrates a Fusion of Cultures," *Globe and Mail*, May 20, 2011, accessed June 10, 2012, http://www.theglobeandmail.com/news/toronto/a-festival-that-celebrates-a-fusion-of-cultures/article598152/.

4 According to page 59 of *The Canada Council 38th Annual Report, 1994–1995*, under the heading "Grants to Professional Dance Companies," there were thirty-seven grants awarded for a total of $7,324,000: twenty-nine modern and contemporary dance companies awarded a total of $2,954,000 combined; five ballet companies awarded $4,275,000 combined; and three multicultural dance companies awarded $95,000 combined. The multicultural dance companies were Vinok Folkdance Society from Edmonton, Alberta ($35,000), Kokoro Dance from Vancouver, British Colombia ($30,000), and Menaka Thakkar and Company from Toronto, Ontario ($30,000). See Canada Council for the Arts, *The Canada Council 38th Annual Report, 1994–1995*, accessed September 5, 2018, https://canadacouncil.ca/-/media/Files/CCA/Corporate/Annual-Reports/en/1994-95-Annual-Report.pdf, 59.

5 Esmeralda Enrique, interview by author, November 17, 2011.

6 This is not to say that there is no innovation in Flamenco, but rather that it is expressed from a different perspective and with a different language than that expressed in dance forms such as contemporary and modern dance.

7 Seika Boye, "Esmeralda Enrique: What is Now is What is Next," *Dance Collection Danse*, no. 67 (Spring 2009): 13.

8 *Firedance*, documentary directed by Vishnu Mathur (Toronto: Silvertouch Production, 2002).

9 Ibid.

10 Ibid.

11 Esmeralda Enrique, personal communication with author, November 17, 2011.

12 "Biographies," Esmeralda Enrique Spanish Dance Company, accessed May 5, 2012, http://www.flamencos.net/company/company-members.html.

13 The Amor de Dios (Love of God) Flamenco arts studio, established in 1953, is still in operation today in Madrid, Spain.

14 Tablao translates as "floorboards." Tablao Flamenco refers to a place where Flamenco shows are performed in a relaxed, restaurant- or café-style atmosphere offering tapas and drinks. It is a venue in which the audience is expected to participate in the form of jaleos, or verbal encouragements.

15 "Biographies," Esmeralda Enrique Spanish Dance Company.

16 According to records at *Dance Collection Danse*, local Spanish dancers and teachers were present in Toronto as early as the 1930s. Although Enrique was not the first woman to found both a company and an academy of Spanish or Flamenco dance in Toronto, in 1982 Paula Moreno was the only other woman to have both a school and a company.

17 DanceWorks, "About DanceWorks," accessed September 5, 2018, http://www.danceworks.ca/.

18 Joanna De Souza, interview by author, June 25, 2012.

19 DanceWorks, "About DanceWorks."

20 De Souza, interview.

21 Ibid.

22 Ibid.

23 Esmeralda Enrique, interview by author, May 25, 2012.

24 Ibid.

25 Miriam Phillips, "Hopeful Futures and Nostalgic Pasts," in *Flamenco on the Global Stage: Historical, Critical, and Theoretical* Perspectives, eds. K. Meira Goldberg, Ninotchka Devorah Bennahum, and Michelle Heffner Hayes (Jefferson, NC: McFarland and Company, 2015), 50.

26 De Souza, interview.

27 Enrique, interview, 2012.

28 Ibid.

29 The original score was created by the Toronto Tabla Ensemble under the artistic

directorship of Ritesh Das in collaboration with Miguel de Cadiz, Paco Fonta, Nicolas Hernandez, Ramesh Misra, Maryem Tollar, and Christopher Ris.

30 Enrique, interview, 2012.

31 Ibid.

32 Refers to the musical metre of a Flamenco song style; it is the rhythmic cycle of a palo.

33 Enrique, interview, 2012.

34 Ibid.

35 Flamenco dancers and musicians from the Esmeralda Enrique Spanish Dance Company, Kathak dancers from Chhandam Dance Company, and musicians from the Toronto Tabla Ensemble in turn put together their own works and are, to this day, hired for weddings and other community events.

REFERENCES

Acheraïou, Amar. *Questioning Hybridity: Postcolonialism and Globalization*. Basingstoke: Palgrave Macmillan, 2011.

Adamson, Lois. "Why Bring Students to the Theatre? An Exploration of the Value of Professional Theatre for Children." MA diss., University of Toronto, 2011.

Albright, Ann Cooper. *Choreographing Difference: The Body and Identity in Contemporary Dance.* Hanover: Wesleyan University Press, 1997.

Anderson, Benedict. *Imagined Communities: Reflections on the Origin and Spread of Nationalism*. London: Verso, 1983.

Andrews, Megan. "Yasmina Ramzy." *The Dance Current.* February 23, 2009. Accessed August 25, 2019. www.thedancecurrent.com/column/yasmina-ramzy.

Arrowsmith, Phyllis M., and Amy Wakefield. Letter to the editor. *Daily Province,* March 26, 1936. LAC, Indian Affairs, RG10, C-II-2, Vol. 11297, [T-16110, 633–34].

Artsayer. "Yvonne Chartrand." Accessed October 3, 2019. http://www.youtube.com/watch?v=SQneXV9CWEU.

Asch, Michael. "Concluding Thoughts and Fundamental Questions." In *Protection of First Nations Cultural Heritage: Laws, Policy and Reform,* edited by Catherine Bell and Robert Patterson, 394–412. Vancouver: UBC Press, 2009.

Atkinson, Michael. "Enduring Bodies in Triathlon." In *Tribal Play: Subcultural Journeys through Sport,* edited by Michael Atkinson and Kevin Young, 295–317. Bingley, UK: Emerald Group Publishing, 2008.

Averbuch, Irit. "Shamanic Dance in Japan: The Choreography of Possession in Kagura Performance." *Asian Folklore Studies* 57, no. 2 (1998): 293–329.

Babette's Feast. Directed by Gabriel Axel. 1987. Copenhagen: Nordisk Film and Det Danske Filminstitut.

Bakht, Natasha. "Mere 'Song and Dance': Complicating the Multicultural Imperative in the Arts." In *Pluralism in the Arts in Canada: A Change is Gonna Come,* edited by Charles C. Smith, 13–26. Ottawa: Canadian Centre for Policy Alternatives, 2012.

———. "Mere 'Song and Dance': Complicating the Multicultural Imperative in the Arts." In *Home and Native Land: Unsettling Multiculturalism in Canada,* edited by May Chazan, Lisa Helps, Anna Stanley, and Sonali Thakkar, 175–83. Toronto: Between the Lines, 2011.

Balme, Christopher. *Decolonizing the Stage: Theatrical Syncreticism and Post-colonial Drama.* Oxford: Oxford UP, 1999.

Baluja, Tamara. "A Festival That Celebrates a Fusion of Cultures." *Globe and Mail,* May 20, 2011. Accessed June 10, 2012. http://www.theglobeandmail.com/news/toronto/a-festival-that-celebrates-a-fusion-of-cultures/article598152/.

Banks, James A. "Multicultural Education: Historical Development, Dimensions, and Practice." In *Handbook of Research on Multicultural Education,* edited by James A. Banks and Cherry A. Mckee Banks, 3–24. New York: Macmillan Publishing Company, 1995.

Bannerji, Himani. *The Dark Side of the Nation: Essays on Multiculturalism, Nationalism and Gender. Toronto: Canadian Scholars' Press, 2000.*

Barnard, Elissa. "Dance Fest Offers Eclectic Mix." *Halifax Chronicle Herald,* February 8, 1999. Accessed July 10, 2016. http://www.elvientoflamenco.com/reviews/reviews.htm.

Bedard, Roger L. "The Cultural Construction of Theatre for Children and Young Audiences: A Captive Eddy of Recursive Harmonies." *Youth Theatre Journal* 23, no. 1 (2009): 22–29.

Behrends, Andrea, Sybille Müller, and Isabel Dziobek. "Moving In and Out of Synchrony: A Concept for a New Intervention Fostering Empathy through Interactional Movement and Dance." *The Arts in Psychotherapy* 39, no. 2 (2012): 107–16.

Bélisle, Rhéal. *Honorable Senator Paul Yuzyk: In the Footsteps of Nationbuilders.* Accessed October 30, 2007. http://www.yuzyk.com.

Bellow, Juliet, and Nell Andrew. "Inventing Abstraction? Modernist Dance in Europe." In *The Modernist World,* edited by Stephen Ross and Allana C. Lindgren, 329–38. Abingdon: Routledge, 2015.

Bender, Thomas, ed. *Rethinking American History in a Global Age.* Berkeley: University of California Press, 2002.

Bennett, Tony. *The Birth of the Museum: History, Theory, Politics.* London: Routledge, 1995.

Bentivoglio, Leonetta. "*Danse d'auteur.*" *Ballet International/Tanz Aktuell* 12, no. 4 (April 1989): 16–20.

Bhabha, Homi. "Cultural Diversity and Cultural Differences." In *The Post-Colonial Studies Reader,* edited by Bill Ashcroft, Gareth Griffiths, and Helen Tiffin, 155–56. London: Routledge, 2006.

———. Foreword to *Debating Cultural Hybridity: Multicultural Identities and the Politics of Anti-Racism,* edited by Pnina Werbner and Tariq Modood, ix-xiii. London: Zed Books, 2015.

Bharucha, Rustom. *Theatre and the World: Performance and the Politics of Culture.* London: Routledge, [1990] 1993.

Binet, Angelique. "Le Flamenco est en ville." *Le Courrier de la Nouvelle Ecosse*, February 18, 2000. Accessed July 10, 2016. http://www.elvientoflamenco.com/reviews/reviews.htm.

Bishop, Clare. "The Perils and Possibilities of Dance in the Museum: Tate, MoMA, and Whitney." *Dance Research Journal* 46, no. 3 (December 2014): 63–76.

Bissoondath, Neil. *Selling Illusions: The Cult of Multiculturalism in Canada*. Toronto: Penguin, 1994.

Boisvert, Richard. "El Viento Flamenco et l'OSQ: rythme, chaleur et jeu de jambe." *Le Soleil*, November 17, 2007; translation by El Viento Flamenco. Accessed July 10, 2016. http://www.elvientoflamenco.com/reviews/reviews.htm.

Boudreau, Tim. "Olé, This Is Hot!" *The Journal*, February 16, 2000. Accessed July 10, 2016. http://www.elvientoflamenco.com/reviews/reviews.htm.

Bouraoui, Hédi. *The Canadian Alternative: Cultural Pluralism and Canadian Unity*. Downsview: ECW Press, 1980.

Bourguignon, Erika. *Religion, Altered States of Consciousness, and Social Change*. Columbus: Ohio State University Press, 1973.

———. "Trance and Ecstatic Dance." In *Moving Histories/Dancing Culture: A Dance History Reader*, edited by Ann Dils and Anne Cooper Albright, 97–102. Durham: Wesleyan Press, 2001.

Bowring, Amy. "Les Feux-Follets: A Canadian Dance Enigma." *Dance Collection Danse Magazine* 60 (Fall 2005): 16–19.

———. "Les Feux-Follets: Popularizing Canadian History." *Dance Collection Danse Magazine* 61 (Spring 2006): 28–35.

———. "Theatrical Multiculturalism: Les Feux-Follets at the Charlottetown Festival." In *Renegade Bodies: Canadian Dance in the 1970s*, edited by Allana C. Lindgren and Kaija Pepper, 83–108. Toronto: Dance Collection Danse Press/Presse, 2012.

Boye, Seika. "Esmeralda Enrique: What Is Now Is What Is Next." *Dance Collection Danse*, no. 67 (Spring 2009): 11–15.

Bracken, Christopher. *The Potlach Papers: A Colonial Case History*. Chicago: University of Chicago Press, 1997.

Brandstetter, Gabrielle. *Poetics of Dance*. Trans. Elena Polzer with Mark Franko. Oxford: Oxford University Press, 2015.

Brannigan, Erin. "Dance and the Gallery: Curation as Revision." *Dance Research Journal* 47, no. 1 (April 2015): 5–25.

Brejzek, Thea. "From Social Network to Urban Intervention: On the Scenographies of Flash Mobs and Urban Swarms." *International Journal of Performance Arts and Digital Media* 6, no. 1 (2010): 109–22.

Brosseau, Laurence, and Michael Dewing. "Canadian Multiculturalism." Background Paper (revised). Ottawa: Library of Parliament, [2009] 2018. Accessed September 23, 2019. http://lop.parl.ca/staticfiles/PublicWebsite/Home/ResearchPublications/BackgroundPapers/PDF/2009-20-e.pdf.

Brubaker, Rogers. "The 'Diaspora' Diaspora." *Ethnic and Racial Studies* 28, no. 2 (2005): 1–19.

———. *Ethnicity without Groups*. Cambridge, MA: Harvard University Press, 2004.

Buckland, Theresa Jill. "Dance, History, and Ethnography: Frameworks, Sources, and Identities of Past and Present." In *Dancing From Past to Present: Nation, Culture, Identities*, edited by Theresa Jill Buckland, 3–24. Madison, WI: University of Wisconsin Press, 2006.

Buford, Kathryn. "What is cultural entrepreneurship?" Quora, May 1, 2017. Accessed March 1, 2019. www.quora.com/What-is-cultural-entrepreneurship.

Burchenal, Elizabeth. *Folk-Dances of Denmark, Collected and Described.* New York: G. Schirmer, 1915.

Burns, John F. "Cameron Criticizes 'Multiculturalism' in Britain." *New York Times*, February 5, 2011. Accessed August 26, 2019. http://www.nytimes.com/2011/02/06/world/europe/06britain.html.

Cameron, Agnes Deans. *The New North: Being Some Account of a Woman's Journey through Canada to the Arctic.* New York: Appleton, 1909.

Campbell, Archibald Glenlyon (Glen), the Chief Inspector of Indian Affairs in Western Canada. Letter to Secretary, Department of Indian Affairs. June 26, 1913. LAC, Indian Affairs, RG10, Vol. 3826, file 60, 511-4, part 1 [C-10145, 7–8].

Campbell, Patricia Shehan. *Lessons from the World: A Cross-Cultural Guide to Music Teaching and Learning.* New York: MacMillan, 1991.

———. *Teaching Music Globally: Experiencing Music, Expressing Culture.* New York: Oxford University Press, 2004.

Canada. "Evaluation of Multicultural Program 2011-12 to 2016-17." Accessed September 20. http://www.canada.ca/en/canadian-heritage/corporate/publications/evaluations/multiculturalism-program.html.

———. *Report of the Royal Commission on Bilingualism and Biculturalism.* Book 1. Ottawa: Queen's Printer, 1967.

———. *Report of the Royal Commission on National Development in the Arts, Letters and Sciences.* Ottawa: King's Printer, 1951.

Canada Council for the Arts. "Glossary." Accessed August 29, 2019. http://canadacouncil.ca/glossary.

———. *The Canada Council 35th Annual Report, 1991–1992.* Accessed September 5, 2018. https://canadacouncil.ca/-/media/Files/CCA/Corporate/Annual-Reports/en/1991-92-Annual-Report-Rapport-annuel.pdf.

———. *The Canada Council 38th Annual Report, 1994–1995.* Accessed September 5, 2018, https://canadacouncil.ca/-/media/Files/CCA/Corporate/Annual-Reports/en/1994-95-Annual-Report.pdf.

Canadian Broadcasting Corporation. "Arabesque." *Dragon's Den*, season 4, episode 3 (2009). Accessed Feb. 28, 2019. www.cbc.ca/dragonsden/pitches/arabesque.

Canadian Charter of Rights and Freedoms, section 27, Part 1 of the *Constitution Act*, 1982, being Schedule B to the *Canada Act 1982* (UK), 1982, c 11.

Canadian Multiculturalism Act, Revised Statutes of Canada (1985), c. 24, 3a. Accessed August 7, 2014. http://laws-lois.justice.gc.ca/PDF/C-18.7.pdf.

Canadian Museum of Immigration at Pier 21. Accessed September 27, 2019. http://pier21.ca/research/immigration-history/order-in-council-pc-1911-1324.

Cantin, Kristina M. "Process and Practice: Groupness, Ethnicity, and Habitus in Carpathian Rus." *Nationalities Papers: The Journal of Nationalism and Ethnicity* 42, no. 5 (2014): 848–66.

Carlinsky, Dan. "Flamenco Dancer: At the Crossroads between Academia and the Life of a Dancer, Evelyne Benaïs-Lemelin Chose Her Passion." *U of T Magazine* (Summer 2015). Accessed July 10, 2016, http://magazine.utoronto.ca/cool-jobs/flamenco-dancer-evelyne-benais-lenelin-cool-jobs/.

Carter, Jill. "Discarding Sympathy, Disrupting Catharsis: The Mortification of Indigenous Flesh as Survivance-Intervention." *Theatre Journal* 67 (2015): 413–32.

Cassin, A. Marguerite, Tamara Krawchenko, and Madine VanderPlaat. *Racism and Discrimination in Canada Laws, Policies and Practices.* Halifax: Atlantic Metropolis Centre, 2007.

Cauthery, Bridget. "Vincent Sekwati Mantsoe: Trance as a Cultural Commodity." In *Fields in Motion: Ethnography in the Worlds of Dance,* edited by Dena Davida, 319–38. Waterloo, ON: Wilfrid Laurier Press, 2011.

———. "Zab Maboungou: An Unshakeable Concern for Art in Life." *The Dance Current* 6, no. 5 (November 2003): 12–15.

Chan, Marty. "Playwright's Note." In *Forbidden Phoenix Study Guide,* by Karen Gilodo and Christina Sangalli, Lorraine Kimsa Theatre for Young People. 2008.

Chartrand, Yvonne. *Eagle Dance.* http://www.vnidansi.ca/media/videos.

Cheung, Wing-Yee, Time Wildschut, Constantine Sedikides, Erusca Hepper, Jamie Arndt, and J. J. M. Vingerhoets. "Back to the Future: Nostalgia Increases Optimism." *Personality and Social Psychology Bulletin* 39, no. 11 (November 2013): 1484–96.

Chin, Daryl. "Interculturalism, Postmodernism, Pluralism." In *Interculturalism and Performance: Writings from PAJ.* Edited by Bonnie Marranca and Gautam Dasgupta, 83–95. New York: PAJ Publications, 1991.

Citron, Paula. "Fresh Moves in the Museum: A New Dance Production Makes Dramatic Use of the ROM Galleries." *Globe and Mail,* May 11, 2010. Accessed October 4, 2015. http://www.theglobeandmail.com/arts/theatre-and-performance/fresh-moves-in-the-museum/article4318459/.

———. "Native-Inspired Performances at Fort York Mostly Hit the Mark with Melancholy Subject Matter." *Globe and Mail,* June 25, 2013. Accessed July 2013. http://www.theglobeandmail.com/arts/summer-entertainment/native-inspired-performances-at-fort-york-mostly-hit-the-mark-with-melancholy-subject-matter/article12815061/.

Clifford, James. "Diasporas." *Cultural Anthropology* 9, no. 3 (1994): 302–38.

———. "On Collecting Art and Culture." *The Predicament of Culture: Twentieth Century Ethnography, Literature and Art.* Cambridge, MA: Harvard University Press, 1988.

———. *Routes: Travel and Translation in the Late Twentieth Century.* Cambridge, MA: Harvard University Press, 1997.

Co.ERASGA. Accessed August 29, 2019. http://companyerasgadance.ca/about/.

Colburn-Roxworthy, Emily. "'Manzanar, the Eyes of the World Are upon You': Performance and Archival Ambivalence at a Japanese American Internment Camp." *Theatre Journal* 59 (2007): 189–214.

Colton, Glenn David. *Newfoundland Rhapsody: Frederick R. Emerson and the Musical Culture of the Island.* Montréal: McGill-Queen's University Press, 2014.

Copeland, Roger. *Merce Cunningham: The Modernizing of Modern Dance.* New York and Abingdon: Routledge, 2004.

Cornell, Katherine. "Dance Defined: An Examination of Canadian Cultural Policy on Multicultural Dance." In *Canadian Dance: Visions and Stories,* edited by Selma Landen Odom and Mary Jane Warner, 415–21. Dance Collection Danse, 2004.

———. "Dance Defined: An Examination of Canadian Cultural Policy on Multicultural Dance." In *Continents in Movement: Proceedings of the Meeting of Cultures in Dance History,* edited by Daniel Tércio, 45–50. Oeiras, Portugal, 1998.

Coulthard, Glen. *Red Skins, White Masks: Rejecting the Colonial Politics of Recognition.* Minneapolis: University of Minnesota Press, 2014.

Courlander, Harold. "Dance and Dance-Drama in Haiti." In *The Function of Dance in Human Society,* edited by Franziska Boas, 41–53. New York: Dance Horizons, 1972.

Crabb, Michael. Joining the Circuit. *International Arts Manager* (May 2005): 3–4.

Cultural Pluralism in the Arts Movement Ontario. Accessed August 29, 2019. http://cpamo.org/what-cpamo-does/.

Currelly, Charles Trick. *I Brought the Ages Home.* Toronto: The Ryerson Press, 1956.

Dance Collection Danse. "Enter Dancing / Narratives of Migration: Zab Maboungou." Accessed September 23, 2018. http://dcd.ca/exhibitions/enterdancing/maboungou1.html.

DanceWorks. "About DanceWorks." Accessed September 5, 2018. http://www.danceworks.ca/.

Davies, Jessi Lynn. *"Binti's Journey" Study Guide.* Theatre Direct 2008. Updated by Lois Adamson. Toronto: Young People's Theatre, 2012.

de Certeau, Michel. *The Practice of Everyday Life.* Berkeley, CA: University of California Press, 1984.

DeFrantz, Thomas, ed. *Dancing Many Drums: Excavations in African American Dance.* Madison, WI: University of Wisconsin Press, 2002.

Department of Indian and Northern Affairs. *The Historical Development of the Indian Act.* Ottawa: Department of Indian and Northern Affairs, 1975.

Desmond, Jane. "Dancing out the Difference: Cultural Imperialism and Ruth St. Denis's 'Radha' of 1906." *Signs* 17, no. 1 (1991): 28–49.

———. ed. *Meaning in Motion: New Cultural Studies of Dance.* Durham and London: Duke University Press, 1997.

———. "Terra Incognita: Mapping New Territory in Dance and 'Cultural Studies.'" *Dance Research Journal* 32, no. 1 (2000): 43–53.

De Souza, Joanna, and Esmeralda Enrique. *Firedance.* Performance presented at the 7th Kala Nidhi International Dance Festival and Conference: A Century of Indian Dance—Phase I, March 23–28, 2004. Harbourfront Centre, Premiere Dance Theatre.

De Souza, Joanna, Esmeralda Enrique, and KELI Company of Kerala. "Process Revealed—Dialogue with Choreographers." Panel discussion presented at the 7th

Kala Nidhi International Dance Festival and Conference: A Century of Indian Dance—Phase I, March 23–28, 2004. Studio Theatre, Toronto.

Dhamoon, Rita. *Identity/Difference Politics*. Vancouver: UBC Press, 2009.

Diamond, Beverley. "Introduction." In *Canadian Music: Issues of Hegemony and Identity*, edited by Beverley Diamond and Robert Witmer, 1–22. Toronto: Canadian Scholars' Press, 1994.

Dickinson, John A., and Brian Young. *A Short History of Quebec* (4th ed.). Montréal/Kingston: McGill-Queen's University Press, 2008.

Dickson, Lovat. *The Museum Makers: The Story of the Royal Ontario Museum*. Toronto: Royal Ontario Museum, 1986.

Dion, Stéphane. "Diversity Is a Fact; Inclusion Is a Choice." Keynote speech for the conference, Inclusive Societies? Canada and Belgium in the 21st Century. Palais des Académies, Brussels, September 22, 2017. Accessed September 28, 2019. http://www.canadainternational.gc.ca/germany-allemagne/highlights-faits/2017/2017-09-26-diversity_fact-diversite_fait.aspx?lang=en#_ftnref19.

Dixon Gottschild, Brenda. *Digging the Africanist Presence in American Performance*. Westport, CT: Praeger, 1998.

Doolittle, Lisa. "Re-imagining the Multicultural Citizen: 'Folk' as Strategy in the Japanese Canadians' 1977 Centennial National Odori Concert." *Discourses in Dance* 5, no. 2 (2013): 73–91.

"Down with the Potlatch." *Daily Province*, February 18, 1936. LAC, Indian Affairs, RG10, C-II-2, Vol. 11297, [T-16110, 630–31].

Drewal, Margaret Thompson. "Symbols of Possession: A Study of Movement and Regalia in an Anago-Yoruba Ceremony." *Dance Research Journal* 7, no. 2 (Spring/Summer 1975): 15–24.

Duffy, Dennis. "Triangulating the ROM." *Journal of Canadian Studies* 40, no. 1 (Winter 2006): 157–81.

Dunae, Patrick A. "Promoting the Dominion: Records and the Canadian Immigration Campaign, 1872–1915." *Archivaria* 19 (Winter 1984–1985): 73–93.

Duran, Anne. "Flash Mobs: Social Influence in the 21st Century." *Social Influence* 1, no. 4 (2006): 301–15.

Dykk, Lloyd. "Exercise in Excellence," *Vancouver Sun*, n.d., 1977.

Ekos Research Associates. *Survey of the Social Impacts of Dance Organizations in Canada*. Ottawa: Canada Council for the Arts and the Ontario Arts Council, 2016.

Ellis, Carolyn, Tony E. Adams, and Arthur P. Bochner. "Autoethnography: An Overview." *Forum Qualitative Sozialforschung/Forum: Qualitative Social Research* 12, no. 1 (2011): 1–13.

Erlien, Tone. "Methods of Disseminating Dance in European Museums." *Acta Ethnographica Hungarica* 60, no. 1 (2015): 93–101.

Esmeralda Enrique Spanish Dance Company. "Biographies." Accessed May 5, 2012. http://www.flamencos.net/company/company-members.html.

Fairclough, Ellen. House of Commons Debates, June 9, 1960, 4711.

———. Letter to John Diefenbaker, November 23, 1961. LAC, RG26, Vol. 100, file 3-15-1, part 8.

Farago, Jason. "A New Type of Museum for an Age of Migration." *New York Times*, July 11, 2018.

Fiji Bureau of Statistics. "Population by Religion and Province." *2007 Census of Population and Housing*. Accessed June 17, 2014. http://www.statsfiji.gov.fj/index.php/2007-census-of-population.

Fiji Government. "Fijian Affairs (Amendment) Decree 2010." *Republic of Fiji Islands Government Gazette*, July 2, 2010. Accessed Aug. 27, 2018. https://countrysafeguardsystems.net/sites/default/files/Fiji%20Fijian%20Affairs%20Amdmt%20Decree%20iTaukei%202010.pdf.

Firedance. Documentary directed by Vishnu Mathur. Toronto: Silvertouch Production, 2002.

Firedance. Video directed by Drew Mullin. Toronto: Paulus Film Group, 2001.

Fischer-Lichte, Erika. "Introduction: Interweaving Performance Cultures—Rethinking 'Intercultural Theatre': Toward an Experience and Theory of Performance beyond Postcolonialism." In *The Politics of Interweaving Performance Cultures: Beyond Postcolonialism*, edited by Erika Fischer-Lichte, Torsten Jost, and Saskya Iris Jain, 1–24. New York and London: Routledge, 2014.

Fish, Stanley. "Boutique Multiculturalism, or Why Liberals Are Incapable of Thinking about Hate Speech." *Inquiry* 23, no. 2 (Winter 1997): 379–95.

Fisher, Jennifer. "Ballet and Whiteness: Will Ballet Forever Be the Kingdom of the Pale?" In *The Oxford Handbook of Dance and Ethnicity*, edited by Anthony Shay and Barbara Sellers-Young, 585–97. Oxford: Oxford University Press, 2016.

Fitzsimmons Frey, Heather. "Dance, Dramaturgy, and Theatre for Young Audiences." *Society for Dance History Scholars Conference Proceedings*. York University, Toronto, 2011.

———. "Forbidden Phoenix and Anime." *Canadian Theatre Review* 139 (Summer 2009): 42–49.

———. "An Interview with Sandra Laronde." *Canadian Theatre Review* 155 (Summer 2013): 90–93.

Fleras, Augie, and Jean Leonard Elliot. *Engaging Diversity: Multiculturalism in Canada*. 2nd ed. Toronto: Nelson, 2002.

Fleras, Augie, and Jean Leonard Elliott, eds. *Unequal Relations: An Introduction to Race, Ethnic, and Aboriginal Dynamics in Canada*. 3rd ed. Scarborough, Ontario: Prentice Hall Allyn and Bacon Canada, 1999.

Flynn, Anne. "Embodying the Canadian Mosaic: The Great West Canadian Folk Dance, Folk Song and Handicraft Festival 1930." *Discourses in Dance* 5, no. 2 (2013): 53–72.

Foley, Kathy. "The Dancer and the Danced: Trance Dance and Theatrical Performance in West Java." *Asian Theatre Journal* 2, no. 1 (1985): 28–49.

"Folk Dances of Many Nations at Ballet Festival." *Globe and Mail*, April 28, 1954, 17.

Foster, Susan Leigh. "Choreographies of Protest." *Theatre Journal* 55, no. 3 (2003): 395–412.

———. "Dance Theory?" In *Teaching Dance Studies*, edited by Judith Chazin-Bennahum, 19–34. New York: Routledge, 2005.

———. "Introduction." In *Choreographing History*, edited by Susan Leigh Foster, 3–21. Bloomington and Indianapolis: Indiana University Press, 1995.

———. *Reading Dancing: Bodies and Subjects in Contemporary American Dance*. Berkeley, CA: University of California Press, 1986.

———. "Worlding Dance—An Introduction." In *Worlding Dance*, edited by Susan Leigh Foster, 1–13. Basingstoke: Palgrave Macmillan, 2009.

Francis, Douglas. "The Philosophy of Railways: The Transcontinental Railway Idea in British North America." Review of *The Philosophy of Railways: The Transcontinental Railway Idea in British North America*, by A. A. den Otter. *Canadian Historical Review* 79, no. 3 (September 1998): 583–86.

Franco, Susanne. "Reenacting Heritage at Bomas of Kenya: Dancing the Postcolony." *Dance Research Journal* 47, no. 2 (August 2015): 3–22.

Franklin, Eric. *Dance Imagery for Technique and Performance*. Champaign: Human Kinetics, 1996a.

———. *Dynamic Alignment Through Imagery*. Champaign: Human Kinetics, 1996b.

Franko, Mark. *Dancing Modernism/Performing Politics*. Bloomington, IN: Indiana University Press, 1995.

Franko, Mark, and André Lepecki. "Editor's Note: Dance in the Museum." *Dance Research Journal* 46, no. 3 (December 2014): 1–4.

Fraser, Kathleen Wittick. "Learning Belly Dance in Toronto: Pyramids, Goddesses and Other Weird Stuff." In *Canadian Dance: Visions and Stories*, edited by Selma Landen Odom and Mary Jane Warner, 423–34. Toronto: Dance Collection Danse Press/es, 2004.

Freire, Paulo. *Pedagogy of the Oppressed*. London: Continuum, 1970.

French, Janet. "Dancin' Round the World." *Dalhousie Gazette*, February 1999. Accessed July 10, 2016. http://www.elvientoflamenco.com/reviews/reviews.htm.

Fulford, Robert. "Can these Two Men Really Figure Out Canada?" *Maclean's*, May 16, 1964, 16–17, 57–58, 60.

Galloway, Gloria "Hate and Hope in Thunder Bay: A City Grapples with Racism Against Indigenous People." *Globe and Mail*, March 27, 2019. Accessed September 9, 2019. http://www.theglobeandmail.com/canada/article-hate-and-hope-in-thunder-bay-a-city-grapples-with-racism-against/.

Garritty, Kim. "Flamenco Captures Halifax." *Nova News Net*, February 15, 2000. Accessed July 10, 2016. http://www.elvientoflamenco.com/reviews/reviews.htm.

Gee, Skana. "Gypsy Time." *Daily News*, May 25, 2004. Accessed July 10, 2016. http://www.elvientoflamenco.com/reviews/reviews.htm.

Gere, David, ed. *Looking Out: Perspectives on Dance and Criticism in a Multicultural World*. New York: Schirmer, 1995.

Ghosh, Ratna. "Public Education and Multicultural Policy in Canada: The Special Case of Quebec." *International Review of Education* 50, no. 5–6 (2004) 543–66.

Gibbon, John Murray. *Canadian Mosaic: The Making of a Northern Nation*. Toronto: McClelland and Stewart, 1938.

Giersdorf, Jens R. "Dancing, Marching, Fighting: Folk, the Dance Ensemble of the East German Armed Forces, and Other Choreographies of Nationhood." *Discourses in Dance* 4, no. 2 (2008): 39–58.

Gilbert, Helen, and Jacqueline Lo. *Performance and Cosmopolitics: Cross-Cultural Transactions in Australasia*. Basingstoke: Palgrave Macmillan, 2008.

Global Centre for Pluralism. Accessed September 9, 2019. http://www.pluralism.ca/.

Goldberg, David Theo, ed. *Multiculturalism: A Critical Reader*. Malden, MA: Blackwell, 1994.

———. *Racist Culture: Philosophy and the Politics of Meaning*. Oxford and Cambridge: Blackwell, 1993.

Gore, Georgiana. "Flash Mob Dance and the Territorialisation of Urban Movement." *Anthropological Notebooks* 16, no. 3 (2010): 125–31.

Gradinger, Malve. "Classical Virtuosity to the Sensitizing of the Body: The Quest of Dance." *Ballet International/Tanz Aktuell* 14, no. 12 (December 1996): 43–45.

Green Thumb Theatre. "Green Thumb Theatre Annual Report." 2010–2011; 2011–2012. Accessed November 4, 2013. https://www.greenthumb.bc.ca/.

Gruen, John. *The Private World of Ballet*. New York: Viking Press, 1975.

Hagood, Thomas K. *A History of Dance in American Higher Education: Dance and the American University*. Lewistown, NY: Edwin Mellen Press, 2000.

Hamilton, William B. *Place Names of Atlantic Canada*. Toronto: University of Toronto Press, 1996.

Hanna, Judith Lynne. *Partnering Dance and Education: Intelligent Moves for Changing Times*. Champaign, IL: Human Kinetics, 1999.

Harbourfront Centre. "Hot & Spicy Food Festival: FlamenKathak Performance." Accessed September 5, 2018. http://www.harbourfront.com/whatson/music .cfm?id=5406.

Harrington, Anne. "Thinking about Trance Over a Century: The Making of a Set of Impasses." In *Hypnosis and Meditation: Towards an Integrative Science of Conscious Planes*, edited by Michael Lifshitz and Amir Raz, 19–30. New York: Oxford University Press, 2016.

Hart, E. J. *The Selling of Canada: The CPR and the Beginning of Canadian Tourism*. Banff: Altitude Publishing, 1983.

Harvie, Jen. *Staging the UK*. Manchester: Manchester University Press, 2005.

Hausmann, Andrea, and Anne Heinze. "Entrepreneurship in the Cultural and Creative Industries: Insights from an Emergent Field." *Artivate: A Journal of Entrepreneurship in the Arts* 5, no. 2 (2016): 7–22.

Hay, Deborah. *Lamb at the Altar: The Story of a Dance*. Durham: Duke University Press, 1994.

Henderson, Stuart. "'While there is still time …': J. Murray Gibbon and the Spectacle of Difference in Three CPR Folk Festivals, 1928–1931." *Journal of Canadian Studies* 39, no. 1 (2005): 139–67.

Hernandez-Ramdwar, Camille. "Feteing as Cultural Resistance? The Soca Posse in the Caribbean Diaspora." *Topia* 20 (Fall 2008): 65–92.

Hetherington, Ralph. *The Sense of Glory: A Psychological Study of Peak-Experiences.* London: Friends Home Service Committee, 1975.

Hill Collins, Patricia, and Sirma Bilge. *Intersectionality.* Cambridge: Polity Press, 2016.

Hill Strategies Research. "Factors in Canadians' Arts Attendance in 2010: An Analysis of Attendance at Art Galleries, Theatres, Classical Music Performances, Popular Music Performances, and Cultural Festivals." *Statistical Insights on the Arts* 11, no. 1 (September 2012).

———. "Factors in Canadians' Cultural Activities: Demographics and Cultural Crossovers Involved in Book Reading, Performing Arts Attendance, Art Gallery Attendance and Movie-Going." *Statistical Insights on the Arts* 6, no. 3 (February 2008).

Hobsbawm, Eric. "The Nation as Invented Tradition." In *Nationalism,* edited by Anthony Smith and John Hutchinson, 198–205. Oxford: Oxford University Press, 1994.

———. "Introduction: Inventing Traditions." In *The Invention of Tradition,* edited by Eric Hobsbawm and Terence Ranger, 1–14. Cambridge: Cambridge University Press, 1983.

Hollihan, K. Tony. "'A Brake upon the Wheel': Frank Oliver and the Creation of the Immigration Act of 1906." *Past Imperfect* 1 (1992): 93–112.

Hollinger, Peggy. "Sarkozy Joins Multiculturalism Attack." *Financial Times,* February 10, 2011. Accessed August 26, 2019. http://www.ft.com/content/05baf22e-356c-11e0-aa6c-00144feabdc0.

Holt, Claire. "Form and Function of Dance in Bali." In *The Function of Dance in Human Society,* edited by Franziska Boas, 55–63. New York: Dance Horizons, 1972.

House of Commons. Standing Committee on Canadian Heritage. "Taking Action Against Systemic Racism and Religious Discrimination Including Islamophobia." 1st Session, 42nd Parliament, February 2018, 4. Accessed September 22, 2019. http://www.ourcommons.ca/Content/Committee/421/CHPC/Reports/RP9315686/chpcrp10/chpcrp10-e.pdf.

"How Rina Singha FOUND her Feet in Canada." *Canada Bound Immigrant,* May 2, 2012. Accessed September 28, 2019. http://www.canadaboundimmigrant.com/successsnapshots/article.php?id=446.

Hsu, James. "The Ming Tomb Gallery." *The Rotunda: The Bulletin of the ROM* 16, no. 1 (1983): 22–23.

Hubbard, Karen W. "Ethnic Dance, the Origins of Jazz: A Curriculum Design for Dance." *Journal of Physical Education, Recreation and Dance* 50, no. 5 (1988): 57–61.

Hubbard, Karen W., and Pamela A. Sofras. "Strategies for Including African and African-American Culture in an Historically Euro-Centric Dance Curriculum." *The Journal of Physical Education, Recreation and Dance* 69, no. 2 (1988): 77–82.

Hughes, Sheila. "Being in the Body: An Assessment of the Extent to Which the Spiritual/Interior Experiences Arising from Specific Physical Activity Can Be Interpreted." PhD diss., University of Surrey, 1998.

Iacovetta, Franca, Paula Draper, and Robert Ventresca, eds. *A Nation of Immigrants: Women, Workers and Communities in Canadian History, 1840s–1960s.* Toronto: University of Toronto Press, 1998.

"Indians Want Their Potlatches to Stand." *Daily Province*, 23 June 1914, n.p., LAC, RG 10, vol. 3826, file 60, 511-3 [C-10145, 102].

If Tate Modern Was Musée de la danse? London: BMW Tate Live, 2015. Accessed November 28, 2018. https://www.tate.org.uk/download/file/fid/48353.

Ivakhiv, Adrian. "Colouring Cape Breton 'Celtic': Topographies of Culture and Identity in Cape Breton Island." *Ethnologies* 27, no. 2 (2005): 107–36.

Jameson, Clifford. *Postmodernism, or the Cultural Logic of Late Capitalism*. Durham: Duke University Press, 1990.

Jervis, John. *Transgressing the Modern: Explorations in the Western Experience of Otherness.* Oxford: Blackwell, 1999.

Jones, Christopher. "ROM Artifacts Inspire Museum Dances." *TO Live with Culture.* Accessed October 7, 2015. http://www.livewithculture.ca/dance/rom-artifacts-inspire-canasian-museum-dances/.

Joseph, Janelle. "Going to Brazil: Transnational and Corporeal Movements of a Canadian-Brazilian Martial Arts Community." *Global Networks* 8, no. 2 (2008): 194–213.

Kaha:wi Dance Theatre. Accessed July 2013. https://www.kahawidance.org.

———. "A Story before Time: Study Guide." Accessed July 2013. http://kahawidance.org/wordpress/wp-content/uploads/2011/04/kdt-asbt-study-guide.pdf.

Kamboureli, Smaro. *Scandalous Bodies: Diasporic Literature in English Canada*. Don Mills: Oxford University Press, 2000.

Kartomi, Margaret, J. "Music and Trance in Central Java." *Ethnomusicology* 17, no. 2 (May 1973): 163–208.

Kealiinohomoku, Joann. "An Anthropologist Looks at Ballet as a Form of Ethnic Dance." In *What Is Dance? Readings in Theory and Criticism*, edited by Roger Copeland and Marshall Cohen, 533–49. Oxford: Oxford University Press, 1984.

Kelley, Ninette, and Michael Trebilcock. *The Making of the Mosaic: A History of Canadian Immigration Policy*. 2nd ed. Toronto: University of Toronto Press, 2010.

Kelly, John D., and Martha Kaplan. *Represented Communities: Fiji and World Decolonization*. Chicago: University of Chicago Press, 2001.

Kerr-Berry, Julie. "African Dance: Enhancing the Curriculum." *The Journal of Physical Education, Recreation and Dance* 65, no. 5 (1994): 25–47.

———. "Afrocentric Forms in 20th Century American Dance History: Transforming Course Content and the Curriculum." In *Focus on Dance XII: Dance in Higher Education*, edited by Wendy Oliver, 53–63. Washington, DC: American Association for Health, Physical Education, and Recreation, 1992.

Kinberg, Judy, and Jodee Nimerichter. *Dance in America*. "Born to be Wild: The Leading Men of American Ballet Theatre." PBS and Universal Music Canada, 2004. DVD.

Knapman, Claudia. *White Women in Fiji, 1835–1930: The Ruin of Empire?* Sydney: Allen and Unwin, 1986.

Knoll, Teri. "Dance in Bali: The Reaffirmation of a Sense of Community." *Journal of the Association of Graduate Dance Ethnologists* 3, no. 3/4 (Fall/Winter 1979–1980): 9–13.

Knowles, Ric. *Performing the Intercultural City*. Ann Arbor: University of Michigan Press, 2017.

———. *Theatre and Interculturalism*. Basingstoke, Hampshire: Palgrave Macmillan, 2010.
Knowles, Ric, and Ingrid Mündel. "Introduction." In *"Ethnic," Multicultural, and Intercultural Theatre,* edited by Ric Knowles and Ingrid Mündel, vii–xvii. Toronto: Playwrights Canada Press, 2009.
Knowles, Valerie. *Strangers at Our Gates: Canadian Immigration Policy, 1540–2007,* Toronto: Dundurn, 2007.
Kobayashi, Audrey. *Women, Work, and Place*. Montréal/Kingston: McGill-Queen's University Press, 1994.
Krawchuk, Peter. *Our History: The Ukrainian Labour-Farmer Movement in Canada, 1907–1991*. Toronto: Lugus Publications, 1996.
Kymlicka, Will. *Multicultural Odysseys: Navigating the New International Politics of Diversity*. New York: Oxford University Press, 2007.
Lal, Brij. "Fiji Islands: From Immigration to Emigration." *Migration Policy Institute* (2003). Accessed March 11, 2014. http://www.migrationpolicy.org/article/fiji-islands-immigration-emigration.
Lambek, Michael. *Human Spirits: A Cultural Account of Trance in Mayotte*. Cambridge: Cambridge University Press, 1981.
Laski, Margaret. *Ecstasy: A Study of Some Secular and Religious Experiences*. New York: Greenwood Press, 1968.
Latcho Drom. Directed by Tony Gatlif. New York: New Yorker films, 1993.
Laurence, Jonathan, and Justin Vaïsse. "The Dis-Integration of Europe." *Foreign Policy,* March 28, 2011. Accessed August 26, 2019. http://foreignpolicy.com/2011/03/28/the-dis-integration-of-europe/.
Lazarevich, Gordana. "The Role of the Canadian Pacific Railway in Promoting Canadian Culture." In *A Celebration of Canada's Arts 1930–1970*, edited by Glen Carruthers and Gordana Lazarevich, 3–13. Toronto: Canadian Scholars' Press, 1996.
Leahy, Helen Rees. *Museum Bodies*. Farnham, Surrey: Ashgate, 2012.
Lepecki, André. "Zones of Resonance: Mutual Formations in Dance and the Visual Arts since the 1960s." In *Move, Choreographing You: Art and Dance since the 1960s,* edited by Stephanie Rosenthal, 152–63. Manchester: Cornerhouse Publications, 2011.
Lethbridge, Gail. "Flamenco in Frogrante Delicto. Ribbit, er, Ole." *Halifax Chronicle Herald,* April 2004. Accessed July 10, 2016. http://www.elvientoflamenco.com/reviews/reviews.htm.
Levitt, Peggy. *Artifacts and Allegiances: How Museums Put the Nation and the World on Display*. Oakland, CA: University of California Press, 2015.
Library and Archives Canada. House of Commons. *Debates, 28th Parliament, 3rd Session,* Volume 8 (October 8, 1971).
Limbertie, Catherine. "Diversity and Toronto: The Transformative Role of The Community Folk Art Council of Toronto." Toronto: Community Folk Art Council of Toronto, n.d.: 1–5. Accessed July 22, 2019. http://cfactoronto.com/wp-content/uploads/2015/05/The-Transformative-Role-of-The-Community-Folk-Art-Council-of-Toronto1.pdf.

Lindgren, Allana C. "Amy Sternberg's Historical Pageant (1927): The Performance of IODE Ideology during Canada's Diamond Jubilee." *Theatre Research in Canada* 32, no. 1 (2011): 1–29.

———. "*Bamboula* Turns 50." *Dance Collection Danse Magazine* 58 (Fall 2004): 14–17.

———. "Beyond Primary Sources: Using Dance Documentation to Examine Attitudes towards Diversity in the Massey Commission (1949-1951)." In *Canadian Performance Histories and Historiographies*, edited by Heather Davis-Fisch, 141–160. Toronto: Playwrights Canada Press, 2017.

———. "Broadcasting Race in Canada: Len Gibson's *Bamboula* (1954)." *Proceedings of the Congress on Research in Dance (CORD) Spring 2005 Conference, Tallahassee, Florida, March 3–6, 2005*. CORD, 2005: 159–65.

———. "Civil Rights Strategies in the United States: Franziska Boas's Activist Use of Dance, 1933–1965." *Dance Research Journal* 45, no. 2 (August 2013): 25–62.

———. "Contextualizing Choreography: Cynthia Barrett's *Eskimo Dances* and National Identity in Post-War Canada." *The Dance Current* 8, no. 2 (Summer 2005): 40–42.

———. "English-Canadian Ethnocentricity: The Case Study of Boris Volkoff at the 1936 Nazi Olympics." In *The Oxford Handbook of Dance and Ethnicity*, edited by Anthony Shay and Barbara Sellers-Young, 412–37. Oxford: Oxford University Press, 2016.

———. "The National Ballet of Canada's Normative Bodies: Legitimizing and Popularizing Dance in Canada during the 1950s." In *Contesting Bodies and Nation in Canadian History*, edited by Patrizia Gentile and Jane Nicholas, 180–202. Toronto: University of Toronto Press, 2013.

Lippa, Kathleen. "Spanish Lady." *The Express*, January 28, 2001. Accessed July 10, 2016. http://www.elvientoflamenco.com/reviews/reviews.htm.

Lippard, Lucy. *Mixed Blessings: New Art in a Multicultural America*. New York: Pantheon Books, 1990.

Littler, William. "Japanese Dances Worth Preserving," *Toronto Star*, section F, June 22, 1977.

Litzenberger, Shannon. "Dance and Cultural Policy in Canada: Celebrating the Canada Council's 50th Anniversary." *The Dance Current* 9, no. 8 (March 2007): 20–24.

Lo, Jacqueline, and Helen Gilbert. "Toward a Topography of Cross-Cultural Theatre Praxis." *TDR* 46, no.3 175 (Fall 2002): 31–53.

Louis Riel Institute. Accessed October 3, 2019. http://www.louisrielinstitute.com/music-a-dance.php.

Lowe, Lisa. *Immigrant Acts*. Durham and London: Duke University Press, 1996.

Luciuk, Lubomyr Y., and Stella Hryniuk. *Canada's Ukrainians: Changing Perspectives, 1891–1991*. Toronto: University of Toronto Press, 1991.

Lupul, Manoly R. *The Politics of Multiculturalism: A Ukrainian-Canadian Memoir*. Edmonton: Canadian Institute of Ukrainian Studies Press, 2005.

Macafee, Michelle. "Flamenco…On the Rock: Evelyne Benais Took Spain's Hottest Dance and Brought It to the Cold North Atlantic." *The Canadian Press*, October 2, 1999. Accessed July 10, 2016. http://www.elvientoflamenco.com/reviews/reviews.htm.

MacDonald, David B. "Aboriginal Peoples and Multicultural Reform in Canada: Prospects for a New Binational Society." *Canadian Journal of Sociology* 39, no. 1 (2014): 65–86.

Macdonald, Sharon, and Gordon Fyfe, eds. *Theorizing Museums.* Oxford: Blackwell Publishers, 1996.

MacKay, D. D. Indian Commissioner for British Columbia. Letter to Secretary, Indian Affairs Branch, Department of Mines and Resources. February 22, 1938. LAC, RG10, C-II-2, Vol. 11297 [T-16110, 589–90].

Mackey, Eva. *The House of Difference: Cultural Politics and National Identity in Canada.* London and New York: Routledge, 1999

Macpherson, Susan. *Inventory of Dance: 'Other Forms'.* Ottawa: Dance Office, Canada Council, 1991.

Major, Alice. *Ukrainian Shumka Dancers: Tradition in Motion.* Edmonton: Reidmore Books, 1991.

Makebe, Tomoko. "Intermarriage: Dream Becomes Reality for a Visible Minority." *Canadian Ethnic Studies* 37, no. 1 (2005): 121–26.

Malarek, Victor. "Edmonton Troupe Marks 25th Anniversary." *Globe and Mail,* March 10, 1984: E3.

Malefyt, Timothy Dewaal. "'Inside' and 'Outside' Spanish Flamenco: Gender Constructions in Andalusian Concepts of Flamenco Tradition." *Anthropological Quarterly* 71, no. 2 (April 1998): 63–73.

Malik, Kenan. "The Failure of Multiculturalism: Community Versus Society in Europe." *Foreign Affairs* 94, no. 2 (March/April 2015): 21–32.

Manning, Susan. "Dance History." In *The Bloomsbury Companion to Dance Studies,* edited by Sherril Dodds, 303–26. London: Bloomsbury, 2019.

———. *Modern Dance/Negro Dance: Race in Motion.* Minneapolis, MI: University of Minnesota Press, 2004.

Marks, Joseph E. III. *America Learns to Dance: A Historical Study of Dance Education in America before 1800.* New York: Dance Horizons, 1957.

Martin, Randy. *Critical Moves: Dance Studies in Theory and Politics.* Durham, NC: Duke University Press, 1999.

Martynowych, Orest T. *The Showman and the Ukrainian Cause: Folk Dance, Film, and the Life of Vasile Avramenko.* Winnipeg: University of Manitoba Press, 2014.

Matsinhe, David M. "Nightlife, Civilizing Process, and Multiculturalism in Canada." *Space and Culture* 12, no. 1 (2009): 116–35.

McCarthy, Pat. *Beneath the Banyan Tree Study Guide.* Toronto: Theatre Direct, 2006.

———. *Raven Stole the Sun Study Guide.* Red Sky Performance, 2008.

McIvor, Charlotte. "Introduction: New Directions?" in *Interculturalism and Performance Now: New Directions?* edited by Charlotte McIvor and Jason King, 1–26. Basingstoke: Palgrave Macmillan, 2019.

McKay, Ian. *The Quest of the Folk.* Montréal/Kingston: McGill-Queen's University Press, 1994.

McKay, Ian, and Robin Bates. *In the Province of History: The Making of the Public Past in Twentieth-Century Nova Scotia*. Montréal/Kingston: McGill-Queen's University Press, 2010.

McNeal, Keith E. *Trance and Modernity in the Southern Caribbean: African and Hindu Popular Religions in Trinidad and Tobago*. Gainesville: University Press of Florida, 2011.

Meer, Nasar, Tariq Modood, and Ricard Zapata-Barrero. *Multiculturalism and Interculturalism: Debating the Dividing Lines*. Edinburgh: Edinburgh University Press, 2016.

Mehra, Samantha. "Dance, Culture and the Printed Word: A Call for the Cosmopolitan Dance Critic." *Forum for Modern Language Studies* 46, no. 4 (September 2010): 431–40.

Meissner, Dirk. "BC Liberals Ethnic Vote Scandal Costs Multiculturalism Minister His Job." *Beacon News*, March 5, 2013. Accessed March 10, 2013. http://beaconnews.ca/blog/2013/03/bc-liberals-ethnic-vote-scandal-costs-multiculturalism-minister-his-job/.

Melnycky, Peter. "Political Reaction to Ukrainian Immigrants: The 1899 Election in Manitoba." In *New Soil—Old Roots: The Ukrainian Experience in Canada*, edited by Jaroslav Rozumnyj, 21–22. Winnipeg: Ukrainian Academy of Arts and Sciences in Canada, 1983.

"Memorandum of the Six Nations and other Iroquois." March 30, 1920. LAC, RG10, Vol. 6810, file 470-2-3, part 7.

Menaka Thakkar Dance. Accessed August 29, 2019. http://www.menakathakkardance.org/.

Merkel, Janet. "Cultural Entrepreneurship." *Cultural Trends* 27, no. 5 (2018): 382–84.

"Merkel Says German Multicultural Society Has Failed." BBC News, October 17, 2010. Accessed August 26, 2019. http://www.bbc.com/news/world-europe-11559451.

Message, Kylie, and Andrea Witcomb. "Introduction: Museum Theory, An Expanded Field." In *The International Handbooks of Museum Studies. Vol. 1, Museum Theory*, edited by Sharon Macdonald and Helen Rees Leahy, xxxv–lxiii. Chichester, West Sussex: John Wiley & Sons, 2015.

Miki, Arthur. *The Japanese Canadian Redress Legacy: A Community Revitalized*. Altona, MB: National Association of Japanese Canadians, 2003.

Misfeldt, Catriona, Jeannie Wassen, Ken Warren, Mark Woloshen, Ruth Sandwell, Shane Gagner, and Tim Thornton. *Early Contact and Settlement in New France*. Vancouver: The Critical Thinking Consortium and Ministry of Education, British Columbia, 2002.

Mitchell, Gillian. *The North American Folk Music Revival: Nation and Identity in the United States and Canada, 1945–1980*. Hampshire, UK: Ashgate Press, 2007.

Mitra, Royona. *Akram Khan: Dancing New Interculturalism*. Basingstoke: Palgrave Macmillan, 2015.

Molnár, Virág. "Reframing Public Space through Digital Mobilization: Flash Mobs and Contemporary Urban Youth Culture." *Space and Culture* 17, no. 1 (2014): 43–58.

Moodley, Kogila, and Heribert Adam. "Shifting Boundaries and Flexible Identities within a Multicultural Canada." *Intercultural Education* 23, no. 5 (2012): 425–36.

Moss, Laura. "Song and Dance No More: Tracking Canadian Multiculturalism over Forty Years." *Zeitschrift für Kanada-Studien* 31, no. 2 (2011): 35–57.

Moss, Suzan. "Learning from Latina Students: Modern Dance Meets Salsa and Merengue." *Journal of Physical Education, Recreation and Dance* 71, no. 3 (2000): 39–42.

Moss, Wendy, and Elaine Gardner-O'Toole. "Aboriginal People: A History of Discriminatory Laws," Government of Canada ([1987] 1991). Accessed September 8, 2019. http://publications.gc.ca/Collection-R/LoPBdP/BP/bp175-e.htm.

Muise, D. A. "Cape Breton Island." In *The Canadian Encyclopedia*. Toronto: Historica Canada, 2006. Accessed January 26, 2015. http://www.thecanadianencyclopedia.ca/en/article/cape-breton-island/.

Müller, Sigurd, Luplau Janssen, and F. C. Lund. *Danske Nationaldragter*. Kolding: P. Blicher, 1916.

Murphy, Marg. *The Ontario Folk Dance Association: Twenty-Five Years, 1969–1994*. Toronto: Ontario Folk Dance Association, 1994.

Murphy, Michael. *Multiculturalism: A Critical Introduction*. London: Routledge, 2012.

"myVancouver: Compaigni V'ni Dansi." Accessed October 3, 2019. http://www.youtube.com/watch?v=znjvfPCmAgs.

Nahachewsky, Andriy. "Conceptual Categories of Ethnic Dance: The Canadian Ukrainian Case." *Canadian Dance Studies* 2 (1997) 137–50.

Nemetz, Andrea. "Spanish Flavour." *Halifax Chronicle Herald*, May 25, 2005. Accessed July 10, 2016. http://www.elvientoflamenco.com/reviews/reviews.htm.

Ness, Sally Ann. "Being a Body in a Cultural Way: Understanding the Cultural in the Embodiment of Dance." In *Cultural Bodies: Ethnography of Theory*, edited by Helen Thomas and Jamilah Ahmed, 121–44. Malden and Oxford: Blackwell Publishing, 2004.

Newland, Lynda. "Religion and Politics: The Christian Churches and the 2006 Coup in Fiji." In *The 2006 Military Takeover in Fiji: A Coup to End All Coups?*, edited by Jon Fraenkel, Stewart Firth, and Brij V. Lal. Canberra: Australian National University Press, 2009.

Newman, Anita F. "The Bridge Between Physical and Conceptual Reality: The Trance Experience of the !Kung Bushmen." *Journal of the Association of Graduate Dance Ethnologists* 3, no. 3/4 (Fall/Winter 1979–1980): 1–7.

Nguyen, Mai, and Garth Stevenson. "Immigration Reform in Canada and the United States: A Comparative Analysis." Paper presented at the annual meeting of the Canadian Political Science Association, Vancouver, British Columbia, June 4, 2008, 38. Accessed September 26, 2019. http://www.cpsa-acsp.ca/papers-2008/Stevenson.pdf.

Niedzvecki, Hal. *Hello, I'm Special: How Individuality became the New Conformity.* Toronto: Penguin Books, 2004.

Noll, William. "Economics of Music Patronage among Polish and Ukrainian Peasants to 1939." *Ethnomusicology* 35, no. 3 (1991): 349–79.

———. "Musical Institutions and National Consciousness among Polish and Ukrainian Peasants." In *Ethnomusicology and Modern Music History*, edited by Stephen Blum, Philip Vilas Bohlman, and Daniel M. Neuman, 139–58. Urbana: University of Illinois Press, 1991.

Obata, Roger. "Final Report of the Centennial Committee." Roger Obata Fonds, 3:1 (1979). Library and Archives Canada.

———. "Japanese Canadian Citizen Association (JCCA) Minutes." Roger Obata Fonds, R9332, 1:5 (1976). Library and Archives Canada.

Oikawa, Mona. "Cartographies of Violence." In *Race Space and the Law: Unmapping a White Settler Society*, edited by S. Razack, 73–98. Toronto: Between the Lines, 2002.

Okin, Susan Moller, ed. *Is Multiculturalism Bad for Women?* Princeton, NJ: Princeton University Press, 1999.

"The Old Timers hold Their First Great Banquet in Calgary." *Calgary Daily Herald*, December 1, 1901, 1.

Ormsby, Kevin A. "Between Generations: Towards Understanding the Difference in Realities and Aspirations of the First and Second Generation of Culturally Diverse Artists." In *Pluralism in the Arts in Canada: A Change is Gonna Come*, edited by Charles C. Smith, 65–78. Ottawa: Canadian Centre for Policy Alternatives, 2012.

Oscroft, Liz. "Dance Melds East, West." *Edmonton Journal*, August 6, 1977.

O'Shea, Janet. *At Home in the World: Bharata Natyam on the Global Stage*. Middletown, CT: Wesleyan University Press, 2007.

Ostashewski, Marcia. "Performing Heritage: Ukrainian Festival, Dance and Music in Vegreville, Alberta." PhD diss., York University, 2009.

———. "A Song and Dance of (Hyper)masculinity: Performing Ukrainian Cossacks in Canada." In "Music, Dance and Masculinities," edited by Marcia Ostashewski and Sydney Hutchinson. Special issue, *World of Music* 3, no. 2 (2014): 15–38.

Overhill, Heidi. "Design as Choreography: Information in Action." *Curator: The Museum Journal* 58, no. 1 (January 2015): 5–15.

Packman, Jeff. "Signifyin(G) Salvador: Professional Musicians and the Sound of Flexibility in Bahia, Brazil's Popular Music Scenes." *Black Music Research Journal* 29, no. 1 (2009): 83–126.

Parameswaran, Uma. "Rina Singha: Seventy Years and Still Dancing." *Dance Collection Danse Magazine* 64 (Fall 2007): 16–22.

Pawlick, George. "The Ming Tomb: Causes of Deterioration in Stone." *The Rotunda: The Bulletin of the ROM* 11, no. 3 (1978): 30–33.

Pedersen, Stephen. "Flamenco Group Dances with Attitude." *Halifax Chronicle Herald*, February 11, 2000. Accessed July 10, 2016. http://www.elvientoflamenco.com/reviews/reviews.htm.

Pepper, Kaija. "View from Vancouver." *Dance International* 33, no. 2 (Summer 2004): 22–23.

Perry, Chas. C., Assistant Indian Commissioner for British Columbia. Letter to the Secretary, Department of Indian Affairs, Ottawa. August 8, 1933. LAC, Indian Affairs, RG10, C-II-2, Vol. 11297, [T-16110, 768-770].

Phillips, Miriam. "Hopeful Futures and Nostalgic Pasts." In *Flamenco on the Global Stage: Historical, Critical, and Theoretical* Perspectives, edited by K. Meira Goldberg, Ninotchka Devorah Bennahum, and Michelle Heffner Hayes, 42–55. Jefferson, NC: McFarland and Company, 2015.

Pietrobruno, Sheenagh. *Salsa and its Transnational Moves*. Lanham, MD: Lexington Books, 2006.

Pohren, D. E. *The Art of Flamenco*. 43rd anniversary ed. Westport, CT: Bold Strummer, 2005.

Pontbriand, Chantal, ed. "Marie Chouinard." In *Festival international de nouvelle danse*, 50–53. Montréal: Éditions Parachute, 1992.

Porter, John A. *The Vertical Mosaic: An Analysis of Social Class and Power in Canada*. Toronto: University of Toronto Press, 1965.

Potter, Russell A. *Spectacular Vernaculars: Hip-Hop and the Politics of Postmodernism*. Albany, NY: SUNY Press, 1995.

Prevots, Naima. "The Role of Dance in Multicultural Education." *Journal of Physical Education, Recreation and Dance* 62, no. 2 (1991): 34–48.

Price, Elizabeth B. "Preserving the Red River Jig for Posterity." *Toronto Star Weekly*, April 7, 1928, 51.

Pritz, Alexandra. "The Evolution of Ukrainian Dance in Canada." In *Visible Symbols: Cultural Expression Among Canada's Ukrainians*, edited by Manoly R. Lupul, 87–101. Edmonton: Canadian Institute of Ukrainian Studies, 1984.

Quick, Sarah. "The Social Poetics of the Red River Jig in Albert and Beyond: Meaningful Heritage and Emerging Performance." *Ethnologies* 30, no. 1 (2008): 77–101.

Ramzy, Yasmina. *Arabesque Canada*. Accessed April 9, 2019. new.arabesquecanada.com.

———. "Artist Interviews." Accessed Feb. 28, 2019. yasminaramzy.com/interviews/index.php.

———. "Feminism and Bellydance," *The Dance Current*, Mar. 1, 2011. Accessed September 25, 2019. www.thedancecurrent.com/feature/feminism-and-bellydance.

———. "Performance." *Arabesque Canada*. Accessed Feb. 28, 2019. arabesquecanada.com/performance/index.php.

———. Personal interview. March 1, 2019.

———. *Yasmina Ramzy Arts*. Accessed Feb. 28, 2019. yasminaramzyarts.com.

Rawlyk, G. A. "Canada's Immigration Policy, 1945–1962." *Dalhousie Review* 42, no. 3 (Autumn, 1962): 287–300.

Ray, John. "In TV Land." Clipping. Gordi Moore Private Papers. Vancouver, British Columbia.

Reed, Susan A. *Dance and the Nation; Performance, Ritual, and Politics in Sri Lanka*. Madison, WI: University of Wisconsin Press, 2010.

Rimsay, Linda L. "Festival of New Dance a Celebration of Talented Newfoundlanders." *St. John's Telegram*, Summer 1998. Accessed July 10, 2016. http://www.elvientoflamenco.com/reviews/reviews.htm.

Rivière, Dominique. "Identities and Intersectionalities: Performance, Power and the Possibilities for Multicultural Education." *Research in Drama Education* 10, no. 3 (2005): 341–54.

Robinson, Andrew M. *Multiculturalism and the Foundations of Meaningful Life: Reconciling Autonomy, Identity and Community*. Vancouver: UBC Press, 2007.

Rollmann, Hans. "Dance—Like You've Never Danced Before," *The Muse* (October 1, 1999). Accessed July 10, 2016. http://www.elvientoflamenco.com/reviews/reviews.htm.

Ross, Janice. *Moving Lessons: Margaret H'Doubler and the Beginning of Dance in American Education*. Madison, WI: University of Wisconsin Press, 2000.

Ross, Stephen, and Allana C. Lindgren. *The Modernist World*. London: Routledge, 2015.

Rouget, Gilbert. *Music and Trance: A Theory of the Relations between Music and Possession*. Chicago: University of Chicago Press, 1985.

Royal Ontario Museum Act, Statutes of Ontario 1912, c. 80, s. 4(b).

Ruitenbeek, Klaas. "The Gallery of Chinese Architecture." *Orientations: The Magazine for Collectors and Connoisseurs of Asian Art*. April 2006: 52–59.

Rutherford, Jonathan. "Interview with Homi Bhabha." In *Identity: Community, Culture, Difference*, edited by Jonathan Rutherford, 207–21. London: Lawrence &Wishart, 1990.

Saint-Fleur, Roger. "Portrait: Evelyne Lemelin." *La Gaboteur*, February 10, 1997. Accessed July 10, 2016. http://www.elvientoflamenco.com/reviews/reviews.htm.

Sansone, Livio. *Blackness without Ethnicity: Constructing Race in Brazil*. New York: Palgrave Macmillan, 2003.

Saunders, John. "Flash Mobs." In *Acts of Citizenship*, edited by Engin F. Isin and Greg M. Neilsen, 295–96. London: Zed Books, 2008.

Saxton, Nadine. "Rina Singha." In *Encyclopedia of Theatre Dance in Canada*, edited by Susan McPherson, 578–80. Toronto: Dance Collection Danse, 2000.

"Scandinavian Dancers of Vancouver. The First Twenty Years: 1970–1990." *Scandinavian Dancers of Vancouver*, BC. Accessed April 3, 2015. http://www.vcn.bc.ca/scandi/First20YearsHistory.pdf.

Schechner, Richard. "Foreword." In *Teaching Performance Studies*, edited by Nathan Stucky and Cynthia Wimmer, ix–xii. Carbondale, IL: Southern Illinois University Press, 2002.

Schmidt, Bettina E., and Lucy Huskinson. *Spirit Possession and Trance: New Interdisciplinary Perspectives*. London: Continuum, 2010.

"School, City Condemn Neo-Nazi Posters Plastered in St. Clair West Area Park." CBC *News*, May 29, 2018. Accessed September 9, 2019. http://www.cbc.ca/news/canada/toronto/neo-nazis-anti-semitic-posters-1.4682529.

Schwartz, Peggy. "Multicultural Dance Education in Today's Curriculum." *Journal of Physical Education, Recreation and Dance* 62, no. 2 (1991): 45–48.

Seiler, Tamara. "Thirty Years Later: Reflections on the Evolution and Future Prospects of Multiculturalism," *Canadian Issues* (February 2002): 6–8.

Sellers-Young, Barbara. *Belly Dance, Pilgrimage and Identity*. Basingstoke, Hampshire: Palgrave Macmillan, 2016.

Sereda, Leslie, and Steven Glassman, dirs. *Dancing on Eggshells: The Making of Ancestors and Elders*. Edmonton, Alberta: Blue Toque Productions, 2019.

Shay, Anthony. *Choreographing Identities: Folk Dance, Ethnicity and Festival in the United States and Canada*. Jefferson, NC: McFarland & Company, 2006.

Shay, Anthony, and Barbara Sellers-Young, eds. *The Oxford Handbook of Dance and Ethnicity*. Oxford: Oxford University Press, 2016.

Shea Murphy, Jacqueline. "Mobilizing (in) the Archive: Santee Smith's *Kaha:wi*." In *Worlding Dance*, edited by Susan Leigh Foster, 32–52. Basingstoke: Palgrave Macmillan, 2009.

———. *The People Have Never Stopped Dancing*. Minneapolis, MI: University of Minnesota Press, 2007.

Shelton, Anthony Alan. "Museums and Anthropologies: Practices and Narratives." In *A Companion to Museum Studies*, edited by Sharon Macdonald, 64–80. Chichester, West Sussex: John Wiley & Sons, 2011.

Sheriff, Robin. *Dreaming Equality: Color, Race, and Racism in Urban Brazil*. New Brunswick, NJ: Rutgers University Press, 2001.

Shipley, Amy. "Grishuk, Platov Repeat as Olympic Champions." *Washington Post*, February 17, 1998.

Shresthova, Sangita. "Bollywood Dance as Political Participation? On Flash Mobs, New Media, and Political Potential." *Convergence: The International Journal of Research into New Media Technologies* 19, no. 3 (August 2013): 311–17.

———. *Is It All about Hips? Around the World with Bollywood Dance*. New Delhi: Sage, 2011.

"Shumka Dancers on Whirlwind Tour." *Student* (February 1979): 4.

Sieg, Katrin. *Ethnic Drag: Performing Race, Nation, Sexuality in West Germany*. Ann Arbor: University of Michigan Press, 2002.

Siegel, Marcia B. "Multicult: The Show." *The Hudson Review* 49, no. 3 (Autumn 1996): 463–67.

Simmel, Georg. "The Sociology of Sociability." Translated by Everett C. Hughes. *American Journal of Sociology* 55, no. 3 (1949): 254–61.

Simpson, Faith. "Trance-Dance: An Ethnography of Dervish Whirling." MA thesis, University of Surrey, 1997.

Simpson, Leanne. "Land as Pedagogy: Nishnaabeg Intelligence and Rebellious Transformation." *Decolonization: Indigeneity, Education & Society* 3, no. 3 (2014): 1–25.

Smith, Donald B. *Calgary's Grand Story*. Calgary: University of Calgary Press, 2005.

Smulders, Marilyn. "Flamenco Dancer from the Rock." *The Daily News*, February 10, 2000. Accessed July 10, 2016. http://www.elvientoflamenco.com/reviews/reviews.htm.

Soja, Edward W. "On the Concept of Global City Regions." *ART-e-FACT: Strategies of Resistance* 4. Accessed July 10, 2016. http://artefact.mi2.hr/_a04/lang_en/theory_soja_en.htm

Sorochan, Cayley. "Flash Mobs and Urban Gaming: Networked Performances in Urban Space." Master's thesis, McGill University, July 2009.

Srinivasan, Priya. *Sweating Saris: Indian Dance as Transnational Labor*. Philadelphia: Temple University Press, 2011.

Statistics Canada. "Ethnic and Cultural Origins of Canadians: Portrait of a Rich Heritage." October 25, 2017. Accessed September 6, 2019. http://www12.statcan.gc.ca/census-recensement/2016/as-sa/98-200-x/2016016/98-200-x2016016-eng.cfm.

———. "Table 35-10-0066-01, Police-reported Hate Crime, by Type of Motivation, Canada (Selective Police Services)." Accessed September 6, 2019. http://doi.org/10.25318/3510006601-eng.

Statutes of Canada. *An Act to Amend the Act Respecting Immigration and Immigrants, Revised Statutes of Canada 1906*, ch. 19, *Statutes of Canada 1910*, ch. 27, section 218.

———. *An Act to Amend The Indian Act, Revised Statutes of Canada 1906*, ch. 81, *Statutes of Canada 1914*, ch. 35, section 8.

———. *An Act to Amend The Indian Act, Revised Statutes of Canada 1927*, ch. 98, *Statutes of Canada 1930*, ch. 25, section 16.

———. *An Act to Amend The Indian Act, Revised Statutes of Canada 1927*, ch. 98, *Statutes of Canada 1932–1933*, ch. 42, section 10.

———. *An Act further to Amend "The Indian Act, 1880," Statutes of Canada 1884*, ch. 27, section 3.

———. *An Act Respecting Immigration, 1919, Statutes of Canada 9-10 Edward II*, ch. 27, section 38.

———. *The Indian Act, Revised Statutes of Canada 1886*, ch. 43, section 114.

———. *Multiculturalism Act, Statutes of Canada 1988*, ch. 31, section 3.1.a.

Spencer, Paul. "Introduction: Interpretations of the Dance in Anthropology." In *Society and the Dance: The Social Anthropology of Process and Performance*, edited by Paul Spencer, 1–46. New York: Cambridge University Press, 1985.

St. Denis, Verna. "Silencing Aboriginal Curricular Content and Perspectives through Multiculturalism: 'There Are Other Children Here.'" *Review of Education and Cultural Studies* 33 (2011): 306–17.

Stein, Janice Gross. "Searching for Equality." In *Uneasy Partners: Multiculturalism and Rights in Canada*, edited by Janice G. Stein, David Robertson Cameron, John Ibbitson, Will Kymlicka, John Meisel, Haroon Siddiqui, and Michael Valpy, 1–22. Waterloo, ON: WLU Press, 2007.

Steinman, Megan M. "The Kinesthetic Citizen: Dance and Critical Art Practices." Master's thesis, University of Southern California, May 2011.

Stoklund, B. "Between Scenography and Science: Early Folk Museums and Their Pioneers." *Ethnologia Europaea* 33, no. 1 (2003): 21–35.

Stuart, Kevin, and Jun Hu. "That All May Prosper: The Monguor (Tu) Nadun of the Guanting/Sanchuan Region, Qinghai, China." *Anthropos* 88, no. 1–3 (1993): 15–27.

Swyripa, Frances A. "Ukrainian Canadians." In *The Canadian Encyclopedia*. Historica Canada, 2012. Accessed November 2, 2015. http://www.thecanadianencyclopedia.ca/en/article/ukrainian-canadians/.

———. "Ukrainians." In *The Encyclopedia of Canada's Peoples*, edited by Paul Robert Magocsi. Toronto: University of Toronto Press, 1999.

———. *Wedded to the Cause: Ukrainian-Canadian Women and Ethnic Identity, 1891–1991*. Toronto: University of Toronto Press, 1993.

Tanaka, Greg. "Dysgenesis and White Culture." In *Measured Lies: The Bell Curve Examined*, edited by Joe Kincheloe, Shirley Steinberg, and Aaron Gresson III, 304–14. New York: St. Martin's Griffin, 1996.

Taras, Raymond. *Challenging Multiculturalism: European Models of Diversity*. Edinburgh: University of Edinburgh Press, 2013.

Taucar, Jacqueline. "(Per)Forming Ourselves and Others in Toronto's Multicultural Caravan Festival." *Canadian Theatre Review* 140 (Fall 2009): 51–56.

Taylor, Diana. *The Archive and the Repertoire: Performing Cultural Memory in the Americas*. Durham: Duke University Press, 2003.

Tembeck, Iro. *Dancing in Montreal: Seeds of a Choreographic History, Studies in Dance History* 5, no. 2 (Fall 1994).

Tessler, Eva Zorilla. "Body and Identity in Afro-Brazilian Candomble." *Choreography and Dance* 5, no. 1 (1998): 103–15.

Teves, Stephanie Nohelani. *Defiant Indigeneity: The Politics of Hawaiian Performance.* Chapel Hill: The University of North Carolina Press, 2018.

Tharp, Twyla. "Twyla Tharp Biography–Academy of Achievement." *Academy of Achievement.* June 25, 1993. Accessed April 10, 2019. https://www.achievement.org/achiever/twyla-tharp/#interview.

Theatre Direct. *Beneath the Banyan Tree,* video. Milk International Children's Festival, Toronto Harbourfront Centre, 2005.

Thobani, Sunera. *Exalted Subjects.* Toronto: University of Toronto Press, 2007.

Thomas, Nicholas. *Entangled Objects: Exchange, Material Culture, and Colonialism in the Pacific.* Cambridge, MA: Harvard University Press, 1991.

———. *In Oceania: Visions, Artifacts, Histories.* Durham: Duke University Press, 1997.

Till, Barry. "A Chinese General's Tomb: Identification of the 'Ming Tomb.'" *The Rotunda: The Bulletin of the ROM* 14, no. 1 (1981): 7–11.

Titley, Brian. *A Narrow Vision: Duncan Campbell Scott and the Administration of Indian Affairs in Canada.* Vancouver: UBC Press, 1986.

Tölölyan, Khachig. "Rethinking Diaspora(s): Stateless Power in the Transnational Movement." *Diaspora* 5, no. 1 (1996): 3–36.

Tomko, Linda. "Teaching Dance History: A Querying Stance as Millennial Lens." In *Teaching Dance Studies,* edited by Judith Chazin-Bennahum, 93–113. New York: Routledge, 2005.

Tomko, Linda J. *Dancing Class: Gender, Ethnicity, and Social Divides in American Dance, 1890–1920.* Bloomington and Indianapolis: Indiana University Press, 1999.

Tomlinson, Matt. *In God's Image: The Metaculture of Fijian Christianity.* Berkeley: University of California Press, 2009.

Torgovnick, Marianna. *Gone Primitive: Savage Intellects, Modern Lives.* Chicago: University of Chicago Press, 1990.

"Truck of Former Reservist with Alleged Neo-Nazi Ties Found Near U.S.-Canada Border." *CBC News,* September 3, 2019. Accessed September 9, 2019. http://www.cbc.ca/news/canada/manitoba/patrik-mathews-neo-nazi-group-recruitment-1.5268780.

Trudeau, Justin. "Diversity Is Canada's Strength." Speech in London, United Kingdom. November 26, 2015. Assessed September 27, 2019. http://pm.gc.ca/en/news/speeches/2015/11/26/diversity-canadas-strength.

Trudeau, Pierre Elliot. "Pierre Elliot Trudeau: Multiculturalism." *Canadian History.* Accessed May 18, 2018 and September 23, 2018. http://www.canadahistory.com/sections/documents/Primeministers/trudeau/docs-onmulticulturalism.htm.

———. Speech. House of Commons, October 8, 1971, 8545. Accessed September 22, 2019. http://parl.canadiana.ca/view/oop.debates_HOC2803_08/811?r=0&s=3.

Underhay, Nicole. "Livin' La Vida Flamenca." *Current,* February 2000. Accessed July 10, 2016. http://www.elvientoflamenco.com/reviews/reviews.htm.

Urciuoli, Bonnie. "Producing Multiculturalism in Higher Education: Who's Producing What and for Whom?" *International Journal of Qualitative Studies in Education* 12, no. 3 (1999): 287–98.

Urszulan, Audrey. "The Danish Folk Dancers of Toronto." In *2012 Heritage Book: Vikings in Canada 2012, Proceedings of the 31st Danish Canadian Conference, Toronto, Ontario, May 24–27, 2012*, edited by Svend Berg, 54–57. Federation of Danish Associations in Canada.

Vachon, André. *Dreams of Empire: Canada before 1700*. Ottawa: Canadian Government Publication Centre, 1982.

Vaughan-Jackson, Mark. "A Spanish Wind: Newfoundland Flamenco Troupe Takes Flight for Mainland Canada and Spain." *St. John's Telegram*, January 8, 1999. Accessed July 10, 2016. http://www.elvientoflamenco.com/reviews/reviews.htm.

Veblen, Kari, Carol Beynon, and Selma Odom. "Drawing on Diversity in the Arts Education Classroom: Educating our New Teachers." *International Journal of Education and the Arts* 6, no. 14 (2005): 1–16.

Venne, Sharon Helen. *Indian Acts and Amendments 1868-1975, An Indexed Collection*. Saskatoon: University of Saskatchewan Native Law Centre, 1981.

Vernon, Charles William. *Cape Breton, Canada, at the Beginning of the Twentieth Century: A Treatise of Natural Resources and Development*. Toronto: Nation Publishing, 1903.

Village Green English Dancers. "Welcome." Accessed September 3, 2019. http://villagegreenenglishdancers.org/.

Visschedyk, Nadine. "El Viento Flamenco Performs to a Packed House." *Lambda*, October 2006. Accessed July 10, 2016. http://www.elvientoflamenco.com/reviews/reviews.htm.

Vissicaro, Pegge. *Studying Dance Cultures around the World*. Dubuque, IA: Kendall/Hunt, 2004.

Vlastos, Stephen, ed. *Mirror of Modernity: Invented Traditions of Modern Japan*. Berkeley: University of California Press, 1998.

V'ni Dansi. "Interview with Yvonne [Chartrand] about Red River Jig," V'ni Dansi. Accessed October 3, 2019. http://www.vnidansi.ca/company/interview-yvonne-about-red-river-jig.

Volk, Terese M. *Music, Education and Multiculturalism: Foundations and Principles*. New York: Oxford University Press, 1998.

Walcott, Rinaldo. "Caribbean Pop Culture in Canada; Or, the Impossibility of Belonging to the Nation." *Small Axe* 5, no. 1 (2001): 123–39.

Walker, Barrington, ed. *The African Canadian Legal Odyssey: Historical Essays*. Toronto: University of Toronto Press, 2012.

Walkowitz, Daniel J. *City Folk: English Country Dance and the Politics of the Folk in Modern America*. New York: New York University Press, 2010.

Ward, Kay-Ann. "Participants Needed for Upcoming Flash Mob." Accessed June 6, 2012. http://www.kayannward.com/uncategorized/participants-needed-for-upcoming-flash-mob/.

Washabaugh, William. "The Flamenco Body." *Popular Music* 13, no. 1 (January 1994): 75–90.

Weaver, Matthew. "Angela Merkel: German Multiculturalism has 'Utterly Failed.'" *The Guardian*, October 17, 2010. Accessed August 26, 2019. http://www.theguardian.com/world/2010/oct/17/angela-merkel-german-multiculturalism-failed.

Wedman, Les. "Bamboula Bows in as Best-Yet Show." *Vancouver Province* (August 28, 1954): 8.

Werbner, Pnina. "Introduction: The Dialectics of Cultural Hybridity." In *Debating Cultural Hybridity: Multicultural Identities and the Politics of Anti-Racism*, edited by Pnina Werbner and Tariq Modood, 1–26. London: Zed Books, 2015.

Whittaker, Herbert. "Showbusiness." *Globe and Mail*, May 4, 1954, 11.

Williams, Denise. "World Dance at Live Art New Dance Festival," reprinted in "Reviews and Articles—Excerpts," El Viento Flamenco. Accessed July 10, 2016. http://www.elvientoflamenco.com/reviews/reviews-excerpts.htm#williams.

Wilcox, Emily. *Revolutionary Bodies: Chinese Dance and the Socialist Legacy*. Oakland, CA: University of California Press, 2018.

Wise, Amanda. "Hope and Belonging in a Multicultural Suburb." *Journal of Intercultural Studies* 26, no. 1–2 (2005): 171–86.

Wise, Amanda, and Selvaraj Velayutham. "Introduction: Multiculturalism and Everyday Life." In *Everyday Multiculturalism*, edited by Amanda Wise and Selvaraj Velayutham, 1–17. Basingstoke, Hampshire: Palgrave Macmillan, 2009.

Wiseman, Nelson. "Ukrainian-Canadian Politics." In *Canada's Ukrainians: Negotiating an Identity*, edited by Lubomyr Y. Luciuk and Stella Hryniuk, 342–76. Toronto: University of Toronto Press, 1991.

Wolf, Sara. "Renegade Gender: Theorizing the Female Body in Extreme Motion." In *Proceedings, Society of Dance History Scholars Conference* (Paris, June 21–24, 2007): 54–58.

Wong, Lloyd, and Shibao Guo. "Revisiting Multiculturalism in Canada: An Introduction." In *Revisiting Multliculturalism in Canada; Theories, Policies and Debates*, edited by Shibao Guo and Lloyd Wong, 1–14. Rotterdam: Sense Publishers, 2015.

Wong, Yutian. *Choreographing Asian America*. Middletown, CT: Wesleyan University Press, 2010.

Wright, Donald, A. "W. D. Lighthall and David Ross McCord: Antimodernism and English-Canadian Imperialism, 1880s–1918." *Journal of Canadian Studies* 32, no. 2 (1997): 134–56.

Wright, Oliver, and Jerome Taylor. "Cameron: My War on Multiculturalism." *The Independent*, February 5, 2011. Accessed August 26, 2019. http://www.independent.co.uk/news/uk/politics/cameron-my-war-on-multiculturalism-2205074.html.

Wulfhorst, Cristina, Cristina Rocha, and George Morgan. "Intimate Multiculturalism: Transnationalism and Belonging amongst Capoeiristas in Australia." *Journal of Ethnic and Migration Studies* 40, no. 11 (2014). Accessed August 9, 2014.

Yablon, Nick. "For the Future Viewer: Salvage Ethnography and Edward Curtis's 'The Oath—Apsaroke.'" *Journal of American Studies* (2019): 1–31.

Youdell, Deborah. "Fabricating 'Pacific Islander': Pedagogies of Expropriation, Return and Resistance and Other Lessons from a 'Multicultural Day.'" *Race Ethnicity and Education* 15, no. 2 (2012): 141–55.

Yúdice, George. *The Expediency of Culture: Uses of Culture in the Global Era.* Durham, NC: Duke University Press, 2003.

Zumba Fitness. "Learn About Zumba." Accessed September 23, 2018. http://www.zumba.com/en-US/about.

CONTRIBUTORS

P. Megan Andrews, PhD, is a settler dance artist/scholar, educator/facilitator, and writer/editor with a portfolio of performance, research, and community engagements. She is currently Associate Artist with Vancouver's Scotiabank Dance Centre and Visiting Scholar at the Institute for Performance Studies at Simon Fraser University (SFU). She teaches in the School for Contemporary Arts at SFU and works as BC Program Manager for the Dancer Transition Resource Centre. As the founding editor of the Canadian dance magazine *The Dance Current,* she led the organization from its grassroots beginnings to become a national multiplatform media company. She acknowledges the unceded Coast Salish territories, colonially known as Vancouver, where she lives and works.

Bridget Cauthery is a dance and cultural studies scholar focusing on the impact of post-/neo-coloniality and the processes of globalization on contemporary and popular dance practices in the Global North. She holds a PhD in Dance Studies from the University of Surrey and is an Assistant Professor in the Department of Dance at York University. She is completing her first book, *Choreographing the North* (McGill–Queen's University Press), which examines eleven contemporary dance works from the northern and southern hemispheres that take the Canadian Arctic as their source and inspiration.

Carolyne Clare completed a master's degree in Museum Studies at the University of Toronto in 2010 and has supported a range of dance legacy projects in Montréal, Toronto, and Vancouver. She is currently a doctoral student at Simon Fraser University, where her research focuses on the use and management of Vancouver-based dance records. She holds a Vanier CGS Scholarship.

Dena Davida, PhD, has practised postmodern dance as a performer, improvisor, teacher, researcher, curator, and writer for fifty years. Born in the US in 1949 into a family of Jewish artists of Eastern European heritage, she immigrated to Canada in 1977, where she co-founded and curated Tangente (1980–2020), Québec's premiere dance performance venue. At the Université du Québec à Montréal, she taught in the Dance Department (1979–2010) and completed her doctorate in artistic dance ethnography (2006) through the Programme d'études et pratiques des arts. She has published widely on dance and culture from a humanistic and politically engaged perspective, co-editing the anthologies *Fields in Motion* (2012) and *Curating Live Arts* (2014).

Eloisa Domenici, PhD, is an Associate Professor of Performing Arts at Federal University of South Bahia. She collaborates in projects and programs for popularization of Brazilian universities. Her work focuses on the so-called popular dances in Brazil with an emphasis on local epistemologies and their dialogues with performing arts. She recently completed the project *Decolonizing the body: non-Eurocentric corporealities in higher education in Brazil*, bringing the contribution of Epistemologies of the South, with the supervision of Boaventura de Sousa Santos, at the Center for Social Studies at the University of Coimbra.

Lisa Doolittle is a dance artist, educator, and scholar. Her research, grounded in collaborations with dance professor Anne Flynn, focuses on performance and social justice. Her work has appeared in numerous journals, including *Dance Research Journal*, *Discourses in Dance*, *Theatre Research in Canada*, and *alt. theatre*, and in the collections *Oxford Handbook of Theatre and Dance*, *Popular Political Theatre and Performance*, and *Performing Utopia*, among others. Locally and internationally, she works in arts-based community initiatives around health promotion, refugee and immigrant communities, and people with disabilities. She is Professor Emerita (Drama) at the University of Lethbridge.

Catalina Fellay is a Toronto-based dance scholar and professional interested in the performance and perception of culture and tradition through dance. Her professional dance experience began with membership in the Esmeralda Enrique Spanish Dance Company and has included Flamenco, classical ballet, baroque, contemporary, and Chinese dance. Her intellectual interest in movement expression prompted the pursuit of a BFA and an MA in dance at York University, an MA in theatre from the University of Toronto, and she is currently a PhD candidate in Dance Studies at York University. Apart from giving lectures, teaching workshops, and performing, she enjoys using her skills as a Certified Movement Analyst (Laban Institute for Movement Studies) to explore dance through writing.

Heather Fitzsimmons Frey is an Assistant Professor of Arts and Cultural Management at MacEwan University in Edmonton. Using archives, qualitative research, performance-based historiography, and practice-based methodologies, her research focuses on arts and performance, for, by, and with young people, in contemporary and historical contexts. Her recent work related to dance and embodiment has been published in *Jeunesse, Journal of Childhood Studies, Performance Research, Theatre Research International, Youth Theatre Journal,* and in *Children's Literature and Imaginative Geography* (2019). She is the editor of the collection *Ignite: Illuminating Theatre for Young People* (2016).

Anne Flynn is a dancer, writer, administrator, and Professor Emerita of Dance at the University of Calgary, where she was instrumental in the creation of its dance degree programs. Her research with Lisa Doolittle is the heart of her scholarly contributions, beginning with the founding of *Dance Connection* magazine in 1987. Their SSHRC-funded and other work has been published in numerous anthologies, such as *The Oxford Handbook of Dance and Theatre* (2015) and *Performing Utopia* (2018). She served as President/Immediate Past-President of the Dance Studies Association (2017–20), and received the association's 2020 Dixie Durr Award for outstanding contributions to dance research.

Suzanne Jaeger is currently the Funded Research Officer in the Faculty of Arts & Science at the University of Toronto. She has a PhD in Philosophy from York University and taught philosophy and humanities at York and at the University of Central Florida in Orlando, Florida. Prior to receiving her academic degrees, she was a professional ballet dancer and teacher. Her published work focuses on art dance aesthetics, philosophies of embodiment, and the nature of meaning making. She danced for a year and a half with the Toronto Danish Folk Dance group, which continues to thrive with regular annual performances.

Steven Jobbitt is an Associate Professor of History at Lakehead University, and Assistant Artistic Director of the Chaban Ukrainian Dance Group in Thunder Bay, Ontario. He is President of the Hungarian Studies Association of Canada, managing editor of *Hungarian Studies Review*, and publishes primarily on Hungarian historical geography.

Janelle Joseph, PhD, is an Assistant Professor of Critical Race Studies in the Faculty of Kinesiology and Physical Education at the University of Toronto, and the Founder and Director of the Indigeneity, Diaspora, Equity and Anti-racism in Sport (IDEAS) Lab. A former SSHRC Banting Postdoctoral Fellow, she is co-editor of two texts that include her ethnographic research on physical activity, transnationality, and racialized communities. Her most recent book is *Sport in the Black Atlantic: Cricket, Canada and the Caribbean Diaspora* (Manchester University Press, 2017).

Evadne Kelly is a Mitacs Elevate Postdoctoral Fellow at Re•Vision: The Centre for Art and Social Justice, University of Guelph. She has a PhD in Dance Studies from York University that builds on her twenty years of professional experience with Canadian choreographer David Earle. Her book, *Dancing Spirit, Love, and War: Performing the Translocal Realities of Contemporary Fiji* (DSA Series, University of Wisconsin Press), addresses histories and legacies of colonialism. She was a leading researcher and co-curator of the exhibition *Into the Light: Eugenics and Education in Southern Ontario,* which won the Lieutenant-Governor's Ontario Heritage Award for Conservation Excellence. The exhibition exposed and countered the ongoing legacies of oppressive ideas and practices that have targeted Indigenous, Black, and other racialized populations, as well as poor and disabled people, for dehumanization and elimination.

Hari Krishnan, PhD, is Chair and Professor of Dance at Wesleyan University and is also the Artistic Director of the Toronto based company, inDANCE. He is a dance artist and scholar whose work focuses on Bharatanatyam, post-colonial dance, queer dance, and the interface between dance and film studies. Krishnan's monograph, *Celluloid Classicism: Early Tamil Cinema and the Making of Modern Bharatanatyam* (2019) recently won a special citation from the 2020 de la Torre Bueno© First Book Award Committee of the Dance Studies Association. The book has been hailed as "an invaluable addition to scholarship on Bharatanatyam."

Allana C. Lindgren is an Associate Professor in the Department of Theatre at the University of Victoria. Her research has appeared in a variety of journals and collections, including *Contesting Bodies and Nation in Canadian History, The Oxford Handbook of Dance and Ethnicity, Dance Research Journal, Journal of Dance and Somatic Practices, American Journal of Dance Therapy,* and *Quarterly Review of Film and Video*. Recent publications include *The Modernist World* (co-edited with Stephen Ross) and *Renegade Bodies: Canadian Dance in the 1970s* (co-edited with Kaija Pepper). She is also the Dance Subject Editor for the Routledge Encyclopedia of Modernism.

Samantha Mehra, MA, is a Toronto-based writer, editor, and creator. She earned an MA in Dance Studies from York University, and a BFA in contemporary dance from Simon Fraser University. Credits include *Canadian Encyclopedia, Feathertale, Oxford Journals,* the *Routledge Encyclopedia of Modernism,* and *Dance Collection Danse Magazine*. She is also an educator, and currently teaches writing, digital storytelling, and communications through the University of Toronto's School of Continuing Studies. She is a National Magazine Award nominee.

Marcia Ostashewski is the Director of the Centre for Sound Communities at Cape Breton University, which she established as part of her Canada Research Chair in Communities and Cultures. It is an arts-led social innovation lab that supports interdisciplinary, technology-enhanced, and community-engaged research among artists, scholars, students, and wider communities. Their research results in innovative outcomes, including public engagement, performances and the production of digital media, as well as publications. As Associate Professor of Ethnomusicology, Ostashewski regularly teaches courses in music, dance, and Indigenous studies. Her most recent publications focus on collaborations with Malian, African Nova Scotian, and Mi'kmaw co-researchers.

Yasmina Ramzy is the Director of Arabesque Canada and Yasmina Ramzy Arts. She has created over 200 ensemble choreographies, including ten full-length productions, for twenty-five dance companies in the United States and Canada, since 1981. Yasmina has produced ten international dance festivals and conferences. She received her essential training from teachers in Egypt and Syria and has performed extensively in the Middle East, primarily with the master musicians of Syria. Some of her productions have toured in the United States, Greece, Lebanon, Jordan, Syria and across Canada. Yasmina has taught in seventy cities around the world and hosts a podcast called *Deeper Dance.*

Danielle Robinson, PhD, is an Associate Professor of Dance at York University in Toronto, Canada, where she is cross-appointed to Theatre and Performance Studies as well as Communication and Culture. She is the author of *Modern Moves: Dancing Race during the Ragtime and Jazz Eras* (2015). Her research has been supported by the Social Sciences and Humanities Research Council (Canada), the Leverhulme Trust (UK), the Arts and Humanities Research Council (UK), and the Institute of Jazz Studies (USA). Between 2005 and 2007, she was a visiting professor of Dance in the School of Dance at the Federal University of Brazil (UFBA). She is currently serving as the director of the Centre for Research on Latin America and the Caribbean at York University.

Clara Sacchetti is an independent scholar and Executive Director for the Community Arts & Heritage Education Project (CAHEP). She is co-editor of *The Economy as Cultural System* (2013) and *Superior Art* (2012). She has written and co-written articles for several edited collections and journals, including *Where Is the Field? Exploring Labor and Migration Studies through the Lenses of Fieldwork* (volume for Studia Fennica Ethnologica, 2012), *Transitions in Marginal Zones in the Age of Globalization: Case Studies from the North and South* (2010), *Expositions: Interdisciplinary Studies in the Humanities, Diskurs, Italian Canadiana, Migration Letters, The Semiotic Review of Books,* and FUSE *Magazine.*

Santee Smith is a multidisciplinary artist, award-winning producer, and Artistic Director of Kaha:wi Dance Theatre. She is from the Kahnyen'kehàka Nation, Turtle Clan, Six Nations of the Grand River. Her passion is creating performance from an Indigenous lens and process. Her training includes

Canada's National Ballet School, Physical Education and Psychology degrees from McMaster University, and a MA in Dance from York University. Kaha:wi Dance Theatre is an internationally renowned company with fourteen productions and numerous short works. Her independent commissions include collaborations with National Arts Centre Orchestra, Canadian Opera Company, and others. She is the Chancellor of McMaster University.

Batia Boe Stolar is Associate Vice-President, Research and Graduate Studies, and an Associate Professor in the Department of English at Lakehead University. She is currently working on a project that explores the gothic in ballet. Her work on the contemporary gothic has been included in such collections as *Werewolves, Wolves and the Gothic,* and *Images of the Modern Vampire: The Hip and the Atavistic.* Her work on immigrant literatures and films has appeared in various journals and collections, including: *Coming Here, Being Here: A Canadian Migration Anthology*; *Austin Clarke: Essays on His Works*; *Image and Territory: Essays on Atom Egoyan*; *Canadian Journal of Film Studies*; and *Downtown Canada: Writing Canadian Cities.* Her work with Clara Sacchetti on image and dance has appeared in journals and collections including *Renegade Bodies: Canadian Dance in the 1970s.*

COPYRIGHT ACKNOWLEDGEMENTS

Davida, Dena. "Croisements cinétiques: Marie Chouinard, Roger Sinha et Maria Castello." *Les cahiers de théâtre* JEU 72.3 (1994): 83–90 in a French translation by Michel Vaïs.

Doolittle, Lisa. "Re-imagining the Multicultural Citizen: 'Folk' as Strategy in the Japanese Canadians' 1977 Centennial National Odori Concert." *Discourses in Dance* 5.2 (2013): 73–91.

Flynn, Anne. "Embodying the Canadian Mosaic: The Great West Canadian Folk Dance, Folk Song, and Handicraft Festival, 1930." *Discourses in Dance* 5.2 (2013): 53–72.

Robinson, Danielle and Eloisa Domenici. "From Inclusion to Integration: Intercultural Dialogue and Contemporary University Dance Education." *Research in Dance Education* 11.3 (2010): 213–21.

INDEX